ON THE TRAIL OF DELUSION

FRED LITWIN

Dear Mr. Frawley: Please enjoy!

fred

NORTHERNBLUES BOOKS

CONTENTS

ALSO BY FRED LITWIN

Conservative Confidential

I Was a Teenage JFK Conspiracy Freak

First North American edition published in 2020 by NorthernBlues Books

Cover design by Kathleen Lynch
Edited by Michael J. Totten

Manufactured in the United States on acid-free paper.

First North American Edition

Litwin, Fred
On the Trail of Delusion

ISBN: 978-0-9948630-4-1

Dedicated to the victims of Jim Garrison
I wrote this book to tell not just the Clay Shaw story, important as it is, but also to highlight the other victims of Garrison's malicious investigation: Edgar Eugene Bradley, Kerry Thornley, Sergio Arcacha Smith, Carlos Quiroga, Carlos Bringuier, and Louis Bloomfield. Lives were ruined, reputations were sullied, and for what?

Let justice be done though the heavens fall.

ABOUT THE AUTHOR

Fred Litwin in New Orleans next to the plaque honoring Clay Shaw

On the Trail of Delusion is Fred Litwin's third book (you can find pictures and updates at onthetrailofdelusion.com. In 2018, he published *I Was a Teenage JFK Conspiracy Freak*, detailing his journey from believing in a JFK conspiracy at eighteen to slowly moving to believe that Lee Harvey Oswald was the lone assassin. In 2015, he released *Conservative Confidential* about his move from left-wing anti-nuclear activist to Conservative Party campaigner.

Fred has written articles for the *National Post*, the *Ottawa Citizen*, the *Toronto Sun*, *C2C Journal*, *iPolitics*, and the

Dorchester Review, and he is often a panelist on the *CTV News Channel*.

In 2000, Fred founded NorthernBlues Music, a cutting-edge blues label that has released over seventy CDs and has garnered twelve Juno Award and more than forty Blues Music Award nominations, three of which have been for album of the year. In 2007, he started the Free Thinking Film Society to showcase films on liberty, freedom, and democracy. The Society has shown over a hundred films and has organized four film festivals.

Fred.Litwin@gmail.com

INTRODUCTION

One of the greatest miscarriages of American jurisprudence occurred on March 1, 1967, when a gay man in New Orleans, Clay Shaw, was charged with conspiracy to assassinate President John F. Kennedy. The prosecutor, Jim Garrison, had no evidence to support the charge other than the recollections of a witness, Perry Russo, who had been interviewed after being injected with sodium pentothal, a so-called truth serum, and then questioned three times under hypnosis. His recovered memory—that he had been at a party where participants had loosely discussed JFK's murder—was enough to ruin Shaw's life.

The case took two years to go to trial, at which time Shaw was acquitted. Garrison then charged him with perjury, and it took another two years for that charge to be quashed. Shortly afterward, Shaw died of cancer, ruthlessly deprived of not only the best years of his retirement but most of his savings too.

I told the story of Clay Shaw in my last book, *I Was a Teenage JFK Conspiracy Freak*. It is an important story because he was victimized a second time when Oliver Stone cast him as the villain while making Jim Garrison the hero of his film *JFK*.

Reaction to my book was quite positive, but there was a group of neo-Garrisonites who took great offense at his portrayal.

James DiEugenio is the author of *Destiny Betrayed*, which argues that Jim Garrison had it right. For a short period, he was obsessed with me. He claimed that I owned a media empire and that I wrote for an alt-right website, and he threatened to start a "Litwin Watch." He was greatly upset when I was interviewed by *TVOntario*'s Steve Paikin for his show "The Agenda," taking particular offense at my claim that there was nothing new in the millions of pages of JFK assassination documents that have been released over the years.

He wrote on an internet forum: "Well, yeah, if you did not read them or choose not to address them, it's nothing. But as I quoted in my article, either Freddie Boy did read them and he does not want anyone to know about them, or he did not read them at all. These documents completely puncture the false image of Garrison and New Orleans that he is trying to peddle."

I have to admit that he was partly right. I had read the Garrison grand jury transcripts that had been made public by the Assassination Records & Review Board (ARRB). But I had not gone to the National Archives to go through what was left of Garrison's papers, nor had I gone through the papers of Clay Shaw and his attorneys. I had mostly relied upon excellent secondary research.

I then received a timely email from a JFK assassination research list, that contained a link to the papers of Jim Garrison, all of which were online at the National Archives website. I decided to have a look. Indeed, there are 202 PDF files online, each file containing up to three hundred pages. I began going through the files and immediately started finding memos that were utterly crazy, and I started putting them aside. The more I read, the more it confirmed the fact that Jim Garrison had nothing. Most of his leads were little more than rumors, which naturally led nowhere.

Garrison spent over two years investigating the JFK assassination and came up empty. He sent his investigators to Miami, Dallas, and even Europe. He had volunteers from various parts of the country assisting his efforts. Prisoners wrote him letters, and all sorts of cranks came out of the woodwork. Con men found him an easy mark. He entertained every crackpot theory; there was nothing too outlandish for his taste. To Garrison, there was no such thing as a coincidence, and there was no conspiracy theory that was too bizarre.

For instance, here is a memo that Jim Garrison wrote to one of his investigators about Jack Ruby, the man who killed Lee Harvey Oswald on November 24, 1963:

June 12, 1967

M E M O R A N D U M

TO: Bill Boxley

FROM: Jim Garrison

RE: Ruby in Houston

Substantial evidence confirms that JACK RUBY was in Houston on November 21, 1963, and that he was engaged in some unusual form of activity (See Secret Service report on this, W.C. exhibits). Although this is "ruled out" in the conclusions of the S/S, for investigative purposes we should assume that he was there -- as numerous witnesses affirm.

It is also to be noted that his attire was unusually casual for him, suggesting the possibility that some form of practice or rehearsal for the shooting may have been under way there. It is further noted that this is the city to which FERRIE drove following the assassination.

JIM GARRISON

Generally speaking, the wearing of casual clothes would be neither indicative of a crime nor a clue pointing to a shooting, but Garrison clearly saw it as such and as a tenuous link between Ruby and suspect David Ferrie.

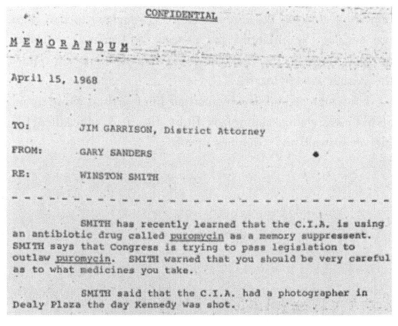

Winston Smith was an alias that Jim Garrison gave to Carl McNabb, a mysterious self-proclaimed CIA contract pilot. Not much of what McNabb said checked out.

Jim Garrison's paranoia (see Chapter Two) infected his staff. In the memo above, a staffer passed on an ominous warning based on an erroneous reading of a study that showed that puromycin injected intracerebrally into mice caused loss of memory. Does this explain why Garrison lost any semblance of critical thinking?

I now have hundreds of these sorts of memos, and while one could find them endlessly amusing, they are actually nothing of the sort. A dangerous mind inhabited the man who sat in the office of the New Orleans DA, and because he couldn't find a conspiracy, he made one up. And in his wake, many lives were broken.

One forgotten victim was Louis Bloomfield, a Montreal lawyer whose papers are housed at the Library and Archives Canada in Ottawa. I had come across his name in my research for my book *I Was a Teenage JFK Conspiracy Freak*, as he was named by the Italian newspaper *Paese Sera* in 1967 as being involved, along with Clay Shaw, in the World Trade Center in Rome, which it claimed was a CIA front. At the time, I didn't consider Bloomfield to be important because so much of what was in *Paese Sera* was just plain false.

Since I live in Ottawa, however, I decided to look for myself. As I suspected, Bloomfield's files and letters showed nothing sinister and confirmed that *Paese Sera* got it all wrong. I learned that Bloomfield was a remarkable person, deeply involved in raising money for hospitals in Montreal, working hard to further ties between Canada and Israel, and cofounding the World Wildlife Fund Canada.

I knew this would make for an interesting article. But combined with the kooky files I was collecting, I realized it was time for a fresh look at Jim Garrison. This project demanded that I examine every primary document I could find.

The first stop was Hood College in Frederick, Maryland, to visit the Harold Weisberg and Sylvia Meagher archives. They were two of the major JFK assassination researchers in the 1960s, and both had had dealings with Garrison. Weisberg had made the trek to New Orleans and actively helped Garrison. Meagher was skeptical of Garrison from the start and never made it down south. Ultimately, Weisberg became critical of Garrison when Oliver Stone's film was being produced, and many of his letters contain important stories about the investigation.

I went to the National Archives in Maryland three times, and I reviewed all of Jim Garrison's files: the files of Edward Wegmann, who was one of Clay Shaw's lawyers; the Garrison files found by his successor as the New Orleans District Attorney, Harry Connick Sr.; the papers of Clay Shaw; and those of the Metropolitan Crime Commission of New Orleans. In addition, I visited to the Library of Congress twice to look at the papers of George Lardner Jr., a terrific *Washington Post* reporter, and the papers of Elmer Gertz, who was the lawyer in a libel lawsuit against Garrison. At Georgetown University I examined the papers of Richard Billings, a *Life* magazine editor who worked with Garrison. And at Baylor University in Waco, Texas, I went through the papers of Gus Russo, one of the best JFK researchers out there.

From there I headed to New Orleans to go through the files of Irvin Dymond, Clay Shaw's trial attorney. His five boxes of material, housed at the New Orleans Historic Collection, were eye-opening. Garrison's complete master file from 1967 was there; it had been given to Shaw's lawyers by William Gurvich, an investigator for Garrison who realized he had no case.[1] While in New Orleans, I stopped in and visited with Harry Connick Sr., who defeated Garrison in 1973 for district attorney and who was in great shape at 93.

Harry Connick Sr. in his home in New Orleans.

As you'll read in this book, Garrison neglected his office to pursue the JFK assassination. Connick told me about the mess he had inherited and how he had to reexamine every open case.

The last part of my journey came just before the coronavirus lockdown. I went to Boston University to examine the papers of James Kirkwood, the author of an excellent account of the Clay Shaw trial, and then I traveled down south to the Sixth Floor Museum in Dallas, where I was privileged to be the first person to review the papers of Patricia Lambert, another author whose book *False Witness* stands out as one of the best on the case.

After examining thousands of pages of Garrison documents, I knew that not only did I have to retell the Clay Shaw story, I had to tell the stories of the other people Garrison had gone after. Ten months after he charged Shaw with conspiracy to kill Kennedy, he indicted another person, Edgar Eugene Bradley, with conspiracy without any indication of how or if the two conspiracies were linked. Garrison Staffer Tom Bethell asked, "Had two entirely separate gangs opened fire simultaneously in Dealey Plaza?" Garrison even tried to go after a man who had committed suicide a year before Kennedy was killed. He charged reporters with fraud and witnesses with perjury. He bribed people to give false statements and threatened others who wouldn't go along.

I've tried to tell all these stories in this book.

After his investigation was finished, Garrison attempted to convince the House Select Committee on Assassinations (HSCA) to follow up on his leads. Once again, his material proved to be worthless. He then wrote a book that was rejected by over a dozen publishers and that Prentice Hall said was unpublishable. One would think all this would have been enough to discredit Garrison permanently.

But a new editor at a radical left-wing publishing house helped rewrite Garrison's book as a first-person narrative, and guess who loved it? Yup, the conspiracy-theorist filmmaker-in-chief himself, Oliver Stone. His film *JFK* portrayed Garrison as a crusading hero and Clay Shaw as the villain.

A new wave of authors believe Garrison had been right all along and that Clay Shaw really was an evil conspirator. They have even come out with a new political magazine, *garrison*, dedicated to exposing the deep politics of our time. In its pages you'll find no shortage of 9/11 truthers and crazy articles that claim, for example, that FDR was murdered, that Courtney Love killed Kurt Cobain, and that the CIA murdered Robert Kennedy.

And Oliver Stone will be back with a new three-part mini-series in late 2020 to try to put "Kennedy's assassination in a far larger context." He has teamed up with James DiEugenio and will use his conspiracy book, *Destiny Betrayed*, as his main source of material to once again foist Jim Garrison on the American people.

So the time is right to have an uncompromising look at Jim Garrison. Fasten your seatbelts. It's going to be a bumpy ride.

PART 1

JIM GARRISON VS. CLAY SHAW

CHAPTER 1

THE TAKING OF NEW ORLEANS 1-2-3

JIM GARRISON WAS BORN in Iowa in 1921. He served with distinction in World War II, flying thirty-five combat missions, and he received the European Theater Campaign Medal with two battle stars. Discharged in 1946, he reactivated his membership in the Louisiana National Guard. Garrison was admitted to the bar in 1949 and received his Master of Laws in 1950. His first job was with the FBI, but he resigned when his Army reserve unit was called to active duty in Korea in 1951. He had a difficult time on his return to the military and was treated for exhaustion. He was discharged on October 31, 1951, for "physical disability."

The psychiatric report stated that Garrison had "a severe and disabling psychoneurosis of long duration. It has interfered with his social and professional adjustment to a marked degree. He is considered totally disabled from the standpoint of military duty and moderately severely incapacitated in civilian adaptability. His illness existed long before his call to active duty July 25, 1951, and is of the type that will require long term psychotherapeutic approach, which is not feasible in a military hospital."

Garrison was put under the care of Dr. Robert Matthews, a neuropsychiatrist at Louisiana State University. He was treated for four and a half years until the spring of 1955, at which time Garrison applied for reentry into the National Guard. Garrison said that his "psychiatric matter" had been cleared up.

He joined the district attorney's office in 1957 and two years later was named assistant city attorney. In 1961 Garrison, along with four other attorneys, formed the "nothing group"—no money, no political prestige, and no political support. Thus, he began his campaign for district attorney.

Garrison had several things going for him. He was 6' 6" tall (people called him the jolly green giant), and he had a deep, booming voice. He had charisma and could charm just about anybody. He dressed impeccably, was well read, and was an excellent speaker who could think on his feet.

But Garrison's campaign went nowhere until he appeared on television. As an article in *Life* magazine enthused, "Always articulate and witty, the TV camera conveyed his sincerity and intelligence. He combined his remarkable appeal with Perry Mason drama." He waited until the last minute in the campaign and used his remaining funds to finance TV commercials, even writing his own scripts. One ad showed a hypodermic needle and some granulated sugar with the tagline "This is what heroin looks like" and Garrison asking why his opponent had not prosecuted more narcotics cases. He referred to Richard Dowling, the incumbent DA, as "the great emancipator—he let everybody go free."

Garrison won the Democratic primary for district attorney. Since Louisiana was a Democratic state, this was akin to winning the election. And while he was elected as a "reformer," it's important to note that in Louisiana, "a reform candidate is someone on the outside looking at all the graft and trying to get in on the inside—to grab his share."

Milton Brener, who briefly supervised the prosecution of

narcotics cases under Garrison, wrote that "By virtue of his office, the District Attorney is potentially the most powerful of the public officials domiciled at Tulane and Broad ... however, until 1962, the full extent of his strength had been convincingly impressed neither upon the community in general, not upon the politicians themselves. It lay largely unused in the statute books. Not until the advent of Jim Garrison was the realization driven home of the large extent to which the DA's power had remained untapped."

And what were these untapped powers?

First, the district attorney had the power to file and dismiss noncapital indictments on his own with just the stroke of a pen. For capital crimes, he had to go to the grand jury and obtain an indictment.

Second, the DA had the power of subpoena and could force a person to appear before the grand jury. While Garrison was in office, his power was augmented, allowing him to subpoena people for questioning. In March 1967 Garrison subpoenaed Donald Dooty, a friend of Clay Shaw's to be interviewed in the DA's office.

Garrison: Where else have you met LAYTON MARTENS [a friend of Clay Shaw's]?

Dooty: I think at another doctor's house.

Garrison: What was the doctor's name?

Dooty: I prefer not saying it because I don't like bringing other people into this.

Garrison: We're trying to keep things simple and we don't plan to be subpoenaing the doctor. At the same time, we've called you in under a subpoena which gives us power to rule you into court on contempt. I'm not threatening you except that if you tell us the doctor's name that is very likely the end of it. But if you didn't, it would

*require us to rule you into court and then it would become
an issue, and frankly this would simplify it and we're not
that interested, but if you balk at a question it causes us to
—of course in a courtroom —*

Dooty: *His name is Rafferty.*

Last, Garrison used the grand jury system as his personal court by packing it with friends and colleagues, many of them from the New Orleans Athletic Club.[1] Witnesses were not allowed to bring their attorneys into grand jury sessions; meetings were held under strict secrecy, and hearsay and opinions were all permitted.

In 1966, a stripper applied for a pardon for obscene dancing. This was opposed by the Metropolitan Crime Commission (MCC), which believed that she had connections to organized crime. Garrison denied the existence of any organized crime in New Orleans. He subpoenaed Aaron Kohn, the head of the MCC, to appear before the grand jury and made him wait for hours before being called in. He did not allow Kohn to present his evidence. Garrison then made a public statement that Kohn was "bluffing" because the grand jury did not return an indictment. Kohn was unable to respond because of grand jury secrecy.

Garrison's favorite maneuver was to subpoena a person to appear before the grand jury and then charge them with perjury. They would then be unable to leave the jurisdiction; they would have to hire a lawyer, and they would have difficulty getting mortgages, a bank loan, or finding a job. It's no wonder that witnesses were afraid of going before the grand jury.

A10   The REGISTER   'Thursday (e) January 25, 1968   *Porter*

Subpoenaed Marina Oswald
Fearful Of Garrison Power

NEW ORLEANS (UPI) —Mrs. gation into an alleged New ciates" when the pair resided
Marina Oswald Porter the wi

On December 1, 1967, presiding Judge Bagert of the Criminal District Court for the Parish of Orleans, said the grand jury system "is more an instrument of oppression than protection" and that a district attorney "can abuse the grand jury by slanting his interpretation of evidence and swaying the jurors who are not knowledgeable about the case." One of Garrison's assistants, Lou Ivon, told staffer Tom Bethell that "It's a lot of power he's got. If all the DAs in the country were like Garrison, things would be in chaos."

Garrison assumed office in May 1962, and his priority was to expand his political power base. That meant going after everybody. His philosophy was simple: "The best way to go from one room to another is through the wall. The best way to get a mule's attention is to hit him between the eyes with a piece of stove wood. Go for the groin."

First up was the previous district attorney, Richard Dowling. One of his assistant DAs had dismissed charges on two cases, and Garrison indicted him for "malfeasance in office," an old statute that had rarely been used before. He also charged Dowling with malfeasance based upon other dismissals. All these charges were dropped or withered with inattention.

Like many reformers, Garrison decided to clean up vice in New Orleans and announced a crackdown in August 1962. The DA's office and the police issued a joint statement that "targets will be police characters, homosexuals, B-drinkers, prostitutes and narcotics violators." Rosemary James, a reporter for the

States-Item, wrote that Garrison's men raided "'gay bars' frequently, arresting 'gay kids' on the streets of the French Quarter. After one such arrest, the New Orleans *States-Item* sent me to the police station to see what the formal charges were. There, on paper, probably was one of the strangest charges in U.S. legal history: 'Being a homosexual in an establishment with a liquor license.'"

Vice squad reports throughout the 1960s referenced the number of homosexuals arrested or the number of crimes against nature. Hugh Murray, a gay man who lived in New Orleans, wrote that Garrison's office "engaged in anti-gay round-ups of single men who might be walking on the street in the wrong part of the French Quarter, or too near one of 'those' bars."

Another major target was B-drinking, where dancers or waitresses would ask customers to purchase a drink in exchange for perhaps going to a booth in the back of the club. As the customer kept on drinking and started getting drunk, the waitresses would stop bringing change. Ultimately, the mark's money disappeared.

In the first week of the summer of 1962, Garrison arrested more than a hundred people, but in the end, only five were ever convicted. Many clubs closed, and Garrison loved all the attention and the headlines. One cab driver complained that "They've got to stop this guy before he turns New Orleans into a Des Moines."

But Garrison had a problem: his undercover investigators were incurring large expenses. They had to pay for drinks with cash, which meant they could not get receipts for their expenditures. This caused an issue with reimbursement, particularly since Garrison wanted more investigators and more raids. A Louisiana statute allowed the district attorney to use funds collected from bond forfeitures and criminal case fines. The law also said that a district judge must approve all spending from the fund. When Garrison took office, the fund had $1,700; by the summer of 1962, it had over $40,000 ($340,000 in 2020 dollars).

Garrison wanted to get new drapes and carpets for his offices, and the judges approved $18,000 ($152,000 in 2020 dollars) for refurbishment. But $14,000 ($119,000 in 2020 dollars) in bills remained unpaid, and three judges decided they would withhold payment until the other judges returned from their summer holidays. They also wanted to work with Garrison on a new system.

In the fall, the judges told Garrison that vice was the jurisdiction of the police, and they were also concerned with the way Garrison had gotten approval for his spending. He went from judge to judge to get approval. "If one judge declined, he went to another until he received an authorization." They decided to fund more office decorations, but funds for vice operations were declined.

The New Orleans police were also unhappy with the system; the investigators they provided to Garrison's office were supposed to be used for trial preparation, not raids on Bourbon Street. Garrison responded by claiming that the police had "monumental disinterest" in fighting vice. The judges also joined in charging that Garrison had established a "second constabulary" and that he was acting more like a police officer.[2]

And then Judge Louis Heyd Sr. complained that the prison was overflowing. Garrison prudently suggested court sessions on Fridays and a reduction in the two-month summer holiday for judges. He publicly remarked that judges were taking too many days off, enjoying 206 days of vacation during the year. He joked that Judge Bernard Cocke "only takes one Friday off each week" and that "the only way to get these sacred cows back to work is by public reaction." What Garrison didn't mention was that judges did not have research assistants, and Judge Cocke could be found every Friday at the library. His rhetoric worked, however, and judges routinely heard people yelling "Moo, moo, moo" at them.

Garrison upped the ante by claiming that their unwillingness to fund his vice raids "raises interesting questions about the racketeer influences on our eight vacation-minded judges."[3] The judges accused Garrison of defamation; during his trial, while in the defendant's chair, he gleefully composed a 3,000-word New Orleans–set parody of Richard III. He was found guilty and fined $1,000. Ultimately the case wound its way to the U.S. Supreme Court, which held that Garrison's conviction violated his "freedom of expression." They said it was impossible to know if "malice was intentional."

This was hailed as a big victory for free speech, although it wasn't planned that way. As author James Savage notes, "Only after his conviction, when the case moved into the appellate process, did Garrison and his attorneys shed their scornful strategy and reformulate the case based on constitutional questions." And, of course, Garrison's political power grew.

Garrison continued his crusade against the police by charging nine officers with brutality. He dropped the charges a week later after a committee examined his charges. Behind closed doors, he admitted that he had no evidence whatsoever to back up his claims. The Catholic *Clarion-Herald* wrote that "Garrison's aggressive if flamboyant actions have been a boost to law enforcement in some areas but henceforth, we feel the DA should reflect before acting."

Next up was the Louisiana State Parole Board. He told the press that "the Louisiana Board of Parole repeatedly has turned loose upon the city of New Orleans hardened criminals convicted of every conceivable offense—including possession of a submachine gun, white slavery, selling narcotics, and cutting off a man's head." Using an old and arcane law, Garrison staged an "open hearing," subpoenaing the board members, who strenuously denied accepting bribes. He put one convict on the stand, John Scardino, who had heard that paroles could be bought, but he had no direct knowledge of such bribes.

Harry Connick told a reporter (not for attribution) that:

"I felt that if Garrison had proof, he should have brought the board to trial. I think he knew he couldn't convict anybody. I think it was an attempt to gain publicity. He could have used his immense influence with McKeithen [the governor of Louisiana] to get legislation. It was a terrible witch-burning. He impugned the parole board— which though not the most professionally competent in the world, was a sincere and honest board."

Garrison quickly ended his hearings and shifted his investigation to the grand jury, but if any evidence was ever developed as a result of the grand jury investigation, it was never made public. Still, Garrison ultimately got his way, and the board was replaced.

His next target was the Louisiana legislature. They had rejected some reforms that Garrison had wanted (concerning bail bondsmen), and Garrison said: "The only way to explain it is wholesale bribery." He was censured and proceeded to scale back his charge, claiming that only some legislators took bribes. Even the mayor of New Orleans wasn't beyond criticism; Garrison said he was using the police as a "political Gestapo."

In November 1964, police superintendent Joseph Giarrusso received information that a $600 payment had been made to the DA's office to destroy evidence of gambling, evidence obtained from a bar safe. Once word of the police investigation got out, Garrison went on a rampage, saying that "I react very strongly to political investigations of my office and I am going to be very aggressive in bringing about the exposure of whoever is responsible for attempting to damage the morale of my office." Garrison started an investigation into what he called "irregularities" in the mayor's office and released a letter containing twenty-one questions, one of which was "Is it not a fact that you have been informed that a high-ranking member of your staff often accepts cash gratuities?" The police investigation into Garrison's office stopped, and so did Garrison's investigation.

Giarrusso issued a statement:

"Mr. Garrison's tactics have been to steam roll over anyone who opposes his views. If, by chance, you are successful in opposing him, his next tactic is to threaten you. If this be unsuccessful, his final tactic is to smoke screen, call press conferences, issue press releases and write letters. He figures, ultimately, he can out word you. Mr. Garrison is obviously not a man to disagree with because if you do, you shall feel the full force of his wrath and fury."

Garrison was able to get away with this sort of behavior because he entertained the population. Rosemary James, a journalist for the *States-Item*, noted that "This has been a community and a state that really enjoyed politicians who would entertain them. Garrison, whatever else he was—nuts, cynical, whatever—he was very entertaining. I think he was allowed to get that far because of his personal charisma."

After fighting city hall (literally), the police, the mayor, and everybody except the dog catchers by the summer of 1966, Jim Garrison was bored. He was interviewed by reporter David Chandler, who asked him why there had been no crime-fighting crusades in the past year:

"Why bother?" he replied. "I cleaned up Bourbon Street and I didn't get any credit. I never get any credit." I said

this was untrue and maybe he was a bit paranoiac about it.
He livened up. "Paranoiac! Paranoiac!" He picked up the
phone and told ... chief assistant Charles Ward to come in.
"Chandler says I'm paranoiac because I say I don't get
any credit. Do I get any credit? Am I paranoiac?" Charlies
said I was wrong. Pleased, Garrison went on. "Another
reason we don't have fights any more is we've beaten the
people trying to stop justice in New Orleans."

Like many Americans, Garrison started reading JFK assassination conspiracy books, notably *Whitewash* by Harold Weisberg, *Inquest* by Edward Jay Epstein, and *Rush to Judgment* by Mark Lane. He also read articles questioning the Warren Report in *Esquire* and *Life* magazine. In late fall, he invited Dean Andrews, a lawyer who was to play a major role in the whole affair, out for a meeting at Broussard's restaurant. Garrison had with him a copy of Harold Weisberg's *Whitewash* and told Andrews that he "was an overlooked witness." Throughout their meeting, Garrison browsed the book. Andrews told NBC that "he didn't even have a copy of the Warren Report."

Garrison knew that Lee Harvey Oswald lived in New Orleans for five months in 1963, and he had also helped investigate some of the early leads in the assassination in late 1963 and early 1964. Perhaps the key to unlocking the JFK mystery was right here in New Orleans. What an opportunity! Garrison could play to a "tremendous resentment [that had] built up in Louisiana, against the Federal government, generally, and Lyndon B. Johnson, particularly [because of] long quarrels over integration, and to a lesser degree over the tidelands oil royalty." Solving the case would bring Garrison the governorship or perhaps a U.S. Senate seat.

He told Richard Billings of *Life* magazine exactly how he would investigate the Kennedy assassination:

"I won't take no for an answer. I've not gonna let somebody lie to me in this case; they lied to the Warren Commission, they lied to the FBI, they're not gonna lie to me. I'm gonna use every legal form of power I have at my disposal. I have the right to make the decision. The people elected me to make the decision. I have the power available, and I'm gonna use it. If they don't like the way I use the power, then the solution is for them not to elect me next time. But until the next election comes up, I have it and I'm going to use it as effectively as possible; and I'm going to use it in new ways, perhaps ways that haven't been used before, and with imagination and if necessary with aggressiveness and audacity in order to get people who have concealed the truth previously, to tell the truth."

And so, Jim Garrison went down the rabbit hole.

The story broke publicly on January 23, 1967, when Jack Dempsey's column in the New Orleans *States-Item* contained an intriguing item: "Did you know? At least five persons have been questioned by the District Attorney's office in connection with another investigation into events linked to the Kennedy assassination." The *States-Item* broke the story wide open on February 17 with a major story by Rosemary James revealing that DA Jim Garrison had spent $8,000 ($61,000 in 2020 dollars) in public money investigating the JFK assassination.[4]

That forced Garrison out into the open, and he boasted that "There will be arrests. Charges will be filed and on the basis of these charges, convictions will be obtained." His prime suspect in the assassination, David Ferrie, died of natural causes on February 22. Two days later, Garrison claimed that "My staff and I solved the case weeks ago. I wouldn't say this if I didn't have evidence beyond the shadow of a doubt. We know the key individuals, the cities involved and how it was done." Mysteriously, he added that "The key to the whole case is through the looking glass. Black is white; white is black. I don't want to be cryptic, but that's the way it is."

On March 1, Jim Garrison arrested businessman Clay Shaw for conspiring to kill President John F. Kennedy.

Garrison announces the arrest of Clay Shaw on March 2, 1967, at a press conference outside his office. CREDIT: Associated Press.

No one was going to stop Garrison. Governor John McKei-then of Louisiana said, "I'm leaving the case alone, I have no criticism of Jim and even if I did, I wouldn't voice it ... I have learned that most of Jim Garrison's political enemies are buried and I don't propose to join the list of the distinguished decedents."

There was an immediate stampede to New Orleans. Entertainer Mort Sahl went right to Jim Garrison's home and introduced himself. He told Garrison, "I want to shake your hand," to which Garrison replied, "I hope you're available to do a lot more than that." He made Sahl an unpaid investigator and even gave him business cards. When James Alcock, second in command to Garrison, heard that Sahl was an official investigator, he commented, "We'll have jugglers and fire-breathers working for us soon." Warren Commission critics Harold Weisberg, Edward Jay Epstein, Raymond Marcus, and Mark Lane all headed to the new Mecca of conspiracy.

On March 29, 1967, Lane called into Sahl's radio show and told him that "I think I can say this, that the evidence is conclusive that no foreign power was involved, none at all, but a very powerful domestic force was involved in planning the events which culminated in the death of President Kennedy and that the persons that actually participated in the conspiracy and in the assassination are known to Mr. Garrison, to his staff, and now to me. The evidence is so conclusive, I believe, that when Garrison walks into that courtroom in New Orleans and presents it, and when the American people learn for the first time who planned the events, which culminated in the death of President Kennedy, they are going to be outraged, absolutely outraged, and shocked and stunned. Then I think that there are going to be some important, drastic changes in this country. There will have to be after that evidence is known."

It was an exciting time to be alive. Jim Garrison was now the most powerful politician in Louisiana, and he was going to reveal the truth. What could possibly go wrong?

CHAPTER 2

A BEAUTIFUL MIND?

SEVERAL RECURRING THEMES colored Jim Garrison's investigation: his mental illness, his bizarre investigative "techniques," his attraction to conspiracy theories, his irrational leftist politics, and his endless paranoia.

The Madness of DA Jim

In 1967, Frank Manning, the chief investigator for Louisiana Attorney General Jack Gremillion, went to the FBI to discuss a serious problem. He had evidence that Jim Garrison was involved in a shakedown racket against homosexuals in the French Quarter. His boss had learned the hard way that it was dangerous to go after Garrison, so Manning was asking for assistance.

UNITED STATES DEPARTMENT OF JUSTICE

FEDERAL BUREAU OF INVESTIGATION

*Reply, Please Refer to
the No.*

WASHINGTON, D.C.   20535

March 6, 1967

ASSASSINATION OF PRESIDENT
JOHN FITZGERALD KENNEDY
DALLAS, TEXAS, NOVEMBER 22, 1963

Mr. Frank W. Manning, Chief Investigator for Attorney General Jack P. F. Gremillion of Louisiana, has advised a representative of this Bureau that he has been extremely concerned over the activities of New Orleans District Attorney James C. Garrison. He stated Garrison has absolutely no basis for his present publicity stunt in claiming that he has reason to believe Oswald acted as a part of a conspiracy in the assassination. Manning stated Garrison is a "psychopath" who has to have publicity, otherwise he falls into "fits of moodiness and depression." Manning commented that he felt Garrison's activities, unless stopped and exposed, are damaging to the FBI and likely to hurt the entire country.

Manning alleged that several years ago he conducted an extensive investigation of Garrison with reference to the prosecution of Garrison for defamation which was handled by Attorney General Gremillion. He advised Gremillion obtained a conviction of Garrison, but the United States Supreme Court reversed the case. Manning commented that he would be glad to make his entire file available to the FBI on a confidential basis and that he is convinced this file contains the ground work for developing a good extortion case on Garrison which would prove that Garrison is involved in a big "shakedown" racket wherein Garrison and a couple of others are "shaking down" hundreds of sex deviates in the New Orleans French Quarter. Manning advised that he has information indicating that Garrison himself might be a sex deviate or at least he is a participant in some deviate activities with other homosexuals.

Manning stated that he did not have a complete case developed to prove the extortion or shakedown activities of Garrison because he stopped his investigation short of that when Attorney General Gremillion had enough evidence on the defamation charge. His investigation into Garrison's activities with sex deviates was designed to give the Attorney General "an ace in the hole" if he should need it. After the Garrison case was reversed on appeal, Attorney General Gremillion washed his hands of any further efforts to "get" Garrison and, therefore, Manning's file on Garrison was closed.

It is alleged by Manning that his file contains the names of several hundred individuals in the French Quarter who were charged by Garrison's office with some sex deviate violation. In many of these cases, Manning found that after the individual was charged, suddenly the case was either dropped by Garrison or the charge was reduced to some minor offense. In still other cases Manning stated that there was a clear-cut indication that Garrison's office had maneuvered the case so that it would be handled by another judge and thereby the individual would be acquitted, the charge dismissed, or he would be given a suspended sentence. Manning advised his investigation led him to believe there are the earmarks of a definite pattern of maneuvering and control by the District Attorney's office and he is convinced that if the FBI dug into these cases and developed a few informants, the FBI would be able without too much difficulty to establish the fact that Garrison was shaking down these individuals for considerable sums of money and after they paid off, Garrison would see that the case was cleared up.

In addition, Manning advised there is another individual named Persian Gervais, who was formerly with the District Attorney's office and was forced to resign after some adverse publicity indicating income tax fraud. According to Manning, the Internal Revenue Service has an extensive file on Gervais which would document this information. Manning stated Gervais is a homosexual and, despite the fact that he was forced out of the District Attorney's office, he still has Garrison "under his thumb." Manning alleged that almost every day Garrison and Gervais can be found in the back room at the Fontainebleau Motel in New Orleans. Manning believes that Gervais could be involved in this shakedown racket with Garrison.

J. Edgar Hoover refused to intervene, claiming that this was a state matter. Ramsey Clark, attorney general of the U.S., also received anonymous complaints.

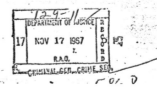

DEAR SIR: anony: 10/14/67

FOR OBVIOUS REASONS, THIS
LETTER MUST BE ANONYMOUS.
    THE PAPERS TODAY NOTE YOU
MAY INDICT MR. GARRISON OF
NEW ORLEANS.
    MR. GARRISON IS NOT JUST
PLAYING WITH THE KENNEDY MURDER.
WITHIN HIS OFFICE GROUP, THEY
ARE RUNNING A HOMOSEXUAL
SETUP - BLACKMAIL BUSINESS WHICH
INCLUDES THE USE OF LOCAL DECOYS
TO LURE NORTHERN CITY VISITORS,
THE SUBSEQUENT CHECKING OF
BANK BALANCES ACROSS STATE
LINES AND THE COOPERATION OF
LOCAL CROOKED ATTORNIES.

RECE'D
NOV 17 1967
CRIMINAL DIVISION

12-9-//
DEPARTMENT OF JUSTICE
17   NOV 17 1967
R.A.O.
CRIMINAL GEN. CRIME SEC.

There was never any investigation into these allegations, so
we don't know if they are true. Historian Alecia Long points
out that "tallies of arrests by vice squad officers for crimes
considered as 'homosexual' were routinely exceeding the
number of arrests for every other category in the book,
including prostitution." She noted that in 1963 alone, "the vice
squad made 249 arrests of homosexuals versus 193 for prostitution."

While Garrison's crackdown on B-drinking abated over time,
his war on homosexuals continued. Rosemary James noted that
"one benefit" of Garrison's raids on homosexuals "may have been
the creation of a body of homosexual informants for the district

attorney's office—informants possibly involved in his Kennedy plot investigation."

Others noticed something deeper that might have been driving his war on gay people. In July 1967 Aaron Kohn, head of the Metropolitan Crime Commission of New Orleans, wrote a memorandum on the "emotional incapacity or perhaps insanity" of Jim Garrison. He commented on Garrison's use of "emotionally disturbed persons (homosexuals, narcotic addicts, sociopaths, extreme neurotics) as witnesses to support his claims and as victims of his prosecutive actions." Kohn consulted with Dr. Harold Lief, a psychiatrist at Tulane Medical School who told him that "he had already concluded Garrison to be paranoid schizophrenic, based upon his personal contacts with Garrison, his knowledge of Garrison's extraordinary personal sex life, indicating him to be obsessed with fear of his own active or latent homosexuality, coupled with the use of his prosecutorial power in an attempt to destroy homosexuals."

Two incidents seem to corroborate the accusation. First, Garrison wrote in his book *On The Trail of The Assassins* about a 1968 incident at the LA airport. He had been in in the baggage claim area and went to buy a magazine. There were no seats in the waiting section, so he decided to go to the men's room to read it. While sitting in an empty stall, he said that he heard the door in the adjoining cubicle open and then close. "Within minutes there were six policemen at the entrance to the men's room ... and they started questioning Garrison. He escaped the situation when two women at the rent-a-car counter recognized him."[1]

It's hard to know if this really happened. Garrison claimed that he "always went to the men's room, sat down in a toilet booth, and read a magazine for ten minutes." Frankly, I'm skeptical. This reminds me of the incident involving Senator Larry Craig in 2007 when he hung out in a stall at the Minneapolis–St. Paul airport and started playing "footsy" with an undercover police officer in the next stall.

A second incident occurred in 1969. Garrison supposedly fondled a thirteen-year-old boy at the New Orleans Athletic Club. Author Patricia Lambert interviewed the victim and his brother in 1993, and they told her that Garrison invited the boy, his older brother, and father into a "slumber room" at the club. The boys weren't interested, but the father thought he might learn something new about the JFK assassination. The room was dark, and Garrison reached over and touched the boy. The family received a lot of pressure not to pursue the case; an attorney warned them "terrible harm" would come to the boy. Worried about his safety, the family dropped the issue.[2]

Jack Anderson Reports From Washington—

New Orleans Atty. Accused Of Molesting 13-Year-Old Boy

By JACK ANDERSON

WASHINGTON — The Orleans Parish grand jury is investigating a charge that New Orleans District Attorney Jim Garrison sexually molested a 13-year-old boy at the city's posh Athletic Club.

man embarrassment, we will leave out names.

Kohn, as director of the privately financed Crime Commission, has often been at odds with Garrison. He would confirm for the record only that the text of the letter obtained by this column was

in the nude at the New Orleans Athletic Club.

"Garrison invited them to relax and take a nap. In that room, Garrison twice fondled the genitals of the younger son, 13 years old (name omitted by this column). The elder son (name omitted) then are

Jack Anderson's nationally-syndicated column from February 23, 1970, which did not run in New Orleans.

Garrison's Theory of Propinquity

Garrison had an important investigative technique to get at the truth: propinquity. A great word, but not such a great concept. Here's how Garrison staffer Tom Bethell described it:

> *"If two people live near one another, say within two or*
> *three blocks, it's suspicious. If any closer—they are*
> *"linked." If, on the other hand, they live at opposite ends of*
> *the city, get a list of friends of each (from their address*
> *books). Two such friends are very likely to live in the same*
> *block, or even know each other. Presto—the link.*

William Gurvich, a Garrison investigator told Shaw's lawyers that "he always said he was going to solve the assassination with an Esso road map and the city directory. And that's all he did all day long. I know. I got him five city directories."

Garrison wrote two memos with the same name to his staff: "Time and Propinquity: Factors in Phase One." His concept of propinquity went beyond geography. Any sort of relationship—numerical, even sexual—was enough to set off alarm bells. Garrison told Tom Bethell, one of his staff members, that "Sooner or later, because people are lazy, you catch them out on propinquity."

Bethell gives a great example of propinquity in his book *The Electric Windmill*:

> *"In Dallas, at the time of the assassination there lived a*
> *Russian-émigré oil geologist named George De*
> *Mohrenschildt who had befriended Lee Harvey Oswald*
> *after Lee returned from the Soviet Union in 1962 (whither*
> *he had defected in 1959). There was another member of*
> *the Dallas émigré community named George Bouhe, who*
> *knew De Mohrenschildt (who knew Oswald). And city*
> *directories showed Bouhe lived right opposite ... Jack*
> *Ruby! (he shot Oswald, just in case you had forgotten.)*

> *And there you have the long-sought Oswald-Ruby link—*
> *based on propinquity."*

Unfortunately, Ruby was dead, little was known about Bouhe, and the lead died.

Lee Harvey Oswald lived on the 4900 block of Magazine Street in New Orleans. Garrison thought it was suspicious that one block toward downtown is the 800 block of Lyons Street. And on *that* block lived two uncles of Layton Martens, a friend of both Shaw and Ferrie. This was enough to link Oswald and Martens. But Garrison went further and investigated all the people who lived on the block. For instance, R. J. Haydel, who had "frequently been in trouble for bad checks, lived in the 5000 block, at least as late as 1962." He concluded that "regardless of the apparently accidental nature of the choice of this apartment by Oswald, it should be assumed for investigative purposes that the selection of this block was meaningful in some way."

Even parts of addresses were enough for a connection. In a memo titled "Time, Place and Number Correlations," Garrison wrote, "Lee Oswald's address book contains the inscription: MIDLAND 2550. Jack Ruby's address book contains the inscription NEWTON 2550. (Midland and Newton are Texas towns.)" Garrison believed these were "call signs" on some radio frequency.

Garrison the Irrational Leftist

Garrison was browsing Harold Weisberg's book *Whitewash* when he interviewed Dean Andrews in the fall of 1966. He relied heavily on several concepts from that book.

Weisberg, like most conspiracy critics, was a leftist, and he not only wanted to prove the existence of a conspiracy but wanted it to be a right-wing plot. That meant that he had to hide

Lee Harvey Oswald's interest in communism and Marxism, which began at the age of fifteen. Oswald wanted to join the New Orleans Amateur Astronomy Association, and its president told the Warren Commission that he was "expounding the Communist doctrine and saying that he was highly interested in communism, that communism was the only way of life for the worker, et cetera, and then came out with a statement that he was looking for a communist cell in town to join but he couldn't find any." At sixteen, he wrote a letter to the Socialist Party of America about his Marxist beliefs.

Oswald defected to the Soviet Union in 1959, at the age of twenty, and came back in 1962 disgusted with what he experienced. He wrote that the "the Soviets have committed crimes unsurpassed even by their early day capitalist counterparts; the imprisonment of their own people, with the mass exterminations so typical of Stalin." But he was still very much a man of the left. Oswald noted that "we have no interest in violently opposing the U.S. government [because] there are far greater forces at work, to bring about the fall of the United States Government."

Oswald's goal was the "emplacement of a separate, democratic, pure communist society, [complete with] union-communes, democratic socializing of production and without regard to the twisting apart of Marxist communism by other powers."

Oswald's interest now turned to Cuba and Fidel Castro. He started a New Orleans chapter of the Fair Play for Cuba Committee. When interviewed on the radio by Bill Stuckey, he said that "You cannot say Castro is a communist at this time because he has not developed his country, his system, thus far. He has not had the chance to become a Communist. He is an experimenter, a person who is trying to find out the best way for his country." Oswald saw Cuba as a chance for that "pure communist society," and he wanted to play a part and influence Castro in the revolution. Oswald even had a picture of Castro on the mantlepiece of his apartment.

So he had to get to Cuba. To help him achieve his goal, he tried to infiltrate anti-Castro groups in New Orleans, where he proceeded to hand out pro-Cuba leaflets on the streets. When anti-Castro groups got wind of this, an altercation ensued. Oswald was arrested, and his arrest made the newspapers and was on the radio. When he went to the Cuban embassy in Mexico City in late September 1963 to get a visa, he showed them his "dossier" to help prove his commitment to the revolution. It didn't work. The Cubans consulted the Russians, and he was turned away. He ended up having a meltdown at the Russian embassy, and he moved to Dallas a deeply bitter and angry man.

But Weisberg ignored all this and wrote that "From boyhood on ... Oswald was anti-Communist" and wondered if he had simply pretended to be pro-Castro. His opinion was that it was all a ruse. Oswald's activities did not make sense "except in terms of what is known in the intelligence trade as 'establishment of a cover.'"

Garrison quickly picked this up as a core theme of his investigation. He told the BBC that "Oswald was not a communist, Oswald was not pro-Castro." Garrison believed that Oswald wanted to get to Cuba to be part of a plot to kill Castro, and when he could not get into Cuba, he turned against Kennedy.

Garrison told an interviewer on May 27, 1969, that "We literally stumbled across Central Intelligence Agency employees in New Orleans who were helping to set Lee Oswald up by giving him intelligence assignments which make it appear as if he were a Communist." Garrison was interviewed for an NBC documentary in June 1967 and he said:

"I think I can tell you that I know but I feel like saying it for the first time, that the Fair Play for Cuba, which he pretended to be so interested in was a cover, for the

operation. Oswald was not a communist, Oswald was not pro-Castro, and as a result of the operation which was working here in the summer of 1963, a spin-off occurred. An unexpected change of direction occurred which, in the fall of 1963, which resulted in the lethal apparatus which was used against President Kennedy and that's what happened, and that's the first time I've ever said this in public."

Garrison went further in his October 1967 interview with *Playboy* magazine:

"I don't believe there are any serious students of the assassination who don't recognize that Oswald's actual political orientation was extreme right-wing. His associates in Dallas and New Orleans—apart from his CIA contacts—were exclusively right-wing, some covert, others overt; in fact, our office has positively identified a number of his associates as neo-Nazis. Oswald would have been more at home with Mein Kampf *than* Das Kapital."

Garrison would never show any evidence of Oswald being a man of the right.

Garrison the Conspiracy Theorist

A staple of conspiracy theorists are pictures showing three tramps (vagrants) being marched away by Dallas police after the assassination. Their arrest records were not in the Warren Commission's twenty-six volumes of evidence, so who were they, and why were they arrested? Dallas Police Sargent D.V. Harkness testified before the Warren Commission that they pulled the tramps and hoboes off a freight train that was about to leave the railway yard. They were taken to the police station, questioned, and then presumably released.

The three tramps. Conspiracy theorists have believed that the tramp on the right was E. Howard Hunt, of Watergate fame. Of course, people were comparing pictures of Hunt in the mid-1970s with a picture taken in 1963.

Conspiracy theorist Richard Sprague believed the pictures of the tramps "might help unlock some mysteries about the assassination. If either the 'tramps' or the officers escorting them could be identified, new avenues for investigation would be opened."

In January 1968, Garrison was scheduled to go on *The Tonight Show Starring Johnny Carson*. Sprague sent him the tramp pictures, and he studied them on the flight to New York. He was immediately suspicious. The tramps had short hair and were clean-shaven; Garrison expected their hair to be "shaggy and overgrown." The soles of their shoes were not thin enough.

He wondered why they weren't handcuffed, and he felt the police officers were not carrying their rifles properly. But what was really strange to him was that the officer who appeared to be in charge was "wearing a miniature radio receiver ear clip—a plastic device less than half an inch by a quarter of an inch in size."[3]

To Garrison, these weren't tramps, and the men in uniform were not Dallas police officers. He "was not sure if the Dallas police force had been penetrated, or impersonated, or both." Garrison noted that "As I put the prints of the shotgun arrests in my briefcase, I resolved that anyone watching the Johnny Carson show the following night was going to get to see them."

Carson challenged Garrison at every turn and put him on the defensive. Toward the end, Carson asked him why the government was concealing evidence. Here's the exchange:

Garrison: Let me show you some pictures, and if you want to reject these, go ahead. In the 26 volumes, there is no reference to any serious sort of arrest. There are a couple of references to short dialogues. And then the indication is that the man wasn't of any value, or of any importance at all. Actually, at Dealey Plaza, there were ten men arrested, and this has been kept secret for more than four years. Here are the pictures of five of them being arrested, [hands photo to Carson] and they've never been shown before.

Carson: No, I don't know any of those men [shows the audience one picture of the tramps].

Garrison: Several of these men arrested have been connected by our office with the Central Intelligence Agency of the United States government. The probability is that this is why Officer Tippit[4] was killed. Is this speculation? Positively, and I want to identify it as that. But the probability appears to be that the killing of Tippit was a diversion which allowed them to turn loose these ten men. Here's some more. [hands photo to Carson]] And here's another ...

Carson: No, really, it won't show Jim [Carson looks at two of the pictures and puts them down].

Garrison: But why aren't they mentioned? Why aren't they mentioned?

Carson: No, but you say speculation and a probability. Who's suppressing all this information, on whose order?

Garrison: I'll tell you who's suppressing it. The federal government is suppressing it.

Carson: Who in the federal government?

Garrison: The administration. The administration of your government is suppressing it because they know that the Central Intelligence Agency ...

Carson: On whose order?

Garrison: On the order of the President of the United States. Who do you think issued—let me finish now— before the advertisement—the executive order, which forbids every person in this audience and every person listening to this program, which forbids him to look at this evidence until September in the year 2039, was issued by the President of the United States. Does that answer your question? He's suppressing it.

Garrison fictionalized this part of the interview in his book *On the Trail of the Assassins*. He claimed he had held up one of the tramp photos and that "it took Carson a moment to recognize the scene, but when he realized what it was, he lunged at my arm like a cobra, pulling it down violently so that the pictures were out of the camera's view." Garrison then concocted a dialogue claiming that after Carson said, "It won't show," he held up the picture and replied, "Sure they do. The camera can pick this up." Then, supposedly Carson yanked his arm down once again and said, "No, it can't."

But it was Carson who showed the first picture and then declined to show the others because he thought the camera wouldn't catch them properly. Garrison wondered, "Why had Carson pulled my arm away so that the photographs were out of camera range? And why had the director and the control room switched off the camera so that the photographs could not be seen?" Garrison also asked, why had newspapers "not seized the opportunity to be first into print with these great photographs?" The only possible answer, to Garrison, was control.

> "[H]ere a call from a high-ranking federal intelligence official explaining to a newspaper publisher the overwhelming national security consequences that might result from irresponsible publication of pictures before the government had studied them; then a call from a Texas politician, a lifelong friend of Lyndon Johnson's, to a network president explains the great harm that could befall the republic if such photographs were shown to the public."

Identifying the tramps became an obsession for Garrison.

The tramps were investigated by the House Select Committee on Assassinations (HSCA) in the late 1970s. The HSCA photographic panel found that "all three men are shabbily dressed, befitting their apparent status as vagrants." They noted that one of the tramps, "from his battered fedora to his worn-out shoes, has managed to achieve a sartorial effect similar to what one would expect had he been fired from a cannon through a Salvation Army thrift shop."

The truth emerged in 1993 when the Dallas City Council released its JFK assassination records. Journalist Mary La Fontaine found arrest records that showed the tramps were exactly that—tramps. Their names were Harold Doyle, John Gedney, and Gus Abrams. Two of the tramps were still alive, and they said that the night before the assassination, they had spent the night at a rescue mission, gotten fresh clothes, showered, shaved, and ate. They went back to the railway yards, and they were arrested after the assassination. John Gedney told the FBI they were held for four to six days and then released.

The Paranoia of Jim Garrison

Garrison was convinced that his phone was tapped by the FBI. In 1967, reporter Hugh Aynesworth visited Garrison to discuss the case. Garrison, he said, would rush off periodically and shout a chess move into the handset of the phone. Aynesworth asked him what was happening, and Garrison replied, "That's the code. The Feebees [FBI] will never break it." He then told Aynesworth he had to take out the kids to play before noon because, as he put it, "There's a torpedo from Miami after me. Everybody knows they sleep till noon." Garrison's aides told the *Times-Picayune* that "He often answered his telephone, F--- you, J. Edgar Hoover."

Garrison decided to raid the local FBI office and retrieve the tapes, which were supposedly kept in the "sound room." He told William Gurvich that there would be "a panel in the wall" and that the room would be "behind a desk or a cabinet or a closet." There would, he added, "be a secret way of opening it." The people who were going to go on this raid were to be armed with red pepper guns that would "immobilize people but would do them no physical harm." Gurvich asked Garrison what would happen if some FBI agents showed up. He told him, "That's the purpose of the red pepper guns." Gurvich asked Garrison if they'd be able to outshoot them with these so-called weapons. "I didn't think of that," Garrison admitted.

Garrison also believed that the CIA was paying the lawyers of several witnesses. On May 28, 1967, he appeared on the ABC show "Issues and Answers", where he alleged that "Every lawyer involved in this case, without exception, involved in the attempt to derail the investigation and to stop the case, has been connected by us with the Central Intelligence Agency." In June 1967, he appeared on NBC:

Question: We now find three people who are outside Louisiana who are fighting their return to the state in connection with your investigation—Gordon Novel, Sergio Arcacha Smith, and Sandra Moffit. Could you briefly discuss these three people and their role in all this?

Garrison: The point that you're going for is that we are in private difficulty for getting them back. That, of course, is because of the intercession of the U.S. government, not necessarily the administration at the topmost level, but certainly, through the intercession of the CIA which has great power because of the millions of dollars, it spends and for other reasons. Sandra Moffit, for example, who has no money, is represented by the very successful lawyer who is Chairman of the 13 State Democratic Regional

Committee. Gordon Novel not only has a very successful lawyer in Ohio he also has a lawyer down here. Mr. Arcacha seems not to have a problem with representation either. He initially announced that he was represented by the Chief Assistant of the District Attorney of Dallas, but he now seems to have private counsel. Similarly, Beauboeuf, who has never been regarded as a crucial witness by us, nor ever been regarded as a great value by us, is represented by a successful and high price lawyer here too. It is obvious that these lawyers are being paid by the Central Intelligence Agency, that the money is being diverted to either people and then coming to them.

Garrison believed that he "never was paranoid enough. I was warned that I should have been."

CHAPTER 3

JIM GARRISON SOLVES THE JFK ASSASSINATION

NEW ORLEANS PLAYED a big part in the life of Lee Harvey Oswald. He was born there in 1939, moved away at the age of six, returned at the age of fifteen, and stayed there for two years before joining the Marines. He defected to the Soviet Union in 1959 and came back to the United States in 1962, living in Dallas—Ft. Worth. Oswald moved back to New Orleans for five months in 1963. It's not surprising then that any investigation into the assassination would start in New Orleans.

Two days after the JFK assassination, Garrison's office got a tip from a local drunk and former felon, Jack Martin, about a New Orleans connection. Martin had a long-standing grudge against David Ferrie, a former Eastern Airlines pilot who had lost his job because of criminal charges related to a homosexual relationship with an underage teenager. Martin thought Oswald's rifle looked similar to the one Ferrie had owned years earlier and recalled that Ferrie had mentioned a short story about a presidential assassination. Martin watched the weekend television coverage and heard that Oswald had been a member of the Civil Air Patrol (CAP) when he was a teenager in New Orleans.

Martin knew that Ferrie had been an instructor in CAP, and that was enough to send him to the telephone.

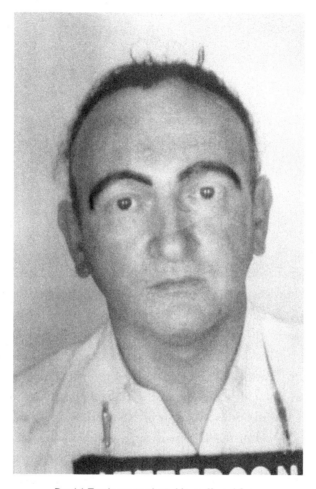

David Ferrie mug shot. He suffered from alopecia, which caused him to lose all body hair. CREDIT: Bettmann.

But Martin had been drinking, and that's when he most suffered from "telephonitis." He called Major Presley Trosclair of the New Orleans Police Intelligence Unit and told him that Oswald was friends with Ferrie. That set off a chain reaction of phone calls in which the FBI and the New Orleans Police

Department were informed. Martin also called and wrote to anybody else he could think of with his stories about Ferrie. FBI special agent Regis Kennedy wrote HQ that "Jack Martin is a well known self -styled New Orleans private eye, personally known to [me] as a psychopathic personality, an individual who is not above furnishing false information ... Martin has an extremely poor reputation for truth and veracity and is regarded by most people who know him as a 'nut.'"

Ferrie was questioned by the FBI and the Secret Service, and he said that while he might have been in CAP at the same time as Oswald, he did not remember him.[1] The weekend of the assassination, he had driven to Houston and had gone ice skating with some friends. His whereabouts were quickly verified, and he was released.

There was another New Orleans connection. Dean Andrews was a short, overweight lawyer who was in the hospital the weekend of the assassination with double pneumonia. He had a high fever and was heavily sedated. On Saturday, November 23, he claimed to have received a call from Eugene Davis, a bar owner in the French Quarter who had previously sent Andrews clients from the gay community. He supposedly told Davis, while still woozy from medication, that he could be famous if he were Oswald's defense attorney. It wasn't long before Andrews phoned his secretary and told her that he had just received a phone call asking him to represent Oswald. When she asked him who had hired him, Andrews just said, "Bertrand."

On Sunday, November 24, Jack Ruby shot Lee Harvey Oswald. That let Andrews off the hook with his crazy story, but it also allowed him to add more details. He started telling people that Oswald had visited his office on at least three occasions in the past seeking legal advice and that he was always accompanied by up to five homosexuals. He then told the FBI and Secret Service that Bertrand's full name was Clay Bertrand, that he was also gay, and that he might have accompanied Oswald on his visits. In one instance, Andrews told the FBI that Bertrand was "a youthful appearing person age 22–23, 5'7", 160 pounds, blonde hair, and crew cut." The FBI, the Secret Service, and Garrison spent several days looking for Bertrand with no success.

(ev. 1-25-60)   FEDERAL BUREAU OF INVESTIGATION

Date ____11/27/63____

1

    JUNIOR O'ROURKE, United Taxi Cab driver, who operates on the corner of Bourbon and Conti Streets, New Orleans, Louisiana, a former New Orleans police officer, retired, who has extensive contacts in the New Orleans French Quarter, particularly among the homosexual element, advised that CLAY BERTRAND was known to him and that inquiry among sources known to him familiar with the French Quarter had been negative to identify this person.

v. 1-25-60)   FEDERAL BUREAU OF INVESTIGATION

Date ____11/27/63____

1

    RAYMOND COMSTOCK, Investigator, District Attorney's Office, advised that DEAN ANDREWS, attorney-at-law, had contacted him, attempting to identify CLAY BERTRAND. COMSTOCK advised he was familiar with a number of homosexuals in the New Orleans French Quarter but has been unable to identify this individual.

FEDERAL BUREAU OF INVESTIGATION

                                        Date November 30, 1963

1

          BETTY PARENT, 935 Dauphine Street, New Orleans,
Louisiana, advised she has numerous acquaintances among
sex deviates of the New Orleans French Quarter and she
advised that she has been unable to determine any information which would identify an individual by the name of
CLAY BERTRAND.

          She advised that the only individual she could
associate with either name was an individual named CLAY
GOULD who associates with the sex deviates in the New
Orleans French Quarter. She advised that she had no reason
to believe that CLAY GOULD is identical to CLAY BERTRAND
other than the similarity of the first name.

*The FBI and the District Attorney's office tried to find "Clay
Bertrand" in late 1963, but to no avail.*

Andrews then backed away from his allegations and told the
FBI that it was all a figment of his imagination (doubtless the
result of the hospital sedation). However, he stuck to his original
story about Oswald visiting his office. In July 1964, Andrews
testified before the Warren Commission and resurrected his
Bertrand story, but he changed his physical description. The
Warren Report spent one paragraph discussing his allegations
and noted that he "was able to locate no records of any of
Oswald's alleged visits" and that his secretary "had no recollection of Oswald being there."

So it was natural that Jim Garrison would start his new investigation by talking to Dean Andrews and seeing if he could shed
any light on Clay Bertrand.[2] But he offered little help, and
Garrison went back to Jack Martin, who was only too happy to
talk. The night of the assassination, Martin had been pistol-
whipped by his boss, the gumshoe Guy Banister. Now Martin
was claiming that he had been beaten because he had made an
off-hand comment about seeing Lee Harvey Oswald, David

Ferrie, and some Cubans in Banister's office in the summer of 1963.[3]

On December 13, 1966, Garrison recorded an interview with Jack Martin and Pershing Gervais, his former chief investigator. Martin now said that Ferrie "was in Dallas at least in Fort Worth two days before the assassination of President Kennedy." He went further, claiming that "I understand he was to fly three people from there to Laredo, Texas, either there or Matamorris [sic], Mexico." This was not true; Ferrie was not in Dallas.

This convinced Garrison that Ferrie's ice-skating trip was perhaps something much bigger: might he have been Oswald's get-away pilot? Richard Billings wrote that "Garrison now believes that Ferrie was the transportation manager in the conspiracy. He was in charge of getting the conspirators in and out of Dallas." Garrison knew that Ferrie had gone to Houston, not Dallas, and thus "He believes Ferrie did not actually fly them himself but knows how it was handled and where the get-away plane is now."

Ferrie was brought in for questioning and told Assistant DA John Volz that he had no recollection of Oswald being in his CAP unit but that it was possible. He had gone ice-skating with two friends, Al Beauboeuf and Mel Coffey, in Houston the weekend of the assassination and then headed to Galveston to check out the nightlife and then to Vinton to do some business for his boss Wray Gill.[4] They then decided to go to Alexandria, Louisiana, for a few days when he called Gill and was told to return because he was wanted for questioning. Ferrie told Volz that Jack Martin was behind all the allegations: "Martin somehow gets to be near the bride at every wedding and the corpse at every funeral." He also told Volz he would take a lie detector test and submit to sodium pentothal, a so-called truth serum.

Ferrie then went to the FBI to tell them what was happening.

This might have been the first time a conspirator to kill JFK went to the FBI on his own volition.

In the meantime, Garrison's men scoured the French Quarter looking for Bertrand, but to no avail.

M E M O R A N D U M

February 25, 1967

TO: JIM GARRISON

FROM:.   LOUIS IVON

RE: CLAY BERTRAND

        To ascertain the location of one CLAY BERTRAND, I put out numerous inquiries and made contact with several sources in the French Quarter area. From the information we have obtained concerning this subject, I'm almost positive from my contacts that they would have known or heard of a CLAY BERTRAND. The information I received was negative results.

        On February 22, 1967, I was approached by "BUBBIE" PETTINGILL in the Fountainbleu Motor Hotel, located on Tulane Avenue, whom I had earlier contacted about CLAY BERTRAND. He stated that DEAN ANDREWS admitted to him that CLAY BERTRAND never existed.

                               LOUIS IVON

Once again Garrison could not find Clay Bertrand. Garrison's note at the bottom reads: "Lou Ivon also has tape in which confidential informant (M.L.) is advised by Prentiss Davis [an investigator for Dean Andrews] that Bertrand apparently did not exist—that Andrews really made no effort to locate him (+ Davis, his investigator, would have known)." The notation above refers to Garrison's interest in using this statement at Andrews' trial for perjury.

Despite all these difficulties, Garrison still managed to figure out Bertrand's identity. Sometime before Christmas 1966, an assistant district attorney had scribbled a note on a copy of the Warren Report next to the paragraph on Dean Andrews. He asked himself who was gay, lived in the French Quarter, and had the first name Clay? Perhaps it was the New Orleans businessman Clay Shaw. Garrison saw the note and knew instantly that Shaw had to be Bertrand. After all, they were both homosexuals, both spoke Spanish, and both had the same first name. Garrison believed that gay people, when using pseudonyms, kept the same first name.

Propinquity naturally played a role in allowing Garrison to fuse the Bertrand and Ferrie connections. Richard Billings wrote that "Then in February, Garrison made a connection he considered very important. Leafing through old New Orleans directories, he found that in 1962 one James Lewallen lived next door to Shaw. Garrison knew Lewallen to be David Ferrie's oldest friend in New Orleans. They had known each other years before in Cleveland and it was at Ferrie's suggestion that Lewallen came south in the 1950s. This convinced Garrison that Shaw and Ferrie were acquainted."

Garrison asked Clay Shaw to drop by for a visit.

"Once I was settled in his office, I wanted to know exactly why I had been asked out there and he explained that the DA's office was still interested in the Kennedy assassination. He told me further that information had been received that during his stay in New Orleans, Oswald had been associating with someone named Clay who lived in the French Quarter and of course they had thought about me. I assured him that I had never met Oswald."

So, who exactly was Clay Shaw? He had served in World War II as aide-de-camp for General Charles Thrasher and was responsible for stockpiling supplies for the Normandy invasion. Shaw was a major at discharge in 1946 and received decorations from three different nations, including the Bronze Star, the Legion of Merit, and Le Croix de Guerre. After the war, he returned to New Orleans and created the Center for International Trade in 1948, becoming its managing director. In 1963, he oversaw the creation of a new Trade Mart building on Canal Street. Shaw retired in 1965, and the City of New Orleans awarded him its international Order of Merit medal.

He authored several published plays, and one, *Submerged*, was performed across the country. Shaw also restored properties in the French Quarter, and several magazines, including *House & Garden*, featured his work. One of his most important renovations was the 1821 residence of naturalist John James Audubon. Shaw was named one of the "most important men in New Orleans" in the March 1967 issue of New Orleans' *Town and Country* Magazine.

Like Garrison, Shaw stood out in New Orleans; he was 6'4" tall, 225 pounds, with a shock of white hair. He had been interviewed on television hundreds of times and was very well known. He was also active in the New Orleans social scene (he was friends with Tennessee Williams), but only those closest to him knew he was gay. He was called the "unlikeliest villain since Oscar Wilde."

Once Garrison figured out that Shaw was Bertrand, he invited Andrews for another dinner to corroborate his thesis, but Andrews refused to play along. Garrison wouldn't let up, and Andrews decided to test him. Andrews noted, "He [wanted] to shuck me like a corn, pluck me like a chicken, stew me like an oyster. I wanted to see if this cat was kosher." He invented a fictitious Cuban acquaintance of Oswald's, Manuel Garcia Gonzalez, and this piqued Garrison's interest.

*Oswald handing out leaflets. The unidentified man on the far
left is who Garrison believed was Manuel Garcia Gonzalez.
CREDIT: Bettmann.*

In the summer of 1963, along with two other men, one of
whom was unidentified (see the arrow above), Oswald handed
out his Fair Play for Cuba leaflets. Garrison became convinced
that this was Manuel Garcia Gonzalez and that he was a trig-
german in the JFK assassination. He sent his men to Miami to
find the elusive Gonzalez.

CITY OF MIAMI, FLORIDA

INTER-OFFICE MEMORANDUM

TO:
Lieut. H. Swilley
Intelligence Unit

DATE: Feb. 20, 1967.   FILE:

SUBJECT: Suspect in
Presidential Assassination

FROM: Sgt. Everett Kay
Intelligence Unit

REFERENCES:

ENCLOSURES:

I received information this date that a possible suspect as an
accomplice in the assassination of President John Kennedy is a
Cuban male, MANUEL (or EMANUEL) GARCIA GONZALEZ.

This subject, GONZALEZ, is unknown to this office, but to the fact
that Sgt. McCracken, on Friday, Jan. 20, 1967, was contacted by
State Attorney Investigator Martin Dardas, who requested that
Sgt. McCracken meet with two investigators from the New Orleans
District Attorney's Office, Det. Lester Otillio, Jr. and Douglas
Ward.

At this meeting the name of EMANUEL or MANUEL GARCIA GONZALEZ was
brought forth by the New Orleans investigators as they were attempting
to locate this man reference narcotics and a possible murder.
Sgt. McCracken made report reference this meeting (report attached).

At no time did the investigators from the New Orleans office indicate
that they were looking for this Cuban male for involvement in the
assassination of the President.

It has been reported to this writer that a group picture showing
this Cuban male, also identifies Harvey Lee Oswald, suspected
assassin of the President.

Attempts are being made by this unit to locate this EMANUEL GARCIA
GONZALEZ, but we have no further information as to the whereabouts
of this subject, physical description, etc. as all this pertinent
information was withheld by the two investigators from the District
Attorney's office in New Orleans. Had we been taken into their
confidence, we could have pursued this matter further.

A private investigator by the name of RICHARD_TORRES is supposedly
working on this assassination plot, being paid by the New Orleans
District Attorney's office. Torres has been active in the Bay of
Pigs organization and other Cuban organizations in Miami, acting
as "Intelligence" for these groups.

ek:rh

*Whenever Garrison's men went to other jurisdictions, they
said they were investigating narcotics.*

The media picked up the story. The *Times-Picayune* wrote
that "Garrison's office is seeking a 'physically powerful and
dangerous' Cuban man who 'is believed to be one of a group of
Cubans who reportedly hid behind a billboard on the parade
route in Dallas Nov. 22, 1963.' Supposedly, the Cuban was

photographed in New Orleans handing out 'Fair Play for Cuba' pamphlets."

Ramparts, a major American left-wing magazine, ran a long article on the Garrison investigation in June 1967, which noted that "A third individual expected to figure prominently in the Garrison inquiry is Manuel Garcia Gonzales. The New Orleans DA has come into possession of a photograph taken at Dealey Plaza just before the assassination which shows several Latin men behind the low picket fence at the top of the famed grassy knoll ... and Garrison thinks Gonzales is one of the men in the photograph. Gonzales has disappeared and has probably fled the country." *Ramparts* included a caricature of Gonzales but had to admit that "his exact features are unknown."

Andrews had all the proof he needed that Jim Garrison was dangerous.

Garrison then asked Andrews to come down to the office and undergo "truth verification" with "memory refreshing procedures." Andrews told NBC that "if they were going to use these techniques for me refreshing to determine Clay Shaw to be Clay Bertrand, they are wasting their time and money."

DISTRICT ATTORNEY
PARISH OF ORLEANS
STATE OF LOUISIANA
2700 TULANE AVENUE
NEW ORLEANS 70119

JIM GARRISON
DISTRICT ATTORNEY

March 6, 1967

HAND DELIVERY

Mr. Sam "Monk" Zelden
Attorney at Law
Suite 1051
National Bank of Commerce Bldg.
New Orleans, Louisiana - 70112

*4:30 P.M.
Zelden agreed to keep confidential
from press.*

Dear Mr. Zelden:

Subsequent to our questioning of your client, Mr. Dean Andrews, who was subpoenaed by the District Attorney's Office on March 2, 1967, you stated to the press that Mr. Andrews had not been asked and had not refused to submit to a polygraph examination.

Since your client, Mr. Andrews, has been unable through failing memory to state that Clay Shaw is not the person who contacted him immediately after the assassination of John F. Kennedy, interceding in behalf of Lee Harvey Oswald, our office has in mind several techniques and procedures which could assist in aiding his memory and arriving at the true facts. I request that Dean Andrews submit to his choice of any one of the following three methods of truth verification and memory refreshing procedures:

1)   Polygraph examination by a qualified expert.
      (A member of the New Orleans Police Department); or

2)   Sodium pentothal (narco-synthesis, a psychiatric technique) under the supervision of the Coroner of the Parish of Orleans and another qualified medical expert; or

3)   Hypnosis under the supervision of the Orleans Parish Coroner and another qualified medical expert.

Mr. Sam "Monk" Zelden
March 6, 1967
Page -2-

Any one of these examinations or techniques which Dean Andrews will submit to will be limited solely for the purpose of determining the issue outlined above. Nothing affecting your client's business or personal life which could in any way embarass him, and which is unconnected to this investigation, would be involved.

Please give me your prompt reply.

Sincerely,

RICHARD V. BURNES
Assistant District Attorney

A similar situation happened with Eleanor Bares, who lived in an apartment to the rear of Clay Shaw's. Investigators came to interview her and tried to obtain a statement to the effect that she had seen David Ferrie in Shaw's apartment. Bares was reportedly shown photographs of Ferrie and Shaw, and she was unable to identify the former. The investigators allegedly suggested that her memory might be "improved" were she to undergo hypnosis and sodium pentothal injections.

Garrison firmly believed that these "memory refreshing techniques" could "objectify" a witness's testimony.

> "[T]here's the fact that we placed a witness under hypnosis. This was done to help objectify his testimony. In other words, when we heard the testimony of this witness, the first thing I said was I want him placed under hypnosis. I want him given sodium pentothal. I want him confirmed with regard to his statements, and I want the kind of confirmation that has a doctor present and not just police officers. So, we thought that we had more or less made history when we made him take hypnosis when we made him take sodium pentothal with two reputable doctors present. We felt that this made history in the sense that a prosecutor was forcing his own witnesses to objectify their testimony."

After the initial story about Garrison's investigation broke in the New Orleans *States-Item* on February 17, Ferrie called the newspaper saying that he was being hounded by Garrison's office and feared arrest. He also told reporter David Snyder that he was physically sick. Snyder went to meet him at his apartment and observed that "his steps were feeble as we climbed the steps to the second floor" and that Ferrie complained of headaches.

Ferrie told Snyder that there was no substance to Garrison's allegations and that he wished he could file a lawsuit against Jim Garrison that would make clear the unjustified harassment to which he was being subjected. He also wanted to sue Jack Martin who had supplied Garrison with a list of names in connection with the assassination. Snyder asked Ferrie "if he thought the Garrison investigation was a phony," and Ferrie replied, "Why certainly, how could it be anything else?"

When the Garrison probe became public on February 19, Ferrie said the investigation was a "big joke." He also told *Washington Post* reporter George Lardner Jr. that "this is not a city prone to knowing what it's doing before it arrests people."

Ferrie was found dead in his apartment on February 22. The coroner determined he died of natural causes from a berry aneurysm, which is caused by a congenital defect. Garrison claimed that it was suicide and that Ferrie had overdosed on Proloid, his thyroid medication, but scar tissue indicated that Ferrie had suffered from an earlier bleed. The toxicology results also came back negative.[5] He called Ferrie "one of history's most important individuals." He issued a press release saying that information caused them to be "concerned as our investigation progressed about the possibility of killing himself, because of this ... [W]e had reached a decision to arrest him early next week, apparently we waited too long."[6]

Two days later, Garrison told the press that he had solved the case, that arrests would be made, that he knew everybody who was involved, and that the assassination had been planned in New Orleans.

More 'Suicides' Predicted

JFK Death Is 'Solved,' New Orleans DA Says

By George Lardner Jr.
Washington Post Staff Writer

NEW ORLEANS, Feb. 24. District Attorney Jim Garrison announced to a corridor jammed with newsmen today that "we have solved the assassination of President Kennedy beyond any shadow of a doubt."

a result of his controversial investigation.

Orleans Parish Coroner

See ORLEANS, A4, Col. 1

Washington Post, February 24, 1967.

But he also indicated that a "premature revelation" of his probe had set back his investigation and that it might take many years to bring the guilty to justice. However, he stated that the only way the conspirators would escape his office's justice was by committing suicide. With that, the press started to pack up and leave.

SAYS JFK DEATH 'SOLVED' *JJ - 2/25/67*

Only Escape for Plotters Suicide, Garrison Claims

District Attorney Jim Garrison says that he has "solved" the Kennedy assassination "plot" and that death is the only escape for those he believes are involved.

Garrison told Hugh Aynesworth, Houston Bureau Chief of Newsweek, that Clay Shaw would commit suicide. "He'll do it, you wait and see. He isn't the type of man who can stand up under the strain. I hope the s.o.b. does kill himself."

Garrison's staff felt this was a propitious time to end the inquiry. "This is your chance ... [Y]ou can drop the faltering investigation and save face. You can say you can't continue because your chief witness is dead. You can write a book about the assassination, and you can even fulfill your dream of running for governor." Garrison yelled back, "Are you crazy? Don't you realize that we are on the verge of solving one of the crimes of the century?"

CHAPTER 4

ENTER STAGE RIGHT: PERRY RUSSO

A TWENTY-FIVE-YEAR-OLD INSURANCE trainee in Baton Rouge, Perry Russo, wrote a letter on February 23 to Jim Garrison saying that he might have some information.[1] Russo then called a local newspaper to say that he knew Ferrie and had heard him talk about how easy it would be to assassinate a president. He also claimed that Ferrie had said "we" will get Kennedy. He did not mention a plot, nor did he mention Oswald, Shaw, or Bertrand. Russo was also interviewed by WAFB in Baton Rouge:

Q: Did he [Ferrie] ever make any more specific threat, like get him?

Russo: Well, right. Now, in late September or during October, the month right prior to the Kennedy assassination in November, Dave Ferrie had occasion to come over to the house on several instances and I went to his place, and just passing, and he made specific references that, in talking about Kennedy, he said: "We will get him and it won't be very long." Now, the last time I can

remember him saying that was sometime in October, but
he was obsessed with the idea.

Q: Did he ever mention Lee Harvey Oswald's name?

Russo: No.

Q; No conversation at all about ...

Russo: No. I had never heard of Oswald until the
television of the assassination.

Assistant DA Andrew Sciambra was sent to Baton Rouge
and spent three hours interviewing Russo. Two days later, he
wrote a 3,500-word memorandum that had nothing about
Oswald, Shaw, Bertrand, or any assassination plot. Toward the
end of the memo, Sciambra wrote: "Russo said the more we talk
the more comes back to me and the name Leon really rings a bell.
He also said that if he were hypnotized, he may have total recall
on names, places, and dates."

Russo was shown a picture of Shaw, and he said that he had
seen him twice, once in a car with David Ferrie and once in May
of 1962 at the Nashville Street Wharf when he went to see JFK
speak. Russo "remembers this guy because he was apparently a
queer. It seems that instead of looking at JFK speak, SHAW kept
turning around and looking at all the young boys in the crowd.
He said that SHAW eventually struck up a conversation with a
young kid not too far from him. It was perfectly obvious to him
that SHAW stared at his penis several times. He said that
SHAW eventually left with a friend. He said that SHAW had on
dark pants that day which fit very tightly and was the kind of
pants that a lot of queers in the French quarter wear."[2]

This description did not fit Clay Shaw, who was a very
conservative dresser and who wasn't known for hanging out with
young boys. Historian Alecia Long noted that "a co-worker from
that era recalled that Shaw 'dressed and carried himself like a
retired German military officer—correct bearing and always

turned out beautifully.'" He was far too much of a gentleman to act inappropriately in public.

Sciambra also showed a picture of Lee Harvey Oswald to Russo, who shook his head.

> "He then said that the picture of LEE HARVEY OSWALD was the person that FERRIE had introduced to him as his roommate. He said the only thing that doesn't make him stand up and say that he is sure beyond the shadow of any doubt is the fact that the roommate was always so cruddy and had a bushy beard. He then drew a beard on the picture of OSWALD and said this was FERRIE's roommate."

The only problem was that Lee Harvey Oswald never had a beard and was known for his good personal hygiene. Sciambra also told Russo that "it was important that these two [Shaw and Ferrie] be linked together. Either physically or through letters or anything."[3] In a hearing conducted in 1971, Russo was questioned by Shaw defense attorney Edward Wegmann:

> Russo: Well, for example, when he left Baton Rouge, during the course of the conversation, I was able to more or less to piece a plot together. I could almost piece it together if I wanted. I could have figured out a plot. No word "conspiracy" was ever used, you know.
>
> Wegmann: You mean, you could piece a plot together of what Sciambra told you?
>
> Russo: Well, I mean a junior, one-year law student and a lot of reading of law books, I mean a man says it's important to link these two together, these two people

have to, you know, it's important to link these two together. Have you ever seen these two together? Where did you see these two together? And it was those types of questions ...

Russo was brought to New Orleans and administered sodium pentothal by Dr. Nicholas Chetta, the New Orleans coroner, on February 27. There is no surviving transcript of this session except a memo written by Andrew Sciambra, who did the questioning. Russo remembered Ferrie having a roommate who was "very dirty and a beatnik-type guy" who "had a bushy beard and his hair was all messed up and he was extremely dirty." Sciambra then "asked him if he could remember any of the details about CLAY BERTRAND being up in FERRIE'S apartment," a fairly leading question. He was priming Russo to fuse the Bertrand and Ferrie connections.

Dr. Chetta later admitted that while sodium pentothal lessens a subject's inhibition as "to expressions of fact," it also lessens inhibitions "as to expressions of fantasy and suggestion." The *Washington Post* carried a letter by Dr. Edwin Weinstein, who wrote that "Under the influence of sodium pentothal, subjects may give highly fictional accounts of past events and describe incidents that never happened. The drug is not a 'truth serum.'"

In 1971, Russo talked about the experience of having been injected with sodium pentothal.

"I just laid there, no effect and they switched bottles, and then my head started spinning as soon as they switched bottles and I started fighting everybody in there, you know. The needle came out of my arm once. I started—not sobering up but straightening up after a swing at

Sciambra, Oser, I was kicking at them and everything and they strapped me down on the table. And they had to strap my arm down on the table. And they had to strap my arm down on his board they stretched out ... all I was saying is leave me alone and just leave me alone, I'd kick at them and even with the straps, there were straps across my chest and the waist and somebody, I think, was holding my legs down."

The seeds of a memory were planted, but Garrison still needed Russo to identify Shaw as Bertrand. So the next day he had Russo walk up to Shaw's house in the guise of selling insurance, and Russo was able to identify Shaw as being Clay Bertrand. The following day, Garrison discussed the case with his office. Charles Ward, who ran the regular caseload while Garrison was investigating JFK, said that

---

"March 1 was the meeting of the twelve people involved in the Shaw investigation in the office, plus eight voluntary investigators. At that meeting, there was a discussion about whether or not there was sufficient evidence to arrest Clay Shaw. Believe me, I wasn't there but I know the vote. It was about 18 to 2 against arresting Shaw. Garrison was one of the two."

Claw Shaw was brought in for further questioning, and he denied knowing Oswald, Ferrie, and Russo. Shaw thought the whole idea of using an alias to be silly. "It would be ridiculous for me to try to use an alias. I am well known in the city. I've been on television, given speeches, my picture has been in the papers over a period of years, and because of my size alone, I couldn't very well get away with something like that."

Garrison's men wanted to administer sodium pentothal, but Shaw refused. Sciambra told an incredulous Shaw that if he refused to comply, he was going to be arrested and charged with conspiring to murder John F. Kennedy. Shaw replied, "You've got to be kidding!"

Rolls 5, 6, 7: Clay Shaw. shots taken through 2-way glass in DA's office. Investigator Louis Ivon, thin tall guy and ADA. Sciambra. questioning clay. also clay alone + eating sandwich. Shaw is very tall, thin, grey hair. They gave him the sandwich first and left him alone. Then Sciambra + Ivon came in. Shaw smoked one cigarette after another.

Life magazine was allowed to take pictures of Shaw through a two-way mirror. Here's their description of photos.

When his lawyer, Sal Panzeca arrived, Garrison asked for a lie detector test. Panzeca agreed, but only if Shaw was given twenty-four hours of rest. Garrison refused, and Shaw was formally charged with conspiring with David Ferrie and Lee Harvey Oswald to kill JFK. He was led away in handcuffs, and it just so happened that the hallway outside Garrison's office was overrun with newsmen, photographers, and cameras. Shaw was pushed and shoved as he made his way to the basement, where he was taken to central lockup. Garrison did not offer to let him use the private elevator in his office.

DISTRICT ATTORNEY
PARISH OF ORLEANS
STATE OF LOUISIANA
2700 TULANE AVENUE
NEW ORLEANS 70119

JIM GARRISON
DISTRICT ATTORNEY

1 March 1967

The first arrest has been made in the investigation of the
New Orleans District Attorney's office into the assasination
of President John F. Kennedy.

Arrested this evening in the District Attorney's office was
Clay Shaw, age 54, of 1313 Dauphine Street, New Orleans,
Louisiana.

Mr. Shaw will be charged with participation in a conspiracy
to murder John F. Kennedy.

It should be pointed out, however, that the nature of this
case is not conducive to an immediate succession of arrests
at this time. However, other arrests will be made at a later
date.

Jim Garrison

Shaw later wondered why he was arrested that day. "My feeling is that Garrison could not bear to be again deserted by the press of the world. He knew he had to produce some sensation to keep their attention and he had decided to do something ... anything ... to make headlines. The other factor is that, in my opinion, Garrison considered himself one of destiny's darlings. It would not be the first time that he had taken a decisive step without knowing exactly what he was going to do next. And it had all come out all right before."[4]

As for Garrison, he told a reporter that "this won't be the first time I've arrested somebody and then built my case afterward." Years later, Charles Ward amended this statement: "Garrison deduced a theory, then he marshaled his facts. And if the facts didn't fit, he'd say they had been altered by the CIA."

The police searched Shaw's home and found a black gown, hood, cape, chains, and five whips.[5] Shaw said these were Mardi Gras costumes and that "they didn't bother taking the Greek or Japanese costumes, which would indicate that the whole thing was simply a residue of carnivals over the past decade."

This was confirmed by his friend Layton Martens in an interview with NBC.

Q: When did you meet Clay Shaw?

Martens: I met Clay Shaw in February; I think it was 1965. It was Mardi Gras day. On that occasion, I remember distinctly meeting Mr. Shaw. He was wearing a long black cloak with a hood with a rope tied around it and he was carrying whips and chains.

Q: Would this have seemed unusual on Mardi Gras day?

Martens: No, hardly. On Mardi Gras day, you'll see everything in New Orleans. This was something Mr. Shaw had apparently picked up in Mexico. There is an order of Monks around Mexico which the Church has tried to disband who dress in this manner with the hoods, with the black cloaks, chains and whips and whatnot and parade as martyrs through the streets and it is quite a colorful spectacle to witness. I understand this is where Mr. Shaw got the idea from for the Mardi Gras costume and that he has worn this costume every Mardi Gras day for at least 12 years.

A few days after Shaw's arrest, investigators visited Mrs. Lawrence Fischer, a friend of Shaw's.

"Wanted to know how long I'd known him. Since he was seventeen. Wanted to know if we'd ever discussed sex." Mrs. Fischer slapped her leg. *"Well, it would be pretty unusual to go for over thirty-five years with a good friend and never bring the subject up, now, wouldn't it? Of course, we had. Then this young man asked, 'Has Mr. Shaw ever told you the intimate details of his sex life?' 'No,' I shot back at him, 'and furthermore, I haven't told him the intimate details of my sex life either. Are you here to discuss his political leanings with reference to the Garrison farce, or are you conducting a sort of Kinsey report?' Then he wanted to get into the black robe and the hood and the black hat and finally I just couldn't take it any longer and I said, 'Listen, my good young man, I don't know whether you've ever heard of it and it's called Mardi Gras! Everybody in town gets dressed up in costumes."*

The affair outed Shaw as a homosexual, and Irvin Dymond, his trial attorney, said that Garrison knew he was vulnerable. Indeed, Clay Shaw was in a tough spot: he was into S&M, and that would have been very hard to admit publicly.

That night, Russo was put under hypnosis by Dr. Fatter, a New Orleans family physician. During the interview, Fatter was quite suggestive.

Dr. Fatter: Continue looking at the television program and Clay, the white-haired man is going to come into the room. You are at Ferrie's apartment and there are many people. Who did he introduce Clay to?

[...]

Dr. Fatter: Let your mind go completely, blank, Perry

—see that television screen again. It is very vivid—now notice the picture on the screen—there will be Bertrand, Ferrie and Oswald and they are going to discuss a very important matter and there is another man and girl there and they are talking about assassinating somebody. Look at it and describe it to me.

It is Dr. Fatter and not Perry Russo who first uses the name "Clay" and the word "assassinating." Surely this a textbook case of creating a memory: a party at Ferrie's apartment where Clay Bertrand (Shaw) and Lee Harvey Oswald discussed killing Kennedy. James Phelan said that "he might as well [have] told Perry Russo that he was a St. Bernard dog and why don't you bark. And Perry would have barked." Russo admitted in 1971 that "the name Bertrand was first voiced by Sciambra."

Russo was hypnotized a second time, but the session was not productive because he regressed too far back and panicked. No known transcript has survived. On March 14, Russo was hypnotized for the third time, and Russo once again described Oswald as having a beard.

Q. Describe him for me. Take a good look at him. Start at the top of his head and describe him.

A. He is dirty. He has brown hair and he's got a beard on, old dirty clothes and rubber tennis shoes.

NBC News consulted with Dr. Jay Katz, an associate professor of law and clinical psychology at Yale. He was shown the transcripts of Russo's two hypnotic sessions.

Q: Does it appear to you that some of the questions of the interviewer, questioning Perry Russo, suggest the answer?

Katz: I wondered about this and I was very much struck that upon many occasions, the hypnotist introduced very leading questions. This was most striking, but just to give one example: When he directly asked him, or in fact not even asked him but told him, to tell him about the conversation that took place in respect to an assassination plot.

Q: Would you comment on the way these interviews were conducted made it more, rather than less, difficult for the subject to separate fact from fantasy?

Katz: Yes, he made no attempt, as far as I can see, to press further, and at least attempt to find out what was fantasy and what was reality.

Not one of Ferrie's friends backed up Russo's story. Layton Martens told researcher Gus Russo that

"Between Morris [Brownlee], Al [Beauboeuf], and Alan [Campbell], one or more of us were at Dave's apartment practically every night that year [1963]. And none of us heard any talk of killing Kennedy, none of us ever saw Clay Shaw, and none of us remember a Perry Russo."

In New Orleans, there were three ways to charge someone with a crime. As mentioned previously, the DA simply had to file a bill of information. He could also opt for a preliminary hearing, or he could go to the grand jury to get his indictment.

Garrison opted for all three. First, he filed his bill of information. Then he opted for a preliminary hearing. James Alcock, second in command to Garrison, told *Life* magazine that this was a "tactical maneuver." A preliminary hearing could be demanded by either the defense or the prosecution, who would then ask a judge to preside. Garrison wanted one of "their" judges rather than a judge who might have been somewhat independent.

Garrison also went to the grand jury to get an indictment. Shaw wrote that "he must have known he was skating on very thin ice, and that if he could not make his charges stick, he would be open to a suit for malfeasance. Such suits are theoretically possible, though very difficult in practice. But Garrison sought to make assurance doubly sure that nothing of this sort would happen to him. If in addition to his bill of information, a grand jury indicted me and a magistrate ordered me bound over for trial, he could certainly argue that he was only doing his duty in trying me."

The night before the preliminary hearing, several of Garrison's assistant district attorneys rehearsed Russo's testimony in a hotel room "using the transcript of the first hypnotic session with Fatter as a script."

Russo: Well, Alcock was gone. Sciambra was like a hound dog about that. He asked me to read it, the transcript of the hypnosis sessions. Or session. No, sessions, because I had two of them, I think, at this time, and that to read that over and he was to ask me questions and I was to give answers.

Wegmann: Based upon ...

Russo: Right.

Wegmann: What had been said in the hypnotic sessions with Dr. Fatter.

Russo: In other words, I was to learn the responses like a parrot. I could learn the responses like a parrot. I could

learn the responses and should Dymond or you or your
brother or Panzeca ask me questions, I knew the answers.

On March 14, 1967, Perry Russo was called to the stand. He testified that in the middle of September 1963, he walked into a party at David Ferrie's apartment. By the end of the evening, only a few people were left, including Leon Oswald (whom Russo claimed was Lee Harvey Oswald), Clem Bertrand,[6] David Ferrie, and Perry Russo. They discussed the assassination of John F. Kennedy, a triangulation of gunshots, and flying the assassin out of the country, and they said that all participants should do something noticeable on the day of the assassination so that they could have alibis. Russo described Oswald as dirty and as having whiskers. He also identified Clay Shaw as Clem Bertrand.

Clay Shaw sat there listening to Russo and later wrote that "aside from any question of guilt or innocence, anyone who knows me knows that I would have better sense than to plot with two nuts like that in the presence of a 22-year-old boy I'd never seen before."

On cross-examination, Russo was asked why he waited until 1967 to report this conversation.

Mr. Dymond: And you did not think it was your duty, as
an American, to volunteer your testimony to that Warren
Commission?

Russo: No, because I had at that time, right after the
assassination, I had an involvement with school, which
was more pressing to me. If they wanted me, ask me
anything, they could.

Mr. Dymond: In your opinion, your little personal
involvements were so important as to keep you from

volunteering to give vital testimony to a commission like the Warren Commission?

Russo: I had other things that were on my mind at the time. One of them was getting out of school and I was sure that the FBI knew what it was doing. I have the highest respect for them and I do now. I just equated them with the Warren Commission, although that is not correct.

Russo also told the court that David Ferrie had never indicated that his plan to kill the president had succeeded, nor did he ever ask Ferrie about the assassination.

On March 17, there was a surprise witness. Vernon Bundy, a prisoner who first came to the attention of Garrison's office just the day before, told the court that in the summer of 1963, he was shooting up heroin on the seawall of Lake Pontchartrain. A black four-door sedan approached, and a distinguished tall man got out. He was approached by a younger fellow, later described by Bundy as a beatnik, who asked the older man what he (the younger of the two) should tell his wife. The older man then gave the younger a roll of money and drove off. A piece of paper fell from the younger man's pockets, and Bundy picked it up. It was a flyer about Cuba. Bundy identified the older man as Clay Shaw and the younger man as Lee Harvey Oswald.[7]

Bundy described the young man as a "junky."

Question: Vernon, describe this second man for us? What did he look like?

Bundy: He was young.

Question: The man who came walking down.

Bundy: Well, he was young, what I would call a junky or a beatnik type of guy.

Question: Why do you say beatnik?

Bundy: Well, from the way he was dressed. He had white jeans on.

Question: What kind of shirt?

Bundy: T-shirt. And what you would call buck shoes, something like what I have on here but they were more of a high top, and he was in pretty nasty shape to tell you the truth about it.

Question: Why do you say he was in nasty shape?

Bundy: Well, he needed a shave; he may have needed a hair cut too. He looks as though he needed everything.

This did not sound like Lee Harvey Oswald, who was always meticulous in his personal hygiene and was invariably clean-shaven.

On cross-examination, Bundy admitted that he had never told this story to anybody until the day before the hearing, so how could Garrison's men have known to seek out Bundy?

Q: Now, when did you first interview anybody from the police department or the district attorney's office?

Bundy: When did they first interview me?

Q: That's right. About this case.

Bundy: Yesterday.

Q: Yesterday?

Bundy: That's right.

Q: Did they come and pick you up or did you get in touch with them?

Bundy: They got in touch with me.

Q: Who got in touch with you?

Bundy: Three guys from the DA's office.

Vernon Bundy also was given a lie detector test on the day of the preliminary hearing. It was conducted by Captain Jim Kruebe of the New Orleans Police Department, who told Garrison that Bundy was lying. Charles Ward, an assistant district attorney, said: "Well, in that case, let's not use him as a witness." Garrison replied, "I don't care if he is lying or not. We are not telling him to lie. We are going to use him."

Jim Garrison did not call Dean Andrews to testify. In June 1967 a reporter asked him if he could identify "Mr. Clem Bertrand." Andrews replied, "Let me put it to you this way. Clay Shaw is not, never has been, or never will be the Clay Bertrand who I identify."

CHAPTER 5

MY SON, THE
CRYPTOGRAPHER

GARRISON CONFISCATED SHAW'S NOTEBOOKS, which led to one of the strangest episodes of the entire affair. A researcher noticed the entry "Lee Odom, P.O. Box 19106, Dallas, Tex" and found that it nearly matched an entry in Lee Harvey Oswald's notebook. Was this perhaps proof that Oswald and Shaw were connected?

Lee Odom notation in Clay Shaw's notebook.

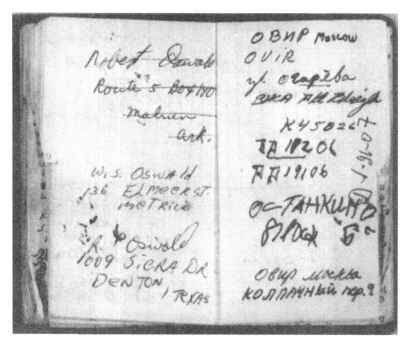

*A page from Oswald's notebook with the two Cyrillic Ds and
"19106."*

Shaw's lawyers said the entry referred to a Dallas businessman who had discussed the possibility of staging a bullfight
in New Orleans in 1966. Further, the Dallas PO box number
19106 was only assigned to Odom in 1965, well after Oswald
had written his notation. And the notation in Oswald's book was
preceded by two Cyrillic Ds, which is not Russian for P(ost)
O(ffice).

Garrison went even further. He believed that Oswald used a
code to hide Jack Ruby's unlisted telephone number. Here is how
Garrison linked Oswald's notation to Jack Ruby's unlisted phone
number:

*"Oswald invariably uses the dial of the telephone as
conversion machinery to convert letters into numbers and*

back again. He systematically adds the number values resulting in a sum which can later be broken down into the real exchange listing." So, the letters 'PO' become the number 13, and Garrison claimed the only telephone exchange in Dallas which the number 13 converts to is WHitehall. If you then unscramble the number in Oswald's notebook, 19106, it then becomes 16901. And if you subtract 1300 (which was a standard coding number in Oswald's notebook) from that you get 1-5601. Ruby's number was WHitehall 1-5601."

Sylvia Meager, a major critic of the Warren Report, thought Garrison's reasoning was faulty and wrote him a registered letter.

16 May 1967

Mr. Jim Garrison
District Attorney
Parish of Orleans
New Orleans, La. 70119

Dear Mr. Garrison,

Two problems arise with respect to the notation "19106" in Oswald's address book which raise a question about its correspondence, when decoded, with the unpublished telephone number WHitehall 1-5601. The symbols which precede the digits "19106" in the notebook (XVI page 58) seem to me to represent the Cyrillic letters "ДД" rather than the English letters "PO". On another page of the address book (XVI page 46) Oswald has written a series of German phrases with their Russian equivalents. The German "Ja" is matched with the Russian "Da" and the "Д" appears to be identical with the symbols which precede the number "19106" on page 58. If the correct reading is "ДД 19106" decoding would not produce the WHitehall exchange.

The second problem is that this notation, which I read as "ДД 19106," appears on a page of the address book which seems to have been written during Oswald's stay in the Soviet Union. This is the inference I draw from the contents, the script, and the consistency of the ink, which is all distinguished from the facing page of the address book which appears to have been written after Oswald's return to the U.S. While it is plausible that Oswald would have recorded a cryptogram of Ruby's telephone number sometime in 1963, it is hard to believe that Oswald would have done so during his time in the Soviet Union.

Perhaps these points had already occurred to you and have been overcome. I take it for granted that, in any case, you would wish me to bring these questions to your attention.

I hope that the material on Bogard and De Brueys has arrived by now. With warm regards,

Yours very sincerely,

Sylvia Meagher
302 West 12 Street
New York, N.Y. 10014

*Courtesy of The Weisberg Collection. Hood College,
Frederick, Maryland. URL: http://jfk.hood.edu/*

Garrison called her the next day and told her he had received her letter but had ignored what she had written. However, he then told her "that he had also decoded from other notations in the same LHO notebook the phone numbers for (1) Clay Shaw (2) the local FBI office (3) the local CIA office." The CIA had put pressure on the press to black this out.

Meagher wrote that "when it was pointed out that it seemed unlikely that Oswald (whose mathematical talent was at a level that caused him to add 20 and 20 in writing) should have memorized a complicated, many-stepped mathematical procedure to encode and decode the number of the FBI's local office, which was published in the telephone directory, Garrison had another quick explanation. Oswald liked to play cops and robbers, or was it cloaks and daggers?"

Garrison never believed the Odom story and said he was "interested in knowing who introduced Mr. Odom to Mr. Shaw, how many bullfights Mr. Odom has actually produced." To make it even sillier, on a memo written in May 1967 about an informant talking about a bullfight in Tampa or Miami, Garrison wrote in longhand: "This is the second time 'Bullfight' has been used as a code word for the assassination."

Richard Billings told yet another code story.

Garrison now has more of his code deciphering for us. He refers to a number in Oswald's notebook, on page 35 of the notebook, which appears on page 50 of Volume 16 of the Warren exhibits. He says you find there the number 6-3-91-92, and if you apply the letter arrangement ADBC, you then get 6139. He says then Oswald subtracted 4900 from that, 4900 being the block on Magazine Street which Oswald lived, and you get the number 1239, which Garrison says is the last four digits of Clay Shaw's phone number, Clay Shaw's number being 522-1239. Asked how 522 might have been part of that code, Garrison says the first letter after the dash is 9, and if you add 5, 2 and 2 -

*- it equals 9. He has no explanation for the 2 that follows
the 9 that follows the dash.*

David Lifton challenged Garrison on the codes and received
an education:

"During one of our conversations, Garrison told me that
his office had established an ironclad link between Ruby
and Oswald. As evidence, he cited the fact that a Ft. Worth
telephone number PE8-1951 was listed in Oswald's
address book and also was found on Ruby's phone bill.
Astonished, I went home and checked it out. That
telephone number, as clearly indicated in Oswald's
address book, is television station KTVT, Channel 11,
Fort Worth Texas.

I confronted Garrison with this the next day. He
became very truculent and annoyed.

"David, stop arguing the defense," he would say.

"But, what does it mean, Jim?" I demanded. "Is there
someone at the TV station whom you can prove knew both
men?"

"It means whatever the jury decides it means," he said,
adding that "Law is not a science."

Finally, I asked: "But what do YOU think, Jim? What
is the truth of the matter?"

His answer is one I will never forget. He said, with
considerable annoyance and contempt, "After the fact,
there IS NO truth. There is ONLY what the jury decides."

Garrison would never let go of this fantasy. He repeated the
story of Oswald's notebook in his book *On the Trail of the Assas-*

sins, still insisting that the Cyrillic Ds were "PO." He ridiculed the innocent explanation of why Lee Odom's PO box was in Shaw's address book: "Once again, the people of this country were being asked to swallow a cannonball, no matter how well lubricated."

CHAPTER 6

JIM GARRISON'S EXCELLENT HOMOSEXUAL ADVENTURE

ALMOST FROM THE start of his probe, Garrison believed that the Kennedy assassination was a homosexual plot. He met journalist Hugh Aynesworth at his home in January 1967 and told him a remarkable story:

"Hugh," he said at last, "you're lucky you're in town today. We've just verified this guy, and believe me, it's dynamite." Explaining no more for the moment, Garrison then called one of his assistant DAs, ex-boxer Andrew Sciambra, known as Moo, who arrived a short while later with this slight little guy from Houston, a piano player, who proceeded to tell us how he knew that Ruby and Oswald were long time gay lovers.

He went into great detail, naming clubs in Dallas and Houston where he said he had been performing when Ruby and Oswald dropped by. He even described one occasion when the owners of a Houston club had booted out the two of them "because," he said, "they had been groping each other all evening long."

Garrison beamed.

"You might be the most important witness we've run across yet," he told the piano player. "And you are certain they were with each other on several occasions?"

The little man vigorously nodded yes, clearly pleased that Garrison was buying his story.

Garrison told James Phelan of the *Saturday Evening Post* a very similar story.

In an effort to get Garrison's story into focus, I asked him the motive of the Kennedy conspirators. He told me that the murder in Dallas had been a homosexual plot.

"They had the same motive as Loeb and Leopold when they murdered Bobby Franks in Chicago back in the twenties," Garrison said. "It was a homosexual thrill-killing, plus the excitement of getting away with a perfect crime. John Kennedy was everything that Dave Ferrie was not—a successful, handsome, popular, wealthy, virile man. You can just picture the charge Ferrie got out of plotting his death.

I asked how he had learned the murder was a homosexual plot.

"Look at the people involved," Garrison said. "Dave Ferrie, homosexual, Clay Shaw, homosexual. Jack Ruby, homosexual."

"Ruby was a homosexual?"

"Sure, we dug that out," Garrison said. "His homosexual nickname was Pinkie. That's three. Then there was Lee Harvey Oswald."

> *But Oswald was married and had two children, I pointed out.*
>
> *"A switch-hitter who couldn't satisfy his wife,"* Garrison said. *"That's all in the Warren Report."* He named two more *"key figures"* whom he labeled homosexual.
>
> *"That's six homosexuals in the plot,"* Garrison said. *"One or maybe two, okay. But all six homosexuals? How far can you stretch the arm of coincidence?"*

Garrison told *Newsweek* that he "had proof that Shaw, Ferrie, and Oswald were conspirators, but was still looking for a 'gay boy' who resembled Oswald and actually fired the fatal shots." Merriman Smith of UPI told the FBI that Garrison had said that some "high-status fags" were involved in the assassination.

Muckraker Jack Anderson, the partner of syndicated columnist Drew Pearson, also spent some time talking to Garrison. According to Pearson's March 24, 1967, diary entry, Garrison told Anderson, "The CIA definitely had a plot to assassinate Castro and had approached Clay Shaw, a reputable, wealthy homosexual businessman, as a man who could execute the plot. Shaw was part of a homosexual ring, including Ferrie and Ruby in Dallas." At this point, Garrison thought the plot was to assassinate Castro, but "when Oswald was refused his visa to Cuba, the conspirators then turned around and decided to assassinate Kennedy. They used Oswald as the patsy. He was the only non-homo member of the ring. They figured he was so mentally disturbed, and so at odds with the world, that he could be used as the fall guy."

Shaw's homosexuality was always on the minds of Garrison and his investigators. Shaw was put under surveillance by the police, and here is a paragraph from one of their reports:

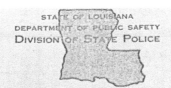

COL. THOMAS D. BURBANK
Director—Superintendent

STATE OF LOUISIANA
DEPARTMENT OF PUBLIC SAFETY
DIVISION OF STATE POLICE

LT. COL. BEN F. RAGUSA
ASSISTANT SUPERINTENDENT

-4-

The undersigned officers recalled that the body of a
W/M was found in Jefferson Parish in 1963, said body cut into
pieces, case as yet unsolved. It was suspected at the time of
the investigation of this murder that homosexuals were involved.
Working on the theory that there might be a connection between
Shaw and his associates and this murder, the undersigned officers
went to Angola, La., on 3-20-67, and obtained a complete Angola
file on one, Kenneth J. Leckie, Angola #51806, victim of this
unsolved murder. Further facts of possible involvment with
Leckie case will follow in next report.

Perry Russo was interviewed by Shaw's lawyers on January 26, 1971. "Russo said also that the D.A.'s office was making every effort to pin two murder charges on Shaw. Those being the killing of a 14 or 15-year-old boy by the name of name Jimmy Rupp and the killing of Dr. [Mary] Sherman on St. Charles Avenue. He said that both of these people belonged to a sex club, and said that at one point the question was asked by someone in the D.A.'s office 'Do we have enough evidence to convict Shaw on these cases?'"

Garrison's theory of propinquity meant that anything related to homosexuality was of interest as evidenced by this memo on investigative leads.

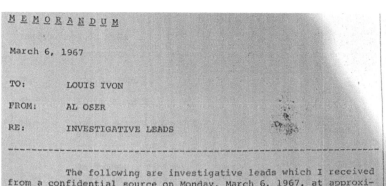

MEMORANDUM

March 6, 1967

TO: LOUIS IVON

FROM: AL OSER

RE: INVESTIGATIVE LEADS

The following are investigative leads which I received
from a confidential source on Monday, March 6, 1967, at approximately 2 P. M. to-wit: 1) one FELIX VALDEZ, owner and operator
of La Casa de Las Marinos, is believed to be a personal friend
and associate of CLAY SHAW. There is a strong possibility that
VALDEZ could give pertinent information regarding the activities
and associates over a considerable period of time. 2) The Elwood
Plantation Restaurant was at one time either owned or leased by
CLAY SHAW from an individual by the name of EDDY, first name
unknown. Approximately ten years ago CLAY SHAW used what is now
known as Elwood Plantation for a sex orgy which resulted in the
Jefferson Parish authorities being summoned to this location.
Further information regarding this said party will be covered
under another memo at the time I receive same. 3) I have been
informed that during the night of the search of CLAY SHAW's
apartment at 1313 Dauphine Street, a white female approached
GEORGE STEIB of the New Orleans Police Department, Bureau of
Identification, and informed him that approximately two weeks
ago members of the New Orleans Police Department were summoned
to the address of 1313 Dauphine Street because CLAY SHAW a white
male and two colored males were in the patio naked and using wine
bottles on each other.

                        ALVIN V. OSER

Does any of this sound like investigative leads?

Garrison's thinking began to change once they found Shaw's
whips and chains, which were "proof of Shaw's position as 'Lord
executioner' in the Society of Sadists + Masochists." Richard
Billings wrote that "Garrison's theory is bolstered somewhat by
the fact that the searchers found hooks bolted into the ceiling
beams and chains fitted with wristbands."

There were indeed two hooks in a beam in Shaw's bedroom.
When I first saw pictures of the hooks (they can be seen in the
Richard Billings papers at Georgetown University), I was dumb-
founded. They were quite tiny and looked more like the small

hooks one would use for plants (which is what Clay Shaw said they were used for) rather than for hoisting people.

Garrison told Billings that he was completely convinced that it was a plot by sadists (he had read the Marquis de Sade and knew that sadists escalated from whipping to killing).

```
M E M O R A N D U M


March 13, 1967


TO:              JIM GARRISON, DISTRICT ATTORNEY

FROM:            JOHN P. VOLZ, ASSISTANT D. A.

_ _ _ _ _ _ _ _ _ _ _ _ _ _ _ _ _ _ _ _ _ _ _ _ _ _

             On March 10, 1967 I brought various
pieces of evidence in the CLAY SHAW matter to Dr. Heath
at Tulane University.

             After he examined it, I had an interview
with him on March 11, 1967 at which time he told me that
SHAW's motive, as you suggested could very possibly have been
rooted in his sadistice, homosexual abnormality.

             He gave me the attached and told me
that he would be happy to discuss it with you.

                     JOHN P. VOLZ
```

Richard Billings's diary quotes Garrison saying that "Shaw is a Phi Beta Kappa sadist." Billings notes that "Whips give away ... Leopold Loeb key to while thing ... Giant convinced." Garrison is again quoted: "I am going to talk to a good psychiatrist—Bob Heath—and I will make sadism relevant ... I'll develop expert testimony that a sadist would have motivation for a Presidential assassination ... He's a sadist, not a masochist ... [T]he robe and hood prove it." Billings also wrote that "Garrison plans to use sadism evidence found in Shaw's apartment to rebut defense contention of good character ... and if defense contends he's a peaceful, law-abiding citizen, Garrison will show human blood on whips (?)" Interestingly, Dr. Robert Heath would later become actively involved in researching gay conversion therapies.

Perry Russo said that Sciambra told him that "Shaw was anti-Kennedy, he enjoys being beat by whips; and Kennedy, (somebody at the D.A.'s office told me this) Kennedy represented youth to him and being as there were never, psychologically be a set of circumstances where he could get whipped by Kennedy, then he would kill him."

Garrison told the *Los Angeles Times* that "besides Cuban refugees and homosexuals, masochists who would do anything for a thrill were part of the alleged plot to kill Mr. Kennedy. If you placed a masochist in a room along with a button that would blow up the White House, he probably would press that button for the thrill of it."

Los Angeles Times, *March 26, 1967, page 1*

S&M was never far from the minds of Garrison and his band of merry investigators. Robert Northshield of NBC informed the FBI that at the preliminary hearing, Shaw was to be portrayed as both a "sadist" and "masochist" who planned the assassination because he wanted to destroy the "world's most handsome man." In a November 1967 memo on his office's current leads, Garrison wrote that "some time ago we received information concerning serious injuries received as a result of beatings by whips. In one instance such injuries occurred in the Biloxi area and in another instance the injury was reported to have occurred in the French

Quarter. Follow-up inquiry should be conducted to determine if any of these reports have any relevance to our case."

In December 1967, Garrison wrote to William Turner and said that Jack Ruby might have been in San Francisco in November of 1963 and suggested that he might wish to check out the area of Eddy and Taylor Streets. He thought that if Ruby had frequented the area, Clay Shaw might have as well. He wondered, "Is this, perhaps, a part of the scene for the S-M swingers?"

Garrison sent William Gurvich to San Francisco (Shaw was there during the assassination) to "look up a shop that catered to sadists and masochists, and sold bullwhips and stuff like that." A January 25, 1968, memo from investigator Gary Sanders noted that "the origins of Shaw's whips (Mexico?) might be interesting since it might lead to some of Shaw's connections outside the U.S."

M E M O R _ _ _ _ _

February 16, 1968

TO: JIM GARRISON, District Attorney

FROM: BILL TURNER

RE: SADO-MASOCHISTS - SAN FRANCISCO
* * * * * * * *************** * ************** * * * * * *

          The following information was furnished by
a woman who was married to one of the subjects. The information contains absolutely no relationship at this point to
the assassination investigation. However, it is being
recorded in the event the names at some time become meaningful

          She said that she was married to a Chinese by
the name of C. TSU PENG who is a scientist at the University
of California Medical Center in San Francisco. PENG is very
close to a STEPHEN WISSIG also employed at the Medical Center.
Both of these men have doctorates. Both are SM. Both have
very definite genocidic and totalitarian tendencies. The
informant stated that WISSIG has boasted about being associated with the CIA. However, she does not know whether this
is true or mere bombast. She said that WISSIG is well to-do
in his own right. Both subjects are associated with a man
by the name of MOHAMMED SCALY originally from Morocco whom
she claims has connections with the Mafia and frequently goes
to Las Vegas, Nevada.

          It is to be pointed out that this informant
is a member of the art colony, quite esoteric in her own
right, and very imaginative. However, the closeness of her
relationship to these people would seem to indicate that her
information about their sexual tendencies is accurate. In
the event any further inquiry is necessary on these people,
I can re-contact her within a day or two.

Garrison always claimed he never talked openly about
Shaw's homosexuality, but his staff certainly understood its
importance. Just take a look at the cover of this pulp magazine
from 1968 with a feature story written by Joel Palmer, who was
working for Garrison. According to his article, Kennedy was the
"victim of a sick and vicious homosexual plot;" Oswald was
"steeped in the homosexual underworld" and had a "bitter
hatred" for Fidel Castro. The homosexual ring consisted of
Oswald, Ruby, Ferrie, Shaw, Russo, and J. D. Tippit, a police

officer whom Oswald killed on the afternoon of the assassination, and he was certain that they were tied together "into one of the most unique and diabolical plots in the history of the world."

Toward the end of the article, Palmer wrote about his visits with Dr. George Barahal, professor of psychology at Wayne State University, who told him that "what you are dealing with here are strong latent homosexual tendencies ... [W]here you have strong latent homosexuality, you also get a paranoid-like reaction ... feelings of persecution ... so there is a connection between paranoia and latent homosexuals."

Might Dr. Barahal have been describing Jim Garrison?

CHAPTER 7

A TOUCH OF BRIBERY

A BOMBSHELL HIT the Garrison investigation with a May 1967 *Newsweek* report by Houston Bureau Chief Hugh Aynesworth. He had uncovered the offer of a bribe to Al Beauboeuf, the friend of David Ferrie who had accompanied him to Houston on the weekend of the assassination. One of Garrison's men, Lynn Loisel, offered Beauboeuf $3,000 ($23,000 in 2020 dollars) and a job in the airline industry on March 17 if he would add certain details to the conspiracy story.

Beauboeuf's lawyer, Hugh Exnicios, taped the conversation.

Exnicios: Now, in other words, what you want him to do, he will come up and give you such evidence that you will be able to couch him in terms of being a hero?

Loisel: That's correct.

Exnicios: And, you'll also—you have an unlimited expense account, you said, and you're willing to help him along?

Loisel: I would venture to say—well, I'm, you know, fairly certain we could put $3,000 on him (sound of snapping of fingers) just like that, you know.

Exnicios: Uh-huh.

Loisel: I'm sure we'd help him financially and I'm sure we—real quick we could get him a job.

But Exnicios wanted specifics about the job offer.

Exnicios: Yes. Now, about the job, what do you mean by that?

Loisel: Al said he'd like a job with an airline.

Exnicios: Uh-huh.

Loisel: And, I feel like the job can be had, you know.

Exnicios: Well, now, these are tough things to come by. What makes you feel that you would be in a position— ...

Loisel: Well, let's say that—well, his connections. For instance, he was talking about a small operation, such as Space Air Freight.

Exnicios: Uh-huh

Loisel: I know with one phone call, he could go out to the Space Air Freight and write his own ticket, you know. That's just Space Air Freight. That's not Eastern or something else. But I feel like we have people who are stepping stones to the larger airlines and so forth.

What did they want Beauboeuf to say?

Exnicios: Well, how is Al supposed to be able to help you with that meeting?

Loisel: *Well, Al is in—Al, being as close to Ferrie—*

Exnicios: *Yes.*

Loisel: *—has to know the whole thing from beginning to end. He has to know it.*

What exactly was that?

Loisel: *We're interested in more than Clay Shaw.*

Exnicios: *Yeah.*

Loisel: *What—to us, Clay Shaw ain't shit, you know.*

Exnicios: *Uh-huh.*

Loisel: *What is he? He was involved in actual talking of it, you know, and—but we want—we want the—the facts, you know, the—all the details.*

Exnicios: *Trying to find out who brought in that crossfire?*

Loisel: *That's right.*

Exnicios: *Do you have any lead on that yet?*

Loisel: *I could tell you something about it, but I'd rather not lie.*

Exnicios: *Well, now, supposing, Lynn—*

Loisel: *I suppose it all could lead to Clay Shaw.*

Exnicios: *Yes. Lynn—Lynn (LAUGHTER). Let me ask you this: Supposing we agree to this and it's all drawn down and after you run Al Beauboeuf through the three deals, it comes out he knows nothing about the whole thing, what—what then? Will you still give him the money and still give him the position?*

Loisel: *No, That's not the deal.*

Exnicios: *What is the deal?*

Loisel: *The deal is that Al fills in the missing links.*

And what were those missing links?

Loisel: I'd like to ask him a few little questions just to satisfy my own curiosity. Not key questions—

Exnicios: Uh-huh.

Loisel: —but something that only a man in his position could know. Then, before we clinch the deal, you know, and answer, I—I have to know what it is before the deal is clinched.

Exnicios: All right. Now, tell me, what the questions you might ask?

Loisel: Well, I'll—I'll ask the questions, you know if— in fact, just let him talk for maybe five seconds, you understand, and my knowledge of the investigation can tell whether or not he knows what we want to know. But anyhow, you could know yourself. I mean, if he tells you, "All right, there was Joe Blow and Joe Blow and Joe Blow present, we talked about this and then we purchased this gun from this place and then we had—it was set up like this and the escape route was this, but it didn't happen, it went this way—"

Once Garrison's office found out about the tape, he had Loisel and Ivon visit Beauboeuf. They told him, "Al, you did us a dirty deal." Toward the end of the conversation, Loisel pointed a finger at Beauboeuf and said, "You are going to get a hot load of lead up your ..."[1] They then threatened to hand out nude pictures of Beauboeuf, supposedly taken by Ferrie. The next day Beauboeuf went to see Garrison and signed a statement denying he was offered a bribe.[2]

Garrison claimed that the tape had been altered.[3] In fact, the

New Orleans police department listened to the tape during their investigation and found that the transcript was accurate and authentic (see below). But while they did acknowledge that Garrison's office may have possessed nude photographs of the witness, they also opined that the investigators in question had not violated the rules governing the code of conduct, in that it was legal to pay for information.

Mr. Hugh Exnicios then played the tape as Major Palmisano and I followed the copy of the transcript and compared the typewritten words with the voices recorded on the tape and concluded that the transcript coincided with the information on the tape. Mr. Exnicios advised us that the tape we were re-viewing at that time was the original tape which had been made of the conversation previously mentioned, and that he had pre-served it and retained it in his exclusive control since it was recorded.

An excerpt from the New Orleans police report dated June 12, 1967.

NBC sent Walter Sheridan, a confidante of Robert Kennedy and a former Department of Justice investigator, to New Orleans to look into the Garrison case. He teamed up with NBC affiliate WDSU reporter Richard Townley. By mid-May, Garrison was so enraged by their poking around that he ordered William Gurvich to arrest them and have them handcuffed, beaten, and dragged to jail. James Alcock, Garrison's second-in-command, asked on what grounds were they to be arrested. Garrison replied, "What do you mean, for what—just arrest them." When Alcock protested, on the basis of the fact that there were no grounds, Garrison replied, "Don't be so blankety-blank legalistic."

The JFK Conspiracy: The Case of Jim Garrison aired nation-wide on June 19, 1967, and exposed Garrison's bribery. The big story was told by John Cancler, aka John the Baptist, who was in prison for burglary. He had a long history of being involved with Garrison; he claimed that he had set up some hold-ups so that Garrison could arrest certain people. He told NBC that Vernon

Bundy said he was lying about seeing Oswald and Shaw on the Lake Pontchartrain seawall. Another prisoner, Miguel Torres, confirmed that Bundy was lying to prevent punishment for parole violation.

Cancler, whom a Garrison assistant called "one of the best—if not the best—active burglar in New Orleans," claimed that Lynn Loisel asked him to break into Shaw's house and plant evidence. He declined the offer. Garrison brought Cancler before the grand jury where he pleaded the Fifth Amendment and received a six-month sentence for contempt of court.[4]

William Gurvich corroborated the basis for the story in an interview with Clay Shaw's attorneys.

"In January, as I recall, yes, it was in January of this year. Loisel told me that Garrison had wanted Shaw's home broken into. And I thought the man was kidding me and I have known Lynn Loisel for ten years or so. He said, "No, I really mean it." I said He couldn't do anything like that. How can he make a case doing things like that? and Loisel said, "What's the difference?" and I said, "The difference is you can't go to Court and taken an oath and swear that this and that happened when you know that it was done this way," and Loisel said to me, "Well, Bill, you certainly can't be that straight," and I said, "that straight? You had better believe that I would never go to Court and lie under oath." And that led me to believe right then and there that certainly Lynn Loisel is one who would lie under oath."

Miguel Torres was of particular interest to Garrison because of his theory of propinquity. Torres once lived with his parents on the 5000 block of Magazine Street, and Oswald had once lived on the 4900 block. Garrison believed that the 4900 block was a "safe block" that was "owned by the CIA, and used as a sort of parking place for agents waiting assignment." Torres was also once the dinner guest of Sergio Arcacha Smith (see Chapter 11) at a cottage on the 1300 block of Dauphine Street, which was just across the street from Shaw (at 1313 Dauphine). To top it all off, Garrison also found it suspicious that Oswald had given the address of 2705 Magazine Street as a reference for employment; Torres had once met his fellow burglar, Emilio Santana, on the 2700 block of Magazine Street. And there were even more instances of propinquity: Santana lived around the corner from Al Beauboeuf, who was friends with David Ferrie.

Torres was brought to Garrison's office a total of four times. In the first meeting, they reminded Torres that "if he did not recall things that he was told to, he would have to serve the full nine-year sentence." He was reminded that Garrison was an extremely powerful and influential man who had the capability of providing help or inflicting harm. He was then supposedly offered some heroin, a Florida vacation, and his freedom. Next, they wanted to hypnotize him, but Torres refused and was persuaded to take a lie detector test.

Was he involved in the JFK assassination? No. Did he kill JFK? No. Did he know Clay Shaw? No. Torres was then told that the lie detector indicated he knew Clay Shaw. The next meeting was with Assistant District Attorney Mike Karmazin.

Torres: Well, he started asking me ... you see I lived in the 1300 block with Charles way back when I first came to the States and then I lived on the 900 block of Esplanade, which you see, puts me in a good position around Mr. Clay's house. And he wanted me to say that I had been approached by Mr. Shaw on a couple of occasions, see. And I refused to say that, I told them, no ... I can't say that.

Q: Approached in what way?

Torres: Homosexual approach and he wanted me to say that Mr. Clay Shaw was Clay Bertrand. In other words, he was, he kept implying for me to say that I knew Clay as Clem.

NBC also talked to Fred Leemans, an operator of a Turkish bath that catered to gay people at night. After being promised financial assistance for his bar, he gave Garrison a statement that said Clay Shaw visited his baths as Clay Bertrand and that he was accompanied by a young man named Lee. Like Russo and Bundy's description of "Lee," this man had a beard and was described as a beatnik. Leemans told NBC he was given some assistance.

Leemans: Then he [Assistant District Attorney Robert Lee] asked me questions about er, couldn't I remember that Clay Shaw had used the name Clay Bertrand when he came to the baths. And the way he asked it I figured he wanted, yes, so I told him yes. And then he asked about how many times he came up and I said, well, once in a while and then he asked did I remember that Clay had come up there in the company of a young fellow and in the company of Cubans. And I told them I wasn't sure, and he said all these things would be helpful to them. So, I told them yes, that they had.

A few weeks before the NBC special, Leemans called Irvin Dymond, Clay Shaw's trial attorney. He had represented Leeman's daughter years earlier on a narcotics charge. She told her father to call him, that he could be trusted, and that it was time for her father to "cleanse his conscience." He told Leemans to write to Garrison, which he did, stating that Clay Shaw had indeed visited his business, but to the best of his recollection, he had done so using his own name and that he had generally arrived alone.[5]

Besides the bribery and intimidation, NBC also disclosed that Perry Russo had been given a lie detector test and that "Russo's general reaction to this series of questions led the polygraph operation to suspect a 'psychopathic personality.'"

In May 1967, Fred Freed, an executive producer at NBC, went to visit Aaron Kohn, head of the Metropolitan Crime Commission. He had been having talks with Roy Jacobs, a polygraph operator with the Jefferson Parish sheriff's office. Jacobs confessed that his conscience had given him no rest since Perry Russo's testimony in the preliminary hearing. He was afraid to speak out since he only had one more year to work in the sheriff's office and felt that if he were to reveal the results of a polygraph test, he would be branded as untrustworthy in the future, and his ability both to obtain business and support his family would be in jeopardy.

Freed showed Kohn the results of Russo's polygraph test. "The reports indicated that when Russo was shown pictures of Clay Shaw and Lee Oswald, in each instance he stated he knew them, but the polygraph reaction indicated that he was emotionally disturbed by his own replies, and might have been lying, but needed further interrogation." The test was abruptly ended before more questions could be asked.

While the test was administered before the preliminary hearing, it was not written up in a memo until May (see below) and probably reflects an attempt to whitewash the whole affair.

```
M E M O R A N D U M


May 9, 1967 (Dictated & transcribed)


TO:         JIM GARRISON, District Attorney

FROM:       ANDREW J. SCIAMBRA, Assistant District Attorney

RE:         PERRY RUSSO
-------------------------------------------------------------------


            In response to our conversation this morning May 9th,
in your office, this is to advise you that PERRY RUSSO was taken
down to Roy Jacobs by me in order to have PERRY undergo a Poly-
graph examination.  I entered the office of William Gurvich,
which is located on Poydras Street, and was met by Roy Jacobs and
Lenny Gurvich.  Jacobs took RUSSO into another office where PERRY
was to undergo the Polygraph examination.  I left PERRY with
Jacobs in the office and came back around one-half hour or forty-
five minutes later.  Jacobs informed me that RUSSO had not taken
the Polygraph examination yet.  He explained to me that PERRY was
extremely nervous and perspiring and that the palms of his hands
were wet and that he was unable to get a reading on PERRY.  Jacobs
said that due to PERRY's extreme nervousness  he did not know
whether or not he could undergo a Polygraph examination; that he
had tried for over an hour to get a reading on PERRY but was
unable to do so.  Jacobs said that it indicated to him that in
his opinion RUSSO was a psychotic.  I asked him the basis of his
evaluation concerning RUSSO and Jacobs said that he was making
this judgment on past experiences.  I asked him if he had had any
psychiatric training and he said "No."  Since it was Jacob's
opinion that any further attempts to have RUSSO take a Polygraph
examination would be futile, it was decided that we would leave
and perhaps try again at a later date.

            When I was taking PERRY back to his automobile, PERRY
told me that he did not particularly care for Jacobs as he felt
a strong feeling of resentment towards Jacobs at the very begin-
ning of his interview with Jacobs prior to PERRY's attempt to take
the Polygraph examination.  PERRY said that Jacobs told him that
he (Jacobs) would have to ask him a few preliminary questions
before he would turn on the machine and that even though Jacobs
did not call him a liar to his face, PERRY had the feeling that
Jacobs was trying to "shoot him down" and did not believe his
story; that Jacobs made a great point of explaining to PERRY how
precise and accurate the Polygraph examination was that that it
would detect the smallest lie.  Jacobs also said that he did not
believe in hypnosis and the only true test of veracity was a
Polygraph examination.
```

But there was also a second attempt at a lie detector test. In June of 1967, Andrew Sciambra asked Lieutenant Edward O'Donnell of the New Orleans Police Department to administer another lie detector test. He stated that the previous test was unsatisfactory and that because of the use of an improper technique, Perry Russo had been antagonised.

O'Donnell interviewed Russo on June 16 and explained the polygraph technique. He attempted to give him a polygraph test on June 19, but "the polygraph tracings were too erratic. He continually moved. So, I took the attachment from the body and continued with my interview." Russo said that "he was under a great deal of pressure, and that he was sorry he ever got involved in this mess."

"So, I then asked him was Clay Shaw there at the David Ferrie apartment, and he asked me if I really wanted to know, and I said yes, of course, that's why you are here, and he said, I don't know. He said again, I don't know. I said, "Well, Perry, Clay Shaw is a big man; he's the type of person who, after you see him, you would probably remember him." I said, was he there, or wasn't he?"

His answer was, "If you really want a yes or no answer, I would have to say no."

O'Donnell went straight to Garrison's office to report what Russo had said. Garrison "became enraged and stated something to the effect that I had sold out to the press, or sold out to someone—sold out to the establishment." O'Donnell prepared a written report, which was ignored. O'Donnell also went to the FBI and told them that Garrison had instructed him to keep his mouth shut and not to say anything about the test or what Russo said.

The results of these lie detector tests were not reported to Clay Shaw's defense team. O'Donnell later approached Shaw's lawyers because he was convinced that Shaw was innocent.

George Lardner of the *Washington Post* was also talking to Russo, who said "without being asked, that there were certain 'weaknesses' or 'holes' surrounding his testimony." But he wasn't going to say anything "without getting something in return," noting that he was dissatisfied with the $300 he had already received from Garrison, supposedly for expenses. Russo ended the interview noting that "if you say anything about this, I'm going to have to call you a liar."[6]

Russo Hints Of Secrets Up for Sale

6/27/67

By George Lardner Jr.
Washington Post Staff Writer

Perry Russo, the star witness in District Attorney Jim Garrison's investigation of President Kennedy's assassination, has repeatedly hinted that he was willing to disclose "weaknesses" in his testimony — for a price.

"I'm looking for guarantees," he told me. "I'm interested in me, my job and money."

The NBC special infuriated Garrison, and on July 7, 1967, he charged Sheridan with bribing and intimidating witnesses (primarily Perry Russo) and subpoenaed him to appear before the grand jury. Only July 11, 1967, he charged Richard Townley with bribing and intimidating witnesses. Their crime (besides their television show) was telling Perry Russo that he could get out of the mess by leaving the state and getting a lawyer. Upon hearing of the indictment, Robert Kennedy issued a statement saying that "I have been fortunate to know and work with Walter Sheridan for many years. Like all those who have known him and his work, I have the utmost confidence in his integrity, both personal and professional ... It is not possible that Mr. Sheridan would do anything which would in the slightest degree compromise the truth in regard to the investigation in New Orleans." The charges against Sheridan and Townley were eventually dropped.

NBC Charges Terror Tactics by Garrison

BY RONALD J. OSTROW
Times Staff Writer

WASHINGTON — The National Broadcasting Co. accused New Orleans Dist. Atty. Jim Garrison Wednesday of trying to intimidate news media critical of his probe into President John F. Kennedy's assassination.

Walter J. Sheridan, NBC special correspondent, said he will return to New Orleans in the next few days to fight Garrison's charges that he attempted to bribe a key witness in the investigation.

Sheridan said his arrest and that of Richard Townley, a reporter for WSDU-TV in New Orleans, "is a blatant attempt to terrorize all those who might criticize Garrison's conduct as district attorney."

Los Angeles Times, *July 13, 1967*

Procedural issues delayed the Clay Shaw trial until February of 1969. This gave Garrison a lot of time to crisscross the nation discussing his ever-growing conspiracy.

CHAPTER 8

THE GREAT ACCUSER

SHAW'S ARREST on March 1, 1967, reverberated around the globe. In Rome, a small Communist Party–controlled[1] newspaper, *Paese Sera*, started a series of articles on March 4 claiming that Clay Shaw had been involved in unsavory activities while serving on the board of Permindex/Centro Mondiale Commerciale (CMC), a corporation founded in the late 1950s to take advantage of the new European common market and make Rome an important trading hub.

Paese Sera alleged that the CMC was a "creature of the CIA ... set up as a cover for the transfer to Italy of CIA-FBI funds for illegal political-espionage activities." The articles repeated a Jim Garrison allegation (supposedly reported in the Italian daily *Il Messaggero*) that "on certain occasions, the International Trade Mart [Shaw's organization in New Orleans] had turned over varying sums of money as contributions to the so-called Cubans in exile." *Paese Sera* also claimed that Garrison "was going through Shaw's account books for information on the financing of the conspiracy."

March 5, 1967, edition of the Paese Sera *newspaper with a Clay Shaw story.*

The *Paese Sera* series was incredibly short on details. Most of the articles focus on the alleged connections of different people associated with Permindex/CMC. For instance, "It is a fact that the CMC is nevertheless the point of contact for a number of persons who, in certain respects, have somewhat equivocal ties whose common denominator is an anticommunism so strong that it would swallow up all those in the world who have fought for decent relations between East and West, including Kennedy."

And it included the false allegation that "Clay Shaw, by his own admission, came to Rome during the time preceding the disbanding of the CMC. According to American sources, Shaw left the U.S. two days after the assassination of Kennedy and came to Europe visiting, among other places, Italy. Shaw's trip lasted about two years, except for a few short visits to the U.S."[2]

The *Paese Sera* narrative traveled quickly. *Pravda* (the official newspaper of the Communist Party of the Soviet Union) published an article by its Italian correspondent on March 7 with the title "Clay Shaw of the CIA." It alleged that "Shaw was given the task of establishing contacts with extreme rightist groups in Rome, including the representatives of the neofascist organizations."

Pravda *story, Clay Shaw of the CIA.*

The story then appeared in *L'Unita* (the newspaper of the Italian Communist Party), *L'Humanite* (the newspaper of the French Communist Party), and then in *Le Devoir* (an influential nationalist and mainstream French-language daily newspaper in Montreal), which ran the *Pravda* article in the March 8, 1967, edition, and then ran a larger article on March 16 written by its New York correspondent Louis Wiznitzer. He mentioned the items confiscated from Shaw's apartment and commented that he was a veritable "Marquis de Sade." Wiznitzer also alluded to Shaw's homosexuality, writing, "Finally, another detail that doesn't lack for a certain spiciness: in his youth Clay Shaw published a story from which John Ford took his film, *Men without Women.*" Ford did produce that film, but it was not based on Shaw's play.

The allegations about Clay Shaw and the CMC had now jumped from communist newspapers into the legitimate press.

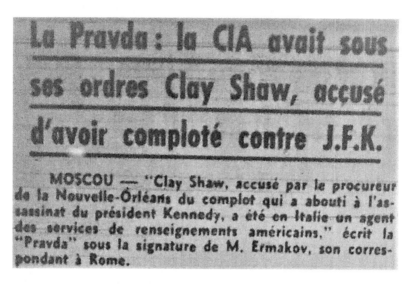

From there it went to *Canadian Dimension*, a small left-wing magazine, whose article "Neo-Fascism and the Kennedy assassins" admitted that the *Le Devoir* articles had a "breezy disregard for documentation." *Ramparts* ran "The Garrison Commission" in the January 1968 issue, which used *Paese Sera* and *Le Devoir* as its sources regarding Permindex/CMC.

Historian Max Holland wrote several articles suggesting that the *Paese Sera* story was planted by the KGB. The Mitrokhin Archive is a collection of notes made secretly by KGB archivist Vasili Mitrokhin documenting the activities of the Soviet Union around the globe. His second book, coauthored with Christopher Andrew, claimed that "In April 1961 the KGB succeeded in planting on the pro-Soviet Italian daily *Paese Sera* a story suggesting that the CIA was involved in the failed putsch mounted by four French generals to disrupt de Gaulle's attempts to negotiate a peace with the FLN which would lead to Algerian independence." The next day *Pravda* repeated the accusations. The entire episode soured French-American relations and helped push France into an antagonistic stance on NATO.

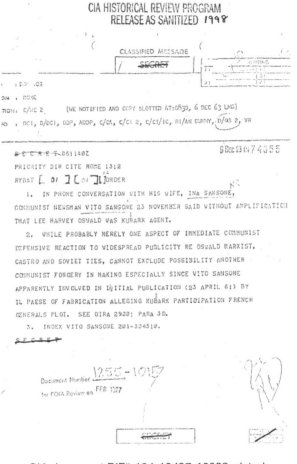

CIA document RIF# 104-10437-10083, dated December 6, 1963. Kubark is a CIA term for itself.

A senior KGB officer, Sergey Kondrashev, told Tennent Bagley, deputy chief of the Soviet Bloc Division in CIA counter-intelligence, that "the most obvious route toward the broad

Western public was, of course, newspapers, and magazines—
planting articles in cooperative papers (of the many Kondrashev
remembers *Paese Sera* in Italy ...)."

Holland's colleague Paul Hoch found a note in the Mitrokhin
Archive saying that "In 1967, Department A of the First Chief
Directorate conducted a series of disinformation operations ...
One such emplacement in New York was through *Paese Sera.*"
Sure enough, an article in the left-wing *National Guardian*
(which was based in New York) discussed Shaw's arrest on
March 19. It added the entirely false allegation that Shaw had
been involved with the planning of Kennedy's trip to Dallas.

National Guardian, *March 1967*

By mid-March 1967, Garrison had received copies of the arti-
cle, quite possibly sent to him by Ralph Schoenman, who was
Bertrand Russell's secretary. We know this from the diary of
Richard Billings, whose entry for March 22 reads, "Story about
Shaw and CIA appears in Humanite [sic], probably March 8 ...
[Garrison] has copy date-lined Rome, March 7th, from la press
Italien [sic]"

Garrison now had a direct link from Shaw to the CIA. This
information, combined with the beliefs of the conspiracy buffs,
helped convince Garrison to move away from the homosexu-
al/S&M angle and to start talking about something bigger.

And boy did it get bigger!

In May 1967, Garrison told the Associated Press that "The
President was killed by a fatal bullet that was fired from the front.
There was a crossfire situation set up which involved at least two
pairs of men in the front, apparently two men behind the stone

wall and two behind the picket fence ... [Y]ou had in effect a group of men operating as a guerilla team."

4A   Columbus Dispatch ··   MON., MAY 22, 1967

Garrison Claims JFK Slain by Angry Cubans

NEW ORLEANS (UPI)—Dist. Atty. Jim Garrison claimed Sunday night that President Kennedy was not killed by Lee Harvey Oswald but by five anti-Castro Cubans angry over the handling of the abortive Bay of Pigs invasion. involved were located both behind the wall at Dealey Plaza and on the grassy knoll the day of the assassination in Dallas.

Itek Corporation, a private company, said last week it had studied films of the as-

---

He then told the *Morning Advocate* in Baton Rouge that he felt that his office had been aware of every principal in the assassination for some time, saying also that "we have even located photographs in which we have found the men behind the grassy knoll and stone wall before they dropped completely out of sight. There were five of them. Three behind the stone wall and two behind the grassy knoll." He further stated that these men were former CIA employees, the identities of whom his office had confirmed in a manner he was not at liberty to reveal (naturally). He ominously noted: "In the final analysis, what it comes down to is whether federal power can be allowed to be totally uncontrolled. If this is so, then we are no different than Nazi Germany or Soviet Russia."

DA Says CIA Hides
Killer's Whereabouts
By LAURA FOREMAN
Associated Press Writer
The CIA is concealing the
whereabouts of the actual as-
sassins of President John F.
Kennedy, Dist. Atty. Jim Garri-
son said Tuesday.

The Times-Picayune, *May 24, 1967*

In a far-ranging interview with Jim Squires of the Nashville
Tennessean in June 1967, Garrison claimed that Kennedy had
been killed by a fourteen-man band of Cuban guerrilla fighters.
Squires noted that "when he talks about this group and what he
contends they did he drops the names of a wide assortment of
Cubans and sometimes it is difficult to follow the thread of the
conspiracy he says occurred."

Trained in U.S.

Cuban Guerrilla Team Killed JFK, Garrison Thinks

By JIM SQUIRES, Staff Correspondent
Copyright 1967 by THE NASHVILLE TENNESSEAN

NEW ORLEANS—District Attorney Jim Garrison
believes President Kennedy was killed by members
of a 14-man band of Cuban guerrilla fighters who
were trained secretly in nearby St. Tammany parish
in the summer of 1963.

Nashville Tennessean, *June 22, 1967, page 1*

Garrison hit the big time in October 1967 with *Playboy*
magazine's longest interview ever. Over five million copies of the
magazine were distributed, and Garrison was sent on a media
tour. The preamble to the interview stated that "the day after

Shaw's arrest Garrison declared that 'Shaw was none other than Clay Bertrand,' the shadowy queen bee of the New Orleans homosexual underworld."[3]

According to Garrison, the assassination was carried out by a guerilla team consisting of a minimum of seven men, including anti-Castro adventurers and members of the paramilitary right. Furthermore, he declared that "We've uncovered additional evidence establishing absolutely that there were at least four men on the grassy knoll, at least two behind the picket fence and two or more behind a small wall to the right of the fence. As I reconstruct it from the still-incomplete evidence in our possession, one man fired at the President from each location, while the role of his companion was to snatch up the cartridges as they were ejected." Sylvia Meagher wrote a letter to *Playboy* saying that "without intending levity on matters as grave as these, I have to admit that Garrison's theory of men on the grassy knoll whose sole function was 'to catch the cartridges as they were ejected from the assassins' rifles' strikes me as comical."

Also, said Garrison, "a number of the men who killed the President were former employees of the CIA involved in its anti-Castro underground activities in and around New Orleans. The CIA knows their identity. So do I—and our investigation has established this without the shadow of a doubt."

1967 Herblock cartoon, ©The Herb Block Foundation

Garrison didn't stop there. He told various reporters that important parts of the Dallas police force were involved in the assassination, ordered and paid for by a few "oil-rich psychotic millionaires." JFK's assassination was carried out by "ultra-militant para-military elements who were patriotic in a psychotic sense." He added that there were more than seven men in radio communication with one another and that Kennedy had been killed because he was pro-Communist.

"The connecting link at every level of operation from the oil-rich sponsors of the assassination down to the Dallas

police department through Jack Ruby and including anti-Castro adventurers at the operating level were Minute Men, Nazi-oriented. It was essentially a Nazi operation."

Dallas Policemen Deeply Involved in Plot, Says DA

JFK Murder Ordered by Millionaires, Charge

District Attorney Jim Garrison said in New York Thursday that "elements of the Dallas police force were deeply involved" in the assassination of President John F. Kennedy.

The assassination, Garrison charged, was ordered and paid for by "a handful of oil-rich psychotic millionaires."

cided to kill Kennedy because they felt he was "selling out to the Communists."

Garrison said there were "considerably more than seven men" involved in the actual assassination in Dallas, adding they were radio-equipped and took virtually no risk of being caught.

"The connecting link at every level of operation from the oil

The Times-Picayune, *September 22, 1967*

And in November 1967, Garrison gave a speech at the 18th Annual Banquet of the Radio and Television News Association of Southern California in which he said,

---

"Who appointed Ramsey Clark, who has done his best to torpedo the investigation of the case? Who controls the CIA? Who controls the FBI? Who controls the Archives—where the evidence is locked up for so long that it is unlikely that there is anybody in this room that will be alive when it is released?

This is really your property and the property of the people in this country. Who has the arrogance and the

brass the prevent the people in this country from seeing that evidence? Who indeed?

The one man who has profited most from the assassination—your friendly President!!

Lyndon Johnson."

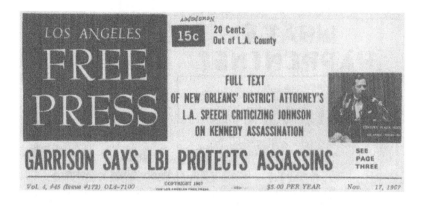

During all his pontificating about the conspiracy, Garrison sent Steve Jaffe, a university student from California, on an important mission to Dallas. He was to check out the possibility that a storm sewer on Elm Street could have been the location of an assassin. Jaffe reported back that "I now believe, without reservation, that it was possible for the storm sewer to have been used in the murder of President Kennedy. I also believe that there is a strong possibility that the fatal shot was fired from this position." Jaffe's letter noted that "a car passing in front of the opening of this drain, at approximately 11 m.p.h. is seen for approximately two seconds. Time enough to aim carefully and fire with a rifle or other type of short-range weapon."

This was more than enough for Garrison. On December 9, he told television interviewer Murphy Martin on WFAA-TV in Dallas that "the man whose bullet delivered the coup de grace to the President of the United States stood in a manhole that connects with a drainage system under Dealey Plaza." He stated that after the assassin fired a .45 caliber pistol, he managed to escape via 18-inch and 30-inch pipes beneath the plaza.

December 18, 1967. Dallas, Texas. New Orleans District Attorney Jim Garrison has released this first of three photos to support his theory that a shot was fired from a storm sewer during the assassination of President John F. Kennedy. Here, an investigator steps into one of the entrances into a sewer complex under Dealey Plaza. This entrance is behind the fence on the top of the "grassy knoll" CREDIT: Bettmann.

*New Orleans District Attorney Jim Garrison
released these two of three pictures to support his
theory that a shot was fired from a sewer during the
assassination of President John F. Kennedy. The
top picture (2) is a sewer opening on the north side
of Elm Street, which can be reached from tunnels
under Dealey Plaza. The bottom photo (3) was
taken from within the sewer as a convertible passed
by. CREDIT: Bettmann.*

Garrison Says Assassin Killed Kennedy From Sewer Manhole

DALLAS, Dec. 10 (AP)—Jim Garrison, District Attorney of New Orleans, said on a television show last night that President Kennedy was killed with a .45-caliber bullet fired by a man standing in a sewer manhole.

wise would not have allowed him to touch it.

The Federal Government, he said, "had to know 10 minutes after the assassination that Lee Oswald could not have done it." "Lyndon Johnson had to know it," he said.

Saying he was "tired of hear-

New York Times, *December 11, 1967*

In January 1968, Monk Zelden, Dean Andrew's lawyer, bumped into Garrison at the New Orleans Athletic Club. "He came in with these long rolled-up documents under his arm. I said 'what's that?'. He said 'Shshshsh,' he looked around the room. Then he leaned over and said, 'these are the official maps of the sewerage system of the city of Dallas.'"

Garrison's theory could never hold much water. "Most of the sewers beneath Dealey Plaza are only 15 inches in diameter, leading to a search for what reporters have called 'the mini-midget.'"

Garrison turned his attention overseas. On Dutch television, in February 1968, he said he had to speak out in Europe, insisting that it was impossible to do so in America. "The U.S. press is controlled to such an extent by the CIA that we can no longer say the truth," he stated. "They throttled us."

He then told the *New York Times* in July of 1968 that "his office had been exchanging information with a foreign intelligence agency that had 'penetrated the forces involved in the assassination ... 'The agency was from a government that was a military ally of the US and that the report, according to Garrison, included an interview with one of the alleged assassins. Garrison now claimed that 'there were four assassination teams, each with one rifleman and one lookout.'"

GARRISON CLAIMS FOREIGN SPY LINK

Says He Exchanged Data About President Kennedy

By PETER KIHSS

District Attorney Jim Garrison asserted yesterday that his office had been exchanging information with a foreign intelligence agency that he said had "penetrated the forces involved in the assassination" of President Kennedy.

New York Times, *July 12, 1968*

Even Robert Kennedy wasn't immune from Garrison's recklessness; Garrison was adamant in his charge that Senator Kennedy was opposed to "the truth being brought out" on the basis of the notion that the facts would interfere with his political career.

Says RFK Obstructs JFK Probe

NEW YORK — (UPI) — Sen. Robert F. Kennedy has "done everything he could to obstruct" the investigation of President Kennedy's assassination, New Orleans District Attorney Jim Garrison charged here yesterday.

Jack Kennedy, would interfere with his political career," the district attorney said.

Garrison said he knows the names of men involved in the alleged plot to assas-

Cleveland Press, *September 22, 1967.*

Who wasn't involved? Veteran reporter James Phelan poked fun with an apt limerick:

> Cried Big Jim, the world owes me praise.
> And I'll get it, come one of these days.
> Earl Warren, the dunce.
> Solved the killing just once.
> But I solved it seventeen ways!

'It say, D. A. Garrison name you, Nanook, in JFK conspiracy'

© Thomas Darcy 1968, courtesy of the Darcy family.

CHAPTER 9

THE TRIAL

THE CASE eventually went to trial in February 1969. It had been a difficult two years for Clay Shaw's defense team. There were no rules for discovery, and his defense team had to run down every rumor brought to their attention. This forced Shaw to spend over $30,000 ($221,000 in 2020 dollars) hiring detectives to investigate potential witnesses.

Shaw's defense team faced two additional problems. First, the state only had to prove that an "overt act" was committed in support of the conspiracy. It did not have to prove that Kennedy was killed as a result of the alleged conspiracy. It was a ridiculously low bar for the prosecution.

Second, the defense team had to file motions to get the prosecution to add details to their bills of information. The indictment charged that "Clay L. Shaw between the 1st day of September and the 10th day of October... in 1963 ... did conspire with Lee Harvey Oswald, David W. Ferrie, Jack Ruby, and others to assassinate John F. Kennedy." They could never find out just who the "others" were, nor could they find out just how many conspiratorial meetings were supposedly held.

Ed Wegmann, one of the defense attorneys, wrote, "We anticipate that we will be confronted with one or more surprise witnesses about whom we know nothing and about whom we will know nothing until they walk into the courtroom, take the witness stand, swear to tell the truth and then proceed to perjure themselves with a story which can only be fictional if it involves the client ... [T]he guilty man is easy to defend because you know what he did. We will not know what Clay did until we hear the witnesses."

But the prosecution also had a problem, and it was a big one: their extremely weak case. Herman Kohlman, an assistant district attorney in Garrison's office, spoke to author Patricia Lambert in 1993.

"Kohlman had heard ... that Garrison was supposed to try the case. And the whole time preceding the trial whenever Alcock or the others asked what the rest of the case consisted of that Garrison said they didn't need to know. He built a Chinese wall between them and "the rest of the case;" only he knew the totality of it. And, so they really thought, like the rest of the world, that he did, in fact, really have something else, they too thought he was really onto something and it would be revealed at the trial. Then, just before the trial, Garrison tells Alcock that he is going to try the case. Alcock says you better tell me the rest of it then and Garrison tells him, that's it, you know it, there isn't anything else."

The first witnesses in the case came from Clinton and Jackson Louisiana, two towns located about 120 miles north of New Orleans. Eight witnesses came forward who saw Clay Shaw and possibly David Ferrie in August and September of 1963 during a voter registration drive. A few witnesses also saw Lee Harvey Oswald, who supposedly wanted a job at a nearby mental hospital. A state representative told him he had to register to vote before he could be hired. He was then seen in a car with Shaw and Ferrie, and he then waited for hours in line before being informed he didn't need to register. Oswald then went to the hospital and filled out a job application.

None of these witnesses came forward before the Garrison investigation. Corrie Collins was asked about this.

Dymond: Now, you were aware that the Warren Commission was conducting an extensive investigation into the assassination of President Kennedy, were you not?

Collins: I was aware they were investigating it.

Dymond: I see. At the time that you were aware of the fact that this investigation was being conducted, you knew that you had seen Lee Harvey Oswald in Clinton, did you not?

Collins: That is true.

Dymond: Did you report this to the Warren Commission or the FBI or any Federal agency?

Collins: No.

Dymond: Why not?

Collins: No one asked me.

Dymond: You didn't consider it your duty to report it?

Collins: Well, I felt like if they wanted to know they would ask me.

There were many problems with the Clinton witnesses. Stephen Roy, the foremost expert on the life of David Ferrie, was convinced that the stories were suspect: the three men visiting were strangers, which would make identification much tougher;

the so-called incident took place four years earlier, and some were basing their identification on pictures; there were differing accounts of the car and what people wore; they only saw the three men for very short periods; and some of the initial accounts included people who later disappeared from their stories. These factors "raise enough reasonable doubt for me to prevent me from regarding the identifications as definitive."[1]

Garrison's lead investigator into the Clinton affair, Anne Dischler, gave her notes to author Patricia Lambert in 1994. She was sent to Clinton, along with state policeman Francis Fruge, to investigate a report that Ferrie, Shaw, Oswald, and Banister had all visited. Ms. Dischler was asked to unearth information about what Oswald had been up to there. Dischler and Fruge started showing people a picture of four men in a Cadillac—Clay Shaw was in the driver's seat along with Oswald—given to her by the DA's office. Some people in town had already seen the picture, but the photograph eventually disappeared and was never mentioned again. Lambert suggested that it would have been a "powerful brainwashing tool."

One witness told Dischler that Oswald had registered to vote and showed her the register. But Oswald's signature was missing, and another name was in its place. When she came back the next day, that page was gone. Oswald's application for employment at the mental hospital was also missing.

Corey Collins testified that Oswald had gotten out of the car to register. Initially, he had told Dischler that two men got out of the car. One of them was "Morgan." Dischler determined that the other person was Winslow Foster, but she was pulled from the case before she could investigate further. What makes this so interesting is that another witness identified Estus Morgan (who also wanted a job at the hospital) as the person standing in line with Oswald. Winslow Foster was a friend of Morgan's. Might they have been the two people getting out of the car?[2] Garrison took Dischler off the case before she and Fruge could talk to Foster.

Hugh Aynesworth drove to Clinton with William Gurvich to investigate for themselves. They talked to several witnesses and were convinced it was a "hoax." Maxine Kemp, a clerk at the hospital, testified at the Shaw trial that she saw an application with the name "Oswald, Harvey." But she told Aynesworth and Gurvich that she had not, that she and a coworker had just found a folder, and that the folder was found in a location where neither applications nor past records would have been filed. They also visited with Corey Collins's father, who seemed scared: "It was simple to see how he had to testify to what Manchester [the town marshal] and the other scrub-nuts wanted him ... [I]n short, being a Negro in Clinton—a hotbed of redneck and the Klan—is not much fun."

One of the major surprises of the trial was New York accountant Charles Spiesel. He claimed that in June 1963 he was at Lafitte's Blacksmith Shop, a bar in the French Quarter, and recognized someone who had served with him in Africa in 1941. He identified this person as David Ferrie (although Ferrie was not in Africa in 1941). Spiesel was asked if he wanted to go to a party, and he left with the man and four others. They went to an apartment in the French Quarter, where he met Clay Shaw and a man who had "dirty blonde hair and a sharp nose" and "a month's growth of beard on his face." Spiesel identified this man as Lee Harvey Oswald. At one point there was a discussion about killing Kennedy with a high-powered rifle. Spiesel "did not consider the overall conversation as too significant or sinister" but became alarmed when the man with the beard stated that he intended to kill the president.

It was quite a story. One person in Garrison's office said, "Well, he'd make a great witness, but he's crazy." They learned that Spiesel actually fingerprinted his own children in the morning to be sure that the government hadn't substituted facsimiles of them during the night. They thought the defense would never ask about something as peculiar as that.

Spiesel took the stand on February 7, 1969. The only people he remembered at the party were David Ferrie and Clay Shaw,[3] and he did not even know who the host was. When asked to describe Ferrie, Spiesel said that he did not notice anything unusual about his appearance other than the fact that his eyebrows were a bit thinner than those of most men.

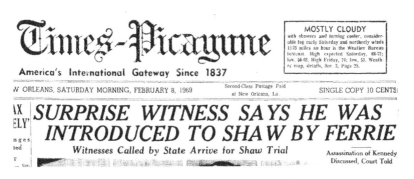

The Times-Picayune, February 8, 1969. You'd have to go to the inside pages to read about Spiesel's hypnosis claims.

Shaw's detectives delivered evidence about Spiesel just in time for cross-examination. Irvin Dymond asked him, "Isn't it true you filed a suit in New York in 1964 against a psychiatrist and the City of New York, claiming that over a period of several years the police and others have hypnotized you and finally harassed you out of business?" Yes, he was sure that he was the victim of a massive conspiracy, perhaps of the "communist" variety, since his father had done some undercover work for the FBI. When he was asked why he had asked for $16 million, he answered, "Well, one million for each year of the conspiracy."

Surprise Witness Says He's Victim of Red Plot

By MARTIN WALDRON   "mystery" witness to bolster
© 1969, New York Times News Service   the case against Shaw a retired

New York Times *News Service, February 8, 1969*

Dymond: How many different people have hypnotized you?

Alcock: Objection!

Dymond: My intent should be fairly obvious to the court.

Judge Haggerty: You may proceed.

Spiesel: It's hard to say. Possibly fifty or sixty.

Dymond: All of these without consent.

Spiesel: Without my consent.

Dymond: Ever happen in New Orleans?

Spiesel: I believe I've been followed down here by people from the detective agencies.

Dymond: I asked if you had been hypnotized in New Orleans?

Spiesel: The point is if I say 'yes' you'll want to know the name of the person and I can't give it to you.

Dymond: Suppose then, I tell you I won't ask you for the person's name.

Spiesel: From time to time, someone has tried to hypnotize me.

Spiesel's claimed that the conspirators "prevented the plaintiff from having normal sex relations, caused psychological terror, caused him to make errors in his work due to hypnotic control." Why, he might even invent stories while hypnotized.

> Dymond: What happens when you are placed under hypnosis?
>
> Spiesel: Certain thoughts are planted or given, and that's what I mean.
>
> Dymond: Do you mean that the thoughts planted give you the impression of being true?
>
> Spiesel: Possibly, yes.

He also confirmed that the prosecution knew about the hypnosis.

> Dymond: Is it not a fact that 15 suits were filed against you for bad tax returns?
>
> Spiesel: Yes, but they were part of the conspiracy against me.
>
> Dymond: When you conferred with the district attorney's office about testifying in this case, did you tell the DA's office about these lawsuits and you're having been under hypnosis?
>
> Spiesel: Yes, I mentioned it.

Garrison wrote years later that after hearing Spiesel's testimony he "was swept by a feeling of nausea. I realized that the clandestine operation of the opposition was so cynical, so sophisticated, and, at the same time, so subtle, that destroying an old-fashioned state jury trial was very much like shooting a fish in a barrel with a shotgun."

Another bizarre moment occurred when a postman, James Hardiman, remembered delivering mail to Clay Shaw's home that was addressed to Clem Bertrand. He also recalled delivering mail to an assortment of other fictitious names.[4] Mr. Hardiman's son was facing charges of theft at the time, and he knew that Garrison could move forward with the charges. After the trial, Hardiman's son was released.

Dean Andrews testified for Clay Shaw and was asked about the phone call he received while being treated in the hospital for double pneumonia.

Mr. Dymond: Was this call to your knowledge from the Defendant Clay Shaw?

Mr. Andrews: No.

Mr. Dymond: Have you ever received a telephone call from Clay Shaw?

Mr. Andrews: No.

Mr. Dymond: Have you ever known Clay Shaw?

Mr. Andrews: No.

Mr. Dymond: Have you ever been introduced to him?

Mr. Andrews: No.

Mr. Dymond: When was the first time that you ever saw Clay Shaw, Mr. Andrews?

Mr. Andrews: When I saw his picture in the paper in connection with the investigation.

And Dean Andrews admitted that he used the name Clay Bertrand as a cover for his client Gene Davis and that it was Davis who called him in the hospital.[5] He also claimed that the request to represent Lee Harvey Oswald was a figment of his imagination—the call was about two people "who were going to sell an automobile and they wanted the title notarized and a bill of sale notarized."

Mr. Alcock: Why is it you called Monk Zelden on Sunday then and asked if he wanted to go to Dallas?

Mr. Andrews: No explanation. Don't forget, I am in the hospital sick. I might have believed it myself, or thought after a while I was retained there, so I called Monk. I would like to be famous too—other than as a perjurer.

[Outburst of laughter]

Bailiffs: Order in the court!

Mr. Alcock: That is going to be difficult.

Mr. Andrews: C'est la vie!

Mr. Alcock: Are you now saying that the call, as far as it regards the representation of Lee Harvey Oswald, is a figment of your imagination?

Mr. Andrews: I have tried to say that consistently, and nobody ever gave me a chance.

And when Perry Russo took the stand, he was forced to admit under cross-examination that the conversations he overheard in Ferrie's apartment might have just been a "bull session." He further conceded there wasn't much of a conspiracy:

Mr. Dymond [Shaw's attorney]: Did Leon Oswald ever, in your presence, agree to kill the President of the United States?

Mr. Russo: No.

Mr. Dymond: Did Clem Bertrand ever agree to kill the President of the United States?

Russo: No.

The party was so mundane that Russo couldn't even remember how he had gotten home.

> Mr. Dymond: *"And you would say that that situation is similar to your not remembering whether or not one of the conspirators to kill the President of the United States rode you home from the conspiratorial meeting?*
>
> *Russo: I don't call them conspirators. No, I don't know who rode me home. I may have caught a bus or hitchhiked or not.*
>
> *Mr. Dymond: You do not call them conspirators?*
>
> *Mr. Russo: I have never used that word.*

A large part of the trial had to do not with Clay Shaw but with Garrison's attempt to discredit the Warren Report. The Zapruder film was shown ten times in court, once in frame-by-frame action. One reporter wrote in his notebook:

> Now playing
> —Criminal Court building—
> the Zapruder Film! Continuous showings—
> in glorious technicolor (Bring the kiddies)

SHAW TRIAL JURY SHOWN MOVIE OF JFK DEATH FRAME BY FRAME
Judge Haggerty Shows Dealey Plaza Exhibit at Trial   Case Dramatically Moves to Dealey Plaza

The Times-Picayune, *February 14, 1967*

James Kirkwood, author of *American Grotesque,* wrote that "If we thought the state's case against the Warren Report would make more sense than the case against Clay Shaw—other than a seriousness to convict—we were mistaken." Critic Sylvia Meagher privately wrote that the "charges against Shaw were nothing but a device by which the W[arren] R[eport] evidence would be tested for the first time in a court of law" and that "Garrison was astonishingly inept and ineffective in challenging the W[arren] R[eport] in the forum of the Shaw trial."

There was one last gasp in the trial. After the Warren Commission rehash was over, Garrison called Nicholas Tadin and his wife Mathilda to the stand. They had just come forward that very day with their story. They testified that their oldest son, who was sixteen in 1964, took flying lessons from David Ferrie. He was deaf, which makes the story unlikely, but there was no time for the defense to check this out. They claimed to have seen Ferrie out at the airport with Clay Shaw. Mrs. Tadin told the court the following:

Mrs. Tadin: So, I can explain myself, we were out there and we were waiting for Dave to come, and he was heading towards us and I noticed a gentleman with Dave and I passed the comment to my husband that it was a distinguished-looking man with Dave and my husband said, "Oh, look, who is with Dave."

Later she said the one thing she remembered was that he was "just a distinguished-looking person." But her statement that morning to the DA's office was slightly different.

Statement from February 27, 1969.

Every single witness in the Garrison investigation came forward after the Warren Commission and the FBI investigation. Perry Russo, Charles Spiesel, and the Clinton and Jackson witnesses hadn't said a word for years before then. "The name Clay Shaw did not emerge in 1963, so a long list of people alleging a relationship between Ferrie and Shaw did not come forward. In short, all that emerged in 1963 were Jack S. Martin and a few people alleging that Ferrie and Oswald may have served in the Civil Air Patrol at the same time, eight years before the assassination."

After just fifty-four minutes of deliberation, the jury found Clay Shaw not guilty. It would have been quicker, but one juror told James Phelan that "we all had to queue up and pee before we got down to business." What was the weakest part of Garrison's case? "Well," a juror said, "the whole thing … [A]fter it was all over, it was like—wow, what happened? What? That's it?" Another said, "It was difficult to determine who was on trial: Shaw, the Warren Report, the Federal Bureau of Investigation, or the Secret Service."

*Clay Shaw holds up a New Orleans newspaper claiming his
innocence at a news conference, Saturday afternoon, March
1, 1969. He is flanked by two of his attorneys, Edward (left)
and William (right) Wegmann. Credit: Associated Press.*

The next day, the New Orleans *States-Item* ran a front-page
editorial calling for Garrison's resignation, saying that Garrison
was "a man without principle who would pervert the legal
process to his own ends." The American Bar Association asked
for an investigation into the DA's office and asked the Louisiana
Bar Association to consider disciplinary action. The *New York
Times* said the prosecution of Shaw was "one of the most
disgraceful chapters in the history of American jurisprudence."

Clay Shaw's nightmare was finally over.

CHAPTER 10

CLAY SHAW V. JIM GARRISON

AS IT TURNED OUT, Clay Shaw's nightmare wasn't quite over after all. On the first business day after the verdict, Garrison charged Shaw with two counts of perjury for his statements that he had never met Lee Harvey Oswald or David Ferrie. The charges carried a twenty-year jail term, equivalent to what he had faced during his conspiracy trial.

ORNING, MARCH 4, 1969   Second-Class Postage Paid at New Orleans, La.   SINGLE COPY 10 CENTS

GARRISON CHARGES SHAW WITH LYING DURING TRIAL

Shaw Released on His Own Recognizance   Perjury Counts Follow Acquittal by Jury

Edward Wegmann said that "Garrison appears to be challenging the credibility of the jury system. I think what the jury said and the manner in which it said it is extremely important. I think the jury spoke." Irvin Dymond added that "the FCC (Federal Communications Commission) wouldn't let you tape" his comment.

It had been a horrible two years for Shaw, catastrophic both psychologically and financially, and he planned to come out of retirement. He also started to drink. "I was up at 6 o'clock and the psychic pain was so intense that I found myself drinking a martini at 6 a.m. Definitely, not a good thing." On many nights, he needed a sleeping pill to nod off.

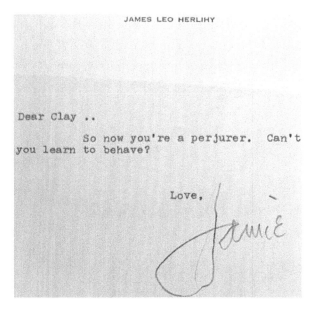

JAMES LEO HERLIHY

Dear Clay ..

        So now you're a perjurer. Can't you learn to behave?

            Love,

James Herlihy, author of Midnight Cowboy, *was a personal friend of Clay Shaw's.*

Shaw's speaking engagements dried up, and his social life took a hit, with people even avoiding him at parties.

"I was talking with Mayor Schiro, when a news cameraman for Channel 12 came over ... and began shooting film of us. Well, Mayor Schiro was too mortified at the idea of being seen on film talking to me that he

*ducked, actually ducked down behind his wife Sunny. I
have not been invited to the city's reception for the
Consular Corps since."*

Shaw wrote in his journal: "When the mind is numbed with
horror, the heart frozen with apprehension, where does one find
words to describe that which is almost indescribable?"

Jim Garrison had his work cut out for him. Once again he
was going to have to find the evidence after the indictment. His
staff redoubled their efforts, and memos started flying in on some
new but mostly old leads, or more accurately, rumors.

"The Show Must Go On — And On — And On — "

A 1969 Herblock cartoon, ©The Herb Block Foundation

The wackiest lead was the "Mardi Gras Ball Caper." In February 1962, over ninety people were arrested at a "fag ball" during Mardi Gras. The party was described as "extremely lewd," and several people were naked. The *Times-Picayune* noted that a policeman's dog "flushed out one man from a sewer pipe after he leaped out a window and attempted to flee."

96 ARE BOOKED AFTER JEFF RAID

Authorities Break Up 'Stag Party'

A "stag party" at the Rambler club was raided Sunday morning by the Jefferson parish sheriff's office.

Ninety-six persons were booked with disturbing the peace and released on $150 bond each.

Capt. San. LeBlanc of the sheriff's office, who led the raid, described the event as a "very lewd party."

The raid was organized after a deputy investigated a complaint on the party.

The Times-Picayune, *February 26, 1962*

A Garrison memo dated March 20, 1969, states that "this lead sounds like an old one which was presumably checked out but its insistent re-appearance suggests that there may possibly be more here than merely smoke. The report is that Ferrie and Shaw were present at a faggot Mardi Gras Ball in Jefferson Parish and that one of them was arrested."

Frederick Soule of the vice squad prepared a list of the people arrested, along with their addresses, noting it was a "party for perverts." Shaw and Ferrie were not on the list. Garrison had to rely on the next best tool: propinquity. David Gentry, a friend of Clay Shaw's, had identified Shaw's friends and acquaintances. Garrison cross-checked the lists and found that Shaw knew a few of the arrested people. But what on earth could be done with that information?

April 7, 1969

TO: Mr. Jim Alcock, A.D.A.   Re: SHAW
                                        Re: PHILIP GERACI
FROM: Capt. F. A. Soule, Sr., Investigator

SUBJECT: Names & Address given by arrested homosexuals who were
          attending a party for perverts on 2/25/62 at 3000 Edenborn
          Street, located in Jefferson Parish.

          All subjects were white males.

1. Donald L. Allen, 5/20/33. 5'11", 165 – 2213 Brainard, born Pass
    Christian.

2. James K. Art, 1/7/29, 6', 175, 832 St. Peter St., born Chicago

3. Gilbert J. Buvens, 9/29/10. 5'10-1/2", 148, 358 W. Moreland, Baton
    Rouge, born, Dallas

Soule listed all ninety-three arrestees from the fag ball.

Propinquity yielded leads from the list of fag ball arrestees. Leonard Frank and Dea Diettrick lived in buildings owned by Shaw; James Mooney lived on the same block as Oswald; William Johnson's address was 935 Burgundy, and Shaw once owned 937 Burgundy; Philip Geraci testified before the Warren Commission that he once met Lee Harvey Oswald when he was fifteen, but this Phil Geraci was forty-nine. There was also a "Long Shot Special:" William Johnson worked at the Dallas International Trade Mart, and Shaw worked at the New Orleans International Trade Mart.

Several memos listed other dubious leads:

- Mrs. J. Fant Taylor "knows a pilot in New York who

is presumably aware of the connection between Shaw and Ferrie."

- Walter Blumstein said that a "faggot" who worked for the Motion Picture Advertising claimed Shaw was introduced to him as Clay Bertrand.
- David Cotter, a close friend of Shaw's, "suddenly left New Orleans when our investigation started and moved to Lacombe."
- Sarah Ryan said that Father Lawrence Toups could give them information on the Mattachine Society (an early gay rights group) and could name the "local members."
- Theresa Claire Fagnant worked at Boeing and on November 22 "left at noon and failed to return. She was missing for a week and on her return claimed that she had gone skiing in New Mexico." A friend of Clay Shaw's stayed in the same apartment building when he returned from a trip to Mexico.
- James Warren "left New Orleans when the probe started. He worked with Clay Shaw. His daughter Phyllis dated Perry Russo and some of his friends."
- Mrs. Jeanne Kelton lived at 905 Governor Nichols from 1963 to 1966. "She said that Shaw used to visit a young man who lived in the apartment building quite often. She said that the young man was 'gay' and referred to Shaw as his 'patron.'"
- Eddie Porter "met Oswald in the summer of 1963 at the Penny Arcade located in the 100 block of Royal Street. Oswald was with a male prostitute by the name of John who, according to Porter, spent most of his time 'hustling the queens' around the arcade."
- "Patsy, a colored female impersonator, said that he has entertained at parties given by Clay Shaw. He

quit working for Shaw because he didn't like his attitude."

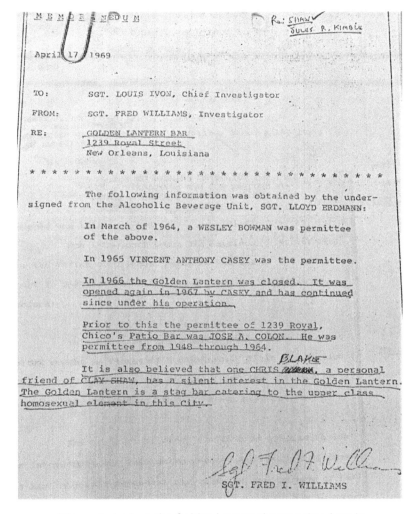

I'll have to look up the Golden Lantern the next time I am in New Orleans. It is still a gay bar.

M E M O R A N D U M

May 7, 1969

TO: SGT. LOUIS IVON, Chief Investigator

FROM: KENT A. SIMMS, Investigator

RE: CLAY BERTRAND LEAD

* *

        Detective Simms on May 5, 1969, contacted MRS. LILLIAN
BISSO in regard to her knowledge of an elevator operator or
building custodian in a downtown office building who stated that
one night a man signed the book as CLAY BERTRAND in the building
where he worked. MRS. BISSO related that she was told the
aforementioned information by a MRS. EVELYN JENKINS, phone number
822-7257, and that she, MRS. BISSO, had no personal knowledge of
the above.

        At this time Detective Simms contacted MRS. EVELYN
JENKINS who stated that she had heard the above information from
a MRS. LILIA CANTRELL employed at Charity Hospital and who resides
at 4308 S. Carrollton Avenue, phone number 486-3610.

        The officer at this point contacted MRS. LILIA CANTRELL
at Charity Hospital who stated that she had heard the above
information from a nurse who was working at Charity Hospital
and since has left her employment at the Hospital. Further that
this was over two years ago since the nurse had told MRS. CANTRELL
the above and that the nurse supposedly heard this from her
mother who lived next door to the elevator operator or building
custodian. MRS. CANTRELL went on to state that she doesn't know
the name of the nurse and that it was stated to her, MRS. CANTRELL
along with other people in general conversation.

        The officer requested from MRS. CANTRELL that if she is
able to remember the name of this nurse, to forward the information to the officer, which she agreed to do.

                            KENT A. SIMMS

An amazing example of the game "telephone."

One of the last lead memos was dated June 20, 1969, and
that appears to have been the end of the investigation. Garrison
had far more pressing issues: he had to start disposing of the other
JFK cases in the queue, an election was coming up for district

attorney, and his first book was coming out in 1970. Compounding all of this were severe back problems, which kept him out of the office.

In October, Harry Connick, who had previously worked for legal aid and the US Eastern District Court, entered the DA race. He campaigned to fix bail bonds; more than 1,100 criminals had jumped bond, and Garrison had neglected to collect $1.2 million in bail bond forfeitures. Connick called Garrison "The Great Accuser" and referring to the Shaw case said, "We can afford only one Mardi Gras and that should be on Canal St. not Tulane and Broad." Still, Garrison beat Connick handily. But Garrison did admit that the JFK investigation had been dead for some time, claiming that it had been very successful, appearances to the contrary.

Ad placed in the Times-Picayune *on March 18, 1969, by the Citizens of New Orleans Committee, Dr. Frank Minyard, chair. It was signed by 250 people. In 1968, Minyard performed a hernia operation on Garrison despite the fact he had never done one. Garrison insisted.*

Garrison spent much of 1970 promoting his new book, *A Heritage of Stone*. Because of the perjury charges, Clay Shaw was not mentioned. Garrison said it depicted "a gradual transition of America from a State controlled by its citizens to a State essentially controlled by its warfare machinery." James Kirkwood, author of *American Grotesque,* said, "I think he's always promising to tell his own story in specifics, but somehow, he just never gets around to it. He uses the word 'they' an awful lot. Now Joyce Carol Oates wrote a book called 'Them.' Garrison's should be called 'They.'"

In February of 1970, Clay Shaw filed a $5 million damage suit against Jim Garrison, Perry Russo, the hypnotist Dr. Fatter, and three people who had funded Garrison's investigation. Shaw alleged he had been deprived of his civil rights and that there was a "scheme designed and contrived" by Garrison and others to "obtain a judicial forum for Garrison's attacks on the Warren Report, the Federal Government, and various high officials." He claimed that funds were provided to Garrison in "support and furtherance of their scheme to misuse and abuse the powers of public office held by the defendant Garrison to conduct the illegal, unwarranted, fraudulent and useless probe of the assassination of John F. Kennedy." In addition, Shaw's suit maintained that Garrison "misused and abused the prosecutorial powers vested in him" and that the prosecution of Shaw "was an unlawful one undertaken in bad faith for the purposes of harassment and served no legitimate interest of the State of Louisiana."

Garrison filed to block the suit on the doctrine of official immunity typically granted to district attorneys. Because of the perjury charges, the suit languished for quite some time.

In January 1971, the Shaw team went to federal court to try to stop Garrison's prosecution on the perjury charges. They believed that if Shaw testified in his own defense that he might again be charged and that it might turn into a never-ending cycle.

Justice Herbert Christenberry denied a motion for a preliminary injunction, but an appellate court ordered him to hold a hearing.

The three-day hearings allowed Shaw's attorneys to turn the tables and cross-examine Garrison, his staff, and his financial backers under oath. A major focus was on Truth and Consequences, the organization set up to privately finance Garrison's probe. About $100,000 ($737,000 in 2020 dollars) had been raised, and Garrison had full control over the money with little oversight.

James Alcock, Garrison's second in command and now a judge, testified that Shaw's perjury charges were unique.

Mr. Wegmann: Now, Mr. Alcock—Judge Alcock, isn't it a fact that during your tenure as assistant District Attorney or as First Assistant District Attorney, that Clay Shaw was the only acquitted defendant who has taken the stand in his own defense and was acquitted and who then subsequently was charged with perjury regarding his testimony given at that trial.

Judge Alcock: Right now, I can't think of any other case, but I feel that there have been some—none that I have personally tried, however.

Wegmann: But you can't specifically tell me of any such cases?

Judge Alcock: No, I can't.

Alcock admitted that the investigation was mostly conducted after Shaw's arrest.

Wegmann: Now, Judge, isn't it a fact that all of these people who had allegedly seen Clay Shaw in the company of Oswald and Ferrie and allegedly seen him sign his name as Clay Bertrand—Vernon Bundy, and so forth, weren't all of these witnesses secured as witnesses after Clay Shaw was arrested?

Judge Alcock: I can't positively state that. Most of them were, yes.

Wegmann: To the best of your knowledge?

Judge Alcock: To the best of my recollection, yes.

Jim Garrison had memory issues when testifying and refused to answer questions he didn't like. But he did admit that he had arrested Shaw before he had investigated the facts:

Wegmann: Let me ask you this question. Isn't it true that most of the investigation concerning Mr. Shaw was conducted after his arrest?

Mr. Garrison: Well, you mean, I presume, as to the testimony of Mr. Alcock. I would say that a great deal— what I am trying to say without trying to fence, Judge, I would say a substantial amount of the corroborative investigation of Mr. Shaw was done afterwards.

Garrison became petulant when asked about witness Vernon Bundy:

Mr. Wegmann: When did Vernon Bundy become a witness?

Mr. Garrison: Mr. Wegmann, the people you are asking me about, to begin with, are not men we intend to use in the perjury case. Secondly, you are going behind the initial, major case, and asking me questions that would again get into the area you referred to before—how did such and such a person become a witness or how did I reach such and such a conclusion. I must reply to you that not only do I consider that irrelevant, but in my judgment, it would be a violation of my duty as Attorney General if I continued to participate with you in a fishing expedition, so I refuse to answer.

Mr. Wegmann: Isn't it a correct statement, Mr. Garrison to say that Vernon Bundy became available to you after the arrest of Clay Shaw on March 1, 1967.

Mr. Garrison: For the reasons I just gave you, I refuse to answer the question.

The Court: I think you should answer the question, Mr. Garrison. The question involves a trial in which the defendant was found not guilty, so I don't think there is any privilege now with respect to that prosecution. You have answered with respect to other witnesses. I don't know why you don't want to this time.

Based on Garrison's non-reply, the court concluded that the "witness was found after Mr. Shaw's arrest."

It didn't take long before he was spouting conspiracy nonsense.

Garrison: The Dallas witnesses were most important to the State's theory of the case, to give it completeness as to the carrying out of the act, but again, that part of the case involving the Dallas witnesses did not involve Mr. Shaw. There was a degree of compartmentalization in what we found to be and what we alleged to be the operation resulting in the President's death.

It is fair to state that the probabilities are that the individuals in New Orleans who set up the role of Oswald as scapegoat, with overtones of leftism and pro-Castroism, were not connected with the individuals who were the housekeepers and those in control of Lee Oswald in Dallas, and secondly that those individuals who were the housekeepers and babysitters, if this is intelligent phraseology, who were in control of Lee Oswald in Dallas, were insulated by the men executing the ambush, so what you have is a potential compartmented operation in a situation like that.

Garrison was asked about O'Donnell's report on Russo's lie detector test.

Mr. Wegmann: Well, the O'Donnell report contained several damaging statements with regard to the veracity of Russo, isn't that correct?

Mr. Garrison: Well, that's correct, yes.

Mr. Wegmann: Did you make a copy of that report available to defense counsel, Mr. Garrison?

Mr. Garrison: I do not recall. I do recall that after interviewing O'Donnell, it was our conclusion that it was not an honest report, and we considered reporting this to the Chief of Police, but then we felt that it would be in effect creating new problems out of a single incident when we were already overloaded with problems, but our evaluation of this report was that it was not accurate and not true.

There was one bombshell moment when Garrison was asked about his book *A Heritage of Stone*.

Mr. Wegmann: Is your investigation still in effect?

Mr. Garrison: I think that if you will read the book, you will find that it is completed. In other words, we reached the conclusion that made further investigation unnecessary.

JFK PROBE IS ENDED, GARRISON DECLARES

Front page, New Orleans States-Item *January 26, 1971. Was Garrison serious? On March 7, 1971, he told a TV reporter that additional arrests would be made.*

Garrison promised during his testimony that he would be putting together a report "to be made available at least to the citizens of New Orleans." We're still waiting.

Judge Christenberry personally noticed the unusual arrest of Clay Shaw.

"Now, this has nothing to do with the outcome of this case, but I saw on television when Shaw was up in Criminal Court, and I thought I recognized the corridor they were in, and Mr. Shaw was surrounded by policemen, deputy sheriffs, I suppose they were, assistant District Attorneys, and others, and they were pushing him, it looked like, from

one side to the other, until there just seemed to be confusion up there. As far as that incident was concerned, I don't think this case was handled in the same way that other criminal cases are handled, or in the customary manner. I just want to say that I saw what I saw, and it didn't appear to be handed in a proper manner at all."

On the last day of the hearing, Perry Russo took the Fifth Amendment.

Mr. Dymond: Mr. Russo, I would like to ask you whether you saw Clay Shaw in David Ferrie's apartment during September of 1963.

Mr. Russo: I can't answer that question on the basis of the Fifth amendment.

Mr. Dymond: Let me get this straight. You refuse to answer, and you are invoking the Fifth amendment because your answer might violate your Constitutional rights and expose you to prosecution?

Mr. Russo: Yes, sir.

Clay Shaw talked about the toll of the trial.

Mr. Wegmann: In what respect and to what extent have you been affected in the pursuit of life, liberty, and happiness as a result of the charges filed against you?

Mr. Shaw: Well, it has been a very agonizing three-and-a-half years. When you are charged with having committed the most heinous crime I suppose that you could be charged with, your life habits suddenly become a lot more restricted, you find yourself being, I guess you would say, hated, shunned, avoided, and just generally your life becomes a great deal more miserable as you try to live with something like that.

Right after the hearings, Perry Russo visited Edward Wegmann for an interview. He asked if Russo now thought that Clay Shaw was the man in Ferrie's apartment, to which Russo replied, "Absolutely not." Wegmann then asked him whether he had ever been positive that Shaw was the man in question, and Russo replied, "Not really." Russo admitted that when he came to New Orleans, Andrew Sciambra showed him Shaw's picture and insisted that "this is the man you saw there" and described his treatment by the DA's office as a complete brainwashing job. Had Russo said any of this at the hearing, Garrison would have certainly charged him with perjury.

New Orleans States-Item, *February 5, 1971. Courtesy of Ralph N. Vinson Collection (MSS 26), Louisiana and Special Collections, Earl K. Long Library, University of New Orleans.*

In May 1971 Judge Christenberry ruled in favor of Clay Shaw and granted a permanent injunction against further prosecution. He noted that "to characterize these facts [of Garrison's investigation] as unique and bizarre is no exaggeration." Garrison, he opined, had "offered no evidence to show any basis or cause for his office's interrogation of the plaintiff concerning such a shocking crime."

Christenberry wrote that "procedures were used to implant into Russo's mind a story implicating the plaintiff in an alleged conspiracy plot. This could have been accomplished by post-hypnotic suggestion." Garrison's arrest of Shaw based solely on

Russo's "questionable, vague story" without "further investigation ... demonstrates ulterior motives." He drew the inference from Russo taking the Fifth, "that even today, he at least has substantial doubts as to the truthfulness of the testimony he gave in state court." The judge concluded that Garrison acted in bad faith, resorting to the use of both hypnosis and drugs in order to fabricate his story.

He also found that Garrison "undertook his baseless investigation with the specific intent to deprive Shaw of his rights under the First, Fifth and Fourteenth Amendments, and that Shaw's arrest and the manner in which [it] was effected was outrageous and inexcusable. The only conclusion that can be drawn from Garrison's actions is that he intentionally used the arrest for his own purposes, with complete disregard for the rights of Clay Shaw." The perjury charges were brought in "bad faith and for the purpose of harassment, being the product of both selective law enforcement and financial interest." Garrison's book *A Heritage of Stone* would be "promoted by the publicity resulting from the continued prosecution of Clay Shaw" and his "desire for financial gain is among the motives" for the perjury charges against Shaw.

> *"Considering all of the evidence adduced at the hearing of this matter the Court finds that the pending prosecution was brought in bad faith and that such bad faith constitutes irreparable injury which is great and immediate."*
>
> *"If the plaintiff is forced to stand trial for perjury, takes the stand and is acquitted, this court has no doubt but that plaintiff will be charged anew on the basis of statements made by him from the witness stand."*

Garrison was furious and issued a statement in which he wondered if Christenberry had actually heard the evidence since, in his words, "his policy is to lean over backward and be as fair as possible to every defendant." He asked if the judge was aware of what "is literally a landmark in fairness in prosecution," that of asking for a preliminary hearing. Garrison promised to "appeal this illegal, biased and distorted opinion ... in the hope that our case will find its way to judges who care about the truth and who are guided by the law."

On June 30, 1971, Jim Garrison and nine other people were arrested in connection with bribery and illegal gambling using pinball machines. The indictment stated that Garrison had been receiving bribes for nine years adding up to over $147,000 (well over a $1 million in 2020 dollars). The main shocker: Pershing Gervais, who had once been Garrison's chief investigator, wore a wire and taped 379 conversations. Gervais would pick up bribe money and deliver it to federal agents who would then substitute marked bills that he would then deliver to Garrison.

Garrison felt that he was being framed and that "he had been predicting that the federal government would take some sort of action against him because of his attacks on the Pentagon, the Central Intelligence Agency, and the 'warfare sector' of the federal government." At least, he mused, this was better than being shot, and it put him "ahead of the game."

In the meantime, in December 1971, Clay Shaw had gone back to work as a project manager for a $2.5 million restoration of the French Quarter at a salary of $24,000. He also started speaking at college campuses about "a creeping erosion of individual rights in this country."

Shaw had more good news on July 31, 1972, when Garrison's appeal was rejected. Judge Wisdom wrote that "it is unnecessary to go beyond the bad faith nature of the perjury prosecution to affirm the judgment." He stated that Garrison's claim that the trial judge had shown bias and prejudice was "totally without merit." Garrison appealed to the Supreme Court, and on November 20, 1972, his case was rejected without comment.

Garrison issued a blistering nine-page statement claiming that the decision "completes the government's circle of deception." He laid out exactly what had happened on November 22, 1963.

"On November 22, 1963, the President of the United States was murdered in a professionally executed guerilla ambush at Dealey Plaza in Dallas. He was killed by riflemen located on the grassy knoll in front of the limousine and in two buildings located behind the limousine ... .A "scapegoat" named Lee Harvey Oswald had been planted in the Texas School Book Depository ... In actuality, Lee Harvey Oswald was a low-level intelligence employee of the United States government ... .The entire operation—from the prior setting-up of the scapegoat in Louisiana to the ultimate assassination in Texas—was carried out by the domestic espionage apparatus of the United States government."

JFK's murder was, according to Garrison, "the product of the top-level military and intelligence sector of the government" and was "instigated by the powerful military chieftains of the Pentagon ... in concert with dominant elements of the Central Intelligence Agency." The Supreme Court decision, he blustered, put the final nail into the coffin of John F. Kennedy.

Journalist Ron Rosenbaum called Garrison to see if he was willing to finally name the gunmen. Garrison told him, "Well, actually, there were more than four. You have four gunmen, but each one had an assistant gunman, and you had to have a man in charge, and you had to have a communications man and—I didn't bother to go into it, but you had two people who created a diversion just as the parade rounded from Main."

And Garrison gave Rosenbaum an actual name: Larry Crafard, a young man who helped manage Jack Ruby's strip club. Since he might have still been alive, Rosenbaum did not mention his name. If you Google his name, a variety of conspiracy theories will appear; some people believed he was a "second Oswald." In the 1980s, he was mentioned in a book about the mob and the assassination. His wife then became paranoid, their marriage broke up, and he lost his job. He died in 2011.[1]

Rosenbaum asked Garrison to identity the "powerful military chieftains," and he replied, "Yes it was the Joint Chiefs ... I don't name 'em by individuals because any time I do that gives them an excuse to file $5 million lawsuits against me all over the country. You can't imagine how that complicates your existence." He ended with some advice: "The Truth is reached only when near-sighted fascination with mere detail is abandoned, and events are looked at in 'perspective' or in 'context."

In October 1973, Garrison's bribery case went to trial. By this time, Frederick Soule, head of the vice squad, pleaded guilty and produced $63,000 from a pickle jar in his backyard.

Some of Gervais's taped conversations[2] were played in court.

Gervais: Let me say this about Freddie [Soule]. Freddie shocked me. You know Freddie been getting money from pinballs as long as we have—
   Garrison: Uh-huh.
   Gervais: Maybe longer.
   Garrison: Uh-huh.
   Gervais: How much you think he's got stashed away?
   Garrison: How much?
   Gervais: Seventy-five thousand dollars.
   Garrison: Jesus Christ!

Gervais: Never, never spent a penny of it. Just salted it
and salted it—seventy-five thousand.
Garrison: Wow—
Gervais: And he's had eight years of it too—

At one point, agents dusted the money and the envelope with fluorescent powder. Garrison locked it in a desk drawer. The next day, when he was arrested, Garrison refused to open the locked drawer, claiming he didn't have a key. But fluorescent powder was found on his hands.

Tom Bethell, one of his staffers, wrote that "once I was with him [Garrison] in New York on one of his jaunts, this time to *Life* Magazine, the editors rolling their eyes as they realized he was making a day of it. Garrison took me to a nearby bar later. When the check came, he produced a thick roll of $50 bills. 'Money doesn't mind who spends it,' he said enigmatically."

In the middle of the trial, Garrison fired his lawyers and took on his own defense. He went back to his old standby: the tapes had been altered. But his expert only examined one fourth of one tape, and when he supposedly found tampering, he decided not to examine the other tapes. In court, he could not even operate the tape recorder. Garrison did not take the stand in his own defense but did deliver a three-hour summary claiming that "the federal government had created a bribery conspiracy where none had existed."

He was acquitted. The jury "recognize[d] the plot against a man who had been criticizing the government. I have only just begun to criticize the government."

Garrison then lost the Democratic primary for district attorney to Harry Connick in December 1973. He had been hurt by the trial, and his coalition of black and blue-collar white voters broke down.

Shaw, meanwhile, was undergoing radiation treatment for

lung cancer. In November 1973, he asked his attorneys to hurry with the civil case. In February 1974 Shaw had a seizure while driving and had a minor accident. One side of his body was partially paralyzed. The cancer continued to spread, and he resigned from his job. By the summer he was mentally incapacitated and unable to give a deposition for his trial against Garrison, which was scheduled for November 1974. In July Shaw suffered from hallucinations, and he died on August 15, 1974. He was only 61.[3]

Even in death, Clay Shaw was not to be spared humiliation. A reporter received a tip that an ambulance had arrived at his house and had brought in a body; perhaps it had been switched with Shaw's. The new coroner, Dr. Frank Minyard, went to Shaw's house and asked to see the body but was refused. "But how can we know for sure the man didn't commit suicide, wasn't given a mercy killing or wasn't murdered?" he asked.

Shaw was cremated and was initially buried in an unmarked grave. Cynthia Wegmann, the daughter of Shaw's attorney said that "we were not having him abused in death as he was in life." Minyard called a judge to get the body exhumed but quickly realized it would be a long process. The police conducted an investigation and found nothing mysterious. A month after Shaw's death, Garrison told reporter Richard Boyle to "look further" and noted the desire of the coroner to have Shaw's body exhumed.

Even beyond death, Clay Shaw's nightmare would continue.

PART 2

JIM GARRISON'S OTHER ZANY EXPLOITS

CHAPTER 11

A TALE OF THREE CUBANS

JIM GARRISON HAD A PROBLEM. He believed that the FBI was listening in on his phone calls and that his office was bugged. One of Garrison's financial backers, Willard Robertson, had just the person to help. Gordon Novel, a bar owner, also owned a company that supposedly had the equipment to find listening devices. Late on the afternoon of February 21, 1967, Robertson got Garrison and Novel together in an insurance company office. Garrison claimed that the FBI was watching every move he made and wondered where he could hold conferences. He was also interested in Novel's equipment to protect against electronic bugging.

Garrison suggested that Novel plant some electronic equipment in Garrison's home and office and then sting the FBI by claiming that only they had such technical ability. Novel turned him down. But he did surprise Garrison by telling him that he knew David Ferrie. Garrison then suggested that Novel fire a dart into David Ferrie to immobilize him and then administer sodium pentothal. Again, Novel refused.

The next day, Novel, never at a loss for words, told Garrison about a raid in 1961 to retrieve explosives from the Schlumberger Corporation in Houma, about fifty miles southwest of New Orleans. Accompanying Novel on this raid were his friend Rance Ehrlinger, David Ferrie, Layton Martens, Sergio Arcacha Smith, and a few others. Garrison granted Novel and Ehrlinger immunity, although it was clear he had no jurisdiction; the so-called burglary had taken place in another parish.

JFK researcher Gus Russo believes the whole operation originated in Guy Banister's office. He was a former FBI agent turned local detective who was involved in the anti-Castro movement. He supposedly obtained a letter of marque from Robert Kennedy's Justice Department that would give legal authority for "quasi-legal actions." (This would have been truly amazing since letters of marque had been issued to privateers during the Age of Sail, and the U.S. has not legally commissioned any privateers since the early nineteenth century). The CIA, Schlumberger, and perhaps the FBI were all supposedly in on it. A couple of cars and a laundry truck were used to transport the explosives back to New Orleans and then on to Miami. The only police report that could be found was dated August 22, 1961, and it said that "Mr. Joe Hanson who works for Schlumberger reported that someone had cut their padlock off the bunker."

Garrison wanted to know more about the laundry truck. His photo expert, Richard Sprague, had identified a laundry truck on a side street during the motorcade in Dallas, and Garrison believed it "had been driven from New Orleans to Dallas and was used in the assassination." Novel said it looked like a Golden Cleaners truck, and Garrison took a picture for the files.

In the meantime, William Gurvich saw Gordon Novel meeting Walter Sheridan, the NBC reporter who was looking into the Garrison investigation, at a restaurant. Novel was also trying to capitalize on the case and was hired to introduce Sheridan to various people in New Orleans. He also sold Sheridan a copy of the Golden Cleaners laundry truck picture he had borrowed from Garrison. Gurvich told Garrison about the meeting, and Garrison cursed violently, "I'll fix him." And Novel instantly became a suspect in the investigation.

```
M E M O R A N D U M


March 27, 1967



TO:        LOUIS IVON

FROM:      FRANK MELOCHE

-----------------------------------------------------------

          Information that Gordon Novel is gay and that when
he gets in trouble which is often, he runs to his mother, Lybil
Reviro, at Coco Beach, Florida.  She lives on Banana Street
and works for Boeing at the Cape.
```

Once the Garrison investigative machinery got going, it found out a great deal about Gordon Novel.

```
M E M O R A N D U M


MARCH 27, 1967


TO:            LOUIS IVON, CHIEF INVESTIGATOR

FROM:          SGT. FENNER SEDGEBEER, INVESTIGATOR

RE:            SPECIAL INVESTIGATION
- - - - - - - - - - - - - - - - - - - - - - - - - - - - - - - - -

              On March 27, 1967 I received an anonymouse telephone
call and learned that GORDON NOVEL in December of 1963 was residing
at 124 Lake Avenue, Metairie - telephone VE-4-8313.  At that time
he was driving a 1963 Black Lincoln automobile, 1963 Louisiana
License 262-626, and had been employed by NASA, Michaud Facility.

              It was learned that NOVEL had been making numerous
obscene telephone calls to a MARLENE A. MANCUSO who was residing
at that time at 6959 Catina Street.  On one occasion, NOVEL followed
Miss MANCUSO to her residence where an argument occured and her
step-father one ALFRED F. BRITSCH and NOVEL began fighting each
other.  On another occasion NOVEL appeared at Michaud and in front
of the building supposedly drank a bottle of ant poison after having
tried to talk to Miss MANCUSO.  Shortly thereafter, either the
latter part of December 1963 or January 1964, NOVEL left for New
York on some business with the World's Fair.


                              SGT. FENNER SEDGEBEER
```

Another important Garrison memo on Gordon Novel.

Garrison was also trying to find Sergio Arcacha Smith, an anti-Castro Cuban who had started the Crusade to Free Cuba in 1960 and bring him in for questioning. Garrison suspected a connection between Arcacha and Oswald. After all, a few of Oswald's pro-Castro leaflets, handed out in August 1963, bore the same address, 544 Camp Street, that Arcacha's organization had back in 1962. And Garrison had two witnesses, Jack Martin and David Lewis, who had seen Oswald and Arcacha together in 1963 at Mancuso's restaurant at the corner of the building.

There were two problems with Garrison's theory. First, Arcacha had left New Orleans in 1962 after being suspected of stealing money from the anti-Cuban organization. Second, Martin and Lewis were two of the shadiest witnesses around.

We've already talked about Martin in Part One—he was the person who had called the New Orleans Police Intelligence Unit about David Ferrie right after the assassination, but Lewis, Martin's roommate, was trying to make money out of the situation. He had asked UPI for $1,000 for this story but was turned down. Merriman Smith, a UPI reporter, said that "Lewis should be locked up inasmuch as he appears to be a dangerous mental case."[1] Lewis originally told Garrison that he had seen Oswald at Mancuso's in 1961 (when he was in the Soviet Union) and then later changed the date to 1963.

In early February 1967, Arcacha's wife was told that two men from New Orleans were looking for him (they were now living in Dallas). She then noticed two men sitting in a car, and when Arcacha went out to talk with them, they sped away. On February 20, Assistant District Attorney James Alcock phoned him and asked him to come to New Orleans. Arcacha couldn't go because of work and because his wife was in the hospital. Four days later, Alcock warned Arcacha that he would receive "bad press" if he didn't cooperate.

Alcock and Gurvich flew out to Dallas the next day, and Arcacha agreed to meet them at police headquarters. Smith did not yet have a lawyer, and he wanted a detective in the room. Alcock and Gurvich refused; they wanted Arcacha alone, and they returned to New Orleans. Garrison then issued a press release saying that Arcacha had refused to talk about the assassination, and his home was thereafter besieged by newsmen and assorted cranks.

On February 27, Arcacha told reporters he would be happy to talk to Garrison as long as either the police or his attorney were present. His lawyer wrote to Garrison and said they would meet anywhere but New Orleans. It was never answered.

On March 31, Garrison charged Novel and Arcacha with conspiring with David Ferrie to "commit simple burglary of a munitions bunker." He wasn't that interested in Houma; he didn't even charge any of the other participants. He just wanted to question Arcacha and harass Novel.[2] Garrison told Richard Billings of *Life* magazine that "by simply enforcing the law, in areas I'm supposed to, I'm going to get results in another area of this case."

On April 2, Arcacha was arrested, fingerprinted, and taken to the Dallas County Jail. Bond was set at $1,500, and he was let go. He told Captain Will Fritz that the Houma incident was not a burglary and that Novel had the key to the bunker. Afterward, he told the press that he was prepared to fight Garrison until he was exposed as a fraud. Holland McCombs, a *Life* magazine reporter, noticed he "had obviously been in tears and was in tears when I left him. He had just talked to his wife and kept asking me how could a thing like this happen in the United States."

Arcacha lost his job. His seven-year-old daughter came home from school one day in tears because her classmates had said that her father had something to do with the assassination of President Kennedy. Arcacha's lawyer later told Gus Russo that "it was very rough on our families. We met our kids' principals and teachers in order to work out special arrangements for their safety. Cops patrolled our neighborhood every 15 minutes."

Fortunately, Governor John Connally refused to extradite Arcacha.

Prior to his belief that there was a homosexual plot, Garrison believed that anti-Castro Cubans were at the center of the JFK conspiracy. So he took a special interest in Carlos Bringuier and Carlos Quiroga, who both met Oswald in 1963.

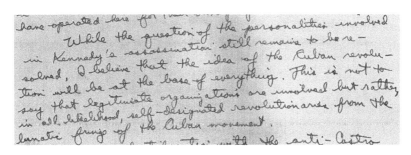

Letter from Jim Garrison to Richard Billings of Life *magazine,*
December 26, 1966.

Carlos Bringuier was the New Orleans delegate of Cuba's Student Revolutionary Directorate (DRE). His father had been a high-ranking judge in Cuba, and he had been in New Orleans since 1961 operating a dry goods shop that catered to merchant mariners and ships.

In the fall of 1961, Bringuier met Arcacha, who told him about David Ferrie and his interest in helping the Cuban cause. Smith took him to meet Ferrie, but Bringuier was turned off by Ferrie's appearance and demeanor. He did not like Ferrie's homosexuality and told Smith he was not the "right man to associate with." This was the end of Ferrie's anti-Castro activities; he was to spend the next couple of years fighting morals charges and trying to get reinstated as a pilot for Eastern Airlines. At this point, Bringuier broke with Arcacha, and they stopped speaking.

On August 5, 1963, Lee Harvey Oswald came into Bringuier's shop and told him he was an ex-Marine and was prepared to train Cubans to fight against Castro. Bringuier replied that he was not involved in military affairs. Oswald then offered him money, which he refused. Oswald, however, returned the next day and left Bringuier his Marine guidebook.

On August 9, Bringuier learned that someone was handing out pro-Castro leaflets on Canal Street. He rushed over and saw that it was Oswald. He then started yelling at Oswald and calling him a Communist. Another Cuban tore up Oswald's literature, and they were all arrested. Three days later, the judge dismissed the charges against the Cubans but fined Oswald ten dollars. Bringuier then sent his friend Carlos Quiroga to Oswald's house posing as a pro-Castro Cuban to get more information. Bringuier last saw Oswald on August 21˙ when he debated him on WDSU radio on the topic of Castro and communism.

Bringuier's brush with Garrison started in December 1966 when David Ferrie came to see him. He believed Garrison was framing him because he "wanted to run for higher office, that he needed publicity." He worried that he could be destroyed by a "bad publicity campaign and hoped that Bringuier could help him find Arcacha to clarify the situation. Bringuier told him that Arcacha was in Houston.

Bringuier then met a television newsman, Sam DePino, who was covering a group of Cubans coming from Mexico. He suggested DePino visit Garrison and ask about his JFK investigation, and he was surprised when DePino replied that he was already supplying information. Bringuier told DePino he was willing to help.

One day later, Assistant District Attorney John Volz visited Bringuier and asked about Arcacha. He told Volz that "Arcacha could have been my foe here in town, my enemy, but I was sure that Arcacha didn't have nothing to do with the whole thing." Volz asked him to come to the DA's office, and once there, he was taken to a conference room with a two-way mirror. Assistant District Attorney James Alcock started questioning Bringuier about a Cuban training camp across Lake Pontchartrain.

In the summer of 1963, about twenty anti-Castro Cubans trained at a small camp. There were only a couple of rifles to practice assembly and disassembly, and no actual shooting occurred. Food was scarce, the men complained bitterly, and after a little more than a month, the Cubans were all sent back to Miami.

Garrison wanted to find what was left of the camp. He told

Merriman Smith of UPI that "a group of local perverts in and around New Orleans eventually infiltrated this group and after a short period of time took over control." He believed that Ferrie, Oswald, and Arcacha were there, and Garrison told reporter Hoke May that the "troops ... went to Dallas" when they left the camp.

Propinquity was also at play: Clay Shaw's mother lived in Hammond, Louisiana, fairly close to where Garrison believed the camps to be. His staff then spent weeks trying to find the camp; he hoped to find 6.5mm Mannlicher-Carcano shells that would prove Oswald had been there.

M E M O R A N D U M

REPORT # 4

January 23, 1967

TO: JIM GARRISON

FROM: ALVIN OSER

RE: INVESTIGATION OF FIRING RANGE AREA LOCATED
         ON JANUARY 19, 1967

Saturday, January 21

As a result of locating the firing range near
Slidell and on the road to the airstrip, I proceeded to investigate this site accompanied by two others.

The purpose of this trip was to possibly find old
cartridges of 6.5mm, 38 cal., 30 cal. and any other type
that may have been fired at this site.

I was able to locate cartridges which appeared to
be of the above types and some of which appeared to have been
there for some time.

Sunday, January 22

In an attempt to locate more cartridges at the site
of this range, a search was made by myself, Fenner Sedgebeer,
Charles Jonau, Jim Conway, and David Levy.

The search concerned itself with both sides of the
range, as the range is divided by the road. All of the
cartridges which were found were turned over to Louis Ivon
upon our return.

We had the occasion to speak with a young white male
who told us that this range was used by various clubs and
people all the time. Also, that many people come to the
range to pick up cartridges either to re-load or to sell.
He said that he had lived near there for nine years and that
when he first moved there, he and his brother had picked up
over two thousand cartridges and sold them. He could give
no information about a group shooting there, other than the
fact that gun clubs come there to shoot.

They eventually found the camp. But Garrison was
convinced there was another, more secret camp, and his men
kept on searching. One day Garrison, while examining aerial
photographs, claimed he had found the camp. Oser and
Gurvich were sent out, and they found the road Garrison had
circled.

*A large sign greeted the two men and informed them
without the necessity of further inquiry what had been*

discovered. This was the location of the Tulane Primate Center maintained by the Tulane University Medical School. Gurvich and the assistant decided to see for themselves despite the "no trespassing" sign. As they wandered into the area, Gurvich pointed to the chimpanzees located within.

"Do they look like Cubans to you, Al?"

"I do have to admit they don't look very Latin to me, Bill," responded Oser.

It was all a delusion. David Ferrie had never been at the camp, nor had Arcacha or Oswald. Carlos Bringuier told Garrison's men that he hadn't been there either. He was then asked what it would mean if somebody was prepared to state that he *had* in fact been there, to which Bringuier replied that "either that somebody is lying or is a son of a bitch."

On February 14, Bringuier met Garrison face-to-face. Garrison told him that Oswald was an anti-communist who had been brought to New Orleans by conservative Americans in the city. Furthermore, said Garrison, "Oswald was receiving training to go to Cuba and try to kill Castro. And that when that plan failed, of Oswald going to Cuba to kill Castro, then some people, not all of the people in the first plan; some of the people in the first plan changed their mind and tried to kill Kennedy."

Bringuier could hardly believe what he was hearing. He told Garrison that this was the most ridiculous thing he had ever heard and that in his opinion someone was giving Garrison false information. After all, he had met Oswald four times and had debated him on WDSU radio. He predicted that "this investigation of yours is going to end in zero because you don't have nothing."

Garrison became angry and insisted Bringuier take a lie detector test. Bringuier agreed and was asked about Clay Shaw,

Clay Bertrand, and Lee Harvey Oswald. Bringuier suggested "the examiner ask him if he thought the investigation was the most ridiculous thing he had ever heard of." A few days later, Garrison told Bringuier he had passed the test and apologized for the way in which he'd treated him previously. Bringuier replied that his "fear was as a Cuban refugee" and that "we don't have power in this country to counter-attack on a smear campaign on us." Garrison's reply: "So far."

THE NEW YORK TIMES, SUNDAY, FEBRUARY 26, 1967

Oswald Inquiry Now Centered on Cuban Refugees

By GENE ROBERTS
Special to The New York Times
NEW ORLEANS, Feb. 25—

might have distributed the literature in an effort to win the confidence of the Cuban Government and gain permis-Latin America as John Smith in the United States.

The District Attorney told the Miami Police that "Gon-show any evidence of the existance of a Clay Bertrand. Today, Mr. Andrews said he had not talked to Mr. Garrison

David Ferrie went back to Bringuier's store on February 20, wondering if he knew on which day the plot against Kennedy supposedly had been created. Ferrie was not well, and Bringuier felt "he looked to me as a person who is destroyed, as a person who is sick." Ferrie died two days later.

At the time, Bringuier's wife was pregnant. He sent his wife and children to Buenos Aires to spare them the pain of seeing him arrested. When he realized that Garrison wasn't going to touch him, they returned to New Orleans. His wife was "crying every night, she was very upset with the situation, and she was very afraid," he said. Unfortunately, she had a miscarriage, and they lost their child.

Carlos Quiroga also met Oswald in August of 1963 when he tried to infiltrate Oswald's one-man New Orleans chapter of the Fair Play for Cuba Committee. His father had been in a Cuban prison since 1961 and was released in 1966. He ran a large poultry business but was jailed when he was caught with munitions a few weeks before the Bay of Pigs invasion.

On January 15, 1967, Quiroga was asked to come down to the DA's office. They wanted to know if he was at the camp (no), and he was asked about several suspects in the case. Quiroga realized that "this investigation was going the wrong way. They were investigating the wrong thing." He decided to "clarify this whole mess" by bringing Garrison a scrapbook containing letters and newspaper clippings about the Crusade to Free Cuba.

Before he could bring it to Garrison, Quiroga received a subpoena to appear for questioning at his office. On January 21, he went down and was put in a small room and told to wait. Right behind him was a rifle with a telescopic sight. He "had a feeling they wanted me to touch it." They left him there for four hours. Quiroga was finally taken into Garrison's office (after being searched for weapons) where he was told that witnesses, viewing him through a two-way mirror, had identified him as being with Oswald in 1961 in the Mancuso restaurant. This was impossible because Oswald was in Russia at the time. Garrison then claimed that Quiroga was at the camp across the lake. No, he wasn't there. Garrison implored him to "tell the truth or I'll bring you to the Grand Jury." Quiroga mentioned the Warren Report, and Garrison said he would "clean his ass" with it. Quiroga replied that he would "clean his ass with your investigation."

Unknown to Quiroga, Garrison taped their interview[3] and had it transcribed. Quiroga got a copy from a journalist and noted that whenever he explained things, the transcript is suddenly "inaudible." It had also been altered because it has Quiroga telling Garrison he worked for the FBI in 1961. And the "clean your ass" comments were deleted.

Two days later, Quiroga's wife received a threatening phone call from Jack Martin. He warned that if Quiroga continued to talk to Garrison, he would kill him, that he had previously killed fifty people, and that one more "would not mean anything to him." Quiroga called the police, and he went with his wife to see Garrison the next day. Louis Ivon played a tape of Martin's voice, and Quiroga's wife identified him. Garrison asked him not to press charges and then proceeded to explain the JFK conspiracy.

> *"He tells me ... he had positively identified one of the Cubans who was in Dealey Plaza ... [T]he Cuban was the same one who was in the photograph with Oswald the day he was distributing communist propaganda in front of the International Trade Mart. This Cuban was Manuel Garcia Gonzalez ... Garrison said he had pictures of Manuel Garcia Gonzalez as being behind the "billboard" close to where President Kennedy was shot ... [H]e had definite proof that Gonzalez was implicated in the assassination."*

Quiroga implored Garrison to "investigate those people who have been lying to you." This information "was nothing but a lie."

Five days later, Quiroga returned with evidence proving he was not at the camp. Jack Martin happened to be there, and Quiroga asked him why he was lying. Martin said "Carlos, I'm sorry. I was drunk." Quiroga asked him more questions and was stopped by Ivon when Martin started fumbling his facts and said that JFK was killed in 1962. Quiroga was told to wait outside. A few minutes later, an agitated Ivon came out and said "that son-of-a-bitch changed his statement he has given us. I'm going to break his head." Ivon took Jack Martin home without charging him with threatening Quiroga.

On April 14, Quiroga was asked to undergo a lie detector test. Garrison had told Richard Billings that he was going to hammer Quiroga and would arrest him if he refused the polygraph test. Quiroga agreed on the provision that he be given copies of the questions to be asked. When he arrived, he was told he could not see the questions, and he refused to be tested. Garrison was called, and he ordered Quiroga to take the test or risk being arrested. Quiroga agreed but resisted signing a statement saying the test was voluntary. His wife started crying, and he finally told the polygraph operator that "I'm signing this paper against my will because if I don't, Mr. Garrison is going to put me in jail. I hereby sign under protest."

Quiroga, in his own words, was "scared, nervous and furious" and was "having stomach pains from all the tension." He was in no state to undergo a polygraph examination, and in any case, the test was rigged. The operator would stop the machine and tell Quiroga in advance what the question would be—for instance, "if he had seen Ferrie and Arcacha together in 1963." Then the machine would be turned on, and the same question would be asked, but without the year. Quiroga stated, with good reason, that this made it impossible for him to answer the question correctly.

The next day, Quiroga was back, and he told Louis Ivon that he was worried. A car was "going around my neighborhood, and they are looking at my kids, and we were scared that my kids were going to be kidnapped." He implored Ivon to have Martin charged.

Quiroga was subpoenaed to appear before the grand jury on May 10. When he arrived, he was taken to a small room by Andrew Sciambra, who told him that in their view, he had lied to them and that not only had he failed the polygraph test, but unless he "changed his story," he could expect to be indicted for perjury by the grand jury. The lie detector test supposedly indicated that Quiroga was lying on several questions, including denying having first-hand knowledge of the JFK conspiracy, denying seeing any of the guns used to assassinate JFK, and that he knew Oswald was anti-Castro.

Quiroga's lawyer suggested he retain another lawyer who was friends with Sciambra, who asked him to take off the pressure. He agreed, but only if Quiroga promised to make no public statement critical of the DA's office.

Quiroga received another subpoena to testify on May 24, 1967. He was intimidated again by the threat that he would be "indicted as an accessory after the fact to the murder of Kennedy, and for perjury" unless he testified "truthfully." Worried about a perjury charge, he declined to answer questions under the Fifth Amendment. Garrison told him he had no legal basis to plead the Fifth and that he must answer the questions or face a contempt charge by the court. That would bring everything out in public, and Quiroga worried about his father in Cuba—might his testimony put him back in prison?

Garrison pressed Quiroga hard to change his answers to the rigged lie detector test. He wouldn't budge and insisted he only wanted to tell the truth. Finally, in disgust, Garrison told him to leave. After ten minutes, he was told he could go home, and as he was walking down the stairs, Garrison told him, "I'm not through with you yet." Garrison did not indict Quiroga for perjury, but Quiroga now had a mission "to prove that not only is Garrison ... without any real substance, but also that Garrison is an insane man."

The Cubans were a stubborn bunch. They wouldn't change their stories for Garrison despite his intimidation. It was time for him to move on to other suspects.

CHAPTER 12

WAS KERRY THORNLEY THE SECOND OSWALD?

RICHARD POPKIN'S *The Second Oswald* and Harold Weisberg's *Whitewash* presented the theory that somebody was impersonating Lee Harvey Oswald in order to incriminate him in the assassination. How else to explain Oswald popping up in so many locations? Jim Garrison went beyond theory and found the imposter.

His name was Kerry Thornley, and he had served for three months with Oswald in the Marines in the spring of 1959. Oswald took an interest in Thornley when he learned he was also an atheist; they then had regular discussions on politics. Oswald told Thornley that "communism was the best—that the Marxist morality was the most rational morality to follow that he knew of."

By this time, Oswald was learning Russian, and he subscribed to a Soviet newspaper. Thornley noticed that "there was someone else in the outfit who spoke Russian" and that "they used to exchange a few comments in the morning at muster and say hello to each other." But Thornley could not remember who this was.

Thornley decided to write a book that would explain the "particular phenomenon of disillusionment with the United States after serving in the Marine Corps overseas in a peacetime capacity." The main character, Johnny Shellburn, was to be based on several Marines, including Oswald. But before Thornley could finish his book, *The Idle Warriors*, Oswald defected to the Soviet Union, and Thornley had to reconsider his ending.

He left the Marines in September 1960 and went to California. He moved to New Orleans in February 1961 and worked at menial jobs while trying to make it as a writer. He left in May 1963 to go back to California, traveling via Dallas. In late August 1963, he went to Mexico City for a week and returned to New Orleans in September. He overlapped with Oswald for just three weeks.

On the day of the assassination, Thornley was working as a waiter, and when another server said the suspect was a Marine who had defected, Thornley knew exactly who it was: Lee Harvey Oswald. That caused a commotion; somebody called the Feds, and the Secret Service came knocking. A few weeks later, Thornley decided that the best way to finish his book was to get away from the distractions of the French Quarter, so he moved to Arlington, Virginia.

By this time, he had shelved his initial concept and decided to write a nonfiction account of Oswald. It was published in 1965 and included a chapter from *The Idle Warriors*. David Lifton, a critic of the Warren Report, read Thornley's book and was angry with its depiction of Oswald as "some type of psychotic idiot who lurked in the woodwork." Thornley lived nearby, and they started meeting to discuss the evidence.

Lifton was interested in the other Marine who spoke Russian. Thornley's memory had been jogged when he had lunch with Warren Commission counsel Albert Jenner, who suggested it might have been John Heindel. What made this interesting to

Lifton was that Heindel's nickname in the Marines was *Hidell*, the same name Oswald had used as an alias.

Might Heindel, like Oswald, have been some sort of government agent? Lifton called Garrison's office and suggested they speak to him. Heindel gave a statement to Garrison saying that he had had only one conversation ever with Oswald at Atsugi Air Base and that he had neither seen nor heard from him since.

Garrison thought Heindel was "lying through his teeth" and that Thornley could perhaps help confront him. Lifton sent Garrison an eleven-page notarized statement from Thornley on September 28, 1967, stating that he was unable to independently recall the name Heindel as the other Marine who had spoken Russian and that "it was Mr. Jenner's mention of this name at lunch that day which caused me to immediately recollect that this was the name I had been groping for, and could not remember."

Three weeks later, Lifton met with Garrison, who revealed a plan. He would subpoena Heindel to the grand jury and then charge him with perjury if he stated he hadn't spoken Russian with Oswald. This would then "persuade Heindel to provide detrimental testimony against his other suspects in the case." Garrison told Lifton to "tell Thornley, that if he cooperates with me, we can throw a couple of bricks through the window of the establishment."

But Lifton then met another Marine, Erwin Donald Lewis, who thought that the man who spoke Russian was "Slavic ... 6 feet tall, stocky, and wears thick glasses." This was certainly not Heindel, and Lifton called Garrison's office and told them that "prudence should be exercised in taking any action regarding John Heindel."

Garrison wanted to speak to Thornley. He sent him a telegram asking him to phone under the name Winston Smith and to ask for Frank Marshall, one of Garrison's pseudonyms. Thornley called using his real name and got an investigator on the phone. He thought he was speaking to Garrison, but the conversation went nowhere because the staffer had no idea who Thornley was. Garrison sent a telegram asking Thornley to try again. By this time, Thornley was tired of the games and was pissed off. He had never thought too much of Garrison. After all, he had lived in New Orleans. He fired off an angry letter to Garrison.

To: archives
Thornley file

Kerry Thornley
726 51st St. So.
Tampa, Florida 33619

24 October 1967

Dear Mr. Garrison:

As a personal favor to Mr. Lifton I spent a whole day with him preparing that damned affidavit. It says everything I know about the subject. I regret that I bothered.

When I said I would speak to you on my terms, as you had apparently offered to do through Mr. Lifton, I meant it. And since you chose, when I called you the first time, not to deal on these terms, to hell with it.

I have no interest to speak of in this matter and from now on intend to keep out of it, as actions on my part can only in my view stimulate the state to violate the rights of others who for all I know may be innocent. "It is far better to reward the guilty than to punish the innocent," said Robert Ingersoll, and every time you subpoena an innocent individual you punish him to the extent that you have violated his precious and unalienable right to liberty.

But what you do is your business, sir, and you are welcome to it.

Sincerely,

Kerry Thornley

Now it was Garrison's turn to be upset, and he "formulated an entirely new theory about Thornley." He told David Lifton the following a few weeks later:

> Garrison: Thornley lied.
>
> Lifton: Why?
>
> Garrison: Thornley lied. Thornley lied when he said he didn't know Oswald in September 1963. We have so many witnesses who saw them together at that time we have stopped looking for more. Thornley's with the CIA.
>
> Lifton: But, why do you say that, Jim?
>
> Garrison: Thornley worked at a hotel in Arlington, Virginia.
>
> Lifton: So, what?

Garrison told Lifton that on the night of the assassination, Thornley had seemed to be happy over the day's events. That was true—Kerry was a libertarian who hated Kennedy's foreign policy—but Garrison believed that Thornley's actions "were those of a member of a conspiracy who was openly applauding the success of a plot of which he was part."

Garrison subpoenaed Thornley to testify before the grand jury, noting that "evidence developed by the District Attorney's office conclusively indicates that Kerry Thornley was a frequent companion of Lee Oswald's in September 1963." Garrison's press release noted that if Albert Jenner, the Warren Commission's lawyer, had shown the slightest interest in what had "really happened to President Kennedy," he would have discovered that Oswald was not always alone in New Orleans. Garrison further stated that "in point of fact, he was in almost continual association with a number of individuals, most of whom were either

Nazi-oriented or connected with the Central Intelligence Agency or both."

Ex-Marine Corps Buddy of Oswald Is Subpenaed

LONGER TUNNEL

Won't Voluntarily Go, Says Tampa Man

The Times-Picayune, *January 10, 1968, page 1*

Thornley went to the DA's office the day before his testimony, and he was asked if he had ever met Clay Shaw.

"Well," Sciambra said, "the man who was your landlord at the time of the assassination was Clay Shaw's best friend."

"Really?"

"Really. And besides that, Shaw was over there helping with an interior decorating project about every other day, in your landlord's living room—across the patio from your apartment."

I remembered that my landlord was redecorating his place, but this did not conjure up any memories of my having met Clay Shaw.

"You'd recall him if you did," said Sciambra. "He's a very impressive person. Big, tanned, with white-silver hair."

"No kidding? I had him pegged from pictures in the news as a little guy."

Thornley offered to take a lie detector test and to be interviewed under sodium pentothal, but the DA wasn't interested. Andrew Sciambra noted in a memo that "he impressed me as a very talkative individual and seemed quite ready to explain anything that we may want him to."

After leaving the DA's office, Thornley remembered a conversation with his girlfriend where she had commented that "so-and-so sure was a handsome man." Could she have been referring to Clay Shaw?

Thornley testified before the grand jury on February 8, 1968. Being completely honest, he admitted to questioning himself in respect to whether he had ever met Oswald.

Garrison: Let me ask you this: are you sure that you never saw Lee Harvey Oswald in New Orleans in 1963, for a while you seemed to be on the fence.

Thornley: No, the only time I ever thought I did was when Barbara Reid was so sure about it, and I became convinced, but I am sure I did not see Oswald and recognize him in New Orleans of 1963.

Garrison: You are telling me that there was a point when she had convinced you that you were with Oswald?

Thornley: Yes, she convinced me, certainly, there was the two hours or so she was talking to me and she said, Kerry, what must have happened was this, you must have walked into the Bourbon House and he must have walked in, you must have seen that his face was familiar, but not recognized him out of uniform and all this stuff, and he must have sat down next to you ... she was so certain, so positive ...

Garrison: Does it seem to you that was possible?

Thornley: It seemed to be possible, when she got all through, until the next day and people began to say

> *Barbara Reid connects herself with everything that happens, then it seemed impossible ...*
> *Garrison: Does it seem possible now?*
> *Thornley: Well, no, it doesn't seem possible to me unless I was drugged or something.*

The next day Thornley was asked to come back to the DA's office to clear some things up. Garrison investigator Lou Ivon entered the room and started yelling at Thornley. "Yeah, if I were on a jury, I'd vote that you were guilty, too. BECAUSE I THINK YOU'RE INVOLVED—AND I AM ONE OF MR. GARRISON'S ADVISORS AND I'M GOING TO ADVISE HIM NOT TO WASTE TIME TALKING TO YOU—BECAUSE I THINK YOU ARE LYING AND SO DOES HE!"

Thornley offered to bring all his friends to Garrison's office to brainstorm a reconstruction of his activities during September 1963 for Garrison's benefit. The offer was refused, and Thornley returned home to Tampa.

Two weeks later, Garrison charged him with perjury for his denial that he had met Oswald. The press release noted that Thornley, in common with other young men who were CIA employees, had a post office box in the federal building. These, the press release went on to state, were "customarily used by federal employees with clandestine assignments as 'message drops.'" According to Garrison, Thornley and Oswald "were both part of the covert federal operation operating in New Orleans," and Garrison accused Thornley of being part of a CIA plot to create a "Communist image" for Oswald. He concluded that "when the time comes that it is desired to determine when we ceased to live in a free society, it will be found that the change occurred on November 22, 1963—the day the credibility gap began."

An appendix to the press release listed excerpts of statements from Marines who had served with Oswald who had not heard him talk about communism. Thornley was noted as the only "former comrade" who described Oswald as a Marxist. "It is particularly thought provoking that this man's associates and pattern of activity in 1963, plainly mark him as an employee, like Lee Oswald, of the Central Intelligence Agency."

This was all patently untrue. Perhaps Garrison didn't read *all* the statements from Marines who had served with Oswald, but here's a sampling: Nelson Delgado said that Oswald owned the book *Das Kapital* and testified that Oswald thought socialism would be a good thing; James Botelho stated that Oswald had referred to "American capitalist warmongers" and that "although he believed in pure Marxist theory, he did not believe in the way communism was practiced by the Russians;" Paul Murphy mentioned that Oswald subscribed to either *The Worker* or the *Socialist Worker* and that "when the paper was identified as being directed to Oswald, few were surprised;" Mack Osborne said that fellow Marines "sometimes jokingly accused him of being a Russian spy"; Dennis Call remembered that when playing chess, "Oswald always chose the red chessmen, making some remark to the effect that he preferred the 'Red Army'"; and Erwin Donald Lewis said that "I know from personal observation that he read *The Daily Worker.*"

As for having a post office box, well, why not? After all, it was only a block or two from Thornley's apartment. Kerry's friend Greg Hill wrote, "nearly every writer in the French Quarter had a box in that post office, since publisher's checks sent to home mailboxes were notoriously subject to being ripped off by desperate junkies."

Propinquity also played a huge role in Garrison's interest in Thornley. He had 'met' Clay Shaw and lived on the same street. He had moved to Arlington, Virginia, right after the assassination —wasn't the CIA located in Virginia? And Thornley showed his book to Martin McCauliffe, who had once assisted an anti-Castro group.

```
                              August 29, 1967

              M E M O R A N D U M


TO:       Tom Bethel

FROM:     Jim Garrison
```

```
I notice that in the phone book there is an EMILE BARRE
listed at 1925 Dauphine Street.  It sticks in my mind
that CARY THORNLEY lived in this block when he was in
New Orleans.  CARY THORNLEY was seen in OSWALD'S company
in the Bourbon House one night by BARBARA REED.

Is this the same BARRE listed in OSWALD'S notebook .
(and who may be a relative of his)?  Can we corroborate
CARY THORNLEY'S address while in New Orleans?
```

Thornley rented an apartment on Dauphine Street in the fall of 1963. Shaw lived several blocks away on the same street.

A warrant was issued for Thornley's arrest. This was a felony charge, and he was put in jail until he posted a $3,000 bond.

The person who claimed to have seen Thornley with Oswald was Barbara Reid, a friend of Thornley's who lived in the French Quarter. She was known as a witch and had a voodoo altar in her apartment. She once told the *Times-Picayune* that "I am not a witch, but I'll show you what a witch can do if you make me out as a kook." Before his testimony, Thornley pleaded with the DA's office to have her investigated: "Send a plainclothes detective out on the streets of the Quarter and just have him ask people about her veracity, for Christsakes!"

FD-302 (Rev. 1-25-60)

FEDERAL BUREAU OF INVESTIGATION

Date ___12/19/63___

1

GUS BEELER, Assistant Manager, Bourbon House
Restaurant and Bar, 700 Bourbon Street, New Orleans,
Louisiana, stated he does not know LEE HARVEY OSWALD or
JACK RUBY and to his knowledge, has never met either
individual.

GUS BEELER advised after viewing photographs
of both LEE HARVEY OSWALD and JACK RUBY, that he could not
identify either person as being a patron of the Bourbon
House Bar.

GUS BEELER stated that there has been considerable
conversation in the Bourbon House regarding LEE HARVEY OSWALD
particularly by the wife of KERRY WENDELL THORNLEY. Both
THORNLEY and his wife, according to BEELER, were regular
patrons of the restaurant and bar and well known to most of
the customers. THORNLEY and his wife separated about the
time of the assassination of President KENNEDY and since that
time, Mrs. THORNLEY has been "running down her husband" and
telling everyone what will listen to her that he, THORNLEY,
was a friend of LEE HARVEY OSWALD.

In addition, BEELER advised that KERRY WENDELL
THORNLEY has made public statements which have appeared
in the local newspaper that he has either written a book
or is writing a book in which he uses LEE HARVEY OSWALD
as a model for a character in the book. BEELER stated that
he did not know if this was true, but it has been the subject
of conversation in the Bourbon House.

BEELER advised that other than the remarks about
KERRY WENDELL THORNLEY which have been passed in the
Bourbon House, he could think of no other individual
frequenting the Bourbon House what might have known LEE
HARVEY OSWALD.

On ___12/13/63___ at ___New Orleans, Louisiana___ File # ___NO 100-16601___

by ___SA REGIS L. KENNEDY :lav___ Date dictated ___12/19/63___

*An FBI report from 1963. Might Thornley's girlfriend [he was
not married at the time] have been the source of the rumors
that he knew Oswald in New Orleans?*

Barbara Reid wasn't just an ordinary witness; she was an
interested party in Garrison's investigation. She attended parties
with Garrison and his investigators and worked with his office to

find new witnesses. In one letter to Harold Weisberg, she wrote that "Joel Palmer [a Garrison investigator] called last night, trying to reach Jim. G. on a non-CIA phone." Weisberg himself wrote that Reid was "an accomplished liar." Thornley's friend, Clint Bolton, remarked that her notions about what constituted reality were extremely fluid and that she'd been seeing "notorious figures" in the French Quarter for as long as she'd been there.

And of course, Oswald did not drink alcohol and was not known to frequent the French Quarter.

M E M O R A N D U M

July 1, 1968

TO: Louis Ivon, Chief Investigator

FROM: WILLIAM BOXLEY, Investigator

RE: BARBARA REED interview

On Wednesday, June 26, 1968, at approximately 3:30 p.m., I accompanied BARBARA REED from her residence to 1914 Magazine Street where she met SAM BRANDENBURG and "CHRIS" CHRISTIAN, former residents of the Quarter whom she felt could substantiate a New Orleans 1963 acquaintance between LEE HARVEY OSWALD and KERRY THORNLEY.

After leaving a portrait with BRANDENBURG for framing, BARBARA asked him if he did recall seeing THORNLEY and OSWALD together in the Bourbon House during the Summer of 1963. BRANDENBURG was extremely nervous during the first ten minutes of the interview; however, he denied recalling seeing THORNLEY and OSWALD together and eventually calmed down to a normal conversational attitude.

He did, however, volunteer in bits of conversation that he had known FBI Agent JOHN QUIGLEY from their days together in Ohio; that QUIGLEY visited his business frequently in the French Quarter and that he had seen QUIGLEY often at the Bourbon House. He said that QUIGLEY knew KERRY THORNLEY, and recalled that just before or shortly after QUIGLEY moved to Dallas in August of 1963 with his wife and family, he (QUIGLEY), inherited a sizable sum of money from an aunt.

Well after Thornley's perjury charge, Garrison was still trying to substantiate Reid's allegation.

Garrison now had to find evidence to back up his indictment. Or find people who "just may have witnessed part of the crime of the century being plotted before their eyes in a restaurant, bar, or some other place." To do this, Thornley said the DA's office would use "all the techniques of encyclopedia salesmen on the make." They'd offer all sorts of inducements to people who would "help" with their investigation. David Lifton called this the Garrison "Witness Recruitment Program."

Not surprisingly, Garrison turned up a witness who "saw Thornley at the Oswald residence a number of times—in fact, they saw him there so much they did not know which was the husband, Oswald or Thornley." This was preposterous—Marina Oswald and Kerry Thornley both testified before the grand jury on February 8, 1968, and neither of them recognized each other. And Thornley's time in New Orleans only overlapped with Oswald's for about three weeks that summer.

As these witnesses piled up, Garrison began to believe that Thornley was the second Oswald. In 1961 two people from an anti-Castro group had ordered ten trucks from a Ford dealership, and one of the people had allegedly used the name Oswald. But Lee Harvey Oswald was then in Russia. Might this have been Thornley? The fact that the incident occurred before Thornley was even in New Orleans didn't matter one iota to Garrison.

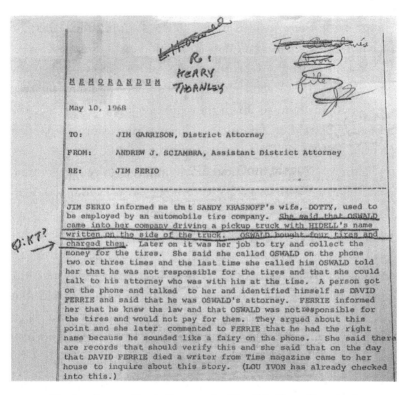

Garrison's question in the margin: Was this Kerry Thornley?

And then Harold Weisberg sent out a letter asking a fellow researcher if he could touch up a Thornley picture to make him look like Oswald. It was sent out on Garrison's letterhead, and the DA's office had to issue a statement saying it was not an official letter. Regardless, Weisberg was out interviewing witnesses, and he claimed that an employee in the print shop where Oswald had picked up his pro-Cuba leaflets had identified Thornley. Unfortunately, evidence of that identification disappeared.

DISTRICT ATTORNEY
PARISH OF ORLEANS
STATE OF LOUISIANA
2700 TULANE AVENUE
NEW ORLEANS 70119

JIM GARRISON
DISTRICT ATTORNEY

March 12, 1968

Mr. Fred Newcomb
4640 Noble Avenue
Sherman Oaks, California

Dear Fred:

Enclosed are four sets of pictures of Kerry Thornley printed
backwards but otherwise entirely untouched. My purpose was
to emphasize the resemblance to Oswald and his receding
hairline, which when his hair is combed the opposite of his
normal fashion is quite emphatic.

What I would like you to do with one of each pair is pretend
you were a make-up man doing the minimum necessary to make
Thornley look as much as possible like Oswald as for example
by pruning off or brushing back the forelock, trimming the
eyebrows, shadowing the chin, etc. I would like you to keep
one pair for your use out there, send one pair to me and
the other two to Jim Garrison, District Attorney, 2700 Tulane
Avenue, New Orleans, La. 70119.

Best to Marlyn and everyone else and many many thanks.

Sincerely,

HAROLD WEISBURG

Garrison now believed that it was Thornley who was in the famous backyard pictures of Oswald holding his rifle. Here's part of a conversation between Garrison and his investigators.

Sciambra: The way Broshears came up with that is that he was shown this—we have this same thing in the office—he was shown this when he came down here. As a result of that, he looked at it and he says "I can see right now that it's Thornley's body, and Oswald's head."

Turner: That's an interesting observation, thought, because look how logical it is.

Sciambra: And so we said, "well how can you be so

sure." He said, "well, I had sex with Thornley and I know
his slender hips."

Garrison: He said his hips were more slender than
Oswald's and also those are Thornley's hands and he
described the hands.

They were referring to Reverend Raymond Broshears, who
had bamboozled Garrison's staff into believing he was once
David Ferrie's roommate. He regaled them with stories of the plot
against Kennedy but couldn't remember any details about
Ferrie's apartment, its furniture, or any of the real details of his
life.

The clincher came from Bill Boxley, a Garrison investigator
you will meet in Chapter 16, who told the group, "We had this
tip from the queer waiter who has since gone to Houston that
Oswald worked at the Sheraton-Charles [Hotel] and wrapped
himself up in a drapery one time to avoid bussing some dishes
out. This must have been Thornley."

If you thought any of this could not get any nuttier, you'd be
wrong. In November 1968, Garrison asked Lou Ivon to write a
memo concerning the height of Lee Harvey Oswald. He listed
the way Oswald was described by various witnesses and by
Oswald himself on various forms, and not surprisingly, they were
not uniform. The conclusion reached was that "the imperson-
ation started in the Marines" and that "the CIA has successfully
put over impersonations so that even mothers are fooled." Ivon
believed that when Oswald returned from the Soviet Union, his
brother "knew this returning defector was not really Lee."

Tom Bethell, a Garrison staffer, recounts a dinner with JFK
buff Jones Harris.

"One day I had dinner with Jones at the Pontchartrain Hotel on St. Charles Avenue in New Orleans and I outlined this and other difficulties with the "second Oswald" theory. There could hardly have been two Oswalds, I said. Jones replied, perfectly seriously: "You're right, Tom. There were three Oswalds."

I gasped, temporarily forgetting my Creole gumbo.

"And two Ruby's" he added.

In March 1969, Thornley called for Garrison to bring him to trial so that he could clear his name. As he said, "I want an opportunity to go into court to answer charges which are utterly ridiculous."

Nothing happened, so Thornley resorted to guerilla tactics.

"Garrison came after me one last time in 1970 just for harassment purposes because I had put an advertisement in a Libertarian magazine that said, "Good-looking, young District Attorney will do anything for, or to, anyone for a chance to jack off to the John Kennedy autopsy photos." [Laughs] This was just to prove I wasn't afraid of him ... It was just my way of saying. "Look, you fucker, you're not going to push me around."

Anyhow, the lawyer I wound up with in this anti-climactic episode, who happened also to be Garrison's brother-in-law, told me in no uncertain terms to stop writing things about Jim. So, I stopped, and never heard from the lawyer again, much less from Garrison."

Ultimately, the charges were dismissed by Harry Connick, who took over from Garrison in 1973.

The Idle Warriors was finally published in 1991, with an introduction by David Lifton, which was highly critical of Garrison. But by this time, Thornley was having his doubts about a conspiracy and wrote in his preface that the case against him nevertheless brought up some "disturbing questions worthy of respect." He had once met Shaw, and he had once met David Ferrie, and his paranoid mind was now questioning what this all meant.

Jonathan Vankin, the author of *Conspiracy, Cover-Ups, and Crimes*, spoke to Thornley in 1989, who told him he believed that

"he and Lee Harvey Oswald were both products of genetic tests carried out by a secret proto-Nazi sect of eugenicists, the Vril Society. He claimed that a bugging device was implanted in his body at birth, and that both he and Oswald were secretly watched and manipulated from childhood by shadowy, powerful Vril overlords. He believes the experiment somehow expanded to include the JFK assassination. He believes the Vril may be monitoring him today.

Paul Hoch wrote that "'Garrison could charm the birds down from the trees,' a staffer once said, and I suppose he would not be the first prosecutor to lead an innocent man to believe his own guilt."

CHAPTER 13

THE BALLAD OF SLIDIN'
CLYDE JOHNSON

AT THE END of March 1967, Reverend Clyde Johnson was in a bar drinking with his wife's cousin, Ed McMillan, and had an idea. Wouldn't "it would be a lot of fun to call up ole Garrison and tell him all about the plot to kill President Kennedy." He called down to New Orleans and told the DA's office that he had information "relative to the assassination of John F. Kennedy." But they'd have to fetch him from Kentwood (about seventy-five miles north of New Orleans) to hear his story.

And what a story it was!

In 1963, the good reverend, also known as Slidin' Clyde Johnson (people viewed him as being shifty), was running for governor of Louisiana. In July or August, he received a telephone page at the Roosevelt Hotel in New Orleans where he was staying. On the line was a Mr. Alton Bernard, who asked to meet him in the Blue Room, where Bernard encouraged him to "keep fighting and making speeches against Kennedy." He then gave Johnson an envelope with $2,000 in cash for his campaign.

Bernard kept on calling Johnson to encourage him, and the conversation always ended up being about Kennedy. In

September 1963, he met Bernard in the lobby at the Capital House Hotel in Baton Rouge. Johnson invited him up to his room, and Bernard brought a friend, whom he introduced as Leon. And then another man by the name of Jack came in accompanied by a tall, big Mexican. Johnson went to the bathroom, and while there he heard one of them say, "Well, he's got to come down from Washington—the pressure is on." The whole idea was that having Johnson "blast" Kennedy would lure him south. Bernard then opened his briefcase and gave envelopes of cash to Leon, Jack, and Johnson (this time $5,000).

After bringing Johnson to New Orleans, the DA's office showed him about thirty-five photographs, and he picked out Lee Harvey Oswald and Jack Ruby as the two men in the room. Alton Bernard was Clay Shaw. Why had Johnson not come forward before? Well, said Johnson, "it was only after I had seen Clay Shaw's picture in the newspaper and on TV that I associated Ruby, Oswald, and Shaw, as being the persons in my room in Baton Rouge."

In April, Ed McMillan stated that he had seen Clay Shaw in Clyde Johnson's hotel room late at night on January 11, 1964. He claimed that Shaw was sitting on one of the beds, and he told Johnson's wife to fix him a drink. Johnson replied, "You get up and fix your own damn drink. My wife is not a barmaid." This was a new twist to the Johnson tale, and Johnson told it to Garrison's investigators on June 5.

All of this was enough for Garrison. In early June, he filed details on the Kennedy conspiracy in court and included this paragraph:

"Clay L. Shaw, traveling from New Orleans to Baton Rouge, Louisiana, in the fall of 1963 and there meeting Lee Harvey Oswald and Jack Ruby at the Capital House

*Hotel and delivering to Lee Harvey Oswald and Jack
Ruby a sum of money."*

Something must have been bothering Garrison, because he
then subpoenaed Johnson for questioning. Johnson fled to a cabin
in southern Mississippi but was located by the press. A *Times-
Picayune* reporter said Johnson "refused to turn on the bedroom
light because he said he was afraid," and the reporter had to stand
in the bathroom and ask questions. He told journalists that he
"was not willing to cooperate any more with Garrison" and
declared himself a "hostile witness. I'll go to Garrison when I
want to and give him what I want to." He added, "You ain't heard
half the truth, baby."

The day before the interview, Johnson had appeared in court
on charges of property damage against Southern Bell Telephone
and Telegraph.

He also told NBC that Clay Shaw had called him on the telephone on the day of the assassination from California. He also
said he knew who the Cuban man was (originally said to be
Mexican) and that he could produce another witness.

Shaw's defense team petitioned the court for more specificity,
and in August the court ordered Garrison to "particularize
further." Garrison gave a date of on or about September 3. They
already knew that Shaw was not in Baton Rouge in early
September, but what about Jack Ruby? They got Hugh
Aynesworth, then Houston bureau chief for *Newsweek*, to do
some investigating, and they reached out to Eva Grant, Jack
Ruby's sister.

February 21st.1968;

...rd F. Wegmann
...orney at Law
...47 National Bank of Commerce Building
...ew Orleans.La. 70112

Dear Sir:

After receiving your letter.I contacted our attorney in Detroit,last September.
Mr. Adleson sent me a copy with what he wrote to you.,.....I believe Mr. Adleson
forgot to mention who you should try to see in Dallas,in regards to the week of
September 1963, that Jim Garrison said,my late brother was at a meeting with
Mr. Clay Shaw, in Baton Rouge, Louisiana....I know,that theres no truth,to Mr.
Garrison accusations. It seems to me,that Mr. Garrison got into what he calls
a conspiracy, after my brother died.

I have read that Mr. Garrison said,my brother and Oswald were acquainted , as
they both were in the (C.I.A.)....My late brother Jack Ruby ,was not in any
                                    arms
branch of our government,other then the Air Force,during world war two..... I
saw the Rampart Magazine of January 1968,.In Mr. Garrison interview.I have read
that on November 21st.1963.I was in Houston, Texas, waiting for our late beloved
president Kennedy to pass me.......I enter the hospital for major surgery the
                                              that
6th.of November 1963.I was there for one week...Following th period,I went to
my apartment,and I was under very heavy sedation from my resent illness....I
was there,until the evening of November 24th.1963.....

I want to go to New Orleans...To help clear my brother name....Please,believe
me.I had not heard of Mr. Clay Shaw name,until some time in February,or March
of (1967). At that time,I went to see Mr. Many Clements with the (F.B. I.)
He told me not to pay any attention to Mr. Garrison. ... Do you think I should
write to the attorney general,Ramsey Clark,for special protection,when I will
appear in the city,where the trial takes place.? I would not want to be put in
jail,because of the shenanigans Garrison is pulling..
334 N. Heliotrope Drive,Los Angles,Calif.90004   Sincerely
                                                        Eva L Grant   Eva L Grant

An investigation showed that Jack Ruby was not in Baton Rouge between September 1 and September 5 in 1963. He made phone calls from Dallas during that period, and on September 5 he purchased a cashier's check from the Merchants State Bank in Dallas. His sister, Eva Grant, was ready to testify that she had seen him in Dallas every day in September, and other friends vouched for his whereabouts.

Garrison should have figured out that Johnson was a scam artist. George Lardner of the *Washington Post* quoted an Orleans Parish official saying, "He's kind of flaky. It's a wonder they didn't elect him governor." He would show up in Garrison's office for small change—$10 to $20—and Johnson would be on his way to Terry's Lounge. His standard line was "What do you want me to say? I'll say it. Where will you put me up tonight?" Garrison was only so happy to do a little coaching.

On one occasion, Johnson was in the office talking to James Alcock, and on his way out he said he wanted to talk about the code. What code? Well, he said, Clay Shaw had given him a code —a phone number when he wanted Johnson to call him (although Johnson never claimed to have phoned him). It was very simple, and Johnson demonstrated it on a pad of paper. He wrote down Clay Shaw's actual phone number but written like division: four numbers on top divided by a line with three numbers. The phone number he wrote down was that of the Monteleone Hotel. Alcock threw it all in the garbage can when Johnson left.

Johnson wasn't just a con man—he was a con. He had been convicted of two felonies, had violated the Dyer Act (interstate transportation), and had served three years for burglary at Parchman, the Mississippi state prison. Before his convictions, he was an inmate at the state hospital at Mandeville, where he was diagnosed as a paranoid schizophrenic.

Johnson's run for governor was a fraud. He never actually filed the proper papers to run. On the day before they were due, he was in a car accident—he claimed he had been shot at—and the papers disappeared. "I had the original papers in a briefcase in my car but they haven't been able to locate the papers or the briefcase." He said he had asked his attorney to file a new set, but he never showed up at the office. As for the reverend's car, well, the police had found four indentations on the car, but the supposed bullets (?) hadn't pierced it.

After his governorship run, in 1964 Johnson decided to run

for Congress but left the race because a fire destroyed his store and he didn't have enough money to run. He then decided to run for the Senate but could not qualify. In March of 1965, he showed people a "special agent ID card" at a truck stop, lined people up, and searched them for weapons. He claimed to have seen a car with a "machine gun and blood smears on the back seat." He was booked for disturbing the peace and impersonating a police officer (the ID card he had was honorary). In 1967, he threatened a black man, Doug Jones, with a shotgun and then hit him with Jones's own walking stick, which resulted in his arrest for aggravated assault and battery.

Despite all this, in the summer of 1968, Clyde Johnson was still on Garrison's list of witnesses for the Clay Shaw trial. And during jury selection for Clay Shaw's conspiracy trial, the prosecutor James Alcock listed six overt acts that the state would prove. Clyde Johnson's meeting with Oswald, Ruby, and Shaw was one of the acts. A few days before the start of the Clay Shaw trial, he told the press that "I'm the ace-in-the-hole in Garrison's case." But he was then arrested for not paying a $162 bill at the Roosevelt Hotel, which he had expected Garrison to pick up, and was criminally charged.[1]

At the start of the Shaw trial, Garrison omitted this overt act, and Clyde Johnson was not called to testify at Clay Shaw's trial. Had he been put on the stand, the defense would have had Ed McMillan testify that he was with Johnson when he drunkenly made the initial call to Garrison.

In July 1969, Clyde Johnson was killed by a twelve-gauge shotgun blast from Ralph McMillan, the brother of Ed, who was subsequently charged with manslaughter. The district attorney of Hammond noted that "some of these things have deep-lying roots." Of course, to the conspiracy theorists, his death is yet again more evidence of something "mysterious."

CHAPTER 14

EDGAR EUGENE BRADLEY WAS A TRAMP

IN SEPTEMBER 1967, former FBI agent Bill Turner, a writer for *Ramparts* magazine and a Garrison investigator, was going through the DA's files. On this day, Turner found gold. A twenty-one-year-old, Thomas Thornhill, had written in with a tip on April 10, 1967, and it sounded promising.

Thornhill supposedly knew of a witness who would testify, he claimed, that a Mr. Edgar Eugene Bradley "tried to hire him to assassinate Mr. Kennedy" in Los Angeles in 1960 during the presidential campaign. Bradley was to "pay him $5,000 before and $5,000 after he did the job," and he would "use the storm-drain system as his escape route after the assassination."

Now we know where Garrison could have gotten his idea of a shot from the Dallas sewer system.

Thornhill also claimed that Bradley had attempted to "recruit" a witness to persuade her husband to kill President Kennedy, which she naturally refused to do. And right after Kennedy was assassinated, another witness overheard a phone conversation between Bradley and his wife, and after the call, his wife "turned to the witness and said 'Guess where Gene is? He's in Dallas.'" Bradley was also supposedly in New Orleans "a short time before the assassination."

Garrison felt that these allegations deserved further investigation.

In mid-December, Bill Turner, Bill Boxley, and Jim Garrison were in Los Angeles. Garrison was registered under the name Clyde Ballou, one of the many pseudonyms he used. A package was delivered to his room, and Boxley thought it was a bomb. He grabbed it and ran into the bathroom and filled the tub with water. When he opened it, it was just a box of books.

Bradley's name came up, and Garrison asked Boxley and Turner to check him out. They drove to visit Tom Thornhill, but he wasn't home, so they talked to Mrs. Carol Aydelotte, who lived in the same house. She had met Bradley through right-wing activity (she was a member of the John Birch Society), and she claimed that he was "constantly harping on the fact that someone should kill Kennedy." Also, she informed them that Bradley had waged a campaign to intimidate and harass her and that the matter was before the court.

Aydelotte said Reverend Wesley Brice would confirm her story about Bradley calling his wife from Dallas on the day of the assassination. She also claimed that Bradley had plans of the storm drain system of the Sears department store complex and shopping center on Laurel Canyon Road and had attempted to convince a Mr. Dennis Mower to "hide in part of this system and take a shot at Kennedy when he came by."

Bradley, she said, was a sadist and "beats his daughter, Jeanine Bradley ... frequently and viciously," and he had "a habit of pinching women to the point where they became black and blue, and while doing so, practically froths at the mouth." When Aydelotte once told Bradley that she owned a .375 Magnum rifle, "he attempted to recruit her to persuade her husband to use the weapon for an assassination attempt" on JFK. Bradley also showed her husband "various assassination devices, including poisons, ground glass and booby traps" at his home.

Aydelotte identified Bradley as being one of the three tramps.

The second tramp in the middle was supposed to be Edgar Eugene Bradley.

Later that afternoon, Boxley and Turner interviewed Thornhill, who confirmed Aydelotte's comments. He had also heard "Bradley boast of a heart attack drug," and shortly thereafter "he had a close friend who suffered one." Thornhill implicated Bradley in two other deaths: an editor of a conservative newspaper who had been hanged and an accidental shooting of someone else. Bradley, said Thornhill, was "sadistic in temperament."

The next day they met with Dennis Mower, who "confirmed that Bradley attempted to recruit him to assassinate President Kennedy," which he duly reported to the FBI. They then met with Reverend Wesley Brice, who claimed that Bradley had left

Dallas the day after the assassination and that he had "stayed at a hotel about a block from Dealey Plaza."

Garrison called his office and told them to file charges against Bradley for conspiring to kill JFK before any of the allegations were checked out. His staff pushed back, but Garrison was insistent and told them the case was solid and that New Orleans could claim jurisdiction. Once again, Garrison would have to investigate after indicting.

The original charge sheet for Edgar Eugene Bradley. Jack Lawrence was a car salesman in Dallas at the time of the assassination. Loran Hall and Lawrence Howard were active, along with Bradley, in the far-right movement that included the Minutemen, John Birchers, the National States Rights Party (NSRP), the California Rangers, the Christian Defense League, and others. Garrison had stumbled into quite a cell of people. Many of them did hate Kennedy, and many were also active in the anti-Castro movement.

On December 20, 1967, Garrison issued a press release stating that Bradley "did willfully and unlawfully conspire with others to murder John F. Kennedy." He provided no details on other conspirators or any overt acts undertaken by Bradley.

At first, Bradley thought it was all a practical joke:

> "[M]y son received a phone call and he thought so little of it he didn't tell me about it until about an hour later and he said, say Dad, we got the strangest phone call a little while ago. He said some man pretending to be from a certain newspaper in New York called and said you were being indicted in a plot to assassinate President Kennedy. And I said somebody just playing more practical jokes and we laughed about it.

When newsmen showed up at his home, Bradley knew it was serious. He told reporters that Garrison "is either being highly paid to do this or he's off his rocker."

Bradley Denies Plot Role, Says DA 'Off Rocker'

Edgar Eugene Bradley, North Hollywood, Calif., radio evangelist's representative, has denied a charge by District Attorney Jim Garrison that he conspired to assassinate President John F. Kennedy at Dallas Nov. 22, 1963.

"This man (Garrison) is either being highly paid to do this or he's off his rocker," Bradley said after the district attorney's office filed the charge late yesterday.

New Orleans States-Item, *December 21, 1967.*

On December 28, Bradley surrendered to the Los Angeles County Sheriff's office and was released on his own recognizance. After the arraignment, he told the press, "I know I am not guilty of any crime. God knows I am not guilty. That's the important thing." He added, "I think the people who should be concerned at this point are those who may have committed perjury or those have apparently conspired to frame me." On the day of the assassination, he said he was in El Paso returning from a visit with his boss, Dr. McIntyre, leader of the American Council of Churches, a small ultra-conservative religious group. The only time he had ever been in New Orleans was in April 1967.

Garrison had stumbled into a massive feud between Bradley and far-right members of the John Birch Society, in particular Carol Aydelotte, who was also involved with the Minutemen and the American Nazi Party. Dennis Mower also had a checkered past. He was currently the leader of the Southern California

Minutemen (a far-right paramilitary organization) and was a KKK organizer north of Los Angeles. He had previously been arrested for armed robbery and for transporting a stolen machine gun across state lines.

It all started when Aydelotte asked Bradley to donate to one of her causes, and when he called her a "kook," she went after him. He wrote to Robert Welch, head of the John Birch Society, to look at what was going on in her chapter, and she was soon downgraded. She sued Bradley for conspiracy to slander, and on December 19, the day before Garrison delivered his indictment, Bradley was being deposed in her lawsuit. Aydelotte claimed to have over four hundred hours of tapes concerning Bradley.

The allegations were preposterous. Dennis Mower was only fourteen in 1960 when Bradley supposedly asked him to kill Kennedy. He said he turned Bradley down and went to the FBI, but the FBI had no record of this. Garrison now had to link the "Bradley conspiracy" to the "Shaw conspiracy." Otherwise, there would have been two competing, independent, successful plots to kill Kennedy.

In January 1968, Garrison filed paperwork in support of extraditing Bradley to New Orleans. He said, "Bradley was seen in New Orleans on other occasions prior to and after the assassination" and "on each occasion" with individuals named as conspirators in the Shaw case. Bradley also "discussed in detail with other individuals the measures to be taken in order to accomplish the assassination of the President." Furthermore, he insisted that Bradley had been in Dallas on the day of the assassination, not in El Paso, and that he "was actively engaged, in participation with other individuals which resulted in the murder of John F. Kennedy."

Two affidavits were submitted in support. Roger Craig, a deputy sheriff in Dallas at the time of the assassination, claimed that he spoke with a man who represented himself as a Secret Service agent outside the Texas School Book Depository and was "positive that this man was Edgar E. Bradley." Max Gonzales, a New Orleans court clerk and pilot, claimed he saw Bradley at Lakefront Airport in New Orleans with David Ferrie on two occasions in the summer of 1963.[1]

It didn't take long for Garrison's case to crumble.

Bradley could hardly be one of the tramps behind the Texas School Book Depository and also impersonating a Secret Service agent in front. Conspiracy theorist Richard Sprague started talking about the possibility of there being multiple Bradleys. When his identification of Bradley as a tramp was questioned, he suggested that Bradley might have since had an operation that altered his appearance. One critic wrote that Sprague was a "threat as long as there are people like Garrison who are easily led."

Roger Craig also had credibility issues. On the day of the assassination, he claimed to have seen Lee Harvey Oswald get into a station wagon fifteen minutes after the assassination, but the evidence is firm that he got away on a bus and in a taxi. In 1967, Craig was fired from the sheriff's department, his marriage fell apart, and he showed clear signs of mental illness.

BULLET MISSES PROBE WITNESS

Craig Tells of Shooting in Interview

A witness in District Attorney Jim Garrison's investigation of the Kennedy assassination said Thursday that a bullet whizzed by his head Wednesday in Dallas, Tex.

He complained of being followed, and on November 1, 1967, he said he was shot at in Dallas. He did not report the incident to the police because he believed that Garrison would be opposed to it.[2]

An extradition hearing was held in June 1968. Bradley's attorney presented over sixty exhibits—including affidavits, hotel registration forms, bus tickets, and telephone records—attesting to his passing through El Paso on the day of the assassination. Further, Bradley never left California in the summer of 1963, and he presented a briefcase of personal records to prove it. The *Los Angeles Times* said the documentation "provide Bradley with an ironclad alibi." Garrison provided no evidence during the hearing.

Ronald Reagan turned down his extradition in November 1968, but the damage had been done. Bradley received hundreds of death threats, mostly by phone, and one day a bullet came

flying through his front window. Journalist Peter Noyes went to
interview Bradley and knocked on the wrong door.

---

*"An elderly man answered, and I asked if he could direct
me to Gene Bradley's house. He responded, "Oh, you mean
the guy who killed Kennedy. He lives a couple of doors
down the street on the next block."*

In May 1969 Bradley wrote Jim Garrison a letter in which he
indicated that he would like to meet him. He hoped that Garrison
would "realize that I am the victim of a terrible injustice." He
wrote Garrison again in September complaining that "Roger
Craig has phoned me collect, twice ... [H]is main interest seems
to be in the money."

September 17, 1969

Mr. Jim Garrison
District Attorney
2700 Tulane Ave.
New Orleans, Louisiana 70119

Dear Mr. Garrison:

Last week, the Midlothian Mirror printed an article about me
that was just as false as everything else that has been
printed concerning me. Perhaps you have seen the article.
Among other things, it states that Craig is being hounded
almost daily by E. E. Bradley of California.

Roger Craig has phoned me collect, twice. This can be proven
by my phone bills. His main interest seemed to be in money.
These are the only two times I have ever been in touch with
him.

Mr. Garrison, this man is not a truthful man and I now doubt
that he saw or talked to anyone in Dallas the day of the
assassination, as he claimed he did.

Mr. Garrison, these irresponsible people aren't going to let
up on their unethical tactics until we can get together and
you are convinced of my innocence. I'm sure you will be, when
you get the complete picture, as I know it.

Please, Mr. Garrison, try to make arrangements to see me as
soon as possible.

Sincerely,

Edgar E. Bradley
12208 Emelita St.
North Hollywood, Calif. 91607

In June 1970, the conspiracy charges against Edgar Eugene

Bradley were dropped because of the death of an unidentified witness. The DA's office refused to divulge any further details.[3]

Roger Craig committed suicide by gunshot in May 1975, leaving a note saying that "he was sorry for what he has to do, but he could not stand the pain." He had been in a serious car accident two years before; the autopsy showed he had been on valium and was drunk. His daughter wrote online that "the man was disturbed. As his daughter, I would place money on the fact that he suffered from either Borderline Personality Disorder or Bi-polar [sic] depression." She also blamed the conspiracy mongers who had encouraged Craig. "It is EXACTLY this kind of dramatic license that killed my father. It fed his disease. It fed his paranoia. And, in the end, it contributed to his self-destruction."

In early 1991, Bradley phoned Garrison and asked him why he had charged him with the assassination. Garrison told him that "his office had misled him and he was very sorry the mistake occurred." He didn't reveal the real reason: in February 1968 Bill Turner admitted to a Garrison staffer that it was all "a gambit in the publicity struggle."

Garrison invited Bradley to New Orleans, and a few months later they had lunch. Afterward, he asked Garrison to autograph a copy of his book *On the Trail of the Assassins*. Bradley told Garrison, "That's a catchy title." I'm not sure that Garrison caught the irony.

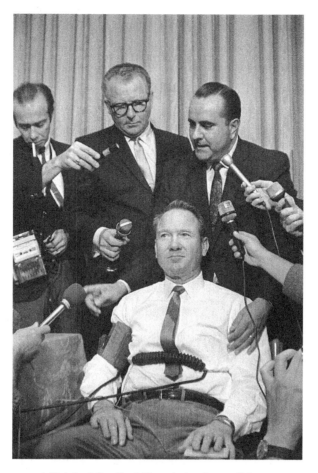

(Original Caption) The photo shows Edgar Eugene Bradley, who was accused by District Attorney Jim Garrison of New Orleans of being a part of the conspiracy to assassinate the late President Kennedy, as he holds a press conference to report the findings of a private lie detector test he had taken to prove his innocence in the case. Posing here only to show the equipment is Bradley. Behind him at left is his attorney, George Jensen, and at right, polygraph expert Major Chris Gugas. January 4, 1968. CREDIT: Bettmann.

CHAPTER 15

FINALLY, A CHAPTER WITH FLYING SAUCERS!

IN MAY 1967 GARRISON RECEIVED AN "IMPORTANT" anonymous letter and handed it to Bill Boxley to investigate.

The writer told a story about someone with "little credibility to his character" and who was "part of the Cuban revolutionary movement." This person claimed that a lot of money had been raised for the Bay of Pigs operation in 1961 and that some of the revolutionaries "decided to flee the country with a good deal of the funds," but they "were arrested in the Miami airport with the money in their possession."

This man was one of those arrested, and he told the anonymous writer the following:

- He knew Clay Shaw.
- He worked for Garrison for a short time as an investigator.
- He saw Oswald in New Orleans and a man "who looked like Ruby."
- He described "the assassination scene in great detail

and told me some facts about it that I had definitely
not heard before."

- He said that Oswald was a "patsy" and that he was a
homosexual "like Shaw, Ferrie, Tippit, and a score of
others."

- The fatal head shot came from the grassy knoll, and a
motorcycle police officer saw a man with a rifle run
from the grassy knoll. Right afterward, the officer
"mysteriously had a very serious accident" and "now
is a near idiot."

- He met Kennedy on several occasions.

The anonymous writer listed five individuals related to his
story and provided Garrison a contact should he require additional information. One of the five men was Thomas Edward
Beckham, a former New Orleans resident and a person of
interest to Garrison since he had hung out with anti-Castro
Cubans in the early 1960s.

Back then, Beckham dressed as a priest, which was a great
help in raising money for his United Cuban Relief Missionary
Force. The money was supposedly going to help anti-Castro
Cubans. The Better Business Bureau of the greater New Orleans
area sent out an alert warning that his fund "has not been granted
a City Solicitation permit," and David Lewis reported him to
the FBI.

Garrison told his men to show Beckham's photograph
around. Charles Spiesel, who embarrassed himself at Shaw's
trial, claimed he saw Beckham at the JFK conspiracy party. A
witness from Clinton, Louisiana, also identified Beckham. A
Garrison memo claimed that "Beckham was among those
handing out Cuban handbills at one time or another."

In November 1967 Garrison located Beckham in Omaha,
Nebraska. He was now referring to himself as Doctor Thomas

Edward Beckham and was involved in several scams. Garrison's file on Beckham revealed a very troubled past.

Beckham started his career as a con artist in 1959 when he promoted a Ricky Nelson show in New Orleans at the age of sixteen. A Ricky Nelson did appear, not the famous star but someone with the same name. Beckham pocketed the money and ran.

In 1961 Beckham and his brother were arrested for stealing $12,000 ($103,000 in 2020 dollars) in cash and merchandise from Halpern's Fabric Store. They were both employees, and they intended to use the goods to open their own store. Beckham's brother received a year of probation, but Thomas's case was continued because he was in a mental institution after trying to hang himself in November 1962. Earlier that year, Beckham was charged with "simple rape contributing to the delinquency of a juvenile," his fourteen-year-old wife.

The Austin Better Business Bureau (BBB) warned people in February 1966 about "Dr." Thomas E. Beckham. He had started the National Institute of Criminology, and those buying an "Honorary Life Membership" for ten dollars would receive the rank of Honorary Colonel. The Lincoln Nebraska BBB sent out an alert on February 15, 1967, about an ad that Beckham had placed in various newspapers.

"Do you have a problem? T. Edward Beckham, DD, PHD announces the opening of his office for the research practice of Metaphysics & Psychology. By appointment only 488-7032."

Garrison's notations are on many of these documents, so clearly none of this fazed him. Noting that Beckham had a mark on his left cheek, Garrison bizarrely wrote that "it should be remembered that one witness who described seeing Jack Ruby meet Oswald at a restaurant shortly before the assassination referred to the fact that Oswald had 'a scar on his left cheek.'"

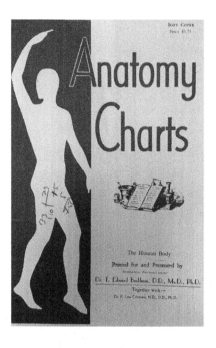

Garrison subpoenaed Beckham to testify before the grand jury in December 1967. He claimed that Beckham was "connected with David Ferrie in that they were both ordained priests in the 'Old Orthodox Catholic Church of North America'" and that he had "knowledge of Central Intelligence Agency–sponsored guerilla training conducted near New Orleans." He also alleged that Beckham was "reported to be in Dallas in November of 1963" and "that a number of persons with whom he was in contact in New Orleans and Dallas have been found to have played a part in the assassination of President Kennedy."

In January 1968, a second anonymous letter arrived asking Garrison to talk with Mr. Fred Crisman. It claimed that

- The first person Clay Shaw phoned "after being told he was in trouble" was Crisman.
- Thomas Beckham also called Crisman the moment he was subpoenaed.
- Crisman had a diplomatic passport issued on the word of a Senate committee chairman.
- Beckham delivered $200,000 of Cuban money to Crisman to recruit people to kill Castro.
- Crisman knew J. D. Tippit.

The letter exhorted Garrison to "keep digging ... [Y]ou have some odd fish on the run."

Two weeks later, investigator Bill Boxley sat down with Robert Lavender, a person who was familiar with Beckham and Crisman. He said that after Garrison's probe had become public, Beckham told him that David Ferrie was a homosexual and in addition that he would be dead within a couple of weeks. Further, an unnamed Associated Press reporter "was killed because of his inside information of the assassination."

Lavender said that Crisman had warned that he would "kill Beckham if I am subpoenaed as a result of anything that he says" while at the same time denying that he had any knowledge of a conspiracy. Crisman also "described himself as being sadistic in sexual practice preferences." Garrison was invariably interested in such things.

And Lavender revealed the secret of the JFK assassination.

"Crisman told him that Arcacha Smith and Louis Rabel said that they had accumulated between four and five hundred thousand dollars in cash from various fund-raising enterprises and private backers. That they as a matter of safe keeping for the money had placed it in Beckham's hands in a suitcase and had sent him aloft

flying around the country from one city to another as custodian of the money. He supposedly flew under the name Mike Nelson and stayed in touch with Arcacha. Eventually, the story goes, Arcacha and Rabel and their backers decided that the money would be used to assassinate President Kennedy. However, in order to throw the authorities off, Beckham was instructed to land at the Miami airport in possession of some $30,000 of the total amount, the rest being stored somewhere else and arrangements were made to have the FBI and the CIA arrest Arcacha and Rabel and Beckham at the Miami airport and confiscate the $30,000, the plan being, it was hoped, that the FBI and CIA would think this was all the money which Arcacha and Rabel had been able to abscond with."

At this point, Boxley had "the distinct feeling that Lavender was on stage reiterating a story which he had been encouraged to tell us." Garrison wrote in the margins that "this is Boxley speaking here. The discreditation line is SOP [standard operating procedure] for him." Boxley thought it should all "be taken with a generous portion of salt" because no one would leave large amounts to money to someone like Beckham. Garrison once again disagreed, saying his remark was a "gratuitous observation" and complained that the original Crisman file "departed with Boxley."

Beckham testified for over six hours on February 15, 1968, and had Garrison flummoxed by his inability to acknowledge anything remotely conspiratorial. He had left school in the seventh grade at the age of fourteen or fifteen(!). He met Jack Martin in 1960 while trying to get into the music business under the name Mark Evans. Martin then introduced him to Guy

Banister, the former FBI agent turned who now ran a detective agency.

Garrison believed Banister had a CIA connection (not true), and he pushed Beckham into also admitting that he worked for the CIA.

Beckham: Mr. Garrison, why are you trying to make me out to be a CIA agent or something, I'm not.

Garrison: You are lying. Now when you come back, I want no more lies. You are dismissed now, come back in an hour, but no more lies because the name of that is perjury. You can go outside.

Garrison wanted to know how much Banister paid Beckham, who was just an errand boy.

"Well, like he would send me to the restaurant to get me a cup of coffee or a coke and bring him back the change and he would say keep it, and I know its costing you money coming down here so here is a buck or five dollars, you know, in that manner."

Beckham said Banister wanted him to watch Jack Martin and report back. "He said keep your eyes and ears open, so one night I was supposed to meet Jack about six o'clock and this is what stands out in my mind, it took him all night to lick a stamp, it took him all night to lick a stamp, he would walk almost anywhere, really he would, he would walk, walk, from that office to Claiborne Towers, he had business up in Claiborne Towers and all, he was licking a stamp ... "

It all turned comedic when Beckham was asked about his priest's outfit.

Juror: No, the church that you did belong to. Was that the Old Orthodox Catholic Church of North America?

Beckham: I think it had Apololectic or Apolostetic or something to it.

Juror: Never mind about that ...

Beckham: I don't know if that is the exact wording of the church, I don't ...

Juror: Maybe this is not the exact wording, but is this the Old Orthodox Catholic Church of North America?

Beckham: I can't answer you.

Juror; Well, suppose you tell me the name of the church you belong to?

Beckham: I got the papers at home, I can show you the papers, but I don't have them with me.

Juror: Well, tell me what you recall that is on the paper?

Beckham: Let me see if I can recall what is on the paper. I don't know, it says that I am an ordained priest within the Holy APOLOTOTIC, or something like that.

Juror: Are you trying to tell me you don't know what church you are a priest in?

Beckham: No, because I wasn't even interested in that, I never even messed with it.

Juror: Were you wearing a habit?

Beckham: At that time, yes.

Juror: While you were wearing the habit what church did you think you belonged to?

Beckham: That's a good question. Ask Mr. Martin. I don't know myself.

A large part of Beckham's testimony concerned Fred Crisman, whom he had met when he answered an ad for the American Association of Parapsychologists, which Crisman headed. They then started an advertising agency together, but Beckham had no idea how much money they generated. Crisman "got" Beckham a PhD "award" from Brackenridge Forest in England, another nonexistent university.

Beckham ended his testimony with a bombshell. Earlier that day, he had told reporter Jack Dempsey that he would blow Garrison "right out of his saddle." He had gone into a tie store, and someone there had told him that they had important information, that Garrison "had some intimate affairs with a gay guy down in the French Quarter." Beckham had this person swear out an affidavit, which said an unnamed person "knows a hustler, a male prostitute who does it for money and was intimate with Mr. Garrison, but he doesn't give the hustler's name."

When Beckham was finished, Assistant DA James Alcock asked staffer Tom Bethell how anybody could believe that "a bum like that" would be working for the CIA.

Throughout 1968, reports flowed into Garrison's office regarding Crisman and Beckham. They were always claiming to possess higher degrees—indeed they loved faking diplomas and certificates. They had also incorporated several businesses, including the Northwest Relief Society, Associated Ambulances, Associated Discount Services, TAB Productions Inc., and the Professional Research Bureau. Their National Association of Criminology advertised that one could obtain a PhD for four hundred dollars, and their Northwest Relief Society placed collection bins in taverns and cafes asking for money.

Crisman appeared to do some good when he wrote a research study on Roma children as part of a new $500,000 Head Start program being instituted in Tacoma. The police viewed it differently, speculating that his real intent was to be hired as the administrator of the program for the purpose of stealing the funds. Crisman was not hired.

This should have been more than enough to give Garrison pause. But what struck him as important was that Lavender said Crisman was "sexually sadistic" and that Raymond Broshears, another con man who claimed to have been David Ferrie's roommate, said Crisman was a homosexual—just like Clay Shaw.

There was another troubling Crisman incident from twenty years earlier.

The flying saucer craze started in June 1947 when pilot Kenneth Arnold said he saw nine UFOs, traveling at what he thought was twelve hundred miles per hour, near Mount Rainier in Washington. The incident garnered national attention, and "flying saucers" entered the lexicon of the day. Ray Palmer, the editor of *Amazing Stories* magazine, saw this an opportunity to boost circulation.

He had earlier published stories by Richard Shaver about a deep cave underworld where there was a war between two robot societies, the Deros and Teros. In 1946 Crisman wrote a letter to the magazine saying it was all true and that he had fought his way out of a cave with a submachine gun fighting these beings during his last combat mission near Burma.

Palmer wrote to Arnold in July 1947 about another sighting, six weeks earlier, near Maury Island in Puget Sound. Harold Dahl, his son, and another harbor patrolman said they saw six doughnut-shaped objects in the sky. One craft was in trouble and excreted some sort of metal that injured Dahl's son and killed his dog. The other harbor patrolman was Fred Crisman, who retrieved some of the debris. Arnold came out to investigate and called Army intelligence to help. Two officers arrived and quickly determined that the material was just slag. Unfortunately, when flying back, their B-25 had engine problems and crashed. The two officers were killed.

The FBI investigated, and Crisman admitted the whole thing

was a hoax. He wasn't a harbor patrolman; he just worked for Dahl salvaging lumber. He had talked Dahl into going along, and he was the one who had talked up the so-called event. For a while, the government considered charging them with fraud but dropped it because of the accidental nature of the two deaths.

To Palmer, the Maury Island incident was a godsend. Supposedly the Deros and Teros beings would occasionally leave their underground world, and Palmer believed that the Arnold sightings and the Maury Island incident proved that they had. His October 1947 issue declared that "a part of the now world-famous Shaver mystery has now been proved."

Crisman never stopped playing up the Maury Island incident. In August 1967, he and Beckham held the "First Midwest UFO Conference," while Crisman later appeared in Seattle claiming he had photos of the ships.

Beckham was sentenced in September 1968 to thirty days in prison for operating an "unlicensed private correspondence school called the American Academy of Professional Arts." He sold a worthless degree to an illiterate California man, who then also started selling degrees, including a "doctor in metaphysics" that allowed people to perform "drugless therapy."

In September, Garrison told his investigators that Crisman was "very important" and that "everything else we've been able to check into about the data from this anonymous source of information has turned out to be true so you have to assume that the rest is true." Crisman, who worked for Boeing for two years in personnel, was linked with other suspects through the aerospace industry. "You dig into Tippit's background, and you find that he used to work for Ling-Temco. You dig into Fred Crisman's background and you find that he used to work for Boeing. You dig into Gene Bradley's background you find that he used to work for Lockheed," said Garrison.

> "I want to just underline that point. That that is the common denominator that I have found, at least in the JFK killing, of virtually anybody who has any role of significance. If they did not work for—it's not just a defense operation but it is one of the elements of the defense operations which got the major bite of the billions. I think we'll find ultimately that the reason for that is because they're almost one with the CIA and vice versa."

Earlier in the year, Garrison had called Warren Hinckle, editor of *Ramparts*, and told him, "This is risky, but I have little choice. It is imperative that I get this information to you now. Important new information has surfaced. Those Texas oilmen do not appear to be involved in President Kennedy's murder in the way we first thought. It was the Military-Industrial Complex that put up the money for the assassination—but as far as we can tell, the conspiracy was limited to the aerospace wing. I've got the names of three companies and their employees who were involved in setting up the President's murder. Do you have a pencil?"

Garrison found more linkages. Oswald greased equipment at the Reily Coffee Company for two months in the summer of 1963 and was then fired for loitering at the garage next door. Garrison found that "every potential witness associated with Oswald at the Reily Coffee Company—almost everybody—now works for aerospace, NASA."[1]

DEPARTURES FROM
REILY COFFEE COMPANY

Lee Oswald leaves on July 19th, 1963.

ALFRED CLAUDE departs later in July	Goes to work at Michoud: CHRYSLER AEROSPACE DIVISION
EMMET BARBEE departs later in July	Goes to work at the NATIONAL AERONAUTICS AND SPACE ADMINISTRATION CENTER
JOHN D. BRANYON leaves shortly afterwards	Goes to work at the NATIONAL AERONAUTICS AND SPACE ADMINISTRATION CENTER
DANTE MARACHINI leaves shortly afterwards	Goes to work at the: CHRYSLER AEROSPACE DIVISION

*Not all of Oswald's associates left to work at
Michoud. For instance, Emmet Barbe was still at
Reily in 1964.*

Garrison wrote a memo entitled "An Analysis of Potential Witnesses Indicating Role of the Military Industrial Complex in the Assassination of President Kennedy." He listed fourteen people who had jobs he found suspicious. But have a look at librarian Norman Gallo:

14.   NORMAN GALLO: Librarian at Napoleon Avenue Branch Library in New Orleans. Oswald visited the library at regular intervals, usually on Thursday. Because libraries are standard "drops" for intelligence operatives, an attempt was made by the New Orleans D.A.'s Office to examine some of the books taken out by Oswald while in New Orleans. It was learned, however, that immediately following the assassination the F.B.I. picked up all available copies of books taken out by Oswald. Subsequent inquiry has brought out that Norman Gallo, one of the librarians at the time, was formerly in Air Force Intelligence in Asia. Gallo spoke Japanese, Italian and Spanish. After serving with Air Force Intelligence in Korea he was engaged in intelligence work for the federal government in Washington, D.C. from 1957 to 1959. Gallo subsequently returned to Japan for governmental work, returning to New Orleans in the Spring of 1962. By 1963 he was librarian at the Napoleon Avenue Branch used by Oswald. This man's history explicitly indicates intelligence work for the government. His presence at the Napoleon Avenue Library and the regularity of Oswald's visits to it indicate the likelihood that this location was a "drop" for an intelligence operation. During the Summer of 1963, Oswald appears to have been using the library in connection with intelligence assignments unrelated to his later role as a decoy on November 22nd. Gallo's last known whereabouts was in the area of Washington, D.C.

Right under Garrison's nose, thousands of good-paying jobs were being created for the space program to go to the Moon. Boeing and Chrysler built huge plants in Michoud, Louisiana, just seventeen miles from New Orleans. Why on earth wouldn't people move?

Workers Reach 4504

If you feel crowded on the Chef Menteur hwy, these days, you should.

This week 4504 workers were trooping back and forth to the Michoud missile plant. The number goes up each week.

Furthermore, the number will get even higher when the plant is going full blast. Chrysler Corporation Space Division will hire about 2700 persons at peak production later this year. The Boeing Company expects to have about 3600 this September.

The rundown this week from the National Aeronautics and Space Administration showed Boeing, 1968 employes; Chrysler, 1818; Mason-Rust Company, 578; NASA, 136, and Vector Corporation, 4.

Boeing estimatees that its peak employment will produce an annual payroll of 35 to 40 million dollars.

The Times-Picayune, *January 27, 1963.*

If you were thinking that this couldn't get any crazier, you'd be mistaken. Garrison's photographic expert, Richard Sprague, argued that Crisman was one of the three tramps. Had they done any real investigation, they would have found that Crisman had an airtight alibi: he was teaching in a high school on November 22, 1963.

COMMITTEE TO INVESTIGATE
ASSASSINATIONS
927 15TH STREET, N. W.
WASHINGTON, D. C. 20005

July 14, 1969

Mr. A. P. Kimbrough
4008 Shannon Lane
Dallas, Texas

Dear Arch:

When I returned home and searched through my files, I discovered that
the enclosed copy of "The Tramp Booklet" was my last copy. So I would
appreciate your returning it when you have finished with it.

As you can see from the opening page, my recommended investigation is
outlined in the text, more or less as I discussed it with you. The witnesses
who might be interviewed if you had the opportunity to do so without
jeopardizing your health or career, are listed on page 5.

As you will notice, I say nothing in this booklet about my beliefs concerning the identities of the three men. However, for your information, I am
convinced by photographic comparisons made in some depth by myself as
well as by Bill Turner and a facial comparison expert, that these three
men are Bradley, Crisman and Slachter.

If you turn to the frontispiece, photo #3, the men from left to right are, in
my opinion, Fred Lee Crisman, Ralph Slachter, and Edgar Eugene Bradley.

If they are, or if even one of the three is correct, then the importance of
these three "tramps" can certainly be seen.

Good luck with whatever efforts you can make in this direction and be careful
who you show the booklet to.

It was a pleasure seeing you again and having dinner and discussion.

Regards,

Dick Sprague

In October, Garrison subpoenaed Fred Crisman, claiming that he "had been engaged in undercover activity for a part of the industrial warfare complex for years" and that this brought him often to Dallas and New Orleans. He was being called to New Orleans, said Garrison, "because our office has developed evidence indicating a relationship on his part to persons involved in the assassination of President John Kennedy." Garrison concluded his press release by stating that Kennedy "was murdered by elements of the industrial warfare complex working in concert with individuals in the United States government."

Echoing the anonymous letter sent to Garrison, Crisman told the press that the FBI was looking for Beckham, who was the "banker" for anti-Castro Cubans, and that he turned over $30,000 to the FBI. He said that Garrison "feels that [Beckham] dropped off ten times that amount in Dallas and that money was used to finance the assassination."

Crisman testified in November after Garrison sent him travel money. He said he had worked for Boeing in its personnel department for two years and had left the company to go into teaching. He had been in New Orleans and Dallas just once, and that was with Beckham in 1966. He did not know anything about the assassination. He testified for just an hour, and Garrison didn't even bother to show up.

The two anonymous letters were most probably written by Crisman, perhaps with Beckham's help. The two con men got what they wanted: lots of headlines and copy in newspapers across the country. They had successfully preyed on the gullibility of a conspiracy theorist. Except they had underestimated their mark. Garrison was a true believer, and he wasn't finished with either of them.

CHAPTER 16

ARSENIC AND OLD PERRIN

WILLIAM WOOD, the editor of the weekly *Houston Tribune*, followed the Garrison investigation with keen interest. He happened to talk with Francis Fruge, a Louisiana state trooper who was conducting field work for the New Orleans investigation, and found himself invited to a job interview with Jim Garrison. Wood had previously worked for the CIA, and Garrison was looking for someone who understood the "mentality of the agency," as he put it. He asked Wood, "When can you start, and do you mind using an alias for operational purposes?" Wood replied, "How about the first of May and what would you like to call me?" They settled on the name Bill Boxley.

He started to educate Garrison about "espionage argot—talk about 'cut-offs, safe houses' etc. and no doubt was largely responsible for getting Garrison to believe what he wanted to believe: that the assassination was engineered by the CIA." Garrison now had an investigator who would "develop the proof" to support the "baseless plots" he continually "dreamed" of.

In February 1968, Garrison fought with his assistant James Alcock.

"You know, Jim, we get disturbed when we see you listening to Boxley, giving you all that bull ..."

"I've learned one thing about Boxley," Garrison replied. *"He's right."*

Wood's real history was far more interesting than Garrison could have imagined. In December 1950 he was granted a covert security clearance by the CIA and was assigned to the island of Saipan as an instructor of clandestine operations. In March 1952 Wood suffered a nervous breakdown and was sent back to Washington. His breakdown had been caused by family problems and alcoholism. He was reassigned in May 1952 to serve as an instructor within the United States.

In December, Wood was found lying on a sidewalk bleeding from the mouth. A month later, he failed to report for duty and was found at home drunk and was told to report for duty the next day. He didn't show up and was admitted to a hospital. The CIA asked for his resignation, and Wood was out by the end of January. In July, Wood called the CIA to inform them he was going to have a brain operation. They informed the hospital that he "had access to highly classified information" and that "he had a history of becoming talkative under anesthesia." The CIA sent in an agent to pose as a doctor.

In the end, Wood just had a spinal tap, and when he woke up, the CIA agent posing as a doctor was in the room, as was his father. He told his father that "he had served overseas with the CIA and had seen many people killed. The CIA are a bunch of dirty cut-throats and I wouldn't be a bit surprised if they sent one of their men to cut mine. They think they are smart but one of these days in the near future I will show them who is the smartest." All of this was reported back to the CIA.

In 1957, Wood offered his services to a Formosan [Taiwanese] intelligence officer. He told his wife they would "receive $700–$1000 per month if this thing goes through." In 1967, the CIA's Domestic Contact Service considered using him as a source (before his employment with Garrison) but was rejected after the FBI determined he was still drinking heavily.

Boxley spent most of his time in the field but returned each week to New Orleans for personal debriefings with Garrison. One lead percolated to the top of the pile, and it concerned a prostitute, Nancy Rich-Perrin, who had supposedly worked behind the bar at Jack Ruby's strip club and tied Ruby in with anti-Castro Cubans. Perrin and her husband had lived in both Dallas and New Orleans. Might this be the link between the planning and execution of the assassination?

Nancy Perrin Rich was interviewed by the FBI in late 1963, and she testified before the Warren Commission in June 1964. She told quite the story. Her marriage to Robert Perrin, who had a history of mental illness, dissolved in 1960, at which point he left. She got wind in 1961 that he was living in Dallas, and she called the police department and just happened to reach officer J. D. Tippit (the policeman Oswald later killed on the afternoon of the assassination). Upon her arrival in Dallas, she went straight to the police station and talked to him.

Nancy Rich reconciled with her husband, who put her to work as a prostitute, and she claimed to have worked for Ruby in the summer of 1963 as a bartender and part-time waitress. After she left his employ, she attended four meetings where she and her husband were offered $10,000 to smuggle rifles to Cuba and bring out refugees. She asked for $25,000, but the deal fell through. Claiming that Jack Ruby had arrived at one of the meetings with a bulge in his pocket, she said he was later called into another room, and the bulge was gone when he emerged. The obvious implication was that he was a financier of the project.

Her story was implausible on its face. During her testimony, she couldn't remember who had taken them to these meetings, who else had attended, or even the location of the apartment. She could barely remember when she had lived in Dallas and New Orleans. And J. D. Tippit never worked behind a desk. There were also significant discrepancies between her FBI statements and her testimony before the Warren Commission.

After speaking to the FBI, Rich was given a lie detector test. The test was inconclusive because she had taken methedrine, but the examiner was still of the opinion that "she has a tendency to delusions of grandeur." The attorney who had represented her on a 1961 vagrancy charge described her "as being a habitual liar, who found it very difficult to tell the truth." Her stories were "so ridiculous that no one could possibly believe them." A Dallas police detective called her a "psychopathic liar who got great delight out of telling wild tales."

None of this mattered to Garrison since she provided crucial evidence tying Ruby to anti-Castro activities. And there was something else that was suspicious. Robert Perrin, her third husband, had called the Louisiana State Police in late August 1962 saying, "I need help. Please send an ambulance right away." Police officers smelled ether in his apartment and found him in bed. There was a suicide note on the dresser. He died a few hours later due to arsenic poisoning, according to the autopsy. His body was identified by one of his friends, who was also a state trooper.

It was all suspicious to Garrison. Propinquity was in place since Perrin once lived on the same block as David Ferrie. He told Boxley, the seasoned pro, to work with Joel Palmer, a volunteer investigator who had previously been a publicist at University City Studios.

Despite two of Perrin's fellow workers identifying him from autopsy photos, Boxley submitted a six-page memo questioning his suicide. Boxley then went to visit Rev. A. Kruschevski, who owned the building where Perrin lived. A fifty-five-year-old man lived opposite Perrin, and he disappeared at the same time. Mysteriously, his apartment was full of radio equipment. To cap it all off, one of the neighbors identified that man as being one of the tramps—perhaps even Edgar Eugene Bradley. Garrison believed this was "the most important break to date in his probe."

Boxley and Palmer were now convinced Perrin's death was faked, that a Venezuelan seaman was killed by the conspirators and buried under Perrin's name, that there was a "secret communications center in that upstairs apartment; and that Perrin was living and writing pulp fiction under the name 'Starr.'" Supposedly, Perrin planned to assassinate Kennedy from his apartment in New Orleans when Kennedy visited the city in 1962. He had the perfect location: his apartment overlooked a one-lane turn on the main route to the Napoleon Street wharf, and the presidential limousine would have to slow down to negotiate the turn. The plan was called off because he could not get the cooperation of the chief of police, so the apartment was used to plan for Dallas some fifteen months before the actual assassination.

Garrison decided that on the fifth anniversary of the assassination, he would charge Perrin, Bradley, and the three tramps. His staff tried to stop him, but all they could do was delay him. He still wanted to charge Bradley and Perrin as assassins on the grassy knoll, and his staff was forced to resort to unorthodox methods to stop him.

Harold Weisberg, a Warren Commission critic who spent a lot of time in the New Orleans office, believed that "if it takes a crook to catch a crook, it could take a nut to reach a nut." He called Vincent Salandria, another critic who was "devoted" to Garrison. "I told him Jim was about to get into real trouble over Boxley and would he please go there with me, so he could persuade Jim after I dug the truth up." He told Salandria that the CIA was trying to "wreck Garrison's investigation from the inside." They caught the same plane to New Orleans to plan their attack.

Once on the ground, they sent out a few of the more dependable investigators to debunk the story from top to bottom. They retrieved the morgue book and found it was all in order, found that the apartment contained beer cans and not radio gear, found the hospital records of Perrin's admission and diagnosis, and found a report by the state trooper whom Perrin had phoned before committing suicide. Weisberg wrote this all up in a report, and the next day Salandria confronted Garrison with assistant DA Andrew Sciambra.

It worked. They convinced Garrison that Boxley was CIA. Salandria said that "When we explained to Garrison why the memorandum had to be a trap for him and had no validity, he immediately agreed." Sciambra was ecstatic and told Weisberg, "Hal, you did it. We are coming to get you and take you to the best Italian dinner you'll ever have."

About six weeks ago there was a monumental reshuffling in New Orleans. JG's staff didn't like the swift pace of his movement and staged a bit of a coup, taking the investigation out of his hands with the threat to resign en mass. Vince Salandria and Weisberg popped up and spread paranoia about Boxley being a CIA agent (if he is, they certainly couldn't prove it) and included Steve Jaffe and myself in the bag. The staff used this to fire Boxley, but they didn't buy the rest of it. Despite word to the contrary circulated by Salandria, who seems to be a pathological case, I am still working with the staff. At this point, however, I think that the Bobby Kennedy murder here in California is ripe for cracking, and I'm concentrating on that.

Excerpt of a letter, dated January 22, 1968, from Bill Turner, a Garrison investigator, to Larry Haapanen, who did some investigative work for Garrison on the west coast. Turner was Boxley's partner in crime in the Edgar Eugene Bradley debacle.

Boxley found out that he'd been fired when he called Garrison's house. Salandria picked up the phone and challenged Boxley's work. Boxley hung up and called back later. Salandria again answered and told Boxley he had been fired.

He hightailed it to Texas[1], fearful of being arrested; his .38 revolver had been stolen, and he thought it might turn up "at the scene of an unsolved crime." He said, "I didn't stop until I got to the Holiday Inn in Orange, Texas. I didn't know what was going on, but I wasn't going to wait around and see. I didn't want to spend the rest of my life in Angola."

Garrison issued a press release announcing the firing of Boxley and told the press that he "was not only a CIA agent, but he was one on a very high level."

DISTRICT ATTORNEY
PARISH OF ORLEANS
STATE OF LOUISIANA
2700 TULANE AVENUE
NEW ORLEANS 70119

JIM GARRISON
DISTRICT ATTORNEY

December 9, 1968

P R E S S   R E L E A S E

The District Attorney's Office today announced the removal of William Boxley from the investigative staff. Boxley was fired after evidence recently developed by the District Attorney's staff indicated current activity by him as an operative of the Central Intelligence Agency. Boxley's initial service with the C.I.A. was in Washington, D.C., where he served for years as an active agent for what was then termed the Department of Covert Activity.

Page 1 of Garrison's press release announcing the firing of Bill Boxley.

Harold Weisberg came to a different conclusion: "Garrison fired Boxley because he could not fire himself."

PART 3

REWRITING HISTORY

CHAPTER 17

GARRISON TAKES THE HSCA FOR A RIDE

IT WAS THURSDAY, March 6, 1975. Like millions of other people across North America, I was watching *Good Night America* with Geraldo Rivera at 11:30 p.m. Geraldo was a new face, avant-garde, on the cutting edge, and it sure didn't hurt that he was easy on the eyes! *Good Night America* was the show to be watching, and we were all in for a shock.

During the last segment, Rivera brought out a then-unknown twenty-nine-year-old man named Robert Groden to show the Zapruder film, probably the most famous twenty-seven seconds of film ever. Abraham Zapruder, a Dallas dress manufacturer, managed to catch the JFK assassination on film. He sold it to *Life* magazine, whose editors agreed that they would not unduly exploit the horribly graphic nature of the film. So it had never been shown publicly.

So there I was, like millions of other people, watching the Zapruder film on American national TV for the first time.

The studio audience gasped at the fatal head shot. So did I. President Kennedy's head moved back and to the left, in an unmistakeable motion. However, Lee Harvey Oswald, the supposed assassin, was in a building behind the motorcade. So why on earth did Kennedy's head go backward?

Geraldo Rivera's show had a national impact. The next day, the *Dallas Morning News* published a front-page article with the headline "Shooting Gory Sight: Kennedy's Head Thrown Backward, Film Shows." The *New York Times* said the show "generated widespread response."

Groden went on a nationwide tour of colleges to show the Zapruder film. He lucked out at the University of Virginia. The son of Congressman Thomas Downing was there and arranged for his father to have a private showing. He then invited his congressional colleagues to see the head snap for themselves. There was already an uproar over the Church Committee investigation into CIA assassination attempts of foreign leaders and the Rockefeller Commission's investigation into illegal domestic CIA activities. Downing then sponsored a bill to create the House Select Committee on Assassinations (HSCA) in 1976 to look into both the John Kennedy and Martin Luther King murders.

Ironically, the HSCA forensic pathology panel concluded that Kennedy was shot from behind. The head motion was caused by a neuromuscular spasm causing involuntary muscle movement. There might also have been some minor movement due to the mass of material exiting from the right front of Kennedy's head.

Two staff members, Jonathan Blackmer and L. J. Delsa, interviewed Garrison for a week in the summer of 1977 about the case. He compiled a list of his outstanding leads and wrote a series of memos to the HSCA on Kerry Thornley, Thomas Beckham and Fred Crisman, and of course Clay Shaw and Perry Russo.

Garrison told the HSCA that he still considered Kerry Thornley to be the second Oswald. He had noticed something peculiar: Oswald had moved out of his apartment in Dallas at the end of April 1963, while in early May, Thornley was leaving New Orleans to go to California. His bus trip had passed through Dallas, and Garrison wondered if he might have stopped. If so, maybe he'd impersonated Oswald in the famous backyard photos. Pictures of Thornley show him to have "an unusual baby face, with rounded features and large lower lip; both features matching the same features in the photograph of LHO." Thornley's father was a photoengraver. Being somewhat coy, Garrison hinted that "I do not, at this late juncture, expect that we would ever be so lucky in this matter as finally to find a bird's nest laying on the ground."

The second Oswald was also seen in Morgan City, Louisiana, on November 14, 1963, by Mrs. Corrine Villard. She saw Oswald with Jack Ruby. But because Oswald was most certainly in Dallas, Garrison believed this must have been the "alternate Oswald" who "might usefully have been brought to Dallas ... for various reasons." Further proof of this hypothesis could be found in the Perry Russo hypnotism sessions. Garrison sent the HSCA transcripts, noting that he now had an explanation for why Russo had gotten Oswald's physical characteristics so wrong. This must have been "someone other than the real Oswald, who was so patently the patsy of the whole affair." He wrote that "it looks like we are dealing with an alternate Oswald" and that we might have "a slightly erroneous game card in our hand."

Rereading the transcripts, Garrison felt that Clay Shaw was not a "mere" coconspirator but someone "bringing down the 'word,' as it were, to men of lesser rank and status in the affair— bringing it down somewhat reluctantly because it forces him to associate too long and too openly with characters who are too common and noisy for him to associate with comfortably." In fact, he was of the opinion that this was only "a segment of the conspiracy" in which Shaw was just the "emissary of elements functioning at a higher level in the operation."

Garrison also tried to pull a fast one on the committee. He

claimed that the two transcripts were from one long hypnosis session with a break between the two. So he reversed the chronology by putting the second session first, lessening the appearance of Russo being led by the hypnotist, Dr. Fatter.

August 16, 1977

-3-

cc: Cliff Fenton
      Gaeton Fonzi
      L.J. Delsa

P.S.   The above-described statement, given by Russo under
       hypnosis, is in two parts - which I have labled
       respectively "A" and "B". Apparently, this was the
       result of a break or rest period interposed by
       Dr. Fatter for the benefit of the subject.

                                              J.G.

Internal markers in the two transcripts prove they came from two different sessions and provide clues as to their dates.

In the first session, it was the hypnotist who first mentions assassination.

"Dr. Fatter: Let your mind go completely blank, Perry—see that television screen again. It is very vivid—now notice the picture on the screen—there will be Bertrand, Ferrie and Oswald and they are going to discuss a very important matter and there is another man and girl there and they are talking about assassinating somebody. Look at it and describe it to me."

Garrison wanted the HSCA to think the leading question above came later, after Russo had talked about Kennedy being killed.

Another memo from Garrison listed twenty-plus leads, but they were all rehashes of rumors with little hard evidence. He even included statements from two prisoners, Edward Whalen and Edward Girnus, which even he had not taken seriously in 1967.

Girnus had been interviewed in the penitentiary in Atlanta, where he was serving a term for interstate transportation of stolen vehicles. He said he "owed the State of Virginia 28 years for various unspecified criminal violations." He claimed to have met Clay Shaw in New Orleans for discussion on running guns and that Lee Harvey Oswald had joined the meeting. Girnus also sent Garrison an FAA flight plan (see below) submitted by David Ferrie with Hidell [Oswald's alias] as a passenger.

Garrison should have realized that the flight plan was bogus; Lee Harvey Oswald was in Dallas on the date in question. Girnus's rap sheet included several forgery offenses, and you'd think that would have alerted Garrison. Nope, he still told the HSCA that the document "looked quite credible, and that it made sense in some ways."

Edward Whalen was forty-three in 1967 and had already spent most of his adult life in prison. He claimed that he went to David Ferrie's apartment in 1965 with Clay Shaw, where he was offered $25,000 to kill Jim Garrison. At the time, Whalen was in and out of mental institutions, and he told doctors that "people were putting things in his food, and that the court, defense and prosecution attorneys and Senator John Tower of Texas were all conspiring against him."

Garrison wrote to the HSCA and said he regretted that he had "aristocratically" dismissed a number of credible sources of information because they were too "raffish," because they were drifters, or because they had criminal records. Now, he felt, they were "giving us the best damned leads we had." An intelligence agent might well "employ as his extension for leg work someone who, while reasonably competent, has accumulated a 'record' suggesting that he is an outright bum." And so, "a record of arrests—bad checks, vagrancy, theft, et cetera—is made particularly attractive by a short spell at a mental institution." Garrison's view was that the agency "taught its operatives how to select competent characters with incompetence written in their records." His advice for the HSCA: "Don't let the bad records here and there stampede you."

There was also more than a tinge of bitterness in Garrison's memos. It was, he said, an impossible task to explain the domestic intelligence operation behind the assassination to a jury in the 1960s, and "we might as well have tried talking to the jury about flying saucers." Garrison charged that Bill Boxley had not only removed files from his office but had "smoothly swiped what was left of our chastity." And to add insult to injury, the establishment of New Orleans had run over him like the proverbial steamroller for even suggesting that Clay Shaw was perhaps not exactly the equal of Albert Schweitzer. He promised to send more leads on "Mr. Spic & Span" if the HSCA could spare the manpower to investigate.

Garrison wanted the HSCA to investigate Fred Crisman and Thomas Beckham. He was sure that Crisman was "one of the three 'tramps' arrested by Dallas police after the assassination" and who in Garrison's mind was linked to Clay Shaw. Right after the assassination, Shaw had traveled from San Francisco to Portland, Oregon. He was to have given a speech there, but it had been canceled. In 1958 Crisman had lived in Turner, Oregon, only some fifty miles away. Garrison wrote that we "have an interesting question of propinquity worthy of a follow through when the opportunity comes for a full inquiry into Crisman and his curious, markedly clandestine patterns of activity." Portland was "essentially Crisman home territory."

Crisman, thought Garrison, deserved "the honor of being a high priority investigative target" because he was a "cut-out for anti-Castro operations." He was "through Shaw ... either exerting a high degree of energizing influence on the New Orleans pre-assassination scene, or, at the very least, monitoring it." Garrison felt that this was a "professionally clandestine operation" and as such that "traditional evidence (fingerprints, footprints, confessions and so on)" just wouldn't work. The only way for investigators to make progress was via "the successive application of models until one finds the one which fits." Once done, he said, "the only reasonable conclusion is that he was (and probably still is, if still around) an operative at a deep cover level in a long-range clandestine, intelligence mission directly related to maintaining national security."

Garrison also had a particular interest in Thomas Beckham, whom he regarded as Crisman's "protégé." During his investigation, he had "come across what quite apparently seemed to be Dr. Beckham himself, wearing glasses, as I recall—in a film taken immediately following the assassination in front of the Book Depository." Unfortunately, this film had vanished, and Garrison was not optimistic over the prospect of its recovery. Garrison found Beckham's stay in a mental institution in 1963 suspicious;

at the very same time, "Shaw and Ferrie" were trying to "plant Oswald" in a job at a mental hospital in Jackson. "Perhaps Beckham had a temporary mental problem or perhaps his new, older friends were toying with the possibility of an alternative patsy in case of a last-minute problem with Lee Harvey Oswald."

Garrison warned the HSCA that if Beckham developed "as a subject for extensive inquiry, then Crisman should be regarded (as his patient mentor and superior through the passing '60s) as ten—or a hundred times—as important, with regard to investigative potential."

In the meantime, Beckham had been arrested in Arkansas for fraud. While using the alias Eggelston Zimmerman, he had promoted a benefit concert for families of law enforcement personnel killed in the line of duty in Mobile, Alabama. The show was never held, and he absconded with the money. In July 1977, Beckham was acquitted—he told the jury that he had worked for the CIA—but was pending transfer to Arkansas on more fraud charges. He had set up his own Chamber of Commerce and sold raffle tickets. He also performed marriages, claiming to be "an ordained bishop of a religious group called Essence Gospel of Peace." Right after his acquittal, HSCA investigators came to interview him.

He had a preliminary discussion with HSCA investigators on October 9, 1977, to determine if he should be granted immunity. Beckham was now ready to spill the beans. He told them about a meeting in Algiers, Louisiana, with Arcacha and a few other people during which they discussed JFK's assassination. A second meeting had taken place with Jack Martin, David Ferrie, and Clay Shaw at the Town and Country Motel in New Orleans where they talked about Cuba and JFK. Two weeks before the assassination, Beckham was given a package to deliver to Dallas that contained pictures of buildings and cars. He also spoke of an "Organization" that was very powerful and that he claimed was even employed by the CIA for missions. A friend of Crisman told him that Oswald and three others were involved in the assassination and that Crisman knew all the details.

The conversation with Beckham was recorded, and word got out that there was a "confession tape." Garrison called radio conspiracy nut Ted Gandolfo in February 1978 and claimed, in his own words, that "I wish I could tell you of the progress they have made. It's past conspiracy. It's past prima facie. It's solid evidence on tape. I mean there's no question about it." In the 1990s, Gandolfo and others charged that the HSCA had covered up the tapes.

The two HSCA investigators assigned to Beckham decided to have him undergo a polygraph test, which was administered in New Orleans in March 1978. However, it was not authorized by the HSCA, and the investigators were suspended for two weeks and then taken off Garrison's leads. Since almost everything Beckham said was a lie, the machine could detect no deviations and hence no untruths.

On May 24, 1978, Beckham was deposed by the HSCA under immunity, but his memory was missing in action. He described meeting Jack Ruby in New Orleans twice. One of those meetings supposedly included Clay Shaw, but he couldn't remember when. Beckham claimed to be a close personal friend of Lee Harvey Oswald's but couldn't remember where he lived, who he lived with, or where he worked. Beckham claimed he had pictures of himself with Oswald, but where on earth were those photographs?

A: Okay. Well, let me tell you what happened, and then you'll know. I was locked up. Well, it's of record. I was arrested and charged with a crime. So when I was in jail, I was worried about what I had, so I have my wife to take—at the time my wife's mother had married, and she still had a lease on an apartment, because she'd remarried, and they hadn't moved yet, because she had a home. So, what they did, I asked her would she take all my stuff and hide it? So she took it over to Tommy Tumberland's, and locked it in, you go downstairs, and there's a washroom, and they have little sections, that you put stuff in –

Q: Uh-huh.

A: - and they put my stuff down there. So I'm in jail during the course of this time.

Q: What year are we talking about?

A: Well, this was—I was in jail, just not too long ago.

Q: 1978?

A: Yeah, right. 1978. But it hadn't been too long ago.

Q: I think I know what you're leading up to.

A: About the—

Q: Just tell us what happened to the pictures.

A: Well, Tommy calls the police and says that someone broke into his place and takes the stuff. And he said he thought it was robbery, but it wasn't no robbery.

Beckham was then asked about the meeting in Algiers.

Q: Okay. Mr. Beckham, please relate to us an incident you have previously described regarding a meeting in the Algiers section of New Orleans.

A: Oh, that was across the bridge. It was at 197— Charlie Marullo.

Q: Let's try to pinpoint the time.

A: It was at night.

Q: Year and month.

A: I can't give you the year and month. I can only

estimate, you know, get an idea. We stopped. We went
over to Algiers. We took a right; we took a left.

Beckham then told the HSCA that "he didn't take for real" the meeting where the assassination was discussed. And as for the package which he'd delivered to Dallas, well, Beckham had mixed up the name of the recipient. They then wanted Beckham to talk about his trip to Miami to deliver cash.

Q: Was this trip—well, in relation to the trip to Dallas, was
it prior to the trip to Dallas, or after the trip to Dallas?
A: I can't put the thing together right.
Q: Well, was it prior to the assassination of President
Kennedy?
A: You mean before?
Q: Yeah.
A: Yeah.
Q: Was it much before.
A: I don't know.
Q: Well, was it a year?
A: I can't be honest with you and tell you.

He couldn't even remember who he had met with.

Q: Who did you meet with when you got to Miami?
A: Oh, Lord. I don't remember now. I can't even
think. A guy got out of the car, got the money. We stood
there. I looked over the car, and I can't think. Honest to
God, I can't. I'm trying to think of your dates, and I'm so
messed up I can't see straight.

Finally, they had had enough and decided to ask Beckham about his aliases.

Q: Have you been known as Eggelston Bryan Zimmerman?

A: That was Alabama.

Q: All right. When? That was when?

A: Let's see. That was a year or two, two years.

Q: Okay. Why did you choose that name? What was the reason?

A: I was hiding out under the names.

Q: Hiding out from whom?

A: Well, I didn't want to run into Jack, or Fred, or any of them, and I figured if I used a different name, they can't find me.

When Beckham testified before the Garrison grand jury, he said he dropped out of school in seventh grade. Turns out that wasn't quite true.

Q: What is the extent of your formal education? In other words, did you graduate from high school?

A: I went through the third grade.

Q: Third grade. And where was that?

A: That was Henry W. Allen.

Q: Henry W. Allen School?

A: Right. New Orleans, Louisiana.

Q: And you dropped out of school after the third grade?

A: That's right.

Q: Okay.

A: Of course, when you've spent three years in each grade, you're not that young when you drop out.

Beckham's lack of formal education did not stop him from receiving higher degrees.

Q: What degrees do you hold?

A: M.D. PhD, and—

Q: All right. Keep going.

A: A bunch of others. I hold a Maryland Medical License from the Maryland State Board of Medical Examiners.

Q: So then, you're a licensed physician for the State of Maryland?

A: That's right.

But wait, there's more!

Q: What other degrees do you hold?

A: I hold an Ms.D., Doctor of Metaphysics.

Q: From where?

A: I hold—oh, boy, I don't know. There's so many on my wall, you'd have to take a look and see.

Q: Where are they hanging now, at your home?

A: Yeah. Medical degrees. United American Medical College, I even got one from there, which was based at Metairie, recently—if you are familiar with the man—

which is also part of the Association. He has also
Louisiana Association of Naturopathic Physicians.

Q: Are you a Naturopathic Physician?

A: I hold an M.D.J., right. I'm a member of the
National Congress of Naturopathic Physicians, American
Coordinated Medical Society, the Georgia Association of
Naturopathic Physicians, Louisiana Association, Texas,
Indiana, Kentucky.

He then told them he was an "ordained priest of about four different Catholic denominations." Everybody laughed when he told them he had "more degrees than a thermometer."

Finally, Beckham started to talk about "The Organization," which consisted, he said, of a coterie of influential men who used their power to accomplish and obtain things desired by others. Beckham claimed that it was an IRS front and that it had been involved in the assassination for money. The whole deposition was well into la-la land.

And that was the end of Beckham's deposition and the HSCA's interest in him.

The House Select Committee on Assassinations issued its final report in 1979. It looked into the allegations concerning Kerry Thornley and found that "his statements have been corroborated and no evidence has been found to contradict him." Fred Lee Crisman died in 1975. Nonetheless, the HSCA spoke to three teachers at Rainier Union High School in Oregon who affirmed that Fred Crisman was teaching on the day JFK was assassinated. He was not one of the tramps. Thomas Beckham wasn't even mentioned.

The HSCA did say that they were "inclined to believe" that Oswald had been in Clinton with David Ferrie "if not Clay Shaw." However, they never interviewed Anne Dischler (see Chapter 9), nor did they review her notes on the witnesses. After the HSCA had acoustical "proof" of a conspiracy (later discredited by the National Academy of Sciences) and concluded that it could not rule out individual members of the Mafia or anti-Castro Cuban groups, it had an interest in tying the assassination to organized crime and anti-Castro Cubans. Ferrie, who did part-time investigative work for crime boss Carlos Marcello and who was associated with the anti-Castro cause in the early 1960s, did just that.

Underlying the entire incident was race relations; Clinton was a hotbed of KKK activity in the midst of a black voter drive. Paul Hoch wrote that "the reality was a bitter struggle marked by official and unofficial intimidation and red-baiting of the disenfranchised blacks and their white supporters. The Clinton story needs to be thought through, with that context in mind." Hoch was disappointed that "the questioning [by the HSCA] was not as critical as it should have been, perhaps subconsciously to avoid having to throw out the Oswald-Ferrie baby with the Shaw bathwater."

However, the HSCA did conclude that the criticism of Garrison for his use of questionable tactics had been fair. Robert Blakey, chief counsel of the HSCA, wrote a book called *Fatal Hour* in 1981 that said "the Garrison case was a fraud." He added that the case against Shaw was "flimsy" and that Perry Russo's testimony was "blatantly concocted."

In the late 1980s, researcher Gus Russo was working on a PBS *Frontline* special on the life of Lee Harvey Oswald. When he heard rumors about a "confession tape," he figured out that it was an interview with Thomas Beckham. He tracked him down to Louisville, Kentucky, and went to visit him.

Beckham basically acknowledged to me being what most people would call a flimflam artist—I remember he pointed to his office walls. They were filled with bogus diplomas from every major university; he was selling them and cheap trinkets, like whoopee cushions, for a living ... He told me he not only recorded but wrote three Number One hits, which he named—"From a Jack to a King" was one. When I told him that I was a former professional musician and recited the names of the real composers, he laughed and said, "Well, I can't fool you."

Beckham went on to finally find the true faith and is now a rabbi ordained through the Union of Yehudite Hebrews, although he admits they "are not one of the largest groups of the Hebrew (Jewish) Faith." He now sings under the name of Wade Hampton, the "singing Jew from the Cajun country of Louisiana."

None of Garrison's leads had panned out, but he had one last trick up his sleeve.

CHAPTER 18

ON THE TRAIL OF DELUSION

HOMOSEXUALS HAVE BEEN PORTRAYED as evil since the story of Sodom and Gomorrah. Easy prey who would not fight back, gays were often the targets of novelists and filmmakers. According to the 1995 documentary *The Celluloid Closet*, gay men were originally portrayed as "pansies" in the 1930s but were portrayed as "sexual perverts, sadists, psychopaths, and social villains" in the 1940s. The famed author Norman Mailer wrote *The Homosexual Villain* in 1954, in which he apologized for purposely making two of his characters evil homosexuals. He wrote, "I have been as guilty as any contemporary novelist in attributing unpleasant, ridiculous, or sinister connotations to the homosexual (or more accurately, bisexual) characters in my novels."

The censorship code began to be liberalized somewhat in the 1950s and 1960s, and there were fewer and fewer wicked homosexuals. Still, some authors couldn't help themselves. In 1988, the right-wing novelist Tom Clancy was profiled in a cover story in *Newsweek*. "A devout and conservative Roman Catholic, he is an unapologetic homophobe: the leaky Congressman in *The*

Cardinal of the Kremlin is gay and the female KGB agent is a lesbian."

But guess who produced a hugely popular modern-day movie about an evil homosexual conspiracy? Well, that would be none other than the leftist film director Oliver Stone. His 1991 film, *JFK*, featured Jim Garrison's ridiculous homosexual plot behind the JFK assassination. And Stone hired heartthrob Kevin Costner to play a heroic Jim Garrison and Tommy Lee Jones a villainous Clay Shaw.

JFK was nominated for eight Academy Awards, and Stone won a Golden Globe for Best Director. More than 25 million people saw *JFK,* and it grossed over $205 million. Warner Brother distributed thousands of study kits to high schools around the country. Ethical questions were pushed aside. One producer told the *New York Times* that "All these guys sit in a room, look at what a picture will cost, look at Oliver's talent and track record, look at the fact they'll get Costner and they say, 'This is a good roll of the dice for us.' All the rest really doesn't count."

It all started in 1970 when Jim Garrison published *A Heritage of Stone*, blaming the CIA for the JFK assassination. Clay Shaw didn't appear once in the book because of ongoing litigation. Ralph Schoenman, former secretary to philosopher Bertrand Russell, wrote Garrison in 1971, proposing a new strategy: "By stopping you from using the courts against Shaw, they have FREED you to put the case into a book. Now it cannot be considered sub judice or prejudicial to a trial. So, I suggest urgently that we take the offensive. Let's get out a book, hard and fast, which nails the case against Shaw that we couldn't get into the courts ... Let's put THEM on the defensive by blowing the Shaw case sky high with a muck-raking book that closes in on the company even closer."

Garrison sent the first five chapters of the book *The Execution* to his publisher, McGraw-Hill, in 1982. He wanted to launch it in November 1983 to commemorate the twentieth anniversary of the assassination, but it was quickly rejected. By 1985 Garrison renamed the book *A Farewell to Justice,* and when he told conspiracy radio host Ted Gandolfo about it, he started receiving letters from would-be purchasers.

Garrison sent back form letters claiming that the book companies were "fearful of the consequences from the federal government of publishing the full truth" about the assassination. He complained that "CIA disinformation machinery" was at work blaming organized crime and Castro for JFK's murder and that there were "many 'authors' who serve as willing prostitutes for the Agency's disinformation operation." Paul Hoch commented on Garrison's letter in his *Echoes of Conspiracy* newsletter in February 1986, noting that a new book, Henry Hurt's *Reasonable Doubt,* discussed the "vulnerability of Clay Shaw due to his apparently irrelevant CIA links and homosexuality." Ted Gandolfo sent a copy to Garrison, who then angrily replied.

Court of Appeal

FOURTH CIRCUIT
STATE OF LOUISIANA
210 CIVIL COURTS BUILDING
421 LOYOLA AVENUE
NEW ORLEANS, LOUISIANA 70112

WILLIAM V REDMANN
CHIEF JUDGE

JAMES C. GULOTTA
PATRICK M SCHOTT
JIM GARRISON
DENIS A. BARRY
ROBERT J. KLEES
WILLIAM H. BYRNES III
PHILIP C. CIACCIO
ROBERT L. LOBRANO
CHARLES R WARD
DAVID R M WILLIAMS
JOAN BERNARD ARMSTRONG
JUDGES

DANIELLE A. SCHOTT
CLERK OF COURT

April 14, 1986

Mr. Ted Gandolfo
1214 First Avenue
New York, New York 10021

Dear Ted:

Thank you for your letter of April 9th, enclosing part of Paul Hoch's recent newsletter.

I have nothing to say concerning his comments about me. Frankly, I found them to be incoherent.

I cannot guess as to the origin of his emotional hang up about me. In any case, I will not attempt to reply to him in a similar vein. I have read some of his research on President Kennedy's assassination and have found it to be quite competent. Moreover -- in view of the solid front presented by the federal government in its cover-up of the assassination -- it seems to me childlike for one assassination critic to attempt to dis-credit another publicly.

One statement of Hoch's, however, does concern me enough to require a comment. He refers to the "vulnerability of Clay Shaw due to his apparently irrelevant C.I.A. links and homosexuality." Mr. Hoch should go straight to the bathroom and wash his mouth with soap.

Throughout our trial, in everything I have ever written and in every public statement I have ever made -- I never once have made any reference to Clay Shaw's alleged homosexuality. What sort of human being is Mr. Hoch that he is impelled to so gratuitously make such a reference in a newsletter which he widely distributes to the public? For all his faults or virtues, Shaw is dead and unable to defend himself from that kind of off the wall canard. No matter how virtuously Hoch might couch it, a smear is still a smear.

Sincerely,

Jim Garrison

1525 Acton St.
Berkeley, CA 94702
July 8, 1986

Judge Jim Garrison
Court of Appeal
210 Civil Courts Building
421 Loyola Avenue
New Orleans, LA 70112

Dear Mr. Garrison:

Ted Gandolfo sent me a copy of your letter to him dated April 14.

I am not quite ready to wash my mouth out with soap, as you suggested.
In this part of the country, a reference to someone's homosexuality ceased
being an "off the wall canard" years ago. At the very least, it is not as
much of a canard as accusing someone of involvement in the assassination of
President Kennedy.

Calling Tony Summers "one of the [CIA's] more accommodating prostitutes"
does, however, sound like a canard to me.

I regret that you found most of the comments about you in my newsletter
"incoherent." Among other things, I offered my $64 question about you: at
the time you arrested Clay Shaw, what serious evidence did you have that he
had in fact conspired with anyone to kill JFK?

None of your many supporters in the critical community have yet provided
me with a good answer. Perhaps you would like to give it a try.

Let me clarify:

The question is about evidence known to you when you decided to arrest
and charge Shaw, not evidence which was developed later.

I am not asking about evidence that Shaw knew Ferrie, that he had been
involved with the CIA, that he used an alias, or even that he had met Oswald.
Nor am I asking about evidence that there was a conspiracy to kill Kennedy,
or that Oswald, Ferrie, and/or the CIA were involved. I am well aware of the
evidence relating to those questions. My question is not even about any
anti-Kennedy opinions or fantasies expressed by Shaw, but about his participation in a criminal conspiracy.

I would be glad to publicize any answer you care to provide.

Sincerely yours,

Paul L. Hoch

Paul L. Hoch

Court of Appeal

FOURTH CIRCUIT
STATE OF LOUISIANA

210 CIVIL COURTS BUILDING
421 LOYOLA AVENUE
NEW ORLEANS LOUISIANA 70112

WILLIAM V. REDMANN
CHIEF JUDGE

JAMES C. GULOTTA
PATRICK M. SCHOTT
JIM GARRISON
DENIS A. BARRY
ROBERT J. KLEES
WILLIAM H. BYRNES III
PHILIP C. CIACCIO
ROBERT L. LOBRANO
CHARLES R. WARD
DAVID R. M. WILLIAMS
JOAN BERNARD ARMSTRONG
JUDGES

DANIELLE A. SCHOTT
CLERK OF COURT

August 8, 1986

Mr. Ted Gandolfo
1214 First Avenue
New York, New York 10021

Dear Ted:

Recently I received a rather strident letter from Mr. Paul Hoch criticizing judgments made by me when I was District Attorney of New Orleans back in the 1960's. I was not aware that Mr. Hoch has had any experience in criminal prosecutions. It has been my policy not to reply to gratuitous critiques of my former office when made by individuals with neither the standing nor the professional experience to make such criticisms.

However, inasmuch as it is not a personal letter - to say the least - and inasmuch as the nature of Mr. Hoch's assault points out a problem which should concern every assassination critic, I pass it on to you. Whether you think it is deserving of reproduction I leave up to you. Because this is 1986 and the forces which killed John Kennedy still remain firmly in control, I personally cannot get too excited about such remote problems as, for example, the pedantic question of how many angels could dance on the head of a pin a number of years ago.

Mr. Hoch has a finely tuned aggression and is wonderfully ferocious. His aggression might be more useful, however, if it were directed not against another critic but against the common foe of us all: the War Machine and its defenders.

The unfortunate thing about the position which Mr. Hoch has taken - attacking a critic who for 17 years has been attempting to point out the culpability of the C.I.A. in the assassination - is that some people who do not know any better might draw the conclusion that his sympathies are really with the Agency.

Regards,

Jim Garrison

Enclosure: Letter from Mr. Paul Hoch

After the letter exchange, Hoch wrote, "Does Garrison now think Shaw was involved in the conspiracy which led to JFK's death? If so, the reference to 'all his faults or virtues' is remarkably mild."

Fred Crisman still played a major role in Garrison's 'conspiracy,' but Garrison needed more information to "complete his book." He wrote researcher Fred Newcombe asking him to hire an investigator who could fill some gaps for him. He wanted to know more about Crisman's ranches and their ownership.

Garrison was not happy with how the HSCA treated his material on Crisman.

```
        As you may know, the House Sub-Committee on
Assassinations developed a spontaneous case of allergy when I
laid the material concerning PC in its collective lap.  The House
Committee - without hearing any sworn testimony from anyone -
simply announced unilaterally in the course of its report that FC
was dead.  It did not mention where, when nor under what
circumstances he died.  It also made a point of misspelling his
name consistently, never once spelling it correctly (which would
greatly impede any search for a record of his death even if one
knew in what county to search).
```

Newcombe asked Larry Haapanen, who had done some investigating in Washington state, to reply. He told Garrison that Crisman was not one of the tramps, that his name was not in Clay Shaw's notebook, and that he was not "an industrial spy" for Boeing. Haapanen wrote that "I'm very doubtful that FC had anything to do with JFK's assassination." He then called Garrison on the phone, who insisted that it was suspicious that Crisman lived fifteen miles from Larry Crafard (who Garrison had told journalist Ron Rosenbaum was on the knoll shooting at Kennedy). Propinquity was always on his mind. Haapanen then fired off another letter to Garrison warning that "including suspicions about Fred Crisman will only serve to weaken the book rather than strengthen it."

Garrison finally hit pay dirt with Prentice Hall Press in 1986 for his newly titled book, *Coup D'état*. He received a $10,000 advance and submitted his manuscript in November. Warren Commission critic Sylvia Meagher served as referee, and she submitted a twenty-six-page analysis, which noted several problems.

Meagher was irked by Garrison's notion that there was something sinister about some people moving from their employment at Reily Coffee (where Oswald had greased the machines for two months) to the aerospace industry. She wondered if "they were perhaps put on the shuttle and dumped into outer space, so that they could never testify to how poorly Oswald aimed his oil can."

She was also not happy with the discussion of Shaw, Ferrie, Banister, Bundy, and Russo, the characters from New Orleans. Meagher noted that "it depends upon identification and allegations elicited years after the fact. Very little value should be attached to material offered by witnesses - and especially identifications—long after the event. The Russo allegations have been largely discredited." Meagher found the chapters dealing with these people to be "dizzying, full of scattershot, and probably irrelevant."

Meagher also disputed Garrison's allegation that the Dallas motorcade route had been changed. Returning to the original testimony of Secret Service agent Forrest Sorrels, she found that Garrison, by quoting that testimony out of context, had "completely distorted and misrepresented the real meaning" of his testimony.

Despite her misgivings, she still recommended that the book be published because Garrison was now claiming that Oswald was totally innocent—a position she had held for many years—as opposed to the Shaw trial, in which Oswald was named as a conspirator.

Philip Pochoda, the publisher of Prentice Hall, wrote to Garrison in January 1987 and said that two "insuperable problems made any attempt at rewriting useless for our purposes." Pochoda agreed with Meagher that Garrison had misrepresented the evidence on the motorcade. He wrote to me in 2020 and said that "it was far too big a blunder to allow into a Simon & Schuster book, much less a manuscript by the person who should have at least known that to be false."

The bigger problem was that Garrison had promised that he "would specify an actual CIA hand in and during the assassination itself: the cut-out agent, Fred Lee Crisman." But Pochoda found that "the Crisman material was much too flimsy to permit inclusion in the book." Thus "without the 'smoking gun' I do not think anybody who doesn't now believe in CIA coordination and involvement will be persuaded by your text." As such, "the evidence you present is really to be found in all the well-known books on the conspiracy." The result is that "what we now have is polemics grappling for confirmation, and a manuscript that is unpublishable." Garrison was told to return his advance. He should have taken Haapanen's advice to take Crisman out of the book.

Garrison replied to Pochoda that the other conspiracy books blame either the mob or Castro, which was, as he put it, "the essential government line as disseminated by the disinformation machinery of our intelligence community." Shortly afterward, he complained in another letter that "my last waltz with an Agency asset has delayed its publication at least another year."

In April 1987, Sheridan Square Publications agreed to publish Garrison's work. This was a good fit as owners Ellen Ray and William Schaap, along with ex-CIA agent Philip Agee, had been involved in *CovertAction Information Bulletin*, a newsletter that documented illegal CIA activities and identified thousands of CIA agents by name.

The Mitrokhin Archive claims that *CovertAction* was founded "on the initiative of the KGB," although there is "no evidence in Mitrokhin's notes that any member of the group running it was conscious of the role" of the KGB, apart from Agee. The first issue of *CovertAction* was launched in Cuba in 1978, and the KGB "assembled a task force ... to keep *Covert Action Information Bulletin* supplied with material designed to compromise the CIA."

Zachary Sklar was named as the new editor of Garrison's book, and he promptly turned it into a first-person narrative. *On the Trail of the Assassins: My Investigation and Prosecution of the Murder of President Kennedy* was published in 1988, and Garrison laid out the same nonexistent case against Clay Shaw.

All of a sudden, many of Garrison's suspects just vanished. Fred Crisman, an important figure in his manuscript submitted to

Prentice Hall, simply disappeared. Thomas Beckham, subject of a long Garrison memo to the HSCA, was left out. The assassin behind the billboard, Manuel Garcia Gonzalez, vanished. Slidin' Clyde Johnson's story of Shaw meeting Ruby just didn't make the cut. There was a nary a mention of Garrison's intent to indict Robert Perrin as a grassy knoll assassin nor the subsequent staff revolt that led to Bill Boxley's "unmasking" as a CIA plant. Garrison's prosecution of Edgar Eugene Bradley as a conspirator didn't get a word. The shot from the sewer—forget about it. And his initial belief in a homosexual thrill killing and an S&M plot—poof, gone into thin air. The Great Accuser was reduced to a shadow of his former self.

What did make the book was a lot of self-pity. He complained that his case had failed because of sabotage by the CIA and other agencies and that he had been infiltrated by a series of people disrupting his investigation from within. As for his star witness, Charles Spiesel, who claimed to have been hypnotized many times over sixteen years, Garrison wrote that the "clandestine operation of the opposition was so cynical, so sophisticated and, at the same time, so subtle, that destroying an old-fashioned state jury trial was very much like shooting in a barrel with a shotgun." In other words, don't blame me.

Garrison included a long list of discredited witnesses and a ton of conspiracy factoids about the case. He now claimed he had heard about Permindex and Shaw's supposed connection with the CIA after the Shaw trial, which was patently untrue. Had he heard about it before, he said, he would have used it. The three tramps made the book: Kerry Thornley was still the Second Oswald, witnesses were still dying mysteriously, the actual killers were protected by the Dallas police, and—of course—the main post office building in New Orleans was a still central meeting place for CIA agents.

He even asserted that he had rejected the idea of giving a lie detector test to Perry Russo when, in fact, Russo was sent twice for a polygraph. And Garrison stubbornly continued with his nonsense about the motorcade route being changed. Paul Hoch wrote this "seems to be typical of the carelessness of his analysis, and of his tendency to obfuscate real issues."

Rosemary James, a reporter for the New Orleans *States-Item*, called his memoir "a great piece of fiction." She clearly wasn't impressed, but guess who was? Yup, Oliver Stone, who felt "it read like a Dashiell Hammett whodunit." And Garrison was "somewhat like a Jimmy Stewart character in an old Capra movie." After reading it three times, he purchased the movie rights for $250,000.

Stone then hired Garrison's editor, Zachary Sklar, to write the screenplay. He also licensed *Crossfire: The Plot That Killed Kennedy* from Jim Marrs, a loony author who would go on to publish such titles as *Our Occulted History: Do The Global Elite Conceal Ancient Aliens?*; *Rule by Secrecy: The Hidden History that Connects the Trilateral Commission, the Freemasons, and the Great Pyramids*; *The Trillion-Dollar Conspiracy: How the New World Order, Man-Made Diseases, and Zombie Banks are Destroying America*; and *The Rise of the Fourth Reich: The Secret Societies that Threaten to Take Over America*.

Stone believed that Garrison had tried to "force a break in the case" and that he was a man out for the truth willing to take on the CIA, the military-industrial complex, and the national security infrastructure. It was "worth the sacrifice of one man," so Stone kept Clay Shaw as the evil gay mastermind along with his band of conspiring homosexuals.

In the early part of his film *JFK*, Garrison has dinner with Dean Andrews, who paints Lee Harvey Oswald as a homosexual.

Garrison: You ever speak to Oswald in Dallas?
Andrews: Hell no. Like, I told that Bertrand cat right

off this ain't my scene, man. I deal in muni court. I'm a
hack. He needs a hot dog.

Garrison: Then how did you get in the Warren
Commission?

Andrews: Like I told to the Washington boys, Bertrand
called that summer and asked me to help the kid upgrade
his Marine discharge. There was no conspiracy, Jim. If
there were, why didn't Bobby Kennedy prosecute as
attorney general? He was his brother, for Christ sake. How
the fuck all these people can keep a secret like that, I don't
know. It was Oswald, he was a fruitcake. He hated this
country.

The scenes from *JFK* in this book are all transcribed directly
from the film, not from the official screenplay, which is far more
homophobic. For instance, in the above scene, the screenplay uses
the word "faggot" instead of "fruitcake."

Perry Russo, the main witness against Clay Shaw, is trans-
formed in *JFK* into a homosexual prostitute, Willie O'Keefe,[1]
who talks to Garrison while in prison. He tells Garrison about a
party at Ferrie's apartment in the summer of 1963 with Ferrie,
O'Keefe, Bertrand, Oswald, and two Cubans.

O'Keefe (voiceover): Dave pulled out some clippings that
he'd been carrying around. He'd been obsessed with Castro
and Kennedy for months. He started in again.

Ferrie: Little ass-wipe closed down the camps! Took all
our C-4! Took 10,000 rounds! 3,000 pounds of
gunpowder! All our fucking weapons! Shit, you want to
free Cuba? You gotta whack out the fucking beard!

First Cuban: Kennedy won't let us. Our hands are
empty. How can we kill him?

Bertrand: Problem is getting to him. Castro has informers on every block.

Ferrie: Bullshit. They got new stuff! I could show you dozens of fucking poisons! Just stick it in his food, he'd die in three days. No trace! Put something in his beard, make his beard fall out. He'd look ridiculous ...

Second Cuban: Fucking Kennedy is doing all kinds of deals with that bastard Khrushchev. Licking his ass (in Spanish). An inspired act of God should happen here and put a Texan in the White House!

O'Keefe (voiceover): Then, the Cubans left. Dave was drunk. Now, really drunk. He started in on Kennedy again.

Ferrie: I will kill! Right in the White House! Stab him in the heart! Somebody got get rid of this fucker!

O'Keefe: C'mon Dave, ain't nobody going to get that son of a bitch!

Ferrie: It won't be long. Mark my words. That fucker will get what is coming to him. It could be blamed on Castro; the country will want to invade Cuba. All we got to do is get Kennedy out in the open.

Bertrand [who is Clay Shaw]: David, David, David. Always some harebrained scheme. [Bertrand looks down at his crotch and sees an erection.] What have we here? Let's have some more champagne, shall we?

O'Keefe: What about the Secret Service? The cops?

Ferrie: If it's planned right, no problem. Look how close they got to De Gaulle. Eisenhower was always riding in an open top. We need three mechanics in three different locations. An office building, with a high-powered rifle. Triangulation of crossfire, that's the key. That's the key. A diversionary shot gets the Secret Service looking the other way. Boom! Get the kill shot. Crucial thing is that one man has to be sacrificed. Then, in the commotion of the crowd, the job gets done. The others fly out of the country, somewhere with no extradition ...

Bertrand: Why don't we drop this subject? It's one thing to engage in badinage [banter] with these youngsters ... but this sort of thing could be so easily misunderstood.

O'Keefe (voiceover): I didn't think much about it at the time. It's just bullshit. You know everybody likes to act more important than they are. Especially in the homosexual underworld. But when they got him (merging to the present) ... man ... I got scared. Real scared. That's when I got popped.

There's the conspiracy, hatched by the "homosexual underworld." Soon afterward, O'Keefe goes to Clay Shaw's house for dinner, Ferrie stops by, they change into costumes, consume some cocaine, and then engage in an orgy with light S&M. This is all a complete Oliver Stone invention.

We see the four men in drag, smiling for the flash camera, champagne bottles in hand. Ferrie sniffs some poppers, then shoves a popper in Shaw's face.

FERRIE: You're mine, Mary. You're mine.

Ferrie forces more poppers on Shaw. The camera moves to Shaw's bedroom, where Ferrie seems to have Shaw in chains.

Ferrie grabs Shaw by his hair: The only way you get this is do what I say. Go on, big boy. You want it.

In another scene, Garrison puts up a distraught David Ferrie in a hotel, and Stone makes up some more incredible dialogue.

Ferrie: I haven't slept since that shit article came out. Why'd you guys have to get me involved, Lou?

Lou: Did we get you involved? Or did Shaw, Dave?

Ferrie: Cocksucking faggot. He got me by the balls.

Lou: What do you mean?

Ferrie: Photographs, compromising stuff. He'll use them, too. Agency plays for keeps. I knew Oswald. He was in my Civil Air Patrol unit. I taught him everything. He was a wannabe, you know. No one really liked him. Thought he was a snitch. But I treated him good. He talked about his kid. He really wanted ... to grow up with a chance. But, what's this? What's going on?

The notes to *JFK: The Documented Screenplay* admit that "At times, however, we had to put words in Ferrie's mouth to write the scene." So now we have Shaw blackmailing Ferrie through the use of photographs and other compromising material. This scene places Shaw, the slave at Ferrie's orgy, as the ringleader of the homosexual cabal.

David Ehrenstein, writing in the *Advocate*, a popular gay magazine, called *JFK* "the most homophobic movie ever to come out of Hollywood." He wrote, "Forget about bullet trajectories and smoke seen coming from the grassy knoll. All Stone has to do is show a sinister Jones [actor Tommy Lee Jones] groping sleazy tootsie Bacon [O'Keefe in the film] and simpering and behaving haughtily toward true-blue Costner [Garrison] and you know who 'really' killed Kennedy." An opinion piece in the *New York Times* added that "Shaw's homosexuality is meant to signify nothing except the fact that he's sinister and capable of murder. The inclusion of the orgy scene is gratuitous. Mr. Stone might as well have shown Jack Ruby bargaining with other Jews in the back row at temple."

Oliver Stone's *JFK*—Pinko Homos Iced the Prez?

THE ADVOCATE

$3.50
$4.50 CAN.
$3.50 U.K.
11.50 NETH.

JANUARY 14, 1992 • THE NATIONAL GAY AND LESBIAN NEWSMAGAZINE • ISSUE 594

An amazing cutline, but slightly wrong: they weren't pinkos.

Stone replied that "the characters of Shaw, Ferrie, and the composite character Willie O'Keefe were historically gay. You cannot be—at the same time, politically correct and a historical revisionist. They were gay, and they were involved in this conspiracy." The Gay & Lesbian Alliance for Defamation disagreed. "Even supposing these men were conspirators, the lurid depiction of their gayness, to augment Stone's portrait of evil, is purely homophobic."

It's almost like Stone had no choice in the matter.

LOS ANGELES TIMES

Gay Rights Activists Protest 'JFK'

■ Movies: One organizaton dubbed the Oliver Stone film 'as homophobic as films get.'

By ANDY MARX
SPECIAL TO THE TIMES

Los Angeles Times, *December 6, 1991.*

But Stone had bigger fish to fry than just a bunch of homosexuals plotting to kill a president, so *JFK* introduced a former military man, X. In the film, Garrison meets him in Washington, and X reveals why Kennedy was killed. "The organizing principle of any society is for war," he tells Garrison, and Kennedy had to be killed because he was going to violate that tenet by pulling troops out of Vietnam and ending the Cold War. Also, X claimed that the 112th Military Intelligence Group (MIG) at Fort Sam Houston was ordered to "stand down" on Kennedy's protection in Dallas and that standard security procedures were violated on November 22.

All of this was pure fabrication.

Kennedy did have plans to remove a thousand troops by the end of 1963, but it was contingent on progress training the South Vietnamese Army. National Security Action Memorandum (NSAM) #273, signed by Lyndon Johnson a few days after the assassination, said that "The objectives of the United States with respect to the withdrawal of U. S. military personnel remain as stated in the White House statement of October 2, 1963." Stanley Karnow, one of the most respected historians on the Vietnam War, wrote that NSAM #273 "perpetuated the Kennedy policy."

In September 1963, Kennedy told CBS reporter Walter Cronkite that "I don't agree with those who say we should withdraw," and he told NBC's Chet Huntley that "we are not there to see a war lost." In the speech he was supposed to give in Dallas, Kennedy was going to say that Vietnam was going to be "painful, risky and costly ... but we dare not weary of the task," adding that "reducing our efforts to train, equip and assist [the allied] armies can only encourage Communist penetration and require in the time the increased overseas deployment of American combat forces." Robert Kennedy also confirmed in an oral history interview in April 1964 that JFK never contemplated pulling out of Vietnam. George Lardner, a reporter for the *Washington Post*, wrote to Harold Weisberg and said that historian William Gibbons had told him that Secretary of Defense Robert McNamara frequently mentioned the possibility of withdrawal to the generals as a way of preempting possible requests for more troops.

This is not to say that Kennedy would have sent half a million ground troops to Vietnam. We just don't know what he would have done in the same circumstances as Lyndon Johnson. It's a left-wing myth that Kennedy wanted to end the Cold War. His planned speech for Austin, Texas, bragged about increases in the military budget.

> *"In the past three years we have increased our defense budget by over 20 percent; increased the program for acquisition of Polaris submarines from 25 to 41; increased our Minuteman missile purchase program by more than 75 percent; doubled the number of strategic bombers and missiles on alert; doubled the number of nuclear weapons available in the strategic alert forces; increased the tactical nuclear forces deployed in Western Europe by 60 percent; added 5 combat ready divisions and 5 tactical fighter wings to our Armed Forces; increased our strategic airlift capabilities by 75 percent, and increased our special counter-insurgency forces by 600 percent."*

Historian Michael Beschloss said Kennedy had initiated "the largest peacetime defense buildup since 1945" and had overseen more "covert action than by any president since the CIA was founded." Kennedy was a Cold Warrior through and through.

So where did Stone get all this nonsense? X was based upon Colonel L. Fletcher Prouty, who worked in the Pentagon's Office of Special Operations before retiring in December 1963.

Prouty's claim about the Military Intelligence Group (MIG) standing down came from a phone call he supposedly made to the commander of the 316th Field Detachment of the 112th MIG. When questioned about this in 1996, he claimed that he was the one who had been called and that not only did he not personally know the caller, he had no recollection of the caller's name. He was unable to name any members of the 112th team, then he admitted, "You know, that phone call has troubled me for a long time. I'm not sure that guy was even authentic."

The commander of the 316th Intelligence Corps Group (the proper name of the group), Colonel Rudolph Reich, said that his unit was not "specially trained" in presidential protection and that neither the 316th or the 112th ever undertook missions of that sort. He thought Prouty had been "smoking something," and he was so incensed that he wrote a letter to the chief of staff of Army Intelligence Support Command asking whether "he could take some sort of legal action against Prouty."

And the regular Secret Service contingent, assigned to protect Kennedy, followed standard operating procedures. Keep in mind that presidential protection was far laxer in the early 1960s than it is today. Prouty's personal knowledge of presidential protection came "entirely from an incident in 1955 when he piloted an aircraft to Mexico City carrying equipment for the Secret Service advance team prior to a trip there by President Eisenhower." He admitted in 1996 that he had "no idea how they [the Secret Service] run their business."

Prouty had a history of crackpot relationships: he consulted for the cult-like Lyndon LaRouche organization, he advised the lawyers working for the Church of Scientology, and he was a speaker at the 1990 Convention of the Liberty Lobby, a far-right organization whose founder, Willis Carto, believed that the Jews were "public enemy number one." Prouty not only appeared on their radio program Radio Free America ten times, he was also an advisory board member of their Populist Action Committee, which had been formed to support a variety of bigoted candidates for public office.

The Institute for Historical Review, a Carto organization that denied the Holocaust, republished Prouty's 1973 book, *The Secret Team: The CIA and Its Allies in Control of the United States and the World* in 1991. According to Edward Jay Epstein, a long-time JFK researcher, "When the Liberty Lobby held its annual Board of Policy convention in 1991, he [Prouty] presented a special seminar, 'Who is the Enemy?' which blamed the high price of oil on a systematic plot of a cabal to shut down oil pipelines deliberately in the Middle East. 'Why?' he asked and explained to the seminar: 'Because of the Israelis. That is their business on behalf of the oil companies. That's why they get $3 billion a year from the U.S. taxpayer.'" In a private letter, Prouty elaborated and said that "major pipelines from Saudi Arabia, Kuwait, Iraq and others are dry because of Israeli threats and unrest."

None of this mattered to Oliver Stone. Robert San Anson wrote a history of the making of the film in *Esquire* magazine, and he recounts that when Prouty was asked about Carto's belief that the Holocaust never happened, he replied that "I'm no authority in that area." He quotes a Stone assistant saying, "If this gets out, Oliver is going to look like the biggest dope of all time." In July 1991, Jane Rusconi, Stone's research assistant, wrote him a memo that said, "Basically, there's no way Fletcher could be unaware of the unsavory aspects of the Liberty Lobby. The Anti-Defamation Leagues keeps a close watch on the Liberty Lobby and are very aware of Fletcher's involvement. It could come back to haunt us if we don't find a way to deal with this."

Stone repeatedly excused Prouty, noting in one forum that "he never made any single one anti-semitic comment" and that "he joined the Liberty Lobby late in life." And while it's true that Prouty was careful with overt statements about Jews, I did manage to find this letter in Richard Sprague's archive in the National Archives. For once, Prouty let his guard down.

The newest and best F-15 goes so fast a human pilot can not sight an enemy and fire his rockets (air to air rockets) in combat. So his fire control system is wired to a computer. The terminal is in his plane. Then he is in contact with the AWACS where there is a big radar and a much bigger piece of the computer. But this is not enough. The AWACS goes to a space satellite and from the satellite back to a massive computer in Southern California. Here the data is rapidly analyzed and instructions sent back to the satellite, then back to AWACS, then over to the F-15's terminal and into the fire control system, to the rocket and when all is lined up...there she goes.

But what about that computer in California? Suppose the guy running it is a Jewish Sgt.? Warfare has become so very complex the whole thing does not make sense anymore. One good bomb fired at that computer might could put all US fighter planes out of action without hitting a one of them.etc.

Excerpt of a letter from Prouty to Charles, dated April 30, 1981, that discusses the problems of military technology. Note the last paragraph: "Suppose the guy running it is a Jewish Sgt.?"

And who do you think introduced Prouty to Oliver Stone? None other than Jim Garrison. In July 1990, Garrison called Prouty and asked him to speak to Stone. As Prouty related it, "A few minutes later, the phone rang and Oliver Stone was telling me he was planning a movie utilizing Garrison's book." Prouty went to Washington one week later to meet Stone, and their relationship blossomed.

The biggest laugh is that Prouty's knowledge about the so-called "organizing principle" of society came from a study that was supposedly suppressed by the Kennedy administration. The Iron Mountain Group report wondered if the U.S. could survive "if and when a condition of permanent peace should arise?" But the report was a complete hoax; it was a spoof written by satirist Leonard Lewin in 1967. Victor Navasky, who went on to become editor of *The Nation*, persuaded the publisher to put it on the nonfiction lists. It certainly fooled a lot of people, but Prouty should have known better. Lewin admitted to the hoax in the *New York Times Book Review* in 1972, where he said his intention "was simply to pose the issues of war and peace in a provocative way."

Prouty's 1992 book, *The CIA, Vietnam, and the Plot to Assassinate John F. Kennedy* (first serialized in *Freedom* magazine, a Church of Scientology publication), refers to the Iron Mountain Group Report over ten times and claims it originated with "an organization whose existence was so highly classified that there is no record, to this day, of [who] the men in the group were or with what sectors of the government or private life they were connected."

It was one thing for Prouty to fall for this nonsense, but Oliver Stone?

Stone wrote the Introduction to Prouty's book. He said the Iron Mountain Report asked "the key question of our time," and Stone accepted the myth that it was "commissioned by Defense Secretary Robert McNamara in August 1963 to justify the big, planned changes in defense spending contemplated by Kennedy." Stone was impressed that "Colonel Prouty points once again to the infusion of Nazi personnel, methods, and ultimately a Nazi frame of mind into the American system." Stone surmised that "If Mr. Hitler had won the Second World War, the version of events now given to us (invasion of Third World lower slave races for mineral-resource conquest and world-round economic-military power) would not be too far off the mark. But instead of Nazi jackboots, we have men in gray suits and ties with attaché cases."

Prouty and Stone went even further with this nonsense. In *JFK*, X talks about his boss General Y, and you briefly see his desk nameplate that reads "M/GEN. E.G." This was Major General Edward Geary Lansdale, whom Prouty believed was one of the organizers of the plot. He went even further, claiming that Lansdale had been in Dealey Plaza on the day of President Kennedy's assassination. Prouty identified him in one of the tramp photos (see below), writing that Lansdale "planned and managed the entire scenario in Dallas" and "masterminded the enormous cover-up."

Prouty had it all wrong.[2] Lansdale was an advocate of a "hearts and minds" approach to counterinsurgency. As Max Boot notes in his 2018 biography of Lansdale, had JFK wanted to reduce troop presence in Vietnam, he "would hardly have objected. He was a critic, not an advocate of the Americanization of the Vietnam War." Lansdale himself wrote that Prouty "had such a heavy dose of paranoia about CIA when he was on my staff that I kicked him back to the Air Force. He was one of those who thought I was secretly running the Agency from the Pentagon, despite all the proof otherwise."

Prouty claimed that the man with his back to us was Major General Edward Lansdale and that the policemen were fake. He wrote to Harold Weisberg and said that the middle tramp "has the trace of a smile on his face. He had just made contact" with the man who was supposed to be Lansdale and had been "reassured." In a letter to Richard Sprague over a decade earlier, Prouty said he was unsure if Lansdale was in the picture, asking "Do you know who he is … or who is supposed to be?" CREDIT: UTA Libraries - FORT WORTH STAR-TELEGRAM COLLECTION.

And if anybody is looking for more craziness about Prouty,

consider that he believed "the Churchill gang" had murdered FDR; he said that he had personally seen a UFO; he wrote that he wouldn't be surprised if the death of Diana, Princess of Wales, was a "Secret Team" operation; he thought that the Jonestown massacre was a plot by the Joint Chiefs of Staff; and he endorsed the ridiculous theory that a bystander at the motorcade holding an umbrella had fired a flechette into Kennedy. Patricia Lambert wrote that Prouty was "another psychologically crippled person that Stone has snatched from well-deserved obscurity and foisted on the American public."

Stone ended *JFK* with two more insinuations about Clay Shaw, whose character had been relentlessly impugned during both his life and in death. The film closed with a note: "In 1979, RICHARD HELMS, Director of Covert Operations in 1963, admitted under oath that CLAY SHAW had worked for the CIA." Shaw did have a relationship with the CIA, but it was as an unpaid domestic contact who reported what he saw on various foreign trips from 1949–1956. All his reports were on international trade. Stone also added that "CLAY SHAW died in 1974 of lung cancer. No autopsy was allowed." This makes it sound suspicious, but the New Orleans police department investigated his death and found that "no evidence has been found to indicate that Mr. Shaw's death was anything but natural." He didn't need an autopsy because his attending physician had been present quite often in the week while his health seriously deteriorated.

There was a massively negative response by critics and others to *JFK*.

Columnist George Will wrote that "Stone falsifies so much he may be an intellectual sociopath, indifferent to truth," and that *JFK* is "an act of execrable history and contemptible citizenship by a man of technical skill and negligible conscience." *Washington Post* reporter George Lardner, the last person to see David Ferrie alive, called the film "Dallas in Wonderland."

Stone spent most of 1991 and 1992 battling *JFK*'s critics. He wrote letters and op-eds and was forced to dive into the minutia of the assassination. It irritated him that people wanted to talk about magical bullets, the backward head snap, and Clay Shaw but not Vietnam. And so, when 9/11 occurred, Stone avoided the truthers. He was far more interested in talking about the results of 9/11, like the Iraq War. Still, he couldn't help but say stupid things. The following discussion took place in October 2001 on "the role of filmmaking in the national debate:"

Stone: There's been conglomeration under six principal princes—they're kings, they're barons! And these six companies have control of the world. Michael Eisner decides, "I can't make a movie about Martin Luther King, Jr.—they'll be rioting at the gates of Disneyland!" That's bullshit! But, that's what the new world order is. They control culture, they control ideas. And I think the revolt of September 11th was about 'Fuck You! Fuck your order —"

Christopher Hitchens: Excuse me, revolt?
Stone: Whatever you want to call it.
Christopher Hitchens: It was state-supported mass murder [by Islamists], using civilians as missiles.

Stone completely lost it in 2010 when he told the *Sunday Times* that Jewish control of the media was preventing an open discussion of the Holocaust and that an upcoming film of his would put Hitler and Stalin in context. To Stone, "Israel had 'f***** up American foreign policy" for years. He apologized for his "clumsy association" about the Holocaust but told the *New York Times* that "I had to apologize because I should not have used the word 'Jewish.' That was the only thing that's frankly wrong in that statement. I was upset at the time about Israel and their control, their seeming control over American foreign policy. It's clear that Jews do not dominate the media ... but certainly AIPAC [American Israel Public Affairs Committee] has an undue influence. They were very much militating for the war in Iraq. They got it."

And he has gone on to kookier and kookier projects, combining his postmodern leftism, his conspiracy groupthink, and his love for dictators. In 2003, he made a fawning documentary, *Commandante*, about Cuban dictator Fidel Castro; in 2012, it was Hugo Chavez's turn with *South of the Border* and once again in 2014 with *Mi Amigo Hugo*; in 2015 he made a film about Ukraine that blamed the CIA for the Maidan protests; and in 2017 he released a four-part laudatory series of interviews with Vladimir Putin.

The hits kept coming. In July 2019, Stone floated the idea of making Putin the godfather of his twenty-two-year-old daughter. Even Putin was taken aback, asking Stone if she wanted to convert to Orthodox Christianity. It was not an issue for Stone, but Putin demurred, saying that perhaps she should be consulted. He then told Putin that "it seems like maybe that's a sensible law" referring to the 2013 Russian law outlawing homosexual propaganda. In October 2019, Stone said that Putin was a "stabilizing force" in Syria, and a few months later he gave an interview to the Russian propaganda arm RT in which he said, "Empires fall, let's pray that this empire [the United States], these evil things ... because we are the evil empire. What Reagan said about Russia is true about us."

One good thing did come out of *JFK*, and that was the creation of the Assassination Records Review Board (ARRB), which declassified thousands and thousands of documents. Anna Nelson, professor of diplomatic history at American University and board member of the ARRB, said that "Jim Garrison had no case. And that it was a show trial." This was not only her personal view. She said all the board members agreed.

> *"And especially when the review board members read parts of Clay Shaw's diary, we were even more convinced that a great misuse of justice, had been carried out by Garrison's wanting to make the headlines, or for whatever reason that he prosecuted Clay Shaw."*

Thanks to the ARRB, we now know a lot more about Garrison's scam prosecution.

A decade later, one of the ARRB's analysts, Douglas Horne, wrote a five-volume work charging that the Zapruder film, as well as the autopsy x-rays and photographs, were altered. Oliver Stone was more than receptive.

Stone seemed to be unaware that in 1996, the ARRB had hired Roland Zavada, an engineer at Eastman-Kodak, to authenticate the Zapruder Film. His 150-page report was quite clear: the

Zapruder film in the National Archives is the original film, and it has not been modified.

Few people know it, but a member of the "team" that supposedly killed JFK confessed to Oliver Stone. A dying man reached out to him in 1993 and told him that he was part of a ten-man squad recruited from a section in the government called "Psychological and Paramilitary." They supposedly went through three months of training, and they were sent to Dallas to protect JFK. Then something happened that was not part of the plan.

"He said it all went crazy. Somebody from his own team, from behind the fence—and he gave me a codename, because he thought he knew who it was—had fired on the President. There was a lot of chaos right away. He never saw that person again, and he barely got out of there in all the confusion. A small plane took him out of Dallas shortly thereafter."

Sounds like a hallucination, no? Not to Stone, who thought it "makes a lot of sense." Stone marveled that "his memory of it was so technical, filled with military jargon, details with radio communications right after the shots." The clincher for Stone? The man was a Buddhist, and "he thought I was an honest man."

It's easy to scoff at Oliver Stone's political delusions. But he's not the first person, and he won't be the last, to use the JFK assassination to make a political point. Many people are now trying to rehabilitate Jim Garrison as a tool for their geopolitical delusions.

CHAPTER 19

GARRISON'S FORGOTTEN VICTIM: MAJOR LOUIS BLOOMFIELD

IN OLIVER STONE'S *JFK,* when Clay Shaw is brought in for questioning, he is asked about the articles in *Paese Sera* tying him to the CIA.

Garrison: Mr. Shaw, this Italian newspaper saying you were a board member of Centro Mondo Commercial [sic] in Italy. That this company was a creature of the CIA for the transfer of funds in Italy for illegal political espionage activities. It says this company was expelled from Italy for these activities.

Shaw: I'm well aware of that asinine article. I'm thinking of suing that rag.

Garrison: It also says this company is linked to the Schlumberger Tool Company, near Houma in Louisiana, which provided arms to David Ferrie and his Cubans.

As was shown in Chapter 8, the *Paese Sera* articles were

published after Shaw's arrest (and not before as the film alleges) and were most certainly planted by the KGB to tie the CIA to the JFK assassination. Historian Max Holland said that "this has to be beyond the KGB's wildest imagination, that their disinformation would be carried in a Hollywood blockbuster."

We have already seen how the story moved from the communist newspapers to *Le Devoir*, a mainstream newspaper in Montreal. *Le Devoir* then ran a second larger article on March 16 written by its New York correspondent Louis Wiznitzer emphasizing a possible Montreal link to the JFK assassination.

So, what was this Montreal connection?

The *Paese Sera* series alleged that retired American Major L. M. Bloomfield held half the shares of the company [CMC] and that "he had participated in the espionage activities of the OSS (now the CIA) during the way." The series also claimed that Bloomfield was currently a banker living in Montreal "who counts among the companies he controls Le Credit Suisse of Canada, Heineken's Breweries, Canscot Realty, the Israel Continental Company, the Grimaldi Siosa Lines, etc."

Le Devoir misspelled his name as "Blumfield" and said he was "a retired army major, served in World War II in the OSS, the precursor of the CIA, and is very well respected in Canada. He was at that time also the main stockholder of a company named 'Permidex' [sic]."

Author and professor Clark Blaise then wrote an article,

"Neo-Fascism and the Kennedy Assassins," in the Sept–Oct 1967 issue of *Canadian Dimension,* a small Canadian left-wing magazine. Blaise "expected to see the story spelled out that afternoon in the *Montreal Star,* or at least to see a solid article or two appear in the liberal journals. Nothing more ever appeared." He was disappointed that the *New York Times* never mentioned any of the details about the activities of the CMC and felt "it was useless" to write to the CBC (the Canadian Broadcasting Corporation) and NBC.

District Attorney Jim Garrison of New Orleans has put forward his own theory of the Kennedy assassination: That it was planned and carried out by a group of anti-Castroites and neo-Fascist anti-Communists, who were based in New Orleans and involved with the C.I.A. They were hostile to Kennedy because of his decision to limit The Bay of Pigs invasion and because of his efforts to establish a Letente with the U.S.S.R. The group included Shaw, Ferrie, Oswald, Ruby and others. Clark Blaise's story, we feel, adds some new evidence supporting Garrison's case.

Neo-Fascism and the Kennedy Assassins

by Clark Blaise

Canadian Dimension *is a far-left magazine that was founded in 1963. It is still published today, although its circulation is only about 3,500.*

Shortly before his *Canadian Dimension* article appeared, Blaise wrote to Robert Scheer, editor of *Ramparts.* Blaise beseeched him to investigate further. Bill Turner, who was reporting on the Kennedy assassination for *Ramparts* (and who was also an investigator for Jim Garrison), sent it to Garrison with a note that said, "This came in while I was gone. There may be some items you don't already have."

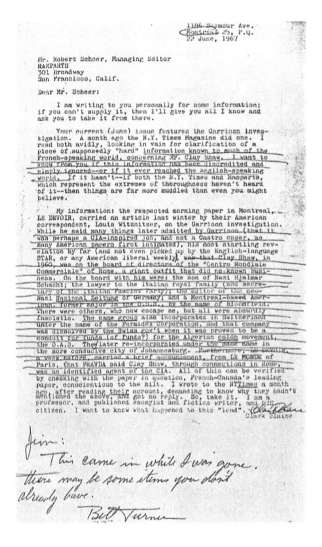

Ramparts then ran "The Garrison Commission" by Bill Turner in the January 1968 issue, which referenced *Paese Sera* and *Le Devoir* as its sources on Clay Shaw and the CMC.

It is now clear that Jim Garrison knew more about Louis Bloomfield then we had previously thought. Here is a letter (found in the donated papers of Bill Boxley, an investigator for Jim Garrison, in the National Archives) from a professor at Sir George Williams University advising Garrison that Bloomfield was a lawyer and noting his exact address. Bloomfield, with his charitable activities, the letter notes, does "great good."

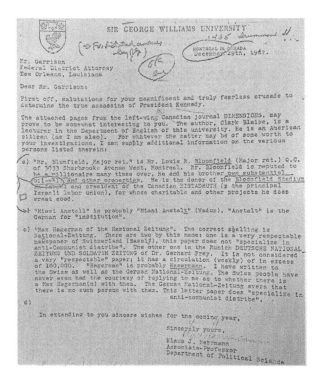

On September 21, 1968, Garrison had a conference with his investigators William Turner and Bill Boxley and conspiracy theorists Richard Sprague and Bernard Fensterwald. At one point, the conversation turned to the topic of James Earl Ray, the assassin of Martin Luther King.

"Garrison: They've got different modes of transportation but Montreal comes up too often. Remember, that's where Bloomfield is who is in this association with Clay Shaw. Now he's a banker in Montreal. He's probably more than a banker. He's in Montreal and everything happens in Montreal. Where does Jules Rocco Kimble go when he

runs away? He goes to Montreal. He went on a plane
flight with Shaw and Ferrie to Montreal." [1]

In 2001, Oliver Stone and Zachary Sklar wrote that Garrison
"had neither the staff nor the resources to go to Europe and
follow up its [*Paese Sera's*] leads." But why didn't Garrison just
fly up to Montreal and speak directly with Bloomfield? Alterna-
tively, he could have just picked up the phone and called him.
No need for a trip to Europe. Was it possible that that Garrison
realized the entire story was ridiculous on its face?

Fantasies about Louis Bloomfield continued in 1969 when
Paris Flammonde, former producer of the Long John Nebel show
—a radio talk show devoted to parapsychology and conspiracy
theories—wrote *The Kennedy Conspiracy: An Uncommissioned
Report on the Jim Garrison Investigation*. The book features a
chapter on the *Paese Sera* articles and also quoted the *Le Devoir*
articles as if they were independent sources. Flammonde noted
that Bloomfield was "active in the espionage arm of the U.S.
government during World War II."

Garrison repeated all of this nonsense in his book *On the
Trail of the Assassins*. "One of the major stockholders of the
Centro was Major L.M. Bloomfield, a Montreal resident originally of American nationality and a former agent with the Office
of Strategic Services, out of which the United States had formed
the CIA." Garrison quotes from *Le Devoir* as if it were a separate
source from *Paese Sera*.

So was Max Holland right about the *Paese Sera* articles?

JFK conspiracy author Joan Mellen claims that the articles had
been in the works for six months before Shaw was arrested. She bases
her claim on an interview conducted by her ex-husband and now
9/11 truther Ralph Schoenman with Giorgio Fanti, *Paese Sera's*
London correspondent at the time. However, three days before that

interview, Fanti told Canadian Historian Paul Mitchinson that he could not remember the Permindex stories. Also, historian Max Holland spoke to Angelo Aver, one of the coauthors of the articles, and he "claimed no such thing when interviewed in 2000, nor did any *Paese Sera* editors I contacted (including Corsini)."

Mellen claims she has found corroboration for the *Paese Sera* allegations in a "CIA document" that was released in 2003. "Dated 6/28/78, it describes Clay Shaw's service to the CIA as running from 1949 through 1972. Shaw was serving the Office of Security, Security Analysis Group (SAG). This document notes a claim 'that CIA used Shaw for services in Italy with U.S. Agent Major Louis Mortimer Bloomfield.'"

9 Mar 67 USSR International Affairs.
    Moscow TASS - 0504 GMT 7 Mar 67.
    Text Moscow-
        Claims CIA used Shaw for services
        in Italy w/ U.S. Agent Major Blumenfeld;
        establishing secret ties w/ Rome's political
        circles & business world. Shaw's task-
        to est. contacts w / extreme rightist groups
        in Rome.
        World Trade Center in Rome a branch of
        Swiss "Permindex" org, allegedly financed
                                    which
        OAS groups in France & is actually
        cover for branch of CIA.

Document RIF #180-10143-10220; Document RIF #104-10246-10040 refers to the above document as notes made by Patricia Orr, a staff member of the House Select Committee on Assassinations. It is not a CIA-originated document.

As is typical with conspiracy authors, Mellen doesn't tell readers that the document (which is merely Patricia Orr's notes for the House Select Committee on Assassinations and not really a CIA document) is merely quoting from a TASS (Soviet wire service) story on March 9, 1967, that traces back to the *Paese Sera* articles.

Mellen and other conspiracy authors believe that two other CIA documents also prove their case.[2]

First, a CIA document stated that Clay Shaw "was a highly paid CIA contract source until 1956." To Garrisonites, this was equivalent to the Rosetta Stone. Jefferson Morley, a former *Washington Post* reporter, made a big deal out of this document on his blog, jfkfacts.org. But there are problems. It seems strange to describe Shaw as a "contract source." He was a *domestic contact source* until 1956. Might the word "contract" have been a typo? In addition, this document is part of a report on a specific set of documents, a collection provided to the House Select Committee on Assassinations (HSCA) for its investigation. But there is no underlying document and no contemporaneous document in that collection that says Shaw was paid. Perhaps a 1955 reference to Shaw as a "valued source of this office" was just misreported.

SECRET

29 contain records from the Office of Legislative Counsel (now OCA), Inspector General, Office of the General Counsel, Directorate of Science and Technology, Office of Security, as well as several boxes of HSCA staff notes and records. Box No. 64 contains 72 microfilm reels (each equivalent to a box of records), which include the Oswald 201 file and Mexico City Station records, as well as other 201 files and information about Cuban exile groups.

4. Organization: The collection is arranged haphazardly, having been gathered in response to a series of HSCA and (in the case of the Oswald 201 file) Warren Commission requests. Although portions of the collection are organized by a variety of systems, there is no overall intellectual control of the entire body of records. We found fifteen indexes to the collection, none of which is adequate for control or retrieval.

5. Sensitivity: Although the collection is almost entirely at SECRET or lower classification, there is a scattering of TOP SECRET and codeword documentation. Materials we consider especially sensitive--more for privacy than national security reasons--include 201 files, phone taps, mail intercepts, security files, photo surveillance, names of sources, watch lists, and MHCHAOS documentation. Such material occurs throughout the collection, usually in response to HSCA requests for name traces. There are 22 microfilm reels of 201 files in addition to the Oswald file, while eight boxes contain security records, including, for example, files on David Atlee Phillips, Martin Luther King, and Clay Shaw.

6. Non-CIA Material: The collection includes a lot of third-agency material, mostly from the FBI. FBI reports dominate the 16 boxes of Oswald's 201 file, and nearly half of the 34 boxes of DO-collected material consists of third-agency material. The collection's remaining 29 boxes contain mostly CIA records, as does the box of microfilm, except for Oswald's 201 file. There is also some documentation of foreign liaison, mainly with the Mexican government.

7. CIA Complicity? Our survey found nothing in these records that indicates any CIA role in the Kennedy assassination or assassination conspiracy (if there was one), or any CIA involvement with Oswald. These records do reveal, however, that Clay Shaw was a highly paid CIA contract source until 1956. While nothing surfaced on Carlos Marcello in the collection, we found substantial documentation on other members of the mob, including Santos Trafficante.

8. Although the results of our survey fully support my earlier recommendation against inviting a panel of historians

2

SECRET

CIA Document RIF #104-10428-10104, dated February 10, 1992, page 3. Section seven notes that "Clay Shaw was a highly paid CIA contract source until 1956." This is probably a mistake; Shaw was a domestic contact until 1956.

But there are also several CIA documents that clearly state that Shaw was not remunerated, like the one below.

```
2.  SHAW HAS A SECURITY STATUS OF "NO INFO" DATED
23 MAR 49; BANISTER, ONE OF NICW) DATED 12 NOV 6J.  AS WE
HAVE ALREADY REPORTED, WE MAINTAINED PROFESSIONAL CONTACT
WITH SHAW FROM 1949 THROUGH 1956 AS MANAGER OF INTERNATIONAL
TRADE MART.  THIS RESULTED IN EIGHT REPORTS OF WHICH SIX
WERE EVALUATED "OF VALUE" AND TWO "OF SLIGHT VALUE."  WE
HAVE NEVER REMUNERATED HIM; HIS NOFO CONTACT WAS HUNTER C.
LEAKE AND THE RELATIONSHIP WAS DISCONTINUED  AS THE "SHOTGUN
APPROACH" TO COLLECTION EFFORTS WANED AND IT BECAME OBVIOUS
THAT SHAW WAS BECOMING MORE AND MORE INTERESTED IN HIS
PRIVATE VENTURES AND LESS AND LESS IN THE ACTIVITIES OF
INTERNATIONAL TRADE MART.  HE RESIGNED AS MANAGER OF
INTERNATIONAL TRADE MART ON 1 OCT 65.
```

CIA document RIF# 1994.04.12.12:16:07:600005, dated October 16, 1967.

Another CIA memo, undated but clearly from 1967 (see below), notes that "Shaw was never asked to use his relationship with the World Trade Center for clandestine purposes." Also, it notes that "all of the *Pravda* charges are untrue."

```
    9.  On 7 March 1967 Pravda published an article
called "Clay Shaw of the CIA" datelined Rome, 6 March
1967, written by V. YERMAKOV.  The article charged that
CIA made use of the services of Clay SHAW for CIA's own
interests in Italy.  The Pravda piece notes that the DA
in New Orleans is accusing SHAW of participation in the
assassination conspiracy.  It says SHAW spent "some years"
in Rome as a World Trade Center leader.  It claims that
the Center was a cover for financing anti-Communist activity.
CIA gave directives to SHAW.  The World Trade Center was
a branch of "Permidex" (sic), "which the newspapers in
Switzerland openly accused of 'criminal operations'...."
(Comment:  It appears that all of the Pravda charges are
untrue, except that there was a CIA-SHAW relationship.  So
far as is known, SHAW was never asked to use his relation-
ship with the World Trade Center for clandestine purposes
and, in fact, he has not been in Italy.)
```

RIF# 104-10013-10308

Second, a recently declassified document written in 1959 notes that Permindex/CMC offered the CIA the opportunity to place an agent on the staff of the company.

MEMORANDUM FOR: Chief, Commercial Staff

SUBJECT: (y) Permindex - World Trade Center

(y)

1. Dr. Ferenc Nagy, former prime minister of Hungary, presently resident in the United States, and a covert associate of IOD is President of Permindex, a Swiss corporation with principal offices in Rome and representatives in various parts of the world. The World Trade Center, in which Nagy is also interested is associated with Permindex. Brochures describing these organizations are attached.

2. Nagy has asked a representative of IOD if CIA would be interested in:

   a) Placing an American businessman on the Board of Permindex.

   b) Placing a CIA agent on the staff of Permindex.

   c) Purchasing some shares in Permindex through the above representative on the Board in order to have a voice in the management of it. (Nagy emphasizes that the firm is well financed and that this is not a pitch for funds).

3. The advantages which in Nagy's judgment Permindex offers to CIA include opportunity to develop information on and contacts in many developing countries of Asia and Africa; cover; and the possibility of influencing the economies of these countries to some extent. (Permindex is reported to have representatives reaching 52 countries, including the Bloc and several countries of Africa and Asia.

4. Permindex has just opened its offices and exhibit halls in Rome and expects to be in full operation in the spring of 1960.

5. Before pursuing this further, IOD would appreciate CI Staff's judgment on the following:

   a) Financial condition of Permindex and the World Trade Center. Dr. Nagy says that Banca Del Laboro, Rome, Italy can supply full details on such matters.

   b) Business potential of Permindex in the exhibit and international trade field; its competition; etc.

SECRET

Page 1 of a CIA memo by Cord Meyer dated November 6, 1959, with the offer of placing a CIA agent on the staff of Permindex.

This memo was included as part of a larger memo (RIF# 104-10181-10114) that was put together by the CIA in March 1967 because of the "Italian aspects of the Clay Shaw Affair." Several other memos from 1959 were attached. But the offer of "placing a

CIA agent on the staff of Permindex" was enough for conspiracy theorists to claim that *Paese Sera* was correct about Clay Shaw.

Of course, the dates don't match. Shaw was named to the board in 1958, and the offer to the CIA was in 1959, so the CIA could not have responded to Nagy's offer by assigning Shaw to be their man on Permindex.

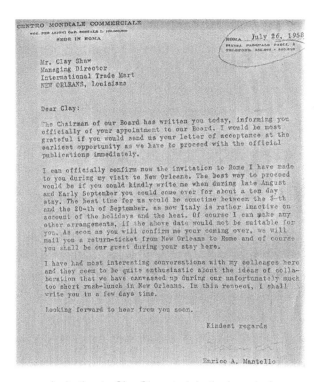

Invitation to Clay Shaw to join the board of
Permindex in 1958.

Given the state of the Cold War in the late 1950s, it is not surprising that the CIA might have been interested in an international trading organization. The memo goes on to note that "the advantages which in Nagy's judgment Permindex offers to CIA include the opportunity to develop information on and contacts in many developing countries of Asia and Africa; cover; and the possibility of influencing the economies of these countries to some extent." However, continued the memo, before going further, the CIA would "need information on the financial condition of Permindex, it's business potential, and further comments on the backgrounds of its management."

According to the original memo above, the CIA then went on to develop more information. Unfortunately, on February 25, 1960, it reported that "we regret to say that up to date information obtained via Agency channels does not provide us with sufficient data to form an opinion." On March 24, 1960, it wrote that "we were hopeful that more valuable information could be obtained through another source. This has now been received and while it is not complete it does furnish considerably more information than heretofore obtained."

The CIA was not impressed with Permindex/CMC. First, it felt that few American tourists would be interested in the Permindex exhibition since it would not allow orders for "over-the-counter" merchandise. Second, there were restrictions on selling that could be done on site (American firms that were not members of European industry organizations were not allowed to take orders), and that was not well understood by management. The CIA noted that "at this stage, the venture seems highly speculative from an investor's point of view. For, if the present exhibitors failed to renew their contracts for space at the end of the first year, the possibility of obtaining replacements and extending the space sold would appear to be rather remote." The CIA concluded that "the prospects for success are precarious and unless exhibitors are found to occupy the whole available space in the exhibition buildings, and soon, the first year's exhibit will be unsuccessful with the consequent result that continuation will not be possible on a profitable basis."

Charles White, on the commercial staff of the CIA, concluded his memo by stating that "it will be noted that no contracts are claimed with any of the Soviet Bloc countries, which may be a consideration in your decision whether to inject anyone into the organization's staff as suggested by the ex-Prime Minister."

There were also concerns about some of the people managing Permindex. One memo described George Mantello, one of the founders, as "being dishonest, unscrupulous and untrustworthy. Subject has firmly established an unsavory business reputation in the transactions he has conducted over the last twenty years. In late 1943 or early 1944, Subject spent a brief time, one source reported that it was two weeks, in a Swiss jail for illegal gold transactions."

Were these allegations about George Mantello (born Gyorgy Mandl) true? The truth begins to come out later in the memo.

"Subject's one determinable loyalty is to his Jewish co-religionists. Beginning in at least September 1944, and perhaps starting a few months earlier, Subject supplied Jews trapped in Hungary with false documentation which enabled them to flee Hungary ... It has been reported that Subject assisted persons not in favor with the Nazis to escape from Germany during World War II. The files indicate that Subject performed most of these services without remuneration, however, at least three un-evaluated reports state or indicate that he sold the false documentation he was able to provide."

Mantello served as a first secretary of El Salvador in Switzer-land and gave out about fifteen thousand Salvadorian citizenship papers to Jews during World War II. In 1944, he publicized the deportation of Hungarian Jews to Auschwitz, through the publi-cation of a thirty-page document called "The Auschwitz Proto-col." This led to over four hundred newspaper articles being published in 120 Swiss newspapers and was a contributing factor in stopping deportations. For his great work for the Jewish people, Mantello received an honorary doctorate from Yeshiva University, he was awarded the 1989 Righteousness Award by the Holocaust Memorial Center in Michigan, and he was nominated for a Congressional Gold Medal in 1989. His partner in the El Salvadoran embassy, Jose Arturo Castellanos, was recognized posthumously by Yad Vashem on May 3, 2010, with the title Righteous Among the Nations.

So where did all the allegations against Mantello come from?

In May 1944, he was arrested by Swiss authorities on the formal charge related to his black-market activities. He had purchased a thousand chronographs, which were sent to New York for British intelligence (they wanted them for fighter planes). But he was also questioned about the sale of Salvadorian papers. He was detained for sixteen days and was only released when he paid two thousand Swiss francs to cover any fines. John Winant, American ambassador to the UK, reported on the results of a State Department investigation in March 1944. He noted that "the consul of San Salvador [Mantello] has acted from pure humanitarian motives and has charged no fee at all."

After the war, the Jewish community of Geneva wrote to Mantello.

"It is impossible for us to adequately express our gratitude to you for the tremendous, altruistic work you have done, sparing neither your time nor your financial resources to come to the aid of the wretched victims of the Nazis. We can, however, bear witness to the fact that your help was entirely without personal motive. Not only have you declined to accept any reimbursement for the innumerable papers you sent to us, but, in your life-saving mission, you have also spent considerable sums of your own money."

Still, rumors abounded about Mantello's supposed profiteering. He wrote to the Federation of Swiss Jewish Communities in September 1945 asking for a formal inquiry. Three judges were named and witnesses were called to either testify or to send affidavits. Wilhelm Fischer, head of the Romanian World Jewish Congress, said that he had sent thousands of names to Mantello and had spent over $20,000 cabling details to Mantello but that nothing was paid for the papers themselves. Rabbi Zvi Taubes, the chief Rabbi of Zurich, said that "Mantello always used to come to me with new plans for the rescue of European Jews ... Since he provided his Salvador papers free of charge, it was a great relief no longer to have to pay for the foreign passports and to be able to obtain as many as possible."

The inquiry ended on June 27, 1946, and completely exonerated Mantello. The judges concluded that "The Commission is of the contrary opinion that *Mr. Mantello organized the entire operation solely for the purpose of assisting his endangered coreligionists in a totally selfless manner.*" [Emphasis in original.]

In the meantime, Mantello was denied entry visas to the UK and France. This was due to the ongoing harassment by Heinrich Rothmund, the anti-Semitic head of the Swiss Alien Police. In 1942, he had addressed a conference of cantonal immigration directors and said that "the Jew is not easily assimilated ... Nor must one forget that many of them pose a danger to our institutions, being used to conditions in which the Jewish instinct for business has a tendency to run free." At one point, Switzerland was ready to expel Mantello from the country, but in October 1948, the Swiss government lifted all restraints on his travel and closed the inquiry on his alleged black-market activities.

When Permindex was trying to get off the ground in Basel in 1957, the American Consulate wrote that a "reliable source" claimed that Mantello "was actively engaged in the wartime Jewish refugee racket, promising to have Jews allowed to escape from Nazi countries for a price which was to be paid to him."

This coincided with a campaign by the press organ of the Social Democratic Party, the *Arbeiter-Zeitung*, against Permindex in general and Mantello's character in particular.

Many conspiracy books use the quotation "Jewish refugee racket" from that consulate dispatch [called a Despatch by the State Department] to besmirch Mantello. For instance, James DiEugenio, author of *Destiny Betrayed*, wrote that "The Board of Directors [of Permindex] was made up of bankers who had been tied up with fascist governments, people who worked the Jewish refugee racket."[3] But they neglect to quote from another consulate dispatch that said, "[I]n connection with these allegations, the Department's attention is drawn to the fact that this Consulate issued Mantello a regular visitor's visa, valid for four years, in November 1957, after the usual security checks produced negative results." They concluded that "none of these charges have been proved."

G. Mandel-Mantello; thwarted the Nazis

ROME (AP)—George Mandel-Mantello, a businessman who helped stop Nazi deportation of thousands of Jews from Hungary during World War II, has died. He was 90.

throughout the 1930s with Salvadoran officials. The relationship led to his appointment as first secretary at the Salvadoran consulate in Geneva, Switzerland, in the early 1940s, after a narrow escape from

Chicago Tribune, May 8, 1992, notice of George Mantello's death in 1992. He was buried in Jerusalem.

It is clear from documents and cables that the CIA and American consulates believed Permindex was indeed trying to set up a center for international trade. There is not a hint that Permindex/CMC could be used, or was used, as a conduit for the financing of anti-communist organizations. No corroboration for the *Paese Sera* allegations can be found in any US government document.

Interestingly, Garrison never mentioned the *Paese Sera* allegations at Clay Shaw's trial in 1969, and his book *On the Trail of the Assassins* erroneously maintained that he didn't know about any of this until after the trial. Was Garrison aware that the sources of the story might be specious? Or as Patricia Lambert believes, "if Shaw's attorneys had exposed the origin" of the articles, "Garrison would have been branded a tool of Communist propaganda." Certainly, KGB disinformation or not, the *Paese Sera* articles were wrong about an awful lot of stuff.

For instance, while Clay Shaw was indeed on the board of the CMC from 1958–1962, he did not come to Rome at all, and he certainly didn't live there for two years. He never attended a board meeting of the CMC, and he wrote to correspondents in 1959 and 1960 and said he was "not familiar with their day-to-day operations." The International Trade Mart had not funded anti-Castro Cubans, and Garrison never found anything in Shaw's notebooks about the funding of any conspiracy, let alone that of the assassination of JFK.

And of course, *Paese Sera* missed the biggest story of all, that Clay Shaw *did* have a real CIA connection. He was an unpaid domestic contact between 1948–1956. His "contacts produced a total of eight intelligence reports which were disseminated to various U.S. Government Agencies." The CIA noted that "six were evaluated as 'of value' and two 'of slight value.'" The CIA discontinued the relationship "as the shotgun approach to collection efforts waned and it became obvious that Shaw was becoming more and more interested in his private ventures and less and less in the activities of the International Trade Mart." There have been over 150,000 other businessmen who have also reported on their trips through the CIA domestic contact program.

Thankfully, we now have additional information to judge the *Paese Sera* articles courtesy of the archives of Louis Mortimer Bloomfield, the corporate lawyer accused of being the major shareholder of Permindex.

Louis Bloomfield donated all his papers to the Public Archives Canada in Ottawa (now known as Library and Archives Canada). He stipulated that they were not to be opened until twenty years after his death, which occurred in 1984. In 2004, a researcher, Maurice Phillips, tried to get access but was told that Bloomfield's widow now wanted the material to remain closed until ten years after her death. Phillips sued and ultimately won access to the files. Still, some material remained restricted, and researcher John Kowalski followed with a new lawsuit to gain access to most of the material. We all owe a debt of gratitude to Maurice Phillips and John Kowalski for prying open these files and helping to put the *Paese Sera* controversy to bed.

I have now gone through most of the Bloomfield archive.[4] His law firm was very busy. In 1960 alone, he sent out over two thousand letters, of which about one hundred were sent to managers and investors of Permindex. Over the years, there were so many letters regarding Permindex that I have lost count, and there is not one mention of Clay Shaw in any business letter, personal letter, cable, notebook, birthday greeting, or journal.

The Bloomfield Archive shows that there was turmoil within Permindex/CMC with a variety of real estate deals going south, new investors coming on board, limited information on new tenants for the exhibition, and general consternation about the running of the company. There is not one piece of evidence that supports anything written in the *Paese Sera* series of articles. Ultimately, the World Trade Center in Rome couldn't pay its rent and was evicted in 1962. It seems ludicrous to believe that the CIA would have used such a troubled organization as its vehicle to finance right-wing extremists.

Bloomfield saw the articles in *Le Devoir* and was deeply troubled by the allegations. He wrote to editor Claude Ryan demanding a retraction. I searched through several months of *Le Devoir,* and I could not find any correction or retraction.

March 20th, 1967

Mr. Claude Ryan,
Editor,
Le Devoir,
434 Notre Dame Street East,
Montreal, Que.

Dear Mr. Ryan:

Mr. Bloomfield has just dittated to me the following message which he asked me to deliver immediately to you -

In accordance with your request during our telephone conversation, I confirm that the exclusive source of the article of March 16th in Le Devoir appears to be an Italian communist newspaper 'Paese Sera' which published a series of false and imaginary articles in Early March.   Other Italian newspapers immediately denied and ridiculed this fantastic story.

Il Tempo (pp.1 & 15) "Fantapolitica su Clay Shaw - una ingarbugliata ed inverosimilii recistruzione di fonte communista."

Il Messaggero (p.8) "Fantasticherie - ma nulla allo stato dei fatti sembra autorizzare illazioni azzardate."

Vita (pp.14 & 16) Un affare sballato - un romanzo alla Fleming."

Some five years ago my attention was drawn to the fact that a former American major, with a name extremely similar to mine, was attached to the U.S. Embassy in Rome and I have reason to believe that misidentification had occurred at that time.   As a matter of fact, the article in Paese Sera referred to a Major L. H. Blumfield, as an American citizen, and not to a Canadian.

I have never been connected, directly or indirectly, with

OSS, CIA or any similar organization and have never been a
director of any of the companies mentioned in your article.

You will appreciate that this article, insofar as it may
identify me with L. H. Blumfield, is causing me terrible damage personally and professionally and I rely upon your integrity to immediately right this wrong.

It would appear that a correspondent of Le Devoir has
an elementary obligation to check the source and veracity of
material of such an incredible nature before flashing headlines involving honourable citizens of Montreal and I declare
that the remarks and insinuations in the article are false
and devoid of any semblance of truth.

I do not want to suffer further harm by keeping this
completely fictitious story alive and for this reason I
would be grateful if you would not refer to this message but
publish a short, dignified retraction consistent with your
integrity and my reputation.

Regards,

Yours sincerely,

Louis M. Bloomfield, Q.C.,
3033 Sherbrooke Street We
Westmount, Quebec.

Presently - in care of
World Jewish Congress,
Geneva, Switzerland.

Louis Bloomfield's letter to Claude Ryan, editor of Le Devoir

Bloomfield's letter referenced *Il Messaggero,* which
presented the facts. There were "stormy financial events," and in
1962, the CMC was evicted from its buildings. Shortly after that,
the company was dissolved, and the members of the board "gave
rise to other initiatives." The articles confirmed that Shaw had
never been to Italy and noted that "there is no trace of his name
in the foreigner's office." Further, "the name of Clay Shaw has
conjured an image of mysterious activity which appears to be
involved with the CIA, that is to say, the headquarters of counter-
intelligence in America, but nothing in the current situation
seems to infer such risky speculation."

Bloomfield also wrote to the editors of *Canadian Dimension*
about the Clark Blaise article. Unfortunately, that letter is not in

his archives, although the reply from associate editor G. David
Sheps contains a full retraction.

DIMENSION

POST OFFICE BOX 1413   ●   WINNIPEG 1

October 22, 1967.

L.M. Bloomfield,
Room 930,
Place Ville Marie,
Montreal, Quebec.

Dear Mr. Bloomfield:

        The editors of Canadian Dimension are
fully satisfied that you are in no way to be
confused with an L.H. Blumfield who is mentioned
on page 26 of Canadian Dimension (Vol. 4, No.6)
in a translated extract from Le Devoir.

        The article in Le Devoir, from which
we quoted, itself appears to be based on dubious
sources and the author of the article in Canadian
Dimension suggested in his article that the
sources were not reliable.

        We sincerely regret any inconvenience
this confusion in identity may cause and apologize
to you for it.

                        Sincerely,

                        G. David Sheps
                        Associate Editor, Canadian
                                            Dimension.

The Bloomfield allegations then took on a more sinister tone.
I went to the Canadian Jewish Archives in Montreal to look at
the Bloomfield file, and it contained an article from a Lyndon
LaRouche publication from 1994 titled "Permindex ties revealed

to JFK murder, 1001 Nature Trust." Lyndon LaRouche was a perennial candidate for the US Presidency, running from 1976–2004 while he headed a cult-like, anti-Semitic conspiratorial organization.

Permindex Ties Revealed to JFK Murder, 1001 Nature Trust

by Joseph Brewda and Jeffrey Steinberg

The Montreal Gazette

Maj. Louis Mortimer Bloomfield of the Permindex assassination bureau which ran the murder of President Kennedy.

Bloomfield figured prominently in LaRouchian propaganda.

Bloomfield was deeply troubled by LaRouche's allegations, and he wrote Isadore G. Alk, a retired friend who had worked in the U.S. Treasury Department, in 1979.

          Zib, there is something I would like you to do
for me and please treat it as a professional matter.
There is an outfit calling itself the North American
Labour Party run by some fellow called Larouche,
apparently whose propaganda is not treated seriously,
but whose propaganda accuses me and other prominent
Canadians of all sorts of heinous crimes. Un particular
I am presumed to have been the head of a CIA Department
in the United States for 30 years with the rank of a Major
in the American Army!

          I am enclosing a copy of a letter which I sent
some time ago to the R.C.M.P. who have this group under
surveillance.

          However, I do believe that they have confused
me with a man called Major L. Blumenfeld who I was
informed was an Attaché to the American Embassy in Rome

in 1966 or 1967. I understand that he probably was
a CIA man attached to the Embassy in Rome. I would
appreciate it very much if you could check as to
whether there was a Major L. Blumenfeld at the American
Embassy in Rome during or around that period of time.

          I am also enclosing a copy of an article
from Maclean's magazine, a most authoratative publication
dated October 29, 1979, which speaks for itself.

Alk wrote back saying that he was on holiday and could see someone in several months when he returned to D.C. It's not known if he ever followed up.

The *Maclean's* article that Bloomfield sent was about the LaRouchians and their book *Dope, Inc.*, which alleged "that Britain is carrying on a $200 billion-a-year opium war against the U.S. much of the operation conducted through Britain's northern 'colony' Canada."

Frontlines

By André McNicoll

Jeffrey Steinberg, director of security and operations for the U.S. Labor Party, is a deeply suspicious man. "Why would Maclean's want to do a story on us?" he keeps asking. For three days now, calls requesting an interview with the USLP's elusive national chairman, L.H. LaRouche, have been unanswered, appointments put off. Finally, a decision is made. One of the three heavy doors opens and the young, stern Steinberg emerges. "Look," he says, "we've been conducting an investigation. You're just a Maclean's

Paranoia and power: the marshalling of a U.S. cult

of the Bronfman family, who the FLQ (Front de Libération du as an extension of earlier effor sassinate de Gaulle." That's no hippie movement was a British resurrection of the ancient cult of Isis (a nature goddess w lowers proved stubbornly resi early Christian teachings), as plot to wreck U.S. social and m ric, and the hit parade has be nized on the same principle cruit youths for deranged D worship.

The USLP's inter

Maclean's *magazine, October 29, 1979.*

Bloomfield also wrote to the commissioner of the Royal Canadian Mounted Police (RCMP).

This book is composed of scurrilous libels against members of the Royal Family, British aristocracy - (Winston Churchill, Sir William Stephenson, Lord Beaverbrook, Lord Caccia, Sir Mark Turner, Lord Trevelyan, etc.) as well as important international personalities - (the Kennedys, Bronfmans, Rothschilds, Rockefellers, etc.) and heads of major British and Canadian Banks and Corporations accused of financing and running the Narcotics business in North America. This wild publication was receeded by a series of propaganda flyers beginning the last week of August 1978 in which the Queen, 14 prominent Canadians, Knights or Officers of the Order of St. John and the R.C.M.P. were accused of complicity in assassination plots. The emphasis in the book has switched from assassination to dope.

In some manner the book has designated me as if I were Major L. Bloomfield of the United States Army and Chief of an F.B.I. division in the U.S. for over 30 years. In order to give credibility to their false and preposterous references the editors obtained certain bits and pieces of my biography which have been mixed, garbled and woven into a fabric of lies, hallucinatory accusations and statements that have no connection with me in any shape or form whatsoever.

Also libeled are the Most Venerable Order of the Hospital of St. John of Jerusalem, Knights of Malta, Canadian Institute of International Affairs and their officers and directors. It should be noted that Business Week of January 22nd, 1979, on page 25, referred to the fact that the Soviets and K.G.B. are apparently behind these operations.

Letter to the commissioner of the RCMP, dated January 25, 1979. Bloomfield also indicated that he had a concern for his safety.

Bloomfield's biography has unfortunately now been corrupted by conspiracy theorists with many factoids, a term

Norman Mailer coined in 1973 to refer to pieces of information that are accepted as true but which are not, seeping into descriptions of his life. And as we have seen, *Paese Sera* was just plain wrong about Bloomfield: he was not a former American major; he was a Canadian war veteran. He wasn't a banker; he was a corporate lawyer. He didn't own half the shares in Permindex; his clients owned a controlling interest, at least for a while. He was never a member of the OSS, nor did he control all the various companies mentioned in their articles.

In real life, Louis Bloomfield was a mensch, the highest compliment you can give a person in the Yiddish language.

During the Second World War, Bloomfield was a lieutenant in the infantry but was moved because of a heart murmur. He was profiled in *Canadian Jewish News* in 1978, and he told the paper that he was moved into "hush hush secret service jobs in a less hectic activity." I realize that this line alone will make conspiracy theorists go crazy, but so be it. His activities included locating German submarines in Mexico, and he said that "his biggest coup came when he was able, because of past dealings with the Polish line, to prevent the Nazis from seizing a number of Polish ships, in New York harbor, by preventing them from sailing into the waiting hands of the German navy."

After the war, he became a lawyer specializing in corporate and international law and was the author of many books and articles. He was on the drafting committee for the Helsinki Rules on the uses of International Rivers in 1966.

He was on the board of governors for several hospitals and raised a lot of money for the Reddy Hospital in Montreal. Bloomfield was the cofounder of the World Wildlife Fund of Canada, and he was active in several charities relating to Israel. He served on the board of governors of the Hebrew University of Jerusalem, the Weizmann Institute of Science, and the Technion in Haifa. He worked hard for a wide variety of Jewish causes, including as honorary counsel for the World Zionist Congress and a judge for its tribunal, and he was the national treasurer of the Canadian Histadrut Campaign, raising money for the Israeli labor union. He and his brother Bernard built a 2,400-seat stadium in Tel Aviv and seventeen trade and vocational schools in Israel.

In 1965, Bloomfield was named the first Jewish Knight of Grace of the Most Venerable Order of the Hospital of St. John of Jerusalem, an organization that teaches first aid around the world. He told the *Canadian Jewish News* in 1978 that "Last year in Canada we trained over 250,000 and in the past 10 years, St. John's Ambulance has trained more than 12% of our population between the ages of 16 and 60. Every morning it's the first thing I do at the office—call and find out how I can help with their problems."

Bloomfield also raised a lot of money for the Progressive Conservative Party in Canada and was a friend of Prime Minister John Diefenbaker. Bloomfield named him the 1962 recipient of the Histadrut Humanitarian Award. Previous recipients included Harry Truman, Eleanor Roosevelt, and U.S. Supreme Court Justices William O. Douglas and Arthur Goldberg.

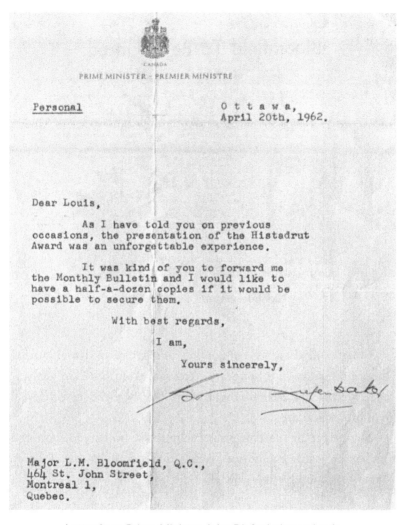

Letter from Prime Minister John Diefenbaker to Louis Bloomfield.

And in 1967, Bloomfield himself was the recipient of the Histadrut Humanitarian Award.

Histadrut Award
Bloomfield To Be Honored

Montreal Attorney and Author Louis M. Bloomfield will be granted the Histadrut Humanitarian Award at a special dinner in his honor Tuesday.

Mr. Bloomfield, president of the Canadian branch of the International Law Association, will be the fifth Canadian to receive the award given for outstanding work in aid of pioneering Israel.

Other recipients of the Histadrut award have included John Diefenbaker, Harry Truman, Eleanor Roosevelt., Arthur J. Goldberg, Samuel Bronfman and Claude Jodoin.

Speakers at the testimonial dinner, set for Tuesday evening at Le Chateau Champlain, are E. Davie Fulton, Progressive Conservative MP and former minister of Justice, and Msgr. Francis J. Smyth, director of the noted Coady Institute of St. Francis Xavier University.

Msgr. Smyth's keynote address will detail the work of the institute, a valuable training school providing social leadership courses for students from underdeveloped countries of Asia, Africa and Latin America.

The banquet is the 43rd annual dinner of the Montreal Histadrut campaign, now in the midst of its 1967 drive.

Mr. Bloomfield, an executive of several hospitals and other public organizations, is the author of "The British Honduras-Guatemala Dispute" and "Egypt, Israel and the Gulf of Aqaba" and co-author of 'Boundary Water Problems of Canada and United States."

LOUIS M. BLOOMFIELD

Montreal Gazette, *April 6, 1967*

Bloomfield died in 1984 while on a trip to Israel during which he received an honorary doctorate from Bar Ilan University. He was just seventy-eight years old, and the world lost a great humanitarian.

Shame on all the conspiracy mongers who have dishonored the legacies and memories of Louis Bloomfield and George Mantello, honorable men both.

מִנְּשָׁרִים קַלּוּ וּמֵאֲרָיוֹת גָּבֵרוּ לַעֲשׂוֹת רְצוֹן קוֹנָם וְחֵפֶץ צוּרָם.
יִזְכְּרֵם אֱלֹהֵינוּ לְטוֹבָה עִם שְׁאָר צַדִּיקֵי עוֹלָם

**They were swifter than eagles and stronger than lions,
to carry out the will of their Creator
and the desire of their Rock.
May our God remember them for good,
together with the other righteous of the world.**

CONCLUSION: THE ATTEMPT TO REHABILITATE JIM GARRISON

SINCE THE RELEASE OF *JFK*, three authors have tried to rehabilitate Jim Garrison and his nonexistent case against Clay Shaw. In 1999, William Davy published *Let Justice Be Done: New Light on the Jim Garrison Investigation*; Joan Mellen released *A Farewell to Justice: Jim Garrison, JFK's Assassination, and the Case That Should Have Changed History* in 2005 and 2013; and James DiEugenio came out with *Destiny Betrayed: JFK, Cuba and the Garrison Case* in 1992 and 2012.

They all suffer from invincible ignorance and peddle ridiculous conspiracy theories. They all believe that federal agencies interfered with Garrison's investigation and that Garrison was betrayed from within by a coterie of spies and agents. And they all propagate the nonsense that Kennedy had to be killed because he was going to end the Cold War, withdraw from Vietnam, and usher in a new era of peace and prosperity. None of this was true.

Of the three, Mellen is the most credulous, believing every Garrison "witness" and buying into every Garrison theory. The centerpiece of her book is Thomas Beckham (see Chapters 16 and 17), and she even includes a picture of Beckham in his rabbi's gown. Well, the con man fooled Garrison, and so it's no surprise that he fooled Mellen. Fred Crisman is in her book, as is Slidin' Clyde Johnson, and even the second Oswald makes an appearance. She regurgitates so many stories of so many conspirators that she can't cobble together any sort of coherent narrative. Patricia Lambert notes that

---

"A Farewell to Justice *is not an easy read. The book's epic-size cast sometimes renders the narrative incoherent. New characters appear at a dizzying rate, vast numbers of whom are said to be CIA connected—CIA operatives, CIA media assets, CIA agents, CIA employees. Affixing the CIA label to as many lapels as possible (regardless of how flimsy the evidence), appears to be a central goal of this book, the assumption being that no such association could possibly be innocent or, God forbid, patriotically inspired."*

The three books are quite incestuous and include many of the same stories, sometimes with absolutely no documentation. Take the story of Slidin' Clyde Johnson as told in Chapter 13. DiEugenio claims that "he was brutally beaten on the eve of the trial and hospitalized." He references Davy (page 310) and Mellen (page 301). Mellen writes that "on the day before he was scheduled to testify, Clyde Johnson was beaten up so badly he had to be hospitalized." Her only reference is to the *Times-Picayune* in July 24, 1969. But they report that a few days before Shaw went on trial, Johnson held a press conference in New Orleans and said, "I'm the ace-in-the-hole in Garrison's case." One day later he was arrested by police for refusing to pay his bill at the Roosevelt Hotel. The Davy book says that "In February of

1969, he was severely beaten and never testified." He offers no footnote.

It takes chutzpah to argue that Clay Shaw was involved in the JFK assassination, but all three books take a shot. This means they thus have to prove that Shaw was Clay Bertrand (see Chapter 3). Unfortunately, they all prefer quantity over quality; they present many witnesses to support their case, but none that have any credibility.

DiEugenio and Mellen claim that Dean Andrews privately admitted to Warren Commission critic Harold Weisberg that Shaw was Bertrand. Remember, Andrews was always adamant that Shaw was *not* Bertrand (see Chapter 3). In May 2001, Joan Mellen wrote to Weisberg and asked him if he remembered the details of his conversation with Andrews. He replied:

"Andrews told me that Shaw was Bertrand without putting it that way. We were in his office discussing some of the evidence, what I now do not recall, when Andrews said, approximately these words, "If the Green Giant gets past that, he is home clear."

Now, Dean Andrews might have been a hip, jive-talkin' attorney, to be sure, but it seems to me that Weisberg read just a little too much into his words.

Another DiEugenio witness is Leander D'avy, whose interview with Garrison's staffers he found to be "utterly fascinating." He worked at a restaurant and bar, The Court of the Two Sisters, and claimed that Oswald walked in one night and asked for Clay Bertrand and that Clay Shaw frequented the place. In 1977, D'avy was deposed by the HSCA, and he recalled that about two weeks before the assassination, he had gone in on a Saturday morning to pick up his check. He was sent to the storeroom, which he said was actually a little apartment, and guess who was there? Lee Harvey Oswald was lying across the bed. David Ferrie was there, and yes, the three tramps were there as well.

He saw other people too. Jack Ruby once parked in a loading zone in front of the restaurant and slapped D'avy in the face when he complained. Fred Crisman came around "almost every week" in 1963. Even Thomas Beckham was in the restaurant. It's not surprising that HSCA investigators thought there were "serious questions about his credibility."

Then there is William Morris who "signed an affidavit he knew Shaw as Clay Bertrand." Morris was interviewed in 1967 while an inmate at the Wynne State Prison Farm in Texas. He claimed that Shaw worked for General Electric and that he lived with his mother, which were both untrue. Morris was six feet tall but said he was taller than Bertrand, forgetting that Shaw was quite tall at 6'4". Further, he claimed that Bertrand brought had Jack Ruby to his apartment. Is there any wonder why he didn't testify at the Shaw trial?

DiEugenio claims that Clay Shaw's maid Virginia Johnson said that "a man who stayed with Shaw on several occasions told her that Shaw had used the name of Bertrand." However, Johnson's statement says something quite different: yes, she had heard the name Bertrand, but she wasn't quite sure of the details. Lots of people were talking to her; she had conversations at a fabric class about the case, but "When asked if Mr. Formadol [sic] [she was clearly talking about Shaw's friend William Formyduval] referred to Mr. Shaw as Bertrand, she stated no." Garrison's investigators went back several months later for another interview, and this time she said that "she had never heard the name, Bertrand."

Then there is Mrs. Jessie Parker, who testified that she had seen Shaw at the Eastern Airlines VIP Room at Moisant Airport and that he had signed the guest book as Clay Bertrand. But

DiEugenio neglects to tell his readers that Shaw was supposedly with a group of visitors from Venezuela who were accompanied by U.S. State Department employees and a military escort. The military man did not recognize a photo of Shaw as the man in the VIP room. One of the State Department employees *did* recognize Shaw's picture but only because he knew Shaw professionally, and he said Shaw was not at the airport.[1]

Yet another DiEugenio witness is Thomas Breitner, who "said that, on Shaw's trip to San Francisco, he visited the University of California and he introduced himself as Bertram." You can see Turner's report below—you have to love the last paragraph. Breitner could only have gotten the name Clem from the media since Perry Russo was the only person to use that name for Clay Bertrand.

```
To: Jim Garrison                    September 23, 1967

From: Bill Turner

Subject: Clay Shaw in San Francisco

        Referring to previous memorandums on the visit of Shaw
to the University of California biological laboratory, as reported
by Thomas Breitner:
        Breitner this date called to advise that he now recalls that
several people employed by the university dropped into the lab
stockroom to meet Shaw, and that Shaw introduced himself as
Clay Bertram. Once, claims Breitner, Shaw introduced himself as
Clem Bertram, but quickly corrected the name to Clay.
        Breitner states that he has read recent stories on the
investigation in which the names Clay and Clem Bertrand have
been mentioned, and that this is what refreshed his memory on
the above.
```

Breitner called the Berkeley Police Department in April 1965 insisting that his wife had attempted to kill him by means of putting "a poisonous powder" in his soup. He made a series of phone calls in February 1968 to the FBI claiming that his life had been threatened by people who were manufacturing miniature darts treated with poison. He wrote another letter in 1969 about CIA harassment. Of course, Garrison did not dare put Breitner on the witness stand.

As for Perry Russo, Garrison's chief witness against Clay

Shaw, DiEugenio completely ignores damaging material. When Russo was first questioned in Baton Rouge, he didn't say a word about Shaw being part of a conspiracy and said he had only briefly met Shaw twice. All that changed when he was brought to New Orleans, administered sodium pentothal, then hypnotized during three sessions. DiEugenio leaves all this out, making it appear that Russo had told one consistent story from the beginning. James Phelan wrote to DiEugenio's publisher and said that "this requires him to censor extensive passages of the trial record and eliminate the cause of Garrison's court disaster."

Since they can't prove that Shaw was Bertrand, well, these authors just make incriminating stuff up. For instance, DiEugenio makes a big deal out of an entry in Clay Shaw's notebook. "Although the entire book listed addresses and phone numbers, on one otherwise blank page were scrawled two abbreviations 'Oct.' and 'Nov.' and next to those, the word 'Dallas.'" This claim was taken, almost word-for-word, from Garrison's book. The actual page from Shaw's notebook is shown below, and it's not quite as advertised. Is there something nefarious that I am missing?

Of course, taking all context out of documents is a DiEugenio specialty. In the summer of 1977, as indicated in Chapter 17, Garrison met with investigators from the HSCA for about a week. Jonathan Blackmer, the lead attorney looking into New Orleans, reported on this in a lengthy memo in which he listed Garrison's main suspects. They were at the front end investigating Garrison's leads, and you can see that when he wrote that "Garrison is putting together a file on Clay Shaw which he will forward to the Select Committee upon completion." Garrison's files on David Ferrie were being indexed by Patricia Orr, an HSCA staffer.

The section on Clay Shaw says that "Garrison believes Shaw was part of a conspiracy whose ultimate goal was the assassination of JFK." Blackmer is just repeating what Garrison told him, and then he writes:

"We have reason to believe that Shaw was heavily involved in the anti-Castro efforts in New Orleans in the 1960's and possibly one of the high-level planners or "cut out" to the planners of the assassination."

The section concludes that "further information about Shaw will be developed as we receive it from Garrison" and that "we are still developing a partial witness list for Shaw."

DiEugenio quotes the statement above about Shaw being a planner and, by removing all context, makes it look like an HSCA conclusion as opposed to a Garrison belief. Needless to say, the HSCA Final Report didn't mention any of this.

Of course, the real reason Garrison lost his case against Shaw was not his lack of evidence. No, DiEugenio believes there was a "three-stage program to destruct Garrison's case and to be make sure Shaw would be acquitted."

The first stage consisted of "singleton" penetrations of his office to disrupt from within. William Gurvich was Garrison's chief investigator who quit in disgust in June 1967. But really, it is claimed, he was CIA. The evidence? Well, his father was an FBI agent, but here's the kicker: Gurvich's niece told a JFK critic whom she had met on holiday that "he did some work for the CIA." Gordon Novel, the scam artist who tricked Garrison into hiring him as his electronic security chief, was an "experienced CIA operative" who "became a good target for Allen Dulles to hire to infiltrate Garrison's office."[2] Nice story, just no evidence. DiEugenio tries to make the case that Novel's lawyers were paid by the CIA. But the papers of Elmer Gertz, Novel's lawyer in his libel case against *Playboy* magazine and Jim Garrison, contain hundreds of letters demanding payment from Novel and threatening to end the case.

The second stage was the use of "intelligence assets/journalists" like James Phelan, Hugh Aynesworth, and Walter Sheridan to wreck Garrison. Sheridan produced the NBC documentary on the Garrison investigation (see Chapter 7). DiEugenio believes that the CIA funneled money to him to defer production costs and that a "covert team was assembled" around Sheridan. But Sheridan was a long-time "trusted Kennedy family operative, loyalist, and staffer for three decades." When he died, Edward Kennedy said he was "an extraordinary investigator and an extraordinary human being. His courage and dedication to justice and the public interest were unmatched by anyone." Incredibly, DiEugenio believes that a long-time friend of the Kennedy family would let JFK's murderers go free.

James Phelan was the journalist Garrison confided in in Las Vegas. He realized that Perry Russo's initial statements in Baton Rouge did not contain the conspiracy story he had spun in New Orleans. But had Phelan wanted to harm Garrison, he could have gone straight to Shaw's attorneys with this information. Instead, he went back to Garrison to confront him with the inconsistent stories. To DiEugenio, Phelan was "on a mission" and was an "intelligence asset." Another nice story and, again, no evidence.

Hugh Aynesworth is one of the finest journalists of our time. He covered every angle of the JFK assassination, from Dealey Plaza to Jack Ruby's trial, and he was also an early confidante of Jim Garrison's. His big crime was helping Shaw's attorneys, and naturally DiEugenio believes Aynesworth was CIA. His proof? Aynesworth tried to get into Cuba in 1962 and told the contact division of the CIA he would provide information (the CIA memo is below).

Chief, Contact Division (LA Branch)   10 Oct 63
VIA   : Chief, Houston Office

'Resident Agent, Dallas

Possibility of Hugh Grant Aynesworth Making Trip to Cuba

1. Hugh Grant Aynesworth, Science-Aviation reporter for the
Dallas Morning News, told me that he had applied for a visa for Cuba
approximately a year ago. He heard nothing for some 11 months and then
in early September of 1963 he received a call from the Czech Embassy in
Washington, D. C., asking him if he was still interested in going. He
replied that he was and asked if his application was going to receive
favorable consideration. The Czech Embassy representative would only
state that it was being considered.

2. Aynesworth has had some 15 years experience as a reporter
and since February 1960 has been the Science-Aviation reporter for the
Dallas Morning News. He has offered his services to us if it develops
that he receives a visa. I am submitting a name check request for
Aynesworth and will keep you advised of developments.

Harold Weisberg wrote to Joan Mellen in April 2000 and
said, "The CIA did not have to penetrate Garrison. He provided
his own endless insanities." In another letter to her, he wrote,
"Nobody had to do a thing to him. He did more than enough to
himself."

David Reitzes, one of the best researchers of the Garrison
fiasco, sums it up best.

---

*"Faced with the fact that several people who worked with
Garrison quit and went public with their disagreement,
the Garrisonites explain that these people were spies
anyway. Faced with Big Jim's wild, constantly changing
theories and enthusiasms, they explain that the spooks
were feeding him disinformation. Faced with the negative
press coverage he garnered, they explain that this was a
"media campaign" against him. Faced with witnesses who*

fled New Orleans and refused to cooperate, they see the nefarious hand of conspirators undermining the DA's case. To vindicate Garrison, they have to implicate virtually everybody else as a spook."

The last stage, according to DiEugenio, was run by the CIA itself through people like James Angleton and Richard Helms. They set up a "Garrison Group" within the CIA, and they "quashed subpoenas," "flipped witnesses," and "physically assaulted witnesses." This was all in CIA documents "that originated in the office of [CIA Director] Richard Helms." Robert Tanenbaum, former deputy chief counsel of the HSCA, told DiEugenio he had seen these documents. Unfortunately, they have simply vanished into thin air.[3]

The CIA, under directions from the Justice Department, did nothing to help Clay Shaw and did not interfere with the Garrison investigation. Here's the real story:

Ramsey Clark, attorney general at the time, took an interest in the Garrison investigation from the beginning and asked the FBI to inform him if anything interesting develops. Lyndon Johnson called up Clark to make sure there was no "interfering or obstruction" of Garrison's investigation, lest he start claiming the government was engaged in a cover-up. If any evidence of value turned up, he wanted to know. Clark called Johnson when David Ferrie died and told him that the Garrison investigation "from every indication ... every piece of evidence that we had indicate[d that] highly erratic people were involved ... [and there's no] factual basis to support any of it."

The CIA was also watching, and a June 1967 memo says Garrison had "attacked CIA more vehemently, viciously, and mendaciously than any other American official or private citizen whose comments have come to our attention. In fact, he outstripped the foreign Communist press, which is now quoting him delightedly."

Clay Shaw's legal team felt he was up against a "stacked deck." In August 1967, they learned that one of their investigators was leaking information back to Garrison. And facing them was a juggernaut: Garrison had private money for his investigation, full control of the New Orleans legal system, and the resources of local and state police on call, all with little oversight. On top of this, Shaw's spiraling costs for private investigators were eating into his nest egg, and his friends and family were scared. Who else might Garrison charge with conspiracy? So Shaw's attorneys decided to go to Washington in September 1967 for help.

Wegmann and Dymond met with Jack Miller, a former assistant attorney general, who agreed to help them. They wanted to meet with anybody at the CIA who could "steer them to the true facts and circumstances" relating to Garrison's charges regarding the agency. Miller then spoke to the CIA's general counsel Lawrence Houston, who then discovered that the Department of Justice did "not want the Agency to contact Shaw's lawyers, but rather to maintain the safety of our executive privilege."

On September 21, 1967, Wegmann and Dymond met with Nathaniel Kossack, the first assistant in the Criminal Division of the Department of Justice, and gave him a list of people that Garrison might involve in the Shaw trial. Ramsey Clark was told that Wegmann and Dymond "presented a strong plea for investigative assistance and cooperation to help them refute charges that are otherwise unanswerable. Ultimately, their objective is access to information in the CIA files. Mr. Kossack said only that he would communicate with them further, without any pledge of assistance."

Donovan Pratt of the CIA wrote a memo for the record saying that "if Garrison learned of federal assistance to Shaw's lawyers, he'd play it to the hilt." He suggested that "Mr. Houston advise Mr. Kossack to tell Mr. Miller to propose to Shaw's lawyers that they study the first volume [of the Warren Report], at least with care ... If Shaw's lawyers are confused by Garrison's smoke screen, a careful study of the report ought to set them straight again."

The CIA had already set up a new committee called the Garrison Group, which met three times in September 1967 to address a major dilemma. Several people involved in the Garrison investigation had links to the CIA from their involvement in the fight against Castro. Others were falsely linked, but the CIA could not deny those claims without addressing the real ones. And the elephant in the room was Clay Shaw's relationship as a contact of the domestic contact service from 1948 to 1956, something that Shaw's lawyers did not even know about.

> *"In view of this dilemma, the Department of Justice has so far taken the position that if any effort is made by either the prosecution or defense to involve CIA in the trial, the Government will claim executive privilege. This, too can be turned by Garrison into a claim that is part of the whole cover up by the establishment and particularly by CIA. No alternative to the claim of privilege appears to be available."*

Therefore, "the Government cannot take any action publicly to refute Garrison's claims and the testimony of his witnesses, as the Louisiana judge would almost certainly take the position that any such public statement would negate the privilege." So "there is no action we can recommend for the Director of the Agency to take."

This presented a problem in that Clay Shaw's "lawyers have

no way of refuting these stories except by attacking the credibility of the witnesses or introducing other witnesses to impeach their stories. They have so far no Government information which they can use for this purpose." Lastly, Houston wrote that "if during the trial it appears that Shaw may be convicted on information that could be refuted by CIA, we may be in for some difficult decisions."

MEMORANDUM FOR: The Director

Attached is a paper which attempts to analyze and predict possible events in the Garrison situation in New Orleans. It also takes the position that there is nothing we can do at the moment. The Department of Justice has seen and agrees. We are following the situation very closely with them.

/s

LAWRENCE R. HOUSTON
General Counsel
2 October 1967
(DATE)

APPROVED FOR RELEASE
CIA HISTORICAL REVIEW PROGRAM 1993

FORM NO. 101 REPLACES FORM 10-101
1 AUG 54   WHICH MAY BE USED.   (47)

Shaw's attorneys also failed with the FBI. On March 9, 1967, Wegmann phoned Robert Wick in the FBI's public affairs office. He wanted Washington HQ to "instruct the New Orleans office ... to cooperate ... in supplying a 'rap sheet' (criminal or arrest record) of the individual Garrison names as the informant against Shaw." The FBI refused to help.[4]

ACTION TAKEN

I told Mr. Wegmann the FBI could not be of any help. I told him that the files of the FBI are confidential by order of the Attorney General and can be made available only to duly authorized persons. He asked if I had any suggestions as to how he could identify and obtain the record and background of the man named by District Attorney Garrison as the informant. I told him I had no suggestions. He stated he believed he would continue pursuing the matter through Attorney General Clark, Sanders and Vinson. He said he believed the FBI should help in this matter since an innocent man is involved.

FBI document 62-109060-4772, dated March 9, 1967.

In April, the FBI learned of Wegmann's wish to travel to Washington in order to discuss "the situation" with the director. He was informed that due to Hoover's busy schedule, other officials at the Bureau handled such matters. The memo concluded by stating that the FBI would be happy to accept any information on the assassination that Wegmann could provide but that "the Bureau would not be able to offer Wegmann any assistance of any kind."

None of this was surprising given that the FBI was sitting on reports that Garrison had falsified his National Guard drill certifications—in other words, he had been fraudulently paid. Two sources reported this to the FBI, but as can be seen below, they decided to do nothing. Garrison resigned his commission.

OBSERVATIONS:

     We have now received from two sources the same basic
allegation of fraud in connection with Garrison's service in the
Louisiana National Guard. The situation today is the same as
existed in April, 1967. Any investigation of the fraud allegation
by the Bureau would become known in the New Orleans area. Rightly
or wrongly, the Bureau would be accused of trying to intimidate
Garrison and engaging in the same tactics which are currently
being charged to Garrison himself.

ACTION:

     It is believed the Bureau's best course of action here
would be to disseminate to Assistant Attorneys General Sanders,
Vinson and Yeagley the information we have received since these
individuals are the normal recipients of all data volunteered to
the Bureau concerning the current Garrison investigation. It would
not be in the Bureau's best interest to voluntarily institute a
fraud investigation of Garrison at this time.

*FBI memo dated May 16, 1967, from Branigan to Sullivan
regarding James C. Garrison's fraud against the government.*

Wegmann told author Patricia Lambert that he had managed
to arrange a meeting with Robert Kennedy but that nothing had
happened. Dymond and Wegmann then drafted a lengthy civil
rights complaint to John Doar, assistant attorney general in the
DOJ's Civil Rights Division, which included details of Garrison's
bribery offers to Leemans and Beauboeuf (see Chapter 7). On
March 21, 1968, they met with Stephen Pollak and John Kirby of
the Civil Rights Division, who told them that "there was no basis
for our conducting an investigation ... that while [the Justice
Department] does not endorse the methods which Wegmann
alleges Garrison has used in this prosecution, that there does not
appear to be a statutory basis for our proceeding at the present
time." Wegmann threatened to go public with his civil rights
complaint, but Pollak agreed to review the materials one more
time.

Wegmann was puzzled about their reasons for refusing to
proceed and wrote them a letter that expressed his anger and
disappointment.

> *"It is my opinion that the facts outlined ... as supported and corroborated by the documents furnished to you, establish beyond any question of a doubt that the District Attorney's case against Clay Shaw is pure fiction and that he is the victim of an unscrupulous and unconscionable public prosecutor ... Certainly there can be no doubt but that the facts presented ... warrant nothing less than an investigation of the situation by the Department or such other government agency as is appropriate."*

On March 28, 1968, Pollak responded and said that "there is presently no basis for departmental investigation of your charges." Shaw's lawyers then filed a forty-five-page complaint in the US District Court in New Orleans asking it to provide "sanctuary" for Shaw and to grant "injunctive relief" against Garrison. Ultimately, this all failed—the court dismissed the complaint, and this was later upheld by the U.S. Supreme Court.

After Shaw was charged with perjury in 1969, Shaw's attorneys filed another civil rights complaint. David Bonderman, part of Richard Nixon's new team at the DOJ, reviewed the request and claimed that "prosecutorial discretion covers at least the right to made bad, erroneous, and even silly decisions," but that "does not extend to bribing witnesses to give false testimony." He believed there was a legal basis for the DOJ to intervene but wished it could have been investigated back in 1967. He decided not to proceed, citing "the general problems in getting involved in the Garrison probe." Patricia Lambert notes that "his memorandum shows Department of Justice officials so determined to keep their distance from Garrison that they abrogated their responsibility, statutory and moral, to Clay Shaw. They simply threw him to the wolves."

Bereft of any sort of valid conspiracy in the assassination, the

Garrisonites cannot sustain their view that Kennedy was a martyr of his politics. Even so, they get his politics all wrong. His administration was waging war against Castro, including assassination attempts against Castro managed by the CIA with help from the mob and anti-Castro Cubans. The CIA was compelled to protect such a potentially explosive secret; it was no wonder that they were watching Garrison.

Garrison was right to think that New Orleans just might have been the incubator for the assassination, but not in the way he imagined. In June 1963, the Kennedy administration decided to step up covert operations inside Cuba. In August, anti-Castro Cubans shelled a Cuban factory. On September 5 two planes dropped bombs on Cuba, after which Fidel Castro gave an important interview on September 7. In it, he denounced "U.S.-prompted raids" and warned that "we are prepared to fight them and answer in kind. United States leaders should think that if they are aiding terrorist plans to eliminate Cuban leaders, they themselves will not be safe."

LA., MONDAY MORNING, SEPTEMBER 9, 1963   SEC

Castro Blasts Raids on Cuba

Says U.S. Leaders Im-|tion. But he said: "We are taking|tial election.
periled by Aid to Rebels|into account the current world| **BOTH 'CHEAP, CROOKED'**
|situation, which of course involves| "I am sure it will be a fight

Castro's interview was reported in the *Times-Picayune*, which Oswald most assuredly read. Author Jean Davison believes that, to Oswald, this might have seemed "like the king's outcry against Becket: Who will rid me of this man?" In late September, Oswald visited the Cuban and Soviet embassies in Mexico City trying to get a visa to Cuba. He was turned away, and this must have added to his anger. He returned to New Orleans, moved to Dallas, and happened to get a job in a building where Kennedy's motorcade would pass.

Strictly by chance, Oswald was able to strike a blow for the revolution.

While this was happening, the CIA was contacting a Cuban official, Rolando Cubela (code-named AM/LASH) to kill Castro and precipitate a coup. He wouldn't proceed until he received a message from top officials in the U.S. government, and one was embedded in Kennedy's speech in Miami on November 18, 1963. A poison pen letter was delivered to Cubela on the same day Kennedy was assassinated.

To be fair, Kennedy also appeared to extend the hand of friendship to Castro through the efforts of William Attwood, who worked in the U.S. mission at the U.N. He had been told that Castro would make "substantial concessions" to the U.S. for normalization. Two journalists, Lisa Howard and Jean Daniel, made contact with Cuban officials. But Richard Helms, director of the CIA, told Congress that the accommodation effort was a "feint" and that the administration's genuine efforts were focused on covert action.

Researcher Gus Russo writes that Garrison came close to figuring it all out but got it backward.

"Garrison was appallingly close to the heart of the coverup, but due to his immense ego and hatred of the government, he chose to see everything in reverse: 544 Camp St. was key to the case, but Garrison refused to see the obvious—Arcacha and the Cuban Revolutionary Council worked hand-in-glove with Bobby Kennedy and the White House; the camps on Lake Pontchartrain of which Garrison was aware, were a cog in the Central American plan of the Artime/Kennedy liaison, not part of an anti-Kennedy clique; Garrison was well-aware of the Rosselli admissions of the White house-backed anti-Castro plots."

Paul Hoch speculated that "the reason the CIA was so upset about Garrison was the threat he posed to the CIA's mob connections, specifically the AM/LASH operation, the efforts to kill Castro, which in 1967 were a big secret. If Garrison pulled on the Anti-Castro Cuban thread there was a risk of unraveling all that."

The viciousness of the Garrisonites had now morphed into anti-Zionism. In 2018, a new book by Michele Metta, *CMC: The Italian Undercover CIA and Mossad Station and the Assassination of JFK*, ties Israel into the Permindex story. Metta quotes a paragraph on George Mantello from a CIA document on Permindex.

5. In 1951, two well-placed sources one of known reliability reported that Subject was closely connected with the Israeli Intelligence Service (IIS). One of these sources, who was of unknown reliability stated that the IIS had separated Subject from their service; no reason was given for this alleged separation. In October 1951 Subject was a partner in the "Banque Pour le Commerce Suisse-Amerique Centrale" of Geneva, which supplied cover employment for IIS agents. Subject's partner in the bank, Jack PAUDA, was closely and actively associated with IIS work.

But why wouldn't the Israelis contact Mantello? He had saved thousands of Jews during the Holocaust and had intimate knowledge of Jewish displaced persons in Europe. From 1948 onward, thousands of Jews left Europe for the new state of Israel. There was nothing shameful about working with the Israelis. The fact that Metta sees this relationship as nefarious tells us more about Metta than Mantello.

Metta goes further and states that in 1967 the brother of Shimon Peres, Gershon Peres, joined the Board of CMC. Why is this relevant? Well, David Ben-Gurion was prime minister of Israel when Kennedy was president. Shimon Peres was his "right-hand man," and "Peres' determination to reach the goal of an

Israeli nuclear arsenal was absolutely no less callous than that of Ben-Gurion himself." Kennedy was opposed to Israel obtaining the nuclear bomb, and "the leaders of the Jewish state saw Kennedy as the enemy."

Nothing could be further from the truth. Israel found itself isolated in the 1950s as the United States under Eisenhower kept its distance. The US-Israel relationship warmed under Kennedy, and Israel started receiving defensive arms from the United States. Facing genocidal neighbors, Israel asked for security guarantees. Kennedy demurred, and Israel made the decision to take her safety and security into her own hands, eventually arming herself with nuclear weapons. No one in Israel saw Kennedy as an enemy.

Metta believes that the people who killed Kennedy were also responsible "for all the wrong-doings that today plague the destiny of Israel, plunging it down into a situation that the Jews exterminated by the gas chambers would certainly be ashamed of." Is it any wonder that he then tells people they should not shout stupid phrases like "Hitler was right" or "Death to Israelis?" What else would he expect when people read that the Mossad was among the conspirators that killed JFK?

And who do you think wrote a blurb for his front cover? None other than Oliver Stone, who called the book "Important ... and it goes to the core of much of my movie I made, which is about fascism." But what on earth does Oliver Stone know about fascism? After all, he believes that Putin has been a "stabilizing force" in Syria, and bombing hospitals doesn't seem to concern him. Iran's support of terrorist groups like Hamas and Hezbollah do not bother him in the least, and he believes that Hugo Chavez was a champion of the people of Venezuela. He actually misses Fidel Castro.

No doubt we'll be hearing a lot more about this because Stone is working with James DiEugenio to adapt *Destiny*

Betrayed into a three-part television documentary scheduled to air in the fall of 2020. He told the press that "This documentary film represents an important bookend to my 1991 film. It ties up many loose threads, and hopefully repudiates much of the ignorance around the case and the movie."

God help us!

As I am writing this, the world is in the grips of the coronavirus pandemic. When we emerge, serious questions will have to be asked about the future of capitalism and global supply chains, how the thuggish and brutal Communist Party of China initially withheld important information about the transmissibility of the virus, and how we can reform the UN and its agencies to properly defend the rights of democratic peoples around the globe. The last thing any country needs is a populace steeped in conspiracy theories.

But Oliver Stone would rather have us tilt at windmills, and I expect many people will lap it up, all too eager to fawn over a filmmaker who glorified Jim Garrison, a man who used his power and influence to ruin the lives of innocent people.

Just then they came in sight of thirty or forty windmills that rise from that plain. And no sooner did Don Quixote see them that he said to his squire, "Fortune is guiding our affairs better than we ourselves could have wished. Do you see over yonder, friend Sancho, thirty or forty hulking giants? I intend to do battle with them and slay them. With their spoils we shall begin to be rich for this is a righteous war and the removal of so foul a brood from off the face of the earth is a service God will bless."

"What giants?" asked Sancho Panza.

"Those you see over there," replied his master, "with their long arms. Some of them have arms well nigh two leagues in length."

"Take care, sir," cried Sancho. "Those over there are not giants but windmills. Those things that seem to be their arms are sails which, when they are whirled around by the wind, turn the millstone."

ACKNOWLEDGMENTS

I really want to thank my dear partner Andrew Yip, who has now heard just about every Jim Garrison story in existence. I'm sure he'd rather do almost anything than listen to yet another ridiculous story related to the case.

This is the third time Michael J. Totten has been my editor, and it's a joy to work with him. He has magical ability—he turns manuscripts into books in short periods of time. Thanks, Michael, and I can't wait till we are out in Oregon again for another one of your amazing tours.

My dear friend Shelley Christina edited my manuscript to improve my English, and boy did she do a great job. She's a tried-and-true friend, and our lunches together are classic.

Paul Hoch has been an amazing resource every step along the way. He has an uncanny ability to find documents and links on the web that are way off in the hinterland. Paul has patiently reviewed my book and notes, and his suggestions have improved this book considerably.

Paul also knows all the major JFK researchers, and he put me in touch with Alecia Long and Don Carpenter. Alecia is an important historian, and her upcoming book on the Garrison case is groundbreaking. She has always been helpful. No one knows more about Clay Shaw than Don Carpenter, and whenever I have a question, I turn to him.

Paul also put me in touch with Larry Haapanen, who volunteered as a researcher on the west coast for Jim Garrison. Larry provided some important documents on Fred Crisman and others caught up in the Garrison investigation, and he patiently answered all my questions.

One of the many blessings of this project was getting to know Hugh Aynesworth. He's been involved in every facet of the JFK assassination, and he loves to regale you with terrific first-hand stories. He's one of the great reporters in America, and it's been an honor to know him.

On a trip to Washington, Andrew and I had a fun lunch with Gus Russo. He's one of the best JFK researchers out there, and he treated us with wonderful stories from his days working on the PBS/Frontline documentary on Lee Harvey Oswald and being on the set of Oliver Stone's film JFK. Gus's papers at Baylor University were a treasure trove of important material for my book.

Todd Vaughan, John McAdams, and Max Holland are three amazing JFK researchers who have always been incredibly helpful. Todd knows the case backward and forward and is always sending me documents. John runs the best JFK assassination web site and has always been supportive. I'm quite proud to have a few of my pieces on his site. Max has done important research on the Permindex story, and I am indebted to him for his help and guidance.

Steve Roe found and donated the papers of Patricia Lambert to the Sixth Floor Museum, an act that greatly furthered research into Jim Garrison. I am indebted to Steve for his gift.

Krishna Shenoy at the Sixth Floor Museum spent three days of her life helping me go through the papers of Patricia Lambert.

She always had a smile on her face, and I greatly appreciate her help. The Sixth Floor Museum is a terrific resource, and all the people there are friendly and supportive. I also want to thank Stephen Fagin, the curator of the Sixth Floor, for including me in their oral history project.

The Mary Ferrell Foundation played an important role in the research for my book, and many documents that I have sourced can be found in their archive. Rex Bradford was always helpful, and he continues to add more Garrison documents. I strongly urge researchers to join the foundation.

David Reitzes has one of the best online resource for information on Garrison and Oliver Stone, and I am heavily indebted to him for his support.

John Kelin generously provided documents from the Sylvia Meagher Archive that were essential to my chapter on Jim Garrison's book.

I visited a variety of archives across the country, and I want to thank the following people: Ted Jackson at Georgetown University, Jennifer Navarre at the New Orleans Historic Collection, Toby Peterson at Hood College, Jane Parr at Boston University, and Amanda Fisher at Baylor University.

Few people know more about Jim Garrison than Stephen Tyler. He was kind enough to give me access to Stephen Roy's manuscript on David Ferrie, an incredible resource that I hope is published soon.

John Kowalski helped me with research at the Library & Archives Canada.

I also want to recognize my buddies from FP4JFK who all met in Dallas in March 2020: F. J. James, Scott Maudsley, Dave Ledbetter, Steve Roe, Bill Brown, Frank Badalson, Matt Douthit, Jerry Dealey (who is one of the best tour guides in Dallas), Ed Murray, Freda Ann Dillard, Chris Peeks, and Joseph Landwermeyer. And a shout out to the founder of FP4JFK, Jim Hess.

Pina Giovannitti translated a paragraph from an Italian newspaper, greatly improving what I had retrieved from Google Translate. Thank you, Pina.

Gil Koltun did superb research work in Israel on George Mantello. Thank you, Gil, and thank you Vera Shalom for putting us in contact.

I also want to thank Scott Lorenz at Westwind Communications, who has been a joy to work with in promoting this book.

Other people who have inspired me along the way include Nick Nalli, Roy Eappen, Tamara and Anthony Fulmes, Terry Glavin, Ron Radosh, Sol Stern, David Roytenberg, Fred Maroun, and Mark and Denise Collins.

Any error or mistake is mine and mine alone.

ADDITIONAL INFORMATION

Here is an annotated list of books, videos, and websites that you would be well-advised to check out.

BOOKS

Hugh Aynesworth, *JFK: Breaking the News,* (IFP, 2003). Aynesworth was a first-hand witness to large parts of the Garrison affair. A terrific book on the JFK assassination.

Tom Bethell, *The Electric Windmill: An Inadvertent Biography,* (Regnery Gateway, 1988). Bethell was on Garrison's staff and this book contains a chapter on the investigation. Worth the price of the book.

Milton Brener, *The Garrison case: A study in the abuse of power,* (C.N. Potter, 1969). Brener worked for Garrison in the beginning and then was the defense lawyer for several of the people involved in the case. Out of print, but available used; this book is indispensable. Highly recommended.

Vincent Bugliosi, *Reclaiming History: The Assassination of*

President John F. Kennedy, (W.W. Norton & Co., 2007). A very important book, with a big chapter on Jim Garrison.

Don Carpenter, *Man of a Million Fragments: The True Story of Clay Shaw*, (Donald H. Carpenter, 2014). A thorough and encyclopedic biography of Clay Shaw. An amazing amount of primary research went into this book.

Edward Jay Epstein, *The Assassination Chronicles: Inquest, Counterplot, and Legend*, (Carroll & Graf, 1992). Epstein witnesses first-hand the craziness of the Garrison investigation. A good buy in that you get all of Epstein's writings on the JFK assassination.

Jim Garrison, *On the Trail of the Assassins*, (Sheridan Square Press, 1988). This is probably the best fictional account available.

Adam Gorightly, *Caught in the Crossfire: Kerry Thornley, Lee Oswald and the Garrison Investigation*, (Feral House, 2014). The complete story of Kerry Thornley—this book contains a lot of documents and some of his writings.

Warren Hinckle, *If You Have a Lemon, Make Lemonade*, (Norton, 1990). Hinckle was the editor of *Ramparts*, a popular left-wing magazine in the 1960s, and his chapter on the JFK assassination 'sleuths' is very funny.

Rosemary James, *Plot or Politics? The Garrison Case and Its Cast*, (Pelican, 1967). James covered the case for the New Orleans States-Item and this book is a useful early primer.

James Kirkwood, *American Grotesque*, (Simon & Schuster, 1970). The best account of Clay Shaw's trial. Kirkwood was a playwright (A Chorus Line) and thus the writing is excellent. Recommended.

David Kranzler, *The Man Who Stopped the Trains to Auschwitz*, (Syracuse University Press, 2000). The story of George Mantello who rescued more than 140,000 Jews from Budapest during World War II.

Patricia Lambert, *False Witness: The Real Story of Jim Garrison's Investigation and Oliver Stone's Film JFK*, (M. Evans & Co.,

1999). Lambert went out and did a lot of original research and it shows. This book is an absolute must-read. Well-researched and well-written.

Alecia P. Long, *Cruising for Conspirators: How the Assassination of John F. Kennedy Became a Sex Crime*, (UNC Press, 2020). A ground-breaking and important book on how sexuality in general, and homosexuality in particular, played a role in shaping people's beliefs on the assassination.

John McAdams, *JFK Assassination Logic: How to Think about Claims of Conspiracy*, Potomac Books, 2011). A handy primer on how to evaluate evidence. Lots of material on Jim Garrison.

James Phelan, *Scandals, Scamps and Scoundrels: The Casebook of an Investigative Reporter*, (Random House, 1982). This book is worth it just for Phelan's chapter on Jim Garrison.

Gus Russo, *Live by the Sword: The Secret War Against Castro and the Death of JFK*, (Bancroft Press, 1998). Russo is a terrific researcher and this book details the Kennedy's war against Castro. Well worth your time.

James Savage, *Jim Garrison's Bourbon Street Brawl: The Making of a First Amendment Milestone*, (the University of Louisiana at Lafayette, 2010). An excellent overview of Garrison's fight with the judges in New Orleans.

Oliver Stone & Zachary Sklar, *JFK: The Documented Screenplay*, (Applause Books, 1992) The annotated screenplay of the film *JFK* along with reactions and commentaries.

WEBSITES

National Archives and Records Administration
    https://www.archives.gov/research/jfk
    You can access the papers of Jim Garrison for free.

The Kennedy Assassination, John McAdams

http://mcadams.posc.mu.edu/home.htm
The best JFK assassination web page with a lot of material on Jim Garrison.

JFK Assassination Resources Online, David Reitzes
http://www.jfk-online.com/home.html
David Reitzes has an amazing collection of original material on the Garrison case. Indispensable.

Mary Farrell Foundation
https://www.maryferrell.org/pages/Main_Page.html
The major repository of JFK documents on the internet. Worthwhile joining.

Washington Decoded, Max Holland
https://www.washingtondecoded.com/
A collection of excellent articles and book reviews with a lot of material on Garrison.

VIDEOS

False Witness, History Channel, 2000. A good documentary based on Patricia Lambert's book.

He Must Have Something, Stephen Tyler, 1992. A very good documentary on the Garrison Affair.
https://vimeo.com/311326731

Notes and Sources

For updates, reviews and pictures about this book, please visit www.onthetrailofdelusion.com
I have included links to many of the documents cited. In several instances, where links are not available, I have linked to a similar article or document.

Interviews for this book include Philip Pochoda, Gary Schoener, Milton Brener, Al Beauboeuf, Larry Haapanen, Steve Burton, Joel Palmer, Harry Connick, Sr., and Gary Cornwell. Joel Palmer was nice enough to offer an extensive narrative on his involvement in the case and I have put his material on my website.

Please note that many Garrison documents can be found in multiple locations. For instance, the Papers of Irvin Dymond in New Orleans include the complete Garrison master file that William Gurvich gave to the Shaw defense team. Many of those documents are also in other collections at the National Archives and Records Administration (NARA), and elsewhere.

Here is a listing of the archives I visited for this book:

Papers of Jim Garrison, NARA, College Park, MD.

Investigative Files received from New Orleans District Attorney Harry Connick, NARA, College Park, MD.

Donated Papers of Edward Wegmann, Clay Shaw's Attorney, NARA, College Park, MD.

Papers of Richard Billings at Georgetown University.

Papers of Richard E. Sprague at Georgetown University; and NARA, College Park, MD.

Jim Garrison Papers at the New Orleans Public Library.

Papers of Irvin Dymond, Clay Shaw's trial attorney, at the New Orleans Historical Association.

Papers of Clay Shaw at NARA, College Park, MD.

Papers of George Lardner, Jr, at the Library of Congress.

The Harold Weisberg Archive at Hood College, MD and online at http://jfk.hood.edu/

Papers of Sylvia Meagher at Hood College, MD.

Papers of James Kirkwood at Boston University.

Papers of Gerald Posner at Boston University.

Papers of Gus Russo at Baylor University.

Papers of Patricia Lambert at the Sixth Floor Museum in Dallas.

Papers of Louis Bloomfield at the Library & Archives Canada, Ottawa.

Papers of Elmer Gertz at the Library of Congress.

Papers of Bill Boxley at NARA, College Park, MD.

Alex Dworkin Canadian Jewish Archives, Montreal.

All the documents from NARA cited or embedded in the text are from the JFK Assassination Records Collection established by the 1992 JFK Act (P.L.-102-526): https://www.archives.gov/research/jfk

NOTES

INTRODUCTION

1. Garrison charged Gurvich with theft of $19 for giving the master file to Shaw's attorneys. He purposely set the value at $19 because a higher amount would have allowed Gurvich to have a trial by jury. There was no discovery in Louisiana courts at the time, and without this information, Shaw would have had a much tougher time defending himself. The charges were eventually dropped.

1. THE TAKING OF NEW ORLEANS 1-2-3

1. David Chandler, a reporter for the *Times-Picayune*, told James Kirkwood that Garrison had "always been successful with his Grand Juries—he begins by seducing them. He is locally famous, and he is friendly with them and takes them to lunch and just does everything he can to win them over."

2. In 1969 when Charles Ward, an assistant district attorney under Garrison, was running for DA, he told a Young Men's Business Club that "today, when you walk down Bourbon Street, I think you'll see it's in the shape it was prior to Garrison's entrance into office. I don't see any change, and I told him this before I left office. I see the same type of strip show. There are the same B-drinking cases. There are the same barkers on Bourbon Street. Why? Why lose interest? No more publicity about raiding Bourbon Street. When there's no publicity, there's no action."

3. The ultimate irony is that Garrison's focus on the JFK assassination meant a rising backlog of other cases. In April 1967, Judge Edward Haggerty threw out seven cases alone. The DA's office docketed 257 fewer cases in the January to March time frame in 1967 than in 1966, 436 few cases than in 1965, and 453 fewer cases than in 1964. "Criminal lawyers have complained privately to reporters that there has been a recent slowdown in the wheels of justice, but none would be quoted. One said he had to deal with the district attorney and he didn't want to anger him." In May 1967, Aaron Kohn talked to Judge Bernhard Bagert, who told him that "In his own section of the court one year ago he had 15 prisoners in custody awaiting trial; that at the present time he has 42 such cases." He also "expressed concern that anything he might say to me would get back to Garrison."

4. The publicity surrounding the use of the funds to investigate the JFK assassination led Garrison to set up a private organization, Truth and Conse-

quences, to finance his probe. Three wealthy individuals donated money, and about $100,000 ($737,000 in 2020 dollars) was raised. There was no public accounting of the disbursement of the funds, and it was all under the control of Garrison. The channeling of funds continued until March of 1969.

2. A BEAUTIFUL MIND?

1. In his book, Garrison claimed his investigator Bill Boxley informed the police when he was flying out of Las Angeles. Boxley would shortly thereafter be accused of being a CIA agent (see Chapter 16). Interestingly, Garrison told the same story to Hugh Aynesworth on the day Shaw was acquitted, except that he said it had occurred two weeks earlier.
2. An FBI memo dated March 10, 1967, contained an allegation that Jim Garrison "was involved in a homosexual affair with a 14-year-old boy, which, according to the source, resulted in a 'big mess.'" The source had no direct knowledge but said that the information came from Irma Fasnacht, the owner of Dixie's Bar of Music.
3. Even after the two arresting officers were identified, Garrison still continued with this nonsense.
4. J. D. Tippit was a policeman who Oswald killed on the afternoon of November 22 in Dallas.

3. JIM GARRISON SOLVES THE JFK ASSASSINATION

1. A picture eventually emerged showing Oswald and Ferrie at a CAP meeting. Stephen Roy wondered in his unpublished manuscript, *Perfect Villain*, if a "CAP officer could have forgotten a cadet? As a high school teacher, Ferrie worked with about 80 students, all boys. As a CAP officer in Cleveland, he had worked with 100 boys. In his first tenure with the CAP/Lakefront in New Orleans, he worked with about 130 boys. As an instructor with CAP/Moisant, he had worked with about 20 boys. On his return to CAP/Lakefront, he worked with about 100 more boys. In his Falcon/IMSU group, he worked with about 15 boys, some new and some holdovers from CAP. That totals about 430-440 boys. Oswald attended 2-4 meetings eight years earlier. Can one believe that Ferrie might have forgotten him?"
2. Prentiss Davis, an investigator for Andrews, testified that "Andrews frequently used the name Bertrand to mask the identity of whomever he might be referring to."
3. The police report from 1963 made no mention of Martin being beaten because of seeing Oswald, Ferrie, and others. Instead, Banister accused Martin of "making some unauthorized telephone calls and run his telephone bill up."
4. Stephen Roy's biography of Ferrie, *Perfect Villain*, notes that "None of Ferrie's acquaintances recall him giving any indication that he knew anything about Oswald or the assassination."

5. Garrison initially believed that Ferrie was murdered, but he quickly moved on to suicide. Oliver Stone's film *JFK* suggests Ferrie was murdered. Dr. Frank Minyard, Garrison's friend and later coroner, believed that bruising on the inside of Ferrie's lip indicated someone had forced something down his throat. But Dr. Ronald Welsh, the pathologist who performed the autopsy, disagreed and told Patricia Lambert that "the whole idea is an absolute fantasy; it doesn't jive with anything." He also questioned Minyard's credentials, noting that "he is not a pathologist. He is an obstetrician/gynecologist and not interested in the anatomical aspects."

6. James Alcock, second in command to Garrison, told author Patricia Lambert in December 1993 that "to my knowledge there was no intent to arrest Ferrie."

4. ENTER STAGE RIGHT: PERRY RUSSO

1. That letter has disappeared and cannot be found. Garrison says he never received it.

2. At the Shaw trial, four witnesses were asked about Shaw wearing tight pants, a euphemism for homosexuality.

3. A June 26, 1967, memo from Tom Bethell to Jim Garrison confirms that Russo did not say anything about a meeting between Shaw, Ferrie, and Oswald until he came to New Orleans. Journalist James Phelan interviewed Russo after the preliminary hearing, and he admitted that he hadn't. Importantly, Bethell talked to Matt Herron who witnessed Russo admitting he had said nothing until New Orleans.

4. Shaw immediately had logistical problems. His lawyers were worried that his house might be "bombed or burned," and he temporarily moved in with a friend. His insurance company agreed, and they cancelled his home insurance. Fortunately, one of Shaw's lawyers was on the board of an insurance firm, and the policy was replaced.

5. Garrison also took a book titled *A Holiday for Murder*, a calorie counter, a copy of the *Wall Street Journal* for Feb. 6, 1961, and Shaw's Olivetti-Underwood typewriter. A list of the contents from the search was released to the press.

6. Russo got mixed up in the hypnosis sessions and erroneously referred to Bertrand as Clem rather than Clay.

7. Carlos Quiroga, an anti-Castro Cuban activist who had been to Oswald's house in 1963, told Aaron Kohn, head of the Metropolitan Crime Commission, that Louis Ivon called him on morning of March 16 and asked him the color of Oswald's leaflet. "I told him it was yellow-orange. He asked me for the size of the leaflet and I told him it was about 4 by 5. I told Mr. Louis Ivon also how in heaven could they be conducting their investigation when they did not have evidence. They didn't have the color, or the size of the leaflet."

7. A TOUCH OF BRIBERY

1. Beauboeuf told Patricia Lambert in 1996 that Ivon stuck a gun in his mouth and told him, "If you don't retract this, we're going to kill you." He confirmed this in a conversation with me in May of 2020. He also said the tape transcript was accurate.

2. Shaw's defense team wanted Beauboeuf to testify, but he chickened out and had "a sudden lapse of memory." He told Dymond that "there was just no way of Ferrie's having had a party like that without him having known about it." He also said he had never seen Clay Shaw or Lee Harvey Oswald before in his life.

3. Garrison claims in his book that the tape never existed. Of course, at the time, he said the tape had been altered. But the New Orleans police listened to the tape as part of their investigation.

4. The charges were dismissed on appeal. A perjury charge by the grand jury might have resulted in a conviction, and that would have been Cancler's fourth felony. He would have faced life imprisonment. His lawyer, Milton Brener, wrote, "Whether Cancler was solicited to commit burglary by one of Garrison's investigators is of considerable importance. His unsupported word is certainly not sufficient proof that he was. Neither, however, are Cancler's character and background conclusive proof that he was not. No serious investigation of the matter has ever been made. Nor has there been a serious denial."

5. In January 1969, Leemans recanted and swore in an affidavit that "the statements I made on the NBC program relative to Garrison's office offering me a bribe for testimony favorable to their case was a lie." But a month earlier, he had again called Dymond and said that "pressure is being put on him to change his story, to repudiate this story." He said his finances were in shambles and that "he had to do something." Interestingly, his affidavit does not mention his story about Shaw, and he was not called as a witness in the trial.

6. Perry Russo told Layton Martens in 1968 that Garrison had promised him $25,000 ($184,000 in 2020 dollars) for his work on the case but that he had only received three or four hundred dollars. He also told Martens that "my main interest is to make some money."

8. THE GREAT ACCUSER

1. *Il Paese* and *Paese Sera* (morning and afternoon editions) were published by Amerigo Terenzi, formerly the director of the official communist newspaper *l'Unita*. He hired Tomaso Smith to run the newspapers, who resigned in 1956 because of differences with the Italian Communist Party over the Soviet invasion of Hungary.

2. Shaw was never in Rome, and he never attended a board meeting of Permindex/CMC. He hated to fly, and he avoided airplanes whenever possible.

3. Shaw's homosexuality was frequently inferred from the allegation that he was Bertrand since Bertrand was gay. At Shaw's trial, Sciambra's memo on

Russo, which included the inference, was read to the jury. Interestingly, author James Kirkwood asked Irvin Dymond why Garrison hadn't openly talked about Shaw's homosexuality at trial. Here is their discussion:

Dymond: I had a little secret weapon.

Kirkwood: Well, what about—what was the secret weapon? Can you tell me?

Dymond: I don't want to put it on tape.

BREAK IN TAPE

Dymond: And I let them know that we were prepared to use that.

9. THE TRIAL

1. Assistant Attorney General of the United States Fred Vinson asked the FBI on April 10, 1968, if it had any information on Oswald being in Clinton or Jackson. The Bureau went through the investigative files of Lee Harvey Oswald and the New Orleans files concerning the assassination and found no indication that Oswald was in either place. In addition, one Clinton witness, Reeves Morgan, said he contacted the FBI after the assassination with information about Oswald. The FBI could not find any record of this, and it had informed the Garrison investigation about this.

2. One witness said that Jack Ruby was the driver of the car and that Guy Banister was one of the passengers. Another witness picked out Clay Shaw from a picture and then said, "Why, yes, that's Mr. Garrison, isn't it?" She also said he was "shabbily dressed," which does not sound like Shaw. Another witness picked out Thomas Beckham, yet another Garrison suspect that you will meet in Chapter 16, as a passenger.

3. A memo written by Jim Garrison dated November 14, 1967, on all the outstanding leads mentions that "Beckham was identified by Charles Speysel [sic] as having been at the party which he attended along with Ferrie and Shaw." Beckham was a person of interest to Garrison in 1968, but there was no mention of Spiesel's identifying him at Shaw's trial.

4. Hardiman remembered delivering mail for Clem Bertrand. But Clem Bertrand was the name that was remembered by Perry Russo. The pseudonym was supposed to be Clay Bertrand.

5. Andrews always told different stories about Clay Bertrand. In April 1967, he told Shaw's investigators that Bertrand was married and had four children and that "he probably will never identify the real Clay Bertrand." One thing is for certain: Dean Andrews never wavered in his belief that Clay Shaw was *not* Clay Bertrand.

10. CLAY SHAW V. JIM GARRISON

1. Bill Boxley, a Garrison investigator, wrote a memo about Larry Crafard on October 2, 1968, and noted that he was "unaccounted for during the morning of the assassination until God-knows-when in the afternoon." He

found it strange that Crafard had talked to a female for over two hours on that Friday night. Boxley felt that the story that Crafard had hitchhiked to Michigan after the assassination and lived there until the Ruby trial was "too Horatio Alger."

2. The tapes picked up one conversation about the JFK assassination. General Charles Cabell, former deputy director of the CIA, was the brother of Earl Cabell, the mayor of Dallas. Garrison asked Gervais to see if General Cabell had perhaps been in New Orleans in November 1963. He told Gervais, "If I can put him in the Fontainebleau Motel, then I've got enough to grab him by the ------balls."

3. Shaw's libel case ended in March 1978 when the Supreme Court overturned previous court rulings that had allowed it to continue. The *New York Times* noted that "the statute is silent on whether such suits survive the death of a plaintiff. Louisiana state law, which the Supreme Court says must apply, allows such suits to proceed only on behalf of surviving relatives. Mr. Shaw, a homosexual whom many think was selected because of his vulnerabilities, left no survivors."

11. A TALE OF THREE CUBANS

1. Carl Pelleck, reporter for the *New York Post*, wrote that Lewis "once tried to tell an editor here he had 'documented' proof that the Vatican was 'sitting' on a big story that Pope John had been canonized, and they didn't want anyone to know."

2. Gordon Novel ultimately fled to Ohio. Garrison half-heartedly tried to have him extradited but never filed proper paperwork. He was a con man; Garrison even told Richard Billings in early March that Novel was a "complete phony." In 1970 he was convicted in Reno for interstate transport of an illegal eavesdropping device. Novel claimed in 1975 that he was about to be named director of the CIA. In 1976, he was arrested by the ATF for possession of an incendiary device and for plotting to firebomb properties in New Orleans. The case was tried three times, and Novel's conviction was ultimately overturned. Over time, he got nuttier and nuttier: Gus Russo interviewed Novel and was "treated to two hours of the most sensational tales imaginable—everything to the truth behind UFO's, Watergate, Hoover, LBJ, the Kennedy Assassination, air-powered engines, etc." In 2008, Novel was plugging anti-gravity devices.

3. While Garrison liked to charge that he was being wiretapped by the FBI (totally false), the truth was that he regularly taped witnesses. He even had a bug installed in Perry Russo's home.

13. THE BALLAD OF SLIDIN' CLYDE JOHNSON

1. Irvin Dymond told James Kirkwood that during jury selection he received several phone calls from Slidin' Clyde "wanting to testify for us." Dymond

said he was "loaded every time he called. And—the wee small hours of the morning, every time." Dymond didn't think it would have been "worthwhile" to talk to him.

14. EDGAR EUGENE BRADLEY WAS A TRAMP

1. Further investigation at Lakefront Airport revealed that there was another Bradley, a Leslie Norman Bradley, who was flying there in 1963. Might this all have been a case of mistaken identity?
2. In early 1971, Roger Craig phoned Irvin Dymond, Clay Shaw's trial attorney. Dymond wrote that he said "he had been intimidated, bribed, and coerced by Garrison to testify at the conspiracy trial." Perhaps he wanted money from Dymond, but there are no memos about any follow-up to the allegation.
3. It was Max Gonzales. Pershing Gervais, Jim Garrison's army buddy and his investigative chief when he first became DA, told Patricia Lambert that Garrison wanted him [Gervais] to "give a false statement that [he] had seen Shaw out at the airport meeting with Ferrie." He refused, and "the next thing I know, Max Gonzales shows up at the Fontainebleau and he was terrified. He told me he signed this affidavit for Garrison ... It terrified him so much that Max borrowed or rented a little plane that had very little gas in it and flew it into the Gulf and nobody's ever seen him since."

15. FINALLY, A CHAPTER WITH FLYING SAUCERS!

1. Mel Coffey, who accompanied David Ferrie to Houston the weekend of the assassination, worked at NASA at Cape Canaveral. Garrison wanted him in for questioning, and he was reluctant. Garrison told William Gurvich, "Well, let's just write him a letter and tell him if he's having any trouble, we'll be glad to contact his employer ... and tell them he's simply wanted in New Orleans as a witness in the investigation ... He would sure as hell have to come or else they would fire him."

16. ARSENIC AND OLD PERRIN

1. Joel Palmer also left. He sent me this message: "Boxley also urged me to think about leaving as they might try to get to him by detaining me. He suggested I head to Texas, specifically Penn Jones' house in Midlothian, which I did several days later."

18. ON THE TRAIL OF DELUSION

1. O'Keefe was a composite character based on Perry Russo, Raymond Broshears, David Logan, and William Morris. All four had credibility issues: Broshears was never David Ferrie's roommate as he claimed; Logan said Shaw owned a nine-foot dinner table, which seems unlikely given the small size of his residence; and William Morris even claimed that Shaw had brought Jack Ruby over for a visit.

2. Prouty was interviewed by the Assassinations Records Review Board in 1996, and it said that "Prouty, in his published work, makes allegations which point clearly to a high level conspiracy. Given the opportunity to document these allegations or in some other fashion uncover the truth, however, Prouty declined to do so, and often retreated from or contradicted his published claims."

19. GARRISON'S FORGOTTEN VICTIM: MAJOR LOUIS BLOOMFIELD

1. Garrison's source, twenty-four-year-old Jules Ricco Kimble, was a Ku Klux Klansman who is currently serving a sentence for murder in Oklahoma. His initial story of the trip to Montreal did not include having Clay Shaw as a passenger.

2. A CIA document also indicates that Clay Shaw may have been connected with the CIA through Project QK/Enchant. But this project does not appear to have been operational; it was used to "provide security approvals for non-Agency personnel and facilities. Such approvals were required so that Agency personnel could meet [these] individuals to discussion proposed projects, activities, and possible relationships." QK/Enchant was started in 1952, and one agency document says that "in all probability, [Shaw] was not cleared by that program." In addition, CIA document # 104-10115-10411 did a trace on Clay Shaw through CIA records, and nothing about Project QK/Enchant showed up, indicating that he might not have been given approval for this project.

3. The main managers and board members of Permindex were not fascists. Ferenc Nagy was a farmer who was jailed by the Gestapo in 1944 and then elected prime minister of Hungary in 1946 as part of an anti-fascist coalition. Nagy resisted, as best he could, the communist takeover of the country. He ended up as a dairy farmer in Virginia. Carlo d'Amelio was a lawyer for the Italian royal family and administrator of its assets. He also represented Guglielmo Marconi and King Farouk of Egypt. He was a councilor of the Bank of Italy and president of Rotary International. Mantello was a war hero. And Bloomfield was an amazing benefactor of hospitals and charities.

4. I am still waiting for the digitization of several of Bloomfield's letter books that were promised in September 2019.

CONCLUSION: THE ATTEMPT TO REHABILITATE
JIM GARRISON

1. Harold Weisberg accompanied Assistant DA Andrew Sciambra in Washington to interview witnesses who were certain they had not seen Shaw. Because of the lack of discovery in Louisiana courts, Shaw's lawyers were not informed of these witnesses.

2. Novel was never an operative for the CIA. A CIA report from May 31, 1967, said that "Gordon Dwane Novel has both claimed and denied affiliation with CIA. A thorough records check has shown no such affiliation." The CIA then used alternate spellings of his name and came up negative. They even asked JMWAVE, a secret covert operations center in Miami, to show Novel's photo "to a well-placed and well-informed asset" to "test the possibility that Novel had been involved in CIA activities under another name." That also came up negative. Novel's lawyer Elmer Gertz wrote Edward Wegmann that "you know him well enough to take what he says with at least one grain of salt; I would say a whole salt shaker."

3. Tanenbaum claimed to have seen a video Ferrie had taken with Oswald, Banister, and others at an anti-Castro training camp. That video has also disappeared. Tanenbaum resigned from the HSCA after Chief Investigator Richard Sprague was forced out early in the probe.

4. Attorney General Ramsey Clark stated on March 2, 1967, that Shaw had been cleared by the FBI in 1963. He misspoke and was referring to the fact that the FBI and Warren Commission had looked into the story about a Clay Bertrand. There are no FBI files from 1963 or 1964 that refer to Clay Shaw, which is to be expected since he was not investigated. Hoover wrote on the memo above that "A.G. made the statement, so it is up to the Dept [of Justice] to wrestle with this."

SOURCES

Introduction

Fred Litwin, *I Was a Teenage JFK Conspiracy Freak*, (NorthernBlues Books, 2018).

James DiEugenio, *Destiny Betrayed: JFK, Cuba, and the Garrison Case*, (Skyhorse Publishing, 2012).

DiEugenio quotes on Fred Litwin: http://educationforum.ipbhost.com/topic/25330-jim-garrison-vs-fred-litwin/?tab=comments#comment-388412

Garrison files at NARA: https://catalog.archives.gov/search?q=*:*&f.parentNaId=641323&f.level=fileUnit&sort=naIdSort%20asc

Garrison memo on Jack Ruby: Papers of Jim Garrison, NARA.

Garrison memo on puromycin: House Select Committee on Assassinations (HSCA) document, RIF # 180-10076-10357, NARA.

Bloomfield Archive in Ottawa: https://www.bac-lac.gc.ca/eng/CollectionSearch/Pages/record.aspx?app=fonandcol&IdNumber=106963&new=-8586146338832466293

Tom Bethell quote: Tom Bethell, *The Electric Windmill: An Inadvertent Autobiography*, (Regnery Gateway, 1988), page 68.

garrison the magazine: http://www.lulu.com/ca/en/shop/midnight-writer-news-publications/garrison-the-journal-of-history-deep-politics-issue-001/paperback/product-24211732.html

Oliver Stone's new series: https://variety.com/2019/tv/global/agc-television-picks-up-worldwide-oliver-stones-jfk-destiny-betrayed-1203368818/

Endnote

Garrison charges Gurvich: http://jfk.hood.edu/Collection/White%20Materials/Garrison%20News%20Clippings/1969/69-09/69-09-08.pdf

THE TAKING OF NEW ORLEANS 1-2-3

Jim Garrison psychiatric reports: The Papers of George Lardner, Library of Congress.

Quote on Garrison being like Perry Mason: Life magazine copy, March 5, 1967, in the Papers of Richard Billings, Georgetown University.

Garrison ad on heroin: Ibid.

Garrison quote on Richard Dowling as the great emancipator: Milton Brener, *The Garrison Case*, (Clarkson Potter, 1969), page 6.

A reform candidate in Louisiana quote: James Kirkwood, *American Grotesque: An Account of the Clay Shaw—Jim Garrison Kennedy Assassination Trial in New Orleans*, (Harper Perennial, 1970), page 79.

Quote on DA being powerful: Milton Brener, op.cit., page 10.

Garrison interview with Donald Dooty: Papers of Irvin Dymond, New Orleans Historic Collection.

Powers of the grand jury: Brener, op. cit., pages 11-12.

Aaron Kohn's appearance at grand jury: Brener, op. cit., pages 40-41.

Judge Bagert's quote on the grand jury system: "End to Grand Juries Urged," *The Times-Picayune*, December 3, 1967. Bagert also said that "a district attorney can abuse the grand jury by slanting his interpretation of evidence and swaying the jurors who are not knowledgeable about the case."

Ivon quote on DA's power: Diary of Tom Bethell, entry for February 11, 1968, NARA; https://mcadams.posc.mu.edu/bethell5.htm

Jim Garrison philosophy: Garrison bio, March 23, 1967, in the Papers of Richard Billings.

Garrison going after Dowling: Brener, op. cit., page. 14.

DA statement joint statement with police: "N.O. Night Clubs Must Light Up, Klein Warns," *The Times-Picayune*, August 9, 1962.

Rosemary James quotes on raiding gay bars: Rosemary James & Jack Wardlaw, *Plot or Politics: The Garrison Case & Its Cast*, (Pelican, 1967), page 21.

Hugh Murray quote: http://hughmurray.blogspot.com/2017/06/a-trail-worth-taking.html

Cab driver quote: Jim Phelan, "The Vice-Man Cometh," *Saturday Evening Post*, June 1963, http://jfk.hood.edu/Collection/Weisberg%20Subject%20Index%20Files/P%20Disk/Phelan%20James/Item%2002.pdf

Funds for Garrison: James Savage, *Jim Garrison's Bourbon Street Brawl: The Making of a First Amendment Milestone*, (University of Louisiana at Lafayette Press, 2010), page 15.

Garrison going from judge to judge: Ibid, page 16.

Garrison on police not fighting vice: Brener, op. cit., page 22.

Garrison on judges: Brener, op. cit., page 16.

People yelling moo, moo, at judges: "Tribunal Hears Garrison Case," *The Times-Picayune*, April 23, 1964.

Garrison quote on racketeer influences on judges: Brener, op. cit., page 18.

Quote on emerging unscathed from the fight with judges: Savage, op. cit., page 25.

Garrison only playing up free speech after appellate process: Savage, op. cit., page 5.

Quote that Garrison should reflect before acting: Catholic *Clarion-Herald*, May 30, 1963; quoted in the Papers of Richard Billings.

Garrison quote about the Louisiana Board of Parole: Garrison bio in the Papers of Richard Billings.

Harry Connick Quote: Ibid; and note in the Billings papers that identifies Connick as the source.

Quote on grand jury on paroles: Brener, op. cit., page 31.

Garrison quote on "wholesale bribery": Garrison bio in The Papers of Richard Billings.

Police as "political gestapo": David Chandler article on Garrison shooting from the hip in the Papers of Richard Billings.

Garrison on a rampage against Giarrusso: Brener, op. cit., page 36.

Garrison's 21 questions: Ibid, page 38.

Giarrusso statement: "If Illegalities, Act, Schiro's Reply to DA," *The Times-Picayune*, June 26, 1965.

Rosemary James quote on Louisiana enjoying politicians who entertain: Rosemary James chapter in *Where Were You? America Remembers The JFK Assassination* by Gus Russo and Harry Moses (Lyons Press, 2013).

David Chandler interview with Garrison on why no crime-fighting crusades: "The Devil's DA" *New Orleans Magazine*, November 1966, http://jfk.hood.edu/Collection/Weisberg%20Subject%20Index%20Files/G%20Disk/Gervais%20Pershing/Item%2016.pdf

Andrews meeting Garrison in late fall: Richard Billings, bio of

David Ferrie, February 13, 1967, in the papers of Richard Billings;

Transcript of NBC interview with Dean Andrews for their documentary The JFK Conspiracy: The Case of Jim Garrison, which aired on Monday, June 19, 1967, at 8:00 PM, Papers of the Metropolitan Crime Commission, NARA; http://www.jfk-online.com/nbctranscript.html; http://jfk.hood.edu/Collection/Weisberg%20Subject%20Index%20Files/N%20Disk/NBC%20Garrison%20Case%20Broadcast%206-16-67/Item%2001.pdf

Quotes on resentment in Louisiana: Clay Shaw's journal, found in the Papers of Clay Shaw.

Garrison quote to Richard Billings on how he would investigate Kennedy's assassination: Billings interview with Jim Garrison found in the Papers of Richard Billings.

Garrison quotes on the investigation: James & Wardlaw, op.cit., page 39 & 47; Jim Phelan, "Rush to Judgment in New Orleans," *Saturday Evening Post,* May 6, 1967; http://jfk.hood.edu/Collection/Weisberg%20Subject%20Index%20Files/P%20Disk/Phelan%20James/Item%2001.pdf

Mort Sahl going to Garrison's home: John Kelin, *Praise from a Future Generation: The Assassination of John F. Kennedy and the First Generation Critics of the Warren Report,* (Wings Press, 2007), page 384.

Alcock quote on jugglers and fire-breathers: The Diary of Tom Bethell, entry for January 25, 1968, at NARA; https://mcadams.posc.mu.edu/bethell4.htm

Mark Lane quote on Garrison's conclusive evidence: Kelin, op.cit., for a partial quote; a complete quote was found in the Harold Weisberg Archive, http://jfk.hood.edu/Collection/Weisberg%20Subject%20Index%20Files/L%20Disk/Lane%20Mark/Lane%20Mark%20Rush%20to%20Judgement/Item%2001.pdf

Endnotes

Chandler's quote on grand juries: James Kirkwood interview with David Chandler in the James Kirkwood Papers at Boston University.

Charles Ward comments on B-drinking: Aaron Kohn memo dated August 21, 1969, with a transcript from a tape recording from August 7th. Retrieved from the files of the Metropolitan Crime Commission, NARA.

The rising backlog of cases because of JFK assassination: Kohn memo, dated June 1, 1967, found in the papers of the Metropolitan Crime Commission: *The Times-Picayune*, April 8, 1967; *New Orleans States-Item*, April 10, 1967, https://www.maryferrell.org/showDoc.html?docId=62411&relPageId=129

Funding of Truth and Consequences: See the various court filings in the Clay Shaw case, and the public hearings held by Judge Christenberry in January 1971, https://www.maryferrell.org/php/showlist.php?docset=2103

A BEAUTIFUL MIND

FBI report on Manning and homosexual shakedown: RIF #179-20001-10409, redacted copy: https://www.maryferrell.org/showDoc.html?docId=60405#relPageId=86

Alecia Long quote on arrests of homosexuals: Alecia Long, *Cruising for Conspirators: How the Assassination of John F. Kennedy Became a Sex Crime*, (UNC Press, to be published Spring 2021), page 136-137.

Hoover refusing to intervene: https://www.maryferrell.org/showDoc.html?docId=60405&relPageId=65&search=%22frank_manning%22

The anonymous letter sent to Ramsey Clark on homosexual shakedown: FBI 62-109060 JFK HQ File, Section 145, https://www.maryferrell.org/showDoc.html?docId=62431#relPageId=220

Rosemary James quote on raids on homosexuals: James & Wardlaw, op. cit., page 21-22.

Aaron Kohn memo on Garrison's use of emotionally disturbed persons: Memo dated July 26, 1967, found in the Papers of the Metropolitan Crime Commission.

Aaron Kohn consultation with Dr. Harold Lief: Ibid.

Lambert discussion of fondling incident: Patricia Lambert, *False Witness: The Real Story of Jim Garrison's Investigation and Oliver Stone's Film JFK* (M. Evans & Company, 1998), page 232-238.

Quote on propinquity: Thomas Bethell, *The Electric Windmill*, op. cit., page 62.

Gurvich quote on city directories: False Witness, page 55; Dean Baquet, "Assistants begged DA to drop case," *The Times-Picayune*, November 20, 1983.

Garrison propinquity memos: Both of these memos are on my website, www.onthetrailofdelusion.com

Bethell example of propinquity: Bethell, *The Electric Windmill*, op. cit., page 63.

Garrison quote on post offices: Garrison memo, "Post Office Boxes," dated February 16, 1968, NARA.

Garrison belief in callsigns or radio frequency: Bethell Diary entry, September 14, 1967, NARA; https://mcadams.posc.mu.edu/bethell2.htm

President of New Orleans Amateur Astronomy Association, William Wulf, on Oswald and communism: Warren Commission, Volume 8, page 15; https://www.maryferrell.org/showDoc.html?docId=36#relPageId=23

Oswald quote about Soviet crimes: Warren Commission Exhibit 97, Volume 16, page 422, https://www.maryferrell.org/showDoc.html?docId=1133#relPageId=446opp

Oswald quote about opposing the U.S. government: Ibid. page 425, https://www.maryferrell.org/showDoc.html?docId=1133#relPageId=449

Oswald quote about the fall of the U.S. government: Ibid, page 426, https://www.maryferrell.org/showDoc.html?docId= 1133#relPageId=450

Oswald interview with Bill Stuckey: https://mcadams.posc. mu.edu/russ/jfkinfo3/exhibits/stuck2.htm

Oswald quote on pure communist society: Warren Commission Exhibit 97, volume 16, page 426, https://www.maryferrell. org/showDoc.html?docId=1133#relPageId=450

Harold Weisberg quote on Oswald's supposed pro-Castro sympathies: Harold Weisberg, *Whitewash: The Report on the Warren Report* (Dell, 1966), page 265.

Weisberg quote on the establishment of a cover: Ibid, page 274.

Garrison quote to the BBC: Papers of the Metropolitan Crime Commission.

Garrison interview of May 27, 1969: "Some Unauthorized Comments on the State of the Union," May 27, 1969, Papers of Jim Garrison, NARA.

Garrison quote for NBC documentary: The JFK Conspiracy: The Case of Jim Garrison, June 19, 1967, page 29, http://jfk. hood.edu/Collection/Weisberg%20Subject%20Index%20Files/ N%20Disk/NBC%20Garrison%20Case%20Broadcast%206-16- 67/Item%2001.pdf

Garrison interview in Playboy Magazine: Playboy Magazine, October 1967, https://www.cia.gov/library/readingroom/docs/ CIA-RDP75-00149R000300040043-1.pdf; http://jfk.hood. edu/Collection/Weisberg%20Subject%20Index%20Files/G% 20Disk/Garrison%20Jim/Garrison%20Jim%20Playboy% 20Interview/Item%2005.pdf

Harkness testimony before the Warren Commission: WC Volume VI, page 312, https://www.maryferrell.org/showDoc. html?docId=35#relPageId=322

Sprague beliefs about the tramps: Garrison, *op. cit.*, page 208.

Garrison's expectation of the tramps and quotes about them: Ibid.

The exchange between Carson and Garrison: Transcript of the Johnny Carson show, found in the Garrison papers at the New Orleans Public Library, https://www.maryferrell.org/showDoc.html?docId=103864#relPageId=116

Garrison's story about being on Carson: Garrison, *On the Trail of the Assassins: My Investigation and Prosecution of the Murder of President Kennedy*, (Sheridan Square Press, 1988), page 210-213.

Garrison quote about why newspapers don't publish these sorts of allegations: Ibid, page 214.

HSCA on the tramps: HSCA Volume VI, page 259, https://www.maryferrell.org/showDoc.html?docId=45#relPageId=107

Tramp arrest records: http://jfk.hood.edu/Collection/Weisberg%20Subject%20Index%20Files/P%20Disk/Pictures%20Tramps%20Dealey%20Plaza/Item%2019.pdf

Aynesworth stories about Garrison's paranoia: Hugh Aynesworth, "The Man Who Saw Too Much," *Texas Monthly*, March 1976; See also Hugh Aynesworth, *JFK: Breaking The News: A Reporter's Eyewitness Account of the Kennedy Assassination and Its Aftermath*, (International Focus Press, 2003), page 233-234.

Aynesworth quote on a torpedo: Warren Rogers, "The Persecution of Clay Shaw," *Look Magazine*, August 26, 1969, http://jfk.hood.edu/Collection/Weisberg%20Subject%20Index%20Files/S%20Disk/Shaw%20Clay%20Trial%20Aftermath/Item%2015.pdf

Quote about Garrison answering the telephone: Dean Baquet, "Assistants begged DA to drop case," *The Times-Picayune*, November 20, 1983.

Gurvich's story about raiding FBI offices: WLOL TV Interview, June 27, 1967. Papers of the Metropolitan Crime Commission; see also Gurvich testimony at Christenberry Hearings, page

342-342,   https://www.maryferrell.org/showDoc.html?docId=217755#relPageId=136&tab=page

Garrison quotes on CIA paying lawyers: NBC interview with Garrison for special on June 19, 1967. Papers of the Metropolitan Crime Commission; Garrison interview, ΛBC, Issues & Answers, May 28, 1967.

Garrison quote on not being paranoid enough: Baquet article, op. cit.

Endnotes

Garrison incident at L.A. airport: Jim Garrison, op. cit., page 188-189.

FBI memo on alleged Garrison homosexual affair: contained in FBI 62-109060 JFK HQ File, Section 121; https://www.maryferrell.org/showDoc.html?docId=62407#relPageId=16&tab=page

Garrison quote on tramps: Garrison, op. cit., page 208.

For more on officer J.D. Tippit: https://www.maryferrell.org/showDoc.html?docId=946&relPageId=189&search=tippit

JIM GARRISON SOLVES THE JFK ASSASSINATION

Secret Service report that Jack Martin has telephonitis: Warren Commission Document 87: Secret Service Report dated December 13, 1963; http://jfk.hood.edu/Collection/Weisberg%20Subject%20Index%20Files/P%20Disk/Phelan%20James/Item%2001.pdf

Regis Kennedy on Jack Martin: FBI memo dated November 25, 1963, retrieved from the Harold Weisberg archive. http://jfk.hood.edu/Collection/Weisberg%20Subject%20Index%20Files/F%20Disk/Ferrie%20David%20William/Item%2036.pdf

Dean Andrews describing Bertrand as young and blonde: https://www.maryferrell.org/showDoc.html?docId=62408&relPageId=89&search=%22a_youthful%20appearing%22

Search for Clay Bertrand documents: Contained in Warren

Commission   Document   #75.   https://www.maryferrell.org/
showDoc.html?docId=10477

Andrew on Bertrand being a figment of his imagination: FBI
105-82555   Oswald   HQ   File,   Section   8;   https://www.
maryferrell.org/showDoc.html?docId=57680&relPageId=107&
search=%22figment_of%20his%20imagination%22

Dean Andrews testimony before the Warren Commission:
Volume XI, page 335, https://www.maryferrell.org/showDoc.
html?docId=45#relPageId=335

Pershing Gervais interview with Jack Martin: Interview
conducted December 13, 1966. Found in the Papers of Richard
Billings, http://jfk.hood.edu/Collection/Weisberg%20Subject%
20Index%20Files/F%20Disk/Ferrie%20David%20William%
20Jack%20Martin/Item%2001.pdf

Richard Billings quote on Ferrie as transportation manager:
Richard Billings' biography of David Ferrie, February 14, 1967,
found in the papers of Richard Billings.

David Ferrie's interview by John Volz: Interview dated
December 15, 1966, Papers of Edward Wegmann, NARA,
http://jfk.hood.edu/Collection/Weisberg%20Subject%
20Index%20Files/F%20Disk/Ferrie%20David%20Garrison%
20Files%20Miscellaneous/Item%2007.pdf

Ferrie going to the FBI: Gus Russo, *Live By The Sword: The
Secret War Against Castro and the Death of JFK*, (bancroft press,
1998), page 402; RIF #124-10369-10029, FBI airtel dated
December   16,   1966,   https://www.maryferrell.org/showDoc.
html?docId=9986&relPageId=270

Lou Ivon memo to Jim Garrison regarding Clay Bertrand:
Found in the Irvin Dymond papers.

Garrison and the scribble on the Warren Report: Gurvich
conference with Shaw's attorneys, August 29, 1967, Papers of
Edward Wegmann.

Billings on propinquity of Shaw and Lewellen: Richard

Billings, "Garrison: The Power of Public Disclosure," found in the Papers of Richard Billings.

Clay Shaw drops in for a visit with Garrison: Clay Shaw Journal, March 1, 1967, found in the Papers of Clay Shaw, NARA.

Biography of Clay Shaw: The best account of the life of Clay Shaw is by Donald Carpenter, *Man of a Million Fragments: The True Story of Clay Shaw* (Donald H. Carpenter, 2014).

Quote about Shaw being unlikeliest villain since Oscar Wilde: Carpenter, op.cit., page 454.

Dean Andrews quote "shuck me like a corn": Lambert, op.cit., page 50.

Fictitious nature of Gonzales: Ibid; See also Robert Wilson interview with Townley and Andrews, April 19, 1967, Papers of Irvin Dymond.

Picture of Oswald handing out leaflets in New Orleans: Pizzo Exhibit 453-B, Warren Commission Volume XXI, page 139, https://www.maryferrell.org/showDoc.html?docId=1138#relPageId=163

Miami Police report on Emanuel Garcia Gonzalez: http://jfk.hood.edu/Collection/Weisberg%20Subject%20Index%20Files/G%20Disk/Gonzalez%20Manuel%20Garcia/Item%2001.pdf

The Times-Picayune quote on "Garrison looking for group of Cubans": February 19, 1967, http://jfk.hood.edu/Collection/FBI%20Records%20Files/62-109060/62-109060%20Section%2012/112J.pdf; https://www.maryferrell.org/showDoc.html?docId=62398&relPageId=155; http://jfk.hood.edu/Collection/White%20Materials/Garrison%20News%20Clippings/1967/67-02/67-02-021.pdf

Ramparts article on the Garrison investigation: William W. Turner, "The Inquest," June 1967, https://archive.org/details/JfkAssassinationTheInquestRampartsJune1967/page/n7/mode/2up

Garrison asks Andrews to undergo "truth verification": Letter to Monk Zelden, March 6, 1967, found in the Papers of Edward Wegmann, NARA.

Quote about Eleanor Bares: Interview of Eleanor Bares from April 19, 1967, found in the Papers of Irvin Dymond.

Garrison quote on "memory refreshing techniques": Garrison interview on *ABC* Issues and Answers, May 28, 1967, http://jfk. hood.edu/Collection/Weisberg%20Subject%20Index%20Files/ G%20Disk/Garrison%20Jim/Garrison%20Jim%20Issues% 20and%20Answers/Item%2001.pdf

David Ferrie quotes by David Snyder: David Snyder story dated February 24, 1967, found in HSCA files; RIF # 180-10111-10065, https://www.maryferrell.org/showDoc.html? docId=197072&relPageId=105

David Ferrie quote by George Lardner: World Journal Tribune, February 23, 1967, https://www.maryferrell.org/ showDoc.html?docId=62496&relPageId=85

Ferrie autopsy report: https://mcadams.posc. mu.edu/ferrie_autopsy.htm

Garrison quote on Ferrie being "one of history's most important individuals": Howard Jacobs, "Mystery Deepens in Death Probe," *The Times-Picayune*, February 26, 1967.

Garrison press release about waiting too long to arrest Ferrie: *The Times-Picayune*, February 23, 1967, https://archive.org/ details/DavidWilliamFerrie/page/n311/mode/1up

Garrison quote about "premature revelation": Brener, op. cit., page 81.

Garrison quote about only escape for plotters is suicide: *New Orleans States-Item*, February 25, 1967, https://www. maryferrell.org/showDoc.html?docId=62422#relPageId=142

Garrison quote to Hugh Aynesworth about Shaw committing suicide: Hugh Aynesworth, "Garrison vs. Shaw: The Big Melodrama in New Orleans," *Newsweek*, January 30, 1969.

Garrison's staff believing this was a good time to end inquiry: Baquet, op. cit. November 20, 1983.

Endnotes

David Ferrie in CAP: Stephen Roy, *Perfect Villain: David Ferrie and the JFK Mystery*, unpublished manuscript; second file, page 49, courtesy of Stephen Tyler.

Prentiss Davis testimony about Andrews using the name Bertrand: "Ruling to be made in Andrews Case," *The Times-Picayune*, August 13, 1967.

The police report of Jack Martin being pistol-whipped: Found in the papers of Gus Russo, http://jfk.hood.edu/Collection/Weisberg%20Subject%20Index%20Files/M%20Disk/May%20Hoke%20Notes/Item%2003.pdf

Ronald Welsh quote to Lambert: *Lambert's notes from talking to Ronald Welsh, December 1, 1993, papers of Patricia Lambert.*

Alcock quote about "no intent" to arrest Ferrie: Patricia Lambert interview of Alcock, December 3, 1993, Papers of Patricia Lambert.

ENTER STAGE RIGHT: PERRY RUSSO

Perry Russo in Baton Rouge newspaper: transcript of Interview of Bill Bankston who worked for the evening newspaper in Baton Rouge, Papers of the Metropolitan Crime Commission.

Perry Russo interview on WAFB in Baton Rouge: Clay Shaw Preliminary Hearing, March 17, 1967, https://www.maryferrell.org/showDoc.html?docId=217744&relPageId=129&search=wafb

Andrew Sciambra's 3,500-word memo on Russo: https://mcadams.posc.mu.edu/russo2.txt

Garrison claim that he never received Russo's letter: Garrison, op. cit., page 151.

Alecia Long on how Shaw dressed: Long, op.cit.

Sciambra telling Russo that Shaw and Ferrie should be linked: Russo interview with Ed Wegmann, March 26, 1971, Papers of the Metropolitan Crime Commission.

Wegmann and Russo quotes on piecing together a plot: Ibid.

Russo administered Sodium Pentothal: Sciambra memo on an interview with Perry Russo, February 26, 1967. Papers of Gus Russo.

Dr. Chetta's admission regarding sodium pentothal: Chetta testimony during the preliminary hearing, March 17, 1967, https://www.maryferrell.org/showDoc.html?docId=217744& relPageId=18&search=%22expressions_of%20fact%22

Quote from Dr. Edwin Weinstein: Washington Post, March 27, 1967, https://www.maryferrell.org/showDoc.html?docId= 62499&relPageId=102

Russo quote about being injected with sodium pentothal: Russo interview with Edward Wegmann and Gurvich, March 26, 1971, Papers of the Metropolitan Crime Commission.

Charles Ward quote on office vote: Aaron Kohn Memo dated August 21, 1969.

Clay Shaw quote on using an alias: Kirkwood, op. cit., page 20.

Sciambra threat to arrest Shaw: Clay Shaw journal, the Papers of Clay Shaw, NARA.

Shaw quote on why he was arrested: Ibid.

Garrison quote on building his case after he's arrested somebody: Warren Rogers, "The Persecution of Clay Shaw," *Look Magazine*, August 26, 1969; http://jfk.hood.edu/Collection/ Weisberg%20Subject%20Index%20Files/S%20Disk/Shaw% 20Clay%20Trial%20Aftermath/Item%2015.pdf;   See   also Patricia Lambert interview with James Phelan, June 8, 1993, Phelan quotes Garrison as saying, "This is not the first time I've charged a person before I've made the case," Papers of Patricia Lambert.

Charles Ward amending Garrison's quote: Dean Baquet, "On trial: Former aides attack Garrison's case against Shaw," *The Times-Picayune*, November 20, 1983.

Shaw's quote on what they didn't take from his home: Clay Shaw journal.

Confirmation by Layton Martens: Transcript of interview for *NBC* documentary June 1967, found in the Papers of the Metropolitan Crime Commission.

Quote from Mrs. Lawrence Fischer: Kirkwood, op. cit., pate 27.

Irvin Dymond quote that Shaw was "vulnerable": Kirkwood interview with Irvin Dymond; "On trial: former aides attack Garrison's case against Shaw," *The Times-Picayune*, November 20, 1983,

Dr. Fatter quotes: Transcript of Perry Russo's first hypnotic session, NARA.

James Phelan's quote on "Perry would have barked": TV interview April 28, 1967, with Bill Slater, NARA.

Russo admission that Bertrand was first voiced by Sciambra: Russo interview with Edward Wegmann, March 26, 1971, Papers of the Metropolitan Crime Commission

Quote from the second Russo hypnotic sessions: Found in a variety of collections at NARA, https://mcadams.posc.mu.edu/session2.htm

Interview with Dr. Jay Katz: Transcript of interview, *NBC*, June 1967, in the Papers of the Metropolitan Crime Commission.

Layton Martens quote to Gus Russo: Russo, op. cit., page 411.

Garrison quote on "tactical maneuver" of the preliminary hearing: Billings note to Angeloff in the Papers of Richard Billings, undated, Folder 46.

Shaw quote on "skating on thin ice": Clay Shaw journal.

Rehearsal of Russo's testimony: Interview of Russo with Edward Wegmann, March 26, 1971, Papers of the Metropolitan Crime Commission; see also Edward Wegmann letter to Elmer Gertz dated February 2, 1971, Papers of Elmer Gertz.

Testimony of Perry Russo at the preliminary hearing: https://

www.maryferrell.org/php/showlist.php?docset=2101

Clay Shaw quote on plotting with "two nuts": Clay Shaw journal entry for March 14, 1967.

Vernon Bundy's story: see Gurvich's memo on an interview with Vernon Bundy, dated 20 April, 1967 based upon an interview on 16 March 1967.

Vernon Bundy lie detector test: See the testimony of Lt. Edward O'Donnell on January 26, 1971, at the Christenberry hearings, https://www.maryferrell.org/showDoc.html?docId=217755#relPageId=95&tab=page

Dean Andrews quote on Clay Bertrand: Interview with Dean Andrews by an unidentified reporter, June 28, 1967, NARA.

Endnotes

Perry Russo's letter to Garrison: Perry Russo testimony, Preliminary Hearing, March 15, 1967.

Usage of term 'tight pants': Questions were asked about tight pants to Lloyd Cobb, Goldie Moore, Clay Shaw, and Jeff Biddison, https://www.maryferrell.org/php/showlist.php?docset=1016

Memo from Tom Bethell corroborating that Russo said nothing about a meeting until New Orleans: Memo dated June 26, 1967, from Tom Bethell to Jim Garrison on an interview with Matt Herron, NARA.

Shaw's logistical problems: Clay Shaw journal, papers of Clay Shaw.

List of Shaw's possessions that were taken by Garrison: Items listed in the Motion for the return of seized property and the suppression of evidence, Case # 198-059. NARA.

Russo using the name 'Clem': Transcript of the first hypnotic session, https://mcadams.posc.mu.edu/session1.htm

Carlos Quiroga's quote about Oswald's leaflet: Aaron Kohn interview with Carlos Quiroga, July 25, 1967, in a memo dated April 18, 1968.

MY SON, THE CRYPTOGRAPHER

Researcher noticing the Lee Odom notation: Edward Jay Epstein, *Counterplot: Garrison Against the World*, published in *The Assassination Chronicles* (Carroll & Graf, 1992), page 187. The researcher was Jones Harris.

Lee Odom notation in Clay Shaw's notebook: Papers of Jim Garrison, NARA.

Oswald notation of DD19106: Warren Commission Volume XVI, page 58, https://www.maryferrell.org/showDoc.html? docId=1133#relPageId=82

Sylvia Meagher's letter to Garrison and his telephone call: Meagher letter to Ray Marcus, dated May 17, 1967; See also Meagher memo "Garrison and the Warren Report Critics: Strangeloves and Surprising Coalitions," dated August 8, 1967, Papers of Sylvia Meagher.

Garrison quote about Mr. Odom and bullfights: New Orleans *States-Item*, May 17, 1967, https://www.maryferrell.org/ showDoc.html?docId=62418#relPageId=142

Garrison document about bullfight as code word: Memo to Garrison from William Martin, dated May 12, 1967; referenced in the Peter Vea Index: Peter Vea, *Chronology and Summaries of Files from the Garrison Investigation*, (self-published, 2000), page 17.

Quote on Garrison link between Ruby and Oswald: Associated Press, "Garrison says 'code' Links Oswald, Shaw, Ruby," *The Evening Star*, May 13, 1967.

Richard Billings code story: Diary of Richard Billings, NARA.

David Lifton's story about Garrison and codes: David Lifton, "Is Garrison Out of His Mind?" *Open City*, an L.A. alternative newspaper, https://mcadams.posc.mu.edu/lifton1.htm

Garrison quote "swallow a cannonball": Garrison, op. cit., page 147.

JIM GARRISON'S EXCELLENT HOMOSEXUAL ADVENTURE

Hugh Aynesworth's story about Ruby and Oswald being lovers: Hugh Aynesworth, *Witness to History*, (Brown Books Publishing, 2013), page 193.

Jim Phelan's story about a homosexual plot: James Phelan, *Scandals, Scamps and Scoundrels: The Casebook of an Investigative Reporter*, (Random House, 1982), pages 150-151.

Garrison telling Newsweek he was looking for a 'gay boy': Hugh Aynesworth, "Assassination: History or Headlines," *Newsweek*, March 13, 1967, http://jfk.hood.edu/Collection/White%20Materials/Sylvia%20Meagher%20Clips/SM-076.pdf

Drew Pearson's March 24, 1967 diary entry: *Drew Pearson Diaries*, Volume 2 1960-1969, University of Nebraska Press, page 470-471.

State police report on death in 1963: Papers of Irvin Dymond, Historic New Orleans.

Perry Russo quote about pinning other crimes on Shaw: Edward Wegmann's memo on an interview with Perry Russo dated January 27, 1971, Papers of Edward Wegmann.

Al Oser memo on Investigative Leads: Papers of Jim Garrison, NARA.

Garrison's thinking of Shaw as "Lord executioner": Richard Billings notes, file on Bertrand/Sadism Inquiry, The Papers of Richard Billings.

Billings on hooks bolted in ceiling beams: Ibid.

Mention of the picture of hooks: There are a couple of photos in the Papers of Richard Billings.

Garrison quote to Billings on sadist plot: Richard Billings diary entry for March 3, 1967, http://www.jfk-online.com/billings3.html

Volz memo on Dr. Heath: The Papers of Richard Billings.

Billings quote on Shaw being a Phi Beta Kappa sadist: Richard Billings diary entry for March 3, 1967.

Billings quote on Garrison's plans to use sadism evidence:
Ibid.

Perry Russo's quote on Shaw being anti-Kennedy: Russo interview with Wegmann, March 26, 1971, Papers of the Metropolitan Crime Commission.

Garrison quote to the L.A. Times: Los Angeles Times, March 26, 1967, page G2.

Robert Northshield informing FBI: Carpenter, op. cit., page 317.

Garrison November 17, 1967 leads memo (#103): Retrieved from the Harold Weisberg Archive; http://jfk.hood.edu/Collection/Weisberg%20Subject%20Index%20Files/G%20Disk/Garrison%20Jim/Garrison%20Jim%20Early%20Statements%20Open%20Leads%2011-14-67/Item%2001.pdf

Garrison letter to William Turner on Jack Ruby and San Francisco: Garrison files in the New Orleans Public Library, letter dated December 29, 1967.

Garrison sending Gurvich to San Francisco: Gurvich deposition, Gordon Novel lawsuit, March 1, 1968. Papers of Elmer Gertz.

Sanders memo on investigating Shaw's whips: Memo from Gary Sanders to Louis Ivon, dated January 25, 1968, NARA.

Turner Memo on Sado-Masochists in San Francisco: Garrison Papers in the Harry Connick collection.

Confidential Magazine cover and article on the "Homosexual Ring": Found in the Papers of the Committee to Investigate Assassinations, Georgetown University, https://archive.org/stream/nsia-PalmerJoelD/nsia-PalmerJoelD/Palmer%20Joel%20D%2015#page/n1/mode/1up

A TOUCH OF BRIBERY

Aynesworth report on Beauboeuf bribery: referred to in Aaron Kohn memo dated May 10, 1967, regarding a phone call from

Hugh Aynesworth.

Transcript of Exnicios, Beauboeuf, and Loisel meeting: https://www.maryferrell.org/showDoc.html?docId= 217758#relPageId=42&tab=page

Loisel and Ivon visit to Beauboeuf after meeting: Aaron Kohn memo dated May 25, 1967 regarding meeting with Burton Klein; Transcript of *NBC* interview with Al Beauboeuf June 1967;

Garrison memo on alteration of Exnicios tape: File found in Folder 5 of the Richard Billings Papers; Garrison rebuttal to NBC show July 1967, https://www.youtube.com/watch?v= Hq02c_SxQag; http://jfk.deeppoliticsforum.com/garrison.htm

New Orleans police department Investigation of Exnicios affair: June 12, 1967, Office of the Deputy Superintendent New Orleans Police Department, found in the Papers of Richard Billings.

Layton Martens quote about Garrison offering him money: Russo, op. cit., page 411; Russo interviewed Layton Martens on February 9, 1994.

Beauboeuf statement to Garrison: Statement dated April 12, 1967, Papers of Jim Garrison, NARA.

Garrison threat to have Sheridan and Townley beaten, etc.: Gurvich testimony, January 26, 1971, during the Christenberry hearings, https://www.maryferrell.org/showDoc.html?docId= 217755&search=gurvich#relPageId=133&tab=page

Alcock and Garrison quotes about arresting Sheridan and Townley: Gurvich conference with Wegmann dated August 29, 1967, contained in a memo written on September 6, 1967, the Papers of Edward Wegmann.

The NBC show, The JFK Conspiracy: The Case of Jim Garrison, aired on Monday, June 19, 1967, at 8:00 PM, http://www.jfk-online.com/nbctranscript.html; http://jfk.hood.edu/ Collection/Weisberg%20Subject%20Index%20Files/N% 20Disk/NBC%20Garrison%20Case%20Broadcast%206-16-67/ Item%2001.pdf

Quote about Cancler being "one of the best" burglars in New Orleans: New Orleans States-Item June 12, 1967; see also Brener, op. cit., page 189, https://www.maryferrell.org/showDoc.html?docId=139370&relPageId=82

Loisel asking Cancler to break into Shaw's home: Defense memo on John Cancler, Papers of Irvin Dymond; Cancler Statement dated April 14, 1967, NBC Special op.cit.

Cancler before Garrison Grand Jury: https://www.maryferrell.org/showDoc.html?docId=1177#relPageId=2&tab=page

Gurvich corroboration of Cancler's story: Gurvich Conference, August 29, 1967, Papers of Edward Wegmann.

Garrison's interest in Torres because of propinquity: Gurvich conference, August 8, 1967;

Garrison's belief that 4900 block of Magazine street was "parking place for agents": Tom Bethell diary entry for March 4, 1968, https://mcadams.posc.mu.edu/bethell7.htm

Torres dinner guest of Arcacha: First Garrison memo on propinquity, op. cit.

Garrison suspicion regarding 2705 Magazine street: Ibid.

Torres meeting fellow burglar on 2700 block: Ibid.

First meeting with Torres: Defense memo on Miguel Torres, Papers of Irvin Dymond; See also NBC Special June 1967.

Torres reminded that Garrison was a powerful man: Ibid.

The offer of heroin, a Florida vacation, and freedom to Torres: "Two Bribe Attempts Claimed in JFK Probe," *New Orleans States-Item*, June 12, 1967, based on a Gene Robert June 12, 1967, report in the *New York Times*; Brener, op. cit., page 191, https://www.maryferrell.org/showDoc.html?docId=139370&relPageId=82

Miguel Torres meeting with Mike Karmazin: NBC Special.

Fred Leemans statement to Garrison: Statement of Interrogation of Fred Leemans, May 5, 1967, in the Papers of Richard Billings.

Leemans' quote from NBC: NBC special, op. cit.

Leemans calling Irvin Dymond: Memo by Irvin Dymond on Leemans phone call in the Dymond Papers.

Leemans' letter to Jim Garrison: Found in the Papers of Irvin Dymond.

Recantation by Leemans: Affidavit signed January 6, 1969. Found in the Papers of Gus Russo.

The disclosure that Perry Russo had undergone a lie detector test: NBC Special, op. cit.

Fred Freed visiting Aaron Kohn: Aaron Kohn memo dated June 15, 1967, regarding information received in late May.

Quote about Jacobs' conscience: Ibid.

Quote about Jacob's future if results were divulged: ibid.

Quote about the results of the polygraph test: Ibid.

Sciambra memo about lie detector test: Found in the Richard Billings Papers.

Second attempt at a Russo lie detector test: Memo from Sgt. Edward O'Donnell to Jim Garrison regarding Perry Russo interview dated June 20, 1967, published in *False Witness*, op.cit., page 287; a copy of the actual report in the Papers of Patricia Lambert.

Quotes on the "polygraph tracings" and Russo quote about "getting involved in this mess": Testimony of Lieutenant Edward O'Donnell at the Christenberry hearings, January 26, 1971, page 295-296, https://www.maryferrell.org/showDoc.html?docId= 217755#relPageId=86&tab=page

Quote about asking Russo if Shaw was at Ferrie's apartment: Ibid, page 296-297.

Quote about Garrison being "enraged": Ibid, page 298-299.

Quote about Garrison telling him to keep his mouth shut: RIF #: 124-10054-10413 https://www.archives.gov/files/research/ jfk/releases/docid-32136896.pdf

George Lardner Jr.'s story about "holes" in Russo's testimony:

"Russo Hints of Secrets Up for Sales," *Washington Post*, June 27, 1967.

Robert Kennedy's statement about Sheridan: Russo, op. cit., page 407.

"NBC Charges Terror Tactics by Garrison": Ronald Ostrow, *Los Angeles Times*, July 13, 1967.

Endnotes

Beauboeuf quote to Patricia Lambert: note regarding telephone call with Beauboeuf March 25, 1996, found in the Papers of Patricia Lambert.

Beauboeuf statement to Irvin Dymond: Irvin Dymond interview with James Kirkwood, the Papers of James Kirkwood.

Garrison's claim in his book that the tape never existed: Garrison, op. cit., page 162.

Brener quote on Cancler: Brener, op. cit., page 191.

Quote about pressure on Leemans: Memo to Irvin Dymond dated December 10, 1968, Papers of Irvin Dymond.

Quote about Perry Russo and Layton Martens: Memorandum for the file: Perry Raymond Russo and Layton Martens, dated January 11, 1968, Papers of Irvin Dymond.

THE GREAT ACCUSER

Paese Sera: Max Holland has written extensively about the *Paese Sera* article and Clay Shaw. See for example, "The Power of Disinformation: The Lie That Linked CIA to the Kennedy Assassination," May 19, 2007, http://www.washingtondecoded. com/site/2007/05/the_power_of_di.html; "The Demon in Jim Garrison," *Wilson Quarterly*, Spring 2001; "Was Jim Garrison Duped by the KGB?" February 11, 2002, http://www. washingtondecoded.com/site/2002/02/was-jim-garriso.html

English translations of Paese Sera articles from Jim Garrison: https://catalog.archives.gov/OpaAPI/media/7564842/content/

arcmedia/dc-metro/jfkco/641323/jfk-garrison-071/jfk-
garrison-071.pdf

Pravda article on Clay Shaw: https://www.cia.gov/library/
readingroom/docs/CIA-RDP75-00149R000700210017-7.pdf;
Garrison translation: https://archive.org/stream/
GarrisonPapers/Shaw%20III-World%20Trade%20Center%20%
28Italy%29#page/n34/mode/1up

Le Devoir article on Clay Shaw: "La Pravda: la CIA avait
sous ses ordres Clay Shaw, accuse d'avoir complote contre J.F.K."
Le Devoir, March 8, 1967; "L'enquete du procureur Garrison sur
l'assassinat de Kennedy conduira-t-elle a Montreal?" *Le Devoir*,
March 16, 1967.

Ford's movie not based on Shaw's play: Carpenter, op. cit.,
page 6.

Clark Blaise, "Neo-Fascism and the Kennedy Assassins,"
Canadian Dimension, Sept-Oct. 1967

Ramparts references Le Devoir: William Turner, "The
Garrison Commission," *Ramparts*, January 1968, http://jfk.hood.
edu/Collection/White%20Materials/Garrison%20News%
20Clippings/1968/68-01/68-01-002.pdf

*Holland's colleague Paul Hoch found a note in the Mitrokhin
Archive*: http://www.psicopolis.com/psipol/Mitrokin/201-
261.htm; Rapporto Impedian numero 222; Oggetto: Operazione
di disinformazione del KGB a mezzo di "Paese Sera"

*Kondrashev's comment to Tennent Bagley regarding Paese
Sera*: Tennent Bagley, *Spymaster: Startling Cold War Revelations
of a Soviet KGB Chief* (Skyhorse Publishing, 2015), page 208.

Quote about KGB story in Paese Sera in Italy in 1961:
Christopher Andrew & Vasili Mitrokhin, *The Mitrokhin Archive
II: The KGB in the World*, (Penguin Books, 2006), page 432.

*Garrison receiving copies of Paese Sera from Ralph
Schoenman*: Joan Mellen, *A Farewell to Justice*, (Potomac Books,
2007), page 136.

Garrison telling Associated Press that JFK was killed by a guerilla team: Laura Foreman, "DA Says CIA Hides Killer's Whereabouts," *The Times-Picayune*, Mary 24, 1967, https://www.maryferrell.org/showDoc.html?docId=62421&relPageId=8

Garrison quoted by newsman Bob Jones: "Garrison's Conspiracy Probe Interview Test Listed," *Baton Rouge Morning Advocate*, May 22, 1967, the text of an interview with Bob Jones of WWL-TV; http://jfk.hood.edu/Collection/Weisberg%20Subject%20Index%20Files/G%20Disk/Garrison%20Jim/Garrison%20Jim%20on%20CIA/Item%2012.pdf

Garrison interview with Jim Squires of the Nashville Tennessean: Jim Squires, "Cuban Guerilla Team Killed JFK, Garrison Thinks," *Nashville Tennessean*, June 22, 1967.

Garrison Playboy Interview: op. cit.

Sylvia Meagher's letter to Playboy: Dated September 12, 1967, found in the Sylvia Meagher Archives at Hood College, MD.

Herblock cartoon: "New Orleans Strip Joint"—published March 1, 1967, courtesy of the Library of Congress.

Garrison quotes "Dallas police force deeply involved"; "a Nazi operation"; "considerably more than seven men": The Times-Picayune, September 22, 1967, https://www.maryferrell.org/showDoc.html?docId=62430&relPageId=135; https://www.maryferrell.org/showDoc.html?docId=62430&relPageId=98

Garrison's speech at the Annual Banquet of Radio and Television News Association of Southern California: full text printed in the *Los Angeles Free Press*, November 17, 1967, https://voices.revealdigital.org/?a=d&d=BGJFHJH19671117.1.1&e=-------en-20--1--txt-txIN--------------1

Steve Jaffe report to Garrison on sewer shot: Letter to Jim Garrison dated November 28, 1967, http://jfk.hood.edu/Collection/Weisberg%20Subject%20Index%20Files/J%20Disk/Jaffe%20Stephen/Item%2007.pdf

Garrison quote on "drainage system under Dealey Plaza" and

"fired a .45 caliber pistol": "Assassins' Names Hidden by U.S., Garrison States," *The Times-Picayune*, December 10, 1967, https://www.maryferrell.org/showDoc.html?docId=62503& relPageId=35; https://www.maryferrell.org/showDoc.html? docId=3914#relPageId=2

Monk Zelden's story about meeting Garrison at the New Orleans Athletic Club: George Lardner Jr. notes from a telephone call with Zelden found in the Papers of George Lardner.

Size of the sewers and the search for the "mini-midget": Hugh Aynesworth, "Garrison vs. Shaw, Part 5: What the Witnesses Will Say." January 30, 1969, *Newsweek*, found in the Papers donated by Harry Connick.

Garrison on Dutch television: Brener, op. cit., page 226; "DA Presents Views to Dutch Interviewer," *The Times-Picayune*, February 22, 1968.

Garrison on "exchanging information with a foreign intelligence agency": Garrison Claims Foreign Spy Link, *New York Times*, July 12, 1968.

James Phelan limerick: Kirkwood, op. cit., page 79.

The story about RFK obstructing Garrison: UPI story carried by many newspapers, https://www.maryferrell.org/showDoc. html?docId=62502&relPageId=35; http://jfk.hood.edu/ Collection/Weisberg%20Subject%20Index%20Files/K% 20Disk/Kennedy%20Bobby/Item%2063.pdf

Endnotes

Origins of Paese Sera: https://it.wikipedia.org/ wiki/Paese_Sera

Shaw was never in Rome and hated flying: See memo from John Volz to Jim Garrison, dated March 27, 1967, regarding State vs. Clay Shaw. "Shaw never traveled by airplane unless it was absolutely necessary no matter how far the distance. (Goldie Moore, Secretary)" There is no evidence Shaw was ever in Rome, and he repeatedly turned down requests to attend Permindex/CMC board meetings.

The Ford film Men Without Women: Carpenter, op.cit., page 6.

Dymond on why Garrison didn't introduce homosexuality at the trial: Kirkwood interview with Irvin Dymond, Papers of James Kirkwood.

THE TRIAL

Shaw spending $30,000 hiring detectives: Irvin Dymond memo on the problems in the Clay Shaw case, Papers of Irvin Dymond.

Problems faced by defense team: Ibid; see also Appendix A to Case #68-1063, "Constitutional Shortcomings of Louisiana Laws" which discusses the conspiracy statute.

Wegmann quote on "surprise witnesses": Letter to Elmer Gertz, dated January 14, 1969, Papers of Elmer Gertz.

Kohlman's quote about the prosecution's weak case: memo dated July 23, 1993, on notes from a conversation with Herman Kohlman; Papers of Patricia Lambert.

Corrie Collins testimony at trial: https://www.maryferrell. org/showDoc.html?docId=1273#relPageId=104&tab=page

Stephen Roy on problems with the Clinton witnesses: http:// www.jfk-online.com/dbtocljac.html

Sylvia Meagher on problems with the Clinton witnesses: "Not with a Roar But a Whimper: The Shaw Trial, the Garrison Wreck" by Sylvia Meagher, March 8, 1969, found in the Sylvia Meagher Archives.

FBI report on Reeves Morgan and his so-called report of Clinton incident: FBI report dated February 10, 1969, found in the Papers of Patricia Lambert; see also https://www. maryferrell.org/showDoc.html?docId=62454&relPageId=73& search=reeves_morgan; https://www.maryferrell.org/showDoc. html?docId=62438&search=reeves_morgan#relPageId=30&

tab=page; Garrison was notified that the FBI had no record of being contacted by Morgan: https://www.maryferrell.org/showDoc.html?docId=9917&relPageId=97&search=reeves_morgan

Patricia Lambert on Anne Dischler: See Chapter 13, "The Clinton Scenario and the House Select Committee" in her book, *False Witness*, op. cit.; see also David Reitzes article on the Clinton witnesses, http://www.jfk-online.com/impeach.html

Garrison taking Dischler off the case: Lambert, op. cit., page 196-197.

Hugh Aynesworth on Clinton witnesses: Aynesworth letter to James Kirkwood, dated October 9, 1969, found in the Papers of James Kirkwood.

The Charles Spiesel story: Memo from James Alcock to Jim Garrison dated July 17, 1967, regarding Charles Spiesel, Papers of Edward Wegmann, NARA.

A person in Garrison's office saying "he's crazy": Tom Bethell, "Conspiracy to End Conspiracies," *National Review*, December 16, 1991; Tom Bethell told NOLA.com that "the prosecution—they knew perfectly well that he was crazy," Adriane Quinlan, "50 years after JFK assassination, New Orleans remains hotbed of conspiracy theories," https://www.nola.com/news/politics/article_8304f408-0f2b-5cb8-92fe-89faa2cbfdf7.html

Spiesel "fingerprints his children": Ibid.

Spiesel testimony at Shaw trial: His testimony was never transcribed and so all we are left with are newspaper accounts of his testimony.

Spiesel only remembering Ferrie and Shaw at a party: "Surprise Witness Says He Was Introduced to Shaw by Ferrie," *The Times-Picayune*, February 8, 1969

Spiesel quote that Ferrie's eyebrows were "a little thinner": Ibid.

Spiesel testimony about the conspiracy against him: Ibid

Dymond-Spiesel exchange about hypnotism in New Orleans:

"Jury Taken to French Quarter," *The Times-Picayune*, February 9, 1969.

Spiesel's claim about "normal sex relations": Ibid.

Dymond-Spiesel exchange about planted thoughts: New Orleans States-Item February 9, 1969.

Dymond-Spiesel exchange about bad tax returns: Ibid.

Garrison quote on Spiesel testimony: Garrison, op. cit., page 237.

James Hardiman testimony: https://www.maryferrell.org/ showDoc.html?docId=1283&search=hardiman#relPageId=2& tab=page; Affidavit dated May 7, 1968, NARA.

James Hardiman's son: Kirkwood, op. cit., page 308.

Dean Andrews testimony: https://www.maryferrell.org/ showDoc.html?docId=1302#relPageId=9&tab=page

Perry Russo testimony: https://www.maryferrell.org/ showDoc.html?docId=1275#relPageId=6&tab=page

Notation in reporter's notebook about Zapruder Film: Kirkwood op. cit., page 332.

Kirkwood quote on the case against the Warren Report: Kirkwood op. cit., page 324.

Sylvia Meagher on Garrison's ineffective and inept challenge to the Warren Report: Meagher memo, March 8, 1969, op. cit.

Testimony of Mrs. Tadin: https://www.maryferrell.org/ showDoc.html?docId=1311

Mrs. Tadin's statement to Garrison's office: Statement dated February 27, 1969, Papers of Jim Garrison, NARA.

Quote on witnesses not emerging during Warren Commission: Stephen Roy, op. cit.

James Phelan's quote about jury queuing up for the bathroom: Telephone conversation between James Phelan and Patricia Lambert dated June 8, 1993, Papers of Patricia Lambert; see also Hugh Aynesworth, "The Garrison Goosechase," *Dallas Times Herald*, November 21, 1982.

Juror quote "wow, what happened": Kirkwood, op. cit.,

page 550.

Juror quote wondering who was on trial: Clarence Doucet, "Garrison Charges Shaw with Lying During Trial," *The Times-Picayune*, March 4, 1969.

New Orleans States-Item quote that Garrison is "a man without principle": "Garrison Should Resign, Orleans Paper Suggests," *Baton Rouge State Times Advocate*, March 1, 1969,

Times-Picayune comment on "flimsy documentary evidence": *The Times-Picayune*, March 2, 1969, "Justice, At Long Last," http://jfk.hood.edu/Collection/Weisberg%20Subject% 20Index%20Files/S%20Disk/Shaw%20Clay%20Trial% 20Aftermath/Item%2017.pdf

American Bar Association asking for an investigation: "Gossett Calls Trial Charade," *The Times-Picayune*, March 2, 1969,

New York Times quote on "one of the most disgraceful chapters": "Justice in New Orleans," The *New York Times*, March 2, 1969, page 12E.

Endnotes

FBI report on Clinton: FBI memo dated April 10, 1968, found in the Papers of Patricia Lambert.

Witness says Jack Ruby was the driver of the car in Clinton: Memo dated January 30, 1968, from Frank Ruiz and Kent Simms to Louis Ivon regarding Interview with Mrs. Andrew H. Dunne found in the Papers donated by Harry Connick.

Witness says Shaw's picture is Mr. Garrison: Memo dated January 31, 1968, from Frank Ruiz and Kent Simms regarding Interview of Mrs. Janie Daniels, found in the Papers donated by Harry Connick.

Witness picks out Thomas Beckham as being in Clinton: Memo dated January 31, 1968, from Frank Ruiz and Kent Simms regarding Interview with William Dunn, found in the Papers donated by Harry Connick.

Garrison memo that mentions Beckham being identified by

"Speysel": Garrison November 17, 1967 leads memo, found in the Harold Weisberg Archive (lead #50).

Dean Andrews's story about Bertrand being married with four children: Defense memo on Richard Townley and Dean Andrews based on a meeting held April 19, 1967, Papers of Irvin Dymond.

CLAY SHAW V. JIM GARRISON

Edward Wegmann's quote on the credibility of jury system: Clarence Doucet, "Garrison Charges Shaw with Lying During Trial," *The Times-Picayune*, March 4, 1969.

Dymond's statement: Ibid.

It was "financially disastrous" for Shaw: Kirkwood, op. cit., page 473.

Shaw quote about "psychic pain": Character Assassination: David Snyder, "The Ordeal of Clay Shaw," *The Times-Picayune*, July 28, 1996.

James Herlihy note to Clay Shaw: Found in the Papers of Clay Shaw.

Quote about Mayor Schiro hiding: Rosemary James, "The Dark Side of 'Not Guilty," *New Orleans Magazine*, March 1971, http://jfk.hood.edu/Collection/Weisberg%20Subject%20Index%20Files/S%20Disk/Shaw%20Clay/Item%2041.pdf

Shaw notation in his journal: Snyder, op. cit.

Garrison had his work cut out for him: Memo from Jim Garrison to Alcock, Sciambra, Alford, and Ivon, dated March 26, 1969, regarding New Files: Shaw II—Statements and Memos.

Herblock cartoon: "The Show Must go on and on and on." Published January 27, 1969, courtesy of the Library of Congress.

The Mardi Gras Caper: Memo from Jim Garrison to James Alcock, dated March 20, 1969, regarding Shaw: Leads Summary, Papers of Jim Garrison, NARA.

Report on the "fag ball": *The Times-Picayune*, February 26,

1962.

Garrison memo from March 20, 1969: Memo from Jim Garrison to James Alcock, regarding Shaw: Leads Summary, Papers of Jim Garrison, NARA.

Soule list of people arrested: Memo from Capt. F. A. Soule to Jim Alcock regarding Names and Addresses given by arrested homosexuals who were attending a party for perverts on 2/25/62, dated April 7, 1969.

David Gentry's identification of Shaw's friends: Garrison cross-checked the above list with a list of Shaw's friends identified in an interview with Gentry, Statement of David Gentry, dated April 18, 1967.

Propinquity leads: Memo from Andrew Sciambra to Jim Garrison dated March 27/28, 1969 regarding The New Shaw Lead File - section IV. Fag Ball in Jefferson parish in 1962.

Several memos listed other dubious leads: Memo dated March 20, 1969, from Jim Garrison to James Alcock—section 2. Mrs. J. Fant Taylor; Memo dated March 25, 1969, from Jim Garrison to Alcock, Sciambra and Ivon, section 2. The Insurance Company Lead, Section 4. The David Cotter Lead; Memo from Andrew Sciambra to Jim Garrison dated March 27/28, 1969 regarding The New Shaw Lead Section XVI—Sarah Ryan; Memo to Sciambra, Alford, Ivon and Garrison-Alcock regarding Shaw Leads Number II dated March 31, 1969—Section IV. Theresa Claire Fagnant, Section IX. James Warren; Memo from Sciambra to Jim Garrison dated April 11, 1969, regarding Shaw Leads II—Section 23. Mrs. Jeanne Kelton; Memo from Sciambra to Jim Garrison dated April 27, 1969, regarding The New Shaw Lead File—Section 41. Eddie Porter Lead, and Section 42 Shaw Parties Lead.

Sgt. Fred Williams memo on the Golden Lantern Bar: Papers of Jim Garrison, NARA.

Kent Simms memo to Louis Ivon regarding Clay Bertrand Lead: Papers of Jim Garrison, NARA.

Last Lead memo: Memo from William Alford to Jim Garrison dated June 20, 1969, regarding Lease of Elmwood Plantation Lead, Papers of Jim Garrison, NARA.

Harry Connick enters DA race: "Connick Makes Entry Official," *The Times-Picayune*, October 21, 1969.

Connick promises to fix bail bonds: "Bond Loss High, Connick Claims," *The Times-Picayune*, October 14, 1969.

Harry Connick calls Garrison "The Great Accuser": "Connick Accords Garrison Label of Great Accuser," *The Times-Picayune*, October 25, 1969.

Connick's quote about affording only one Mardi Gras: "Connick Urges Public to Think," *The Times-Picayune*, October 8, 1969.

Garrison admission that the JFK investigation has been dead: *The Times-Picayune*, November 9, 1969, with results of the election.

Dr. Minyard performing a hernia operation on Garrison: "Minyard Won't Back Candidate," *The Times-Picayune*, November 4, 1969.

Garrison quote about his book, A Heritage of Stone: Jim Garrison testimony, Christenberry Hearings, January 26, 1971, https://www.maryferrell.org/showDoc.html?docId=217755& relPageId=61

Kirkwood's quote on Garrison's book should be called "They": "Kirkwood Face, Topic Contrast," *The Times-Picayune*, December 1, 1990.

Clay Shaw lawsuit against Jim Garrison: Docket #70-466 Clay L. Shaw v. Jim Garrison et al. Shaw asked for $5 million which consisted of $1 million for loss of reputation; $2 million for mental anguish and continuous harassment; and $2 million for pain and suffering and irreparable damage to health.

Shaw team going to Federal Court to stop Garrison: Docket # 71-135 Clay L. Shaw v. Jim Garrison, individually and as District Attorney for the Parish of Orleans.

Three-day hearings: United States District Court, Eastern District of Louisiana, New Orleans Division; Docket #71-135. Proceedings of January 25, 26, and 27, 1971 in open court; https://www.maryferrell.org/php/showlist.php?docset=2103

Garrison promising more arrests: Interview with Ron Hunter of *WWL-TV* on Sunday, March 7, 1971; Court filing by the Shaw defense team; #71-135, the reply of the plaintiff to defendant's memo, Papers of Edward Wegmann, NARA.

Judge Christenberry on Shaw's arrest: January 25, 1971, page 196 in the Christenberry hearings, https://www.maryferrell.org/showDoc.html?docId=217754&relPageId=194&search=Mr._Shaw%20was%20surrounded%20by%20policemen

Perry Russo interview with Edward Wegmann: Memo dated January 27, 1971, regarding a visit of Perry Russo, found in the Papers of Edward Wegmann.

The ruling of Judge Christenberry: Docket #71-135, Decided May 27, 1971; http://www.jfk-online.com/christenberry2.html

Garrison statement regarding Christenberry decision: Press release dated May 31, 1971, Harry Connick Papers donated to NARA, the complete statement is in the following news report, https://www.maryferrell.org/showDoc.html?docId=62462&search=garrison_statement+on+christenberry#relPageId=55&tab=page

The indictment of Jim Garrison for bribery: Press release by Department of Justice dated June 30, 1971; United States of America v. Jim Garrison and others, the indictment was found in the Papers of Elmer Gertz, http://jfk.hood.edu/Collection/Weisberg%20Subject%20Index%20Files/G%20Disk/Garrison%20Jim/Garrison%20Jim%20DoJ%20Graft%20Charges%20Gervais/Item%2001.pdf

Garrison's bribes over nine years: The indictment claims that the pinball dealers gave Garrison $10,000 during his 1961 campaign for DA and that starting in 1962 they paid Pershing Gervais $3,600 every two months. Sometimes the amounts were as low as $2,700 bi-monthly and as high as $4,400 bi-monthly. Gervais retained $700 from each bi-monthly payoff and he passed the rest to Jim Garrison (his payoff would rise or fall depending on the total amount); "Garrison 'Prays' for Acquittal in Case, Jury Resumes Deliberation Today," *The Times-Picayune*, September 26, 1973, this article puts the total as $147,825.

Garrison quote that this was a "frame-up" and his prediction the government would take some sort of action: The Times-Picayune, July 1, 1971, "Frame-Up, Says DA of Charges," by Clarence Doucet.

Clay Shaw going back to work: Gene Bourg, "The return of Clay Shaw as a force in the city," *New Orleans States-Item*, December 16, 1971. Clay Shaw's salary was disclosed in a legal brief.

Clay Shaw lecturing at Colleges: "Clay Shaw is Touring Colleges Lecturing on 'Erosion of Rights," *New York Times*, September 27, 1970.

Rejection of Garrison's appeal: Docket #71-2422 United States Court of Appeals, Fifth Circuit, Shaw v. Garrison, Decided November 20, 1972.

Garrison's nine-page statement: Press Release titled "Reply To the Federal Supreme Court Decision of November 20 Preventing the Prosecution of Clay L. Shaw for Perjury." http://jfk.hood.edu/Collection/Weisberg%20Subject%20Index%20Files/S%20Disk/Shaw%20Clay%20Perjury%20Trial%203-4-69/Item%2037.pdf

Ron Rosenbaum called Garrison: Ron Rosenbaum, "Garrison & JFK's Assassination: The whole story & nothing but the whole story," *The Village Voice*, January 18, 1973, http://jfk.hood.edu/Collection/Weisberg%20Subject%20Index%20Files/S%20Disk/Shaw%20Clay%20Perjury%20Trial%203-4-69/Item%2043.pdf

Larry Crafard: Ron Rosenbaum, "Taking a Darker View," *Time Magazine*, January 13, 1992, http://jfk.hood.edu/

Collection/Weisberg%20Subject%20Index%20Files/S%20Disk/
Stone%20Oliver%20JFK%20Movie/Reviews%20Comments%
20Stories%2001-11-92%20--/Item%2026.pdf

Gervais taped conversations: From the indictment, op. cit.

Garrison and fluorescent powder: "Marked Money Seized, Agents Say," *The Times-Picayune*, September 11, 1973.

Tom Bethell and Garrison's roll of $50 bills: Tom Bethell, "Jim Garrison's Great Escape," *The American Spectator*, December 1998, https://www.unz.com/print/AmSpectator-1998dec-00020/

Garrison's claim that the tapes were altered: "Garrison v. Everybody," *Time Magazine*, October 8, 1973.

Garrison's three-hour summation and quote about creating a conspiracy: John McMillan and Don Hughes, "Garrison Asks for Acquittal, Jury Retires for Evening," *The Times-Picayune*, September 26, 1973.

Garrison quote about acquittal: John McMillan and Don Hughes, "Jury Acquits Garrison, Nims, Callery in Pinball Bribe Case," *The Times-Picayune*, September 28, 1973.

Shaw undergoing radiation for lung cancer: Carpenter, op. cit., page 484.

Shaw's seizure in February 1974: Ibid, page 495.

Death of Clay Shaw: "Clay Shaw Final Rites To Be Today," *The Times-Picayune*, August 16, 1974.

The tip about an ambulance: Don Gross, "Anonymous Tip Told of Body," *The Times-Picayune*, August 20, 1974.

Minyard quote on suicide or murder: Richard Boyle, "The Strange Death of Clay Shaw," *True Magazine*, April 1975, http://jfk.hood.edu/Collection/Weisberg%20Subject%20Index%20Files/S%20Disk/Shaw%20Clay%20Death%20of/Item%201.pdf

Cynthia Wegmann quote: Adriane Quinlan, "After JFK assassination, DA Jim Garrison ripped into life of Clay Shaw," *The Times-Picayune*, November 21, 2013, https://www.nola.com/

news/politics/article_07ba6d76-8ca8-5341-86d2-
3e85eac1aad3.html

Garrison exhortation to look into Shaw's death: Boyle, op. cit.

Endnotes

Boxley memo on Larry Crafard: Dated October 2, 1968,
memo from Wm. C. Boxley to Jim Garrison regarding Larry
Crafard; http://jfk.hood.edu/Collection/Weisberg%20Subject%
20Index%20Files/B%20Disk/Boxley%20Memos%
20Miscellaneous/Item%2007.pdf

Garrison and Gervais discussing the Cabell's: Iris Kelso,
"Garrison Planned to Link General to JFK slaying," The *Washington Post*, September 16, 1973.

Supreme Court ruling on Shaw's libel case: "Clay Shaw's
Lost Cause," *New York Times*, June 20, 1978, https://www.
nytimes.com/1978/06/20/archives/clay-shaws-lost-cause.html

A TALE OF THREE CUBANS

Garrison's belief the FBI was listening on his phone calls: Gurvich
conference with Edward Wegmann, September 6, 1967, Papers
of Edward Wegmann, NARA; Brener, op. cit., page 81; Gurvich
testimony in the Christenberry hearings, January 26, 1971, page
341,   https://www.maryferrell.org/showDoc.html?docId=
217755#relPageId=135&tab=page

Garrison's interest in equipment to protect against bugging:
Elmer Gertz letter to Edward Jay Epstein regarding Gordon
Novel, dated June 10, 1968, Papers of Elmer Gertz, Library of
Congress.

*Novel meeting with Garrison and Robertson on February 21,
1967*: Gordon Novel interview for *NBC* Special June 1967, transcript in the Papers of the Metropolitan Crime Commission;
Brener op. cit., page 81.

Garrison quote that the FBI is "scrutinizing every move": FBI

report dated March 29, 1967; http://jfk.hood.edu/Collection/
Weisberg%20Subject%20Index%20Files/N%20Disk/Novel%
20Gordon/Item%20012.pdf

Garrison suggestion that Novel plant equipment in his office:
Gordon Novel interview for NBC special mentioned above.

Garrison suggestion that Novel fire a dart gun into Ferrie:
Washington Post, April 25, 1967, "Novel Charges Garrison Plan
to Stun Ferrie." Garrison admitted he discussed this with Novel,
although he said it was Novel's idea: "Gurvich Blasts Investigation," *The Times-Picayune*, June 28, 1967, http://jfk.hood.edu/
Collection/Weisberg%20Subject%20Index%20Files/N%
20Disk/NBC%20Clips/Item%20076.pdf

Garrison granting Novel and Ehrlinger immunity: Gurvich
conference, August 29, 1967, Papers of Edward Wegmann,
NARA.

Gus Russo on Houma operation: Russo, op. cit., page
150-153.

Garrison believing laundry truck used in the assassination:
Gurvich conference with Edward Wegmann, August 29, 1967,
Papers of Edward Wegmann, NARA; FBI document, Airtel
from SAC, NO to DIRECTOR, FBI 2/23/67 RIF # 124-10040-
10268,   https://www.maryferrell.org/showDoc.html?docId=
9986#relPageId=158&tab=page; Diary of Richard Billings, entry
for February 23, 1967, http://www.jfk-online.com/billings3.html

Richard Sprague identifying a laundry truck in Dealey Plaza:
Richard Sprague monograph, "The Kennedy Assassination:
What The Photographs Show," October 15, 1967.

Novel said it looked like a Golden Cleaners Truck: Diary of
Richard Billings, entry for March 16, 1967, http://www.jfk-
online.com/billings3.html

It was a Golden Cleaners truck: Memo from George Eckert to
Jim Garrison, dated March 27, 1967, regarding Golden Cleaners, Papers of Irvin Dymond,

Garrison took a picture of a Golden Cleaners Truck: Diary of

Richard Billings, entry for February 23, 1967, http://www.jfk-online.com/billings3.html

Sergio Arcacha Smith: A good summary of Sergio Arcacha Smith and 544 Camp Street can be found in Volume X of the HSCA Report Appendix Volumes: https://www.maryferrell.org/showDoc.html?docId=1212#relPageId=127&tab=page

Two witnesses to see Arcacha and Oswald together: Statement of David Lewis, December 15, 1966, Papers of Gus Russo; Statement of Jack Martin, December 14, 1966.

Lewis trying to sell a story to UPI: FBI Memo dated February 28, 1967, from C.D. De Loach to Mr. Tolson regarding the assassination: https://www.maryferrell.org/showDoc.html?docId=60404&search=%22merriman_smith%22#relPageId=134&tab=page

Lewis originally saying he saw Oswald in 1961: Diary of Tom Bethell, entry for September 9, 1967, https://mcadams.posc.mu.edu/bethell1.htm

Gurvich seeing Novel meet with Walter Sheridan: Gurvich conference with Edward Wegmann, August 29, 1967, Papers of Edward Wegmann, NARA.

Garrison quote about Novel breaking contract: Gurvich conference with Edward Wegmann, August 29, 1967, Papers of Edward Wegmann, NARA.

Garrison cursing violently and saying "I'll fix him": https://www.maryferrell.org/showDoc.html?docId=56288&search=%22gurvich_continued+that+Jack+S.+Martin%22#relPageId=68&tab=page

Two memos on Gordon Novel: Papers of Jim Garrison, NARA.

Garrison was also trying to find Arcacha: Memo from William Gurvich to Jim Garrison dated January 6, 1967, NARA.

Two men looking for Arcacha: Sergio Arcacha Smith affidavit dated May 22, 1967; Dallas Municipal Archives and Record

Center, https://texashistory.unt.edu/ark:/67531/
metapth339537/?q=arcacha

Alcock phone call to Arcacha on February 20, 1967: ibid.

Alcock warning about 'bad press': Ibid.

Gurvich and Alcock flying to Dallas: Memo from William
Gurvich to Jim Garrison regarding Sergio Arcacha Smith -
February 25, 1967, dated April 4, 1967, Papers of Jim Garrison,
NARA.

A Garrison press release that Arcacha had refused to talk:
Arcacha affidavit.

*Arcacha telling reporters he'd be happy to speak with
Garrison*: Ibid.

Garrison charged Novel and Arcacha with burglary: Charge
sheet for Gordon Novel and Sergio Arcacha Smith, Papers of
Gus Russo.

*Garrison quote about getting results in another area of the
case*: Richard Billings interview with Jim Garrison, Papers of
Richard Billings: see also Gurvich conference, August 8, 1967, in
which he said Garrison was just interested in the laundry truck.

Arcacha quote that he would fight Garrison: Holland
McComb memo to Will Lang at Life Magazine dated April 4,
1967, Papers of Richard Billings.

Arcacha in tears: Ibid.

Arcacha's seven-year-old daughter: Ibid.

Quote from Arcacha's lawyer: Russo, op. cit., page 410.

*Letter from Jim Garrison to Richard Billings, December 26,
1966*: Papers of Richard Billings.

Elmer Gertz on taking Novel with a whole salt shaker: Gertz
letter to Edward Wegmann, February 24, 1972, Papers of Elmer
Gertz.

Carlos Bringuier and Lee Harvey Oswald: Warren Report,
page 728, https://www.maryferrell.org/showDoc.html?docId=
946#relPageId=752

Ferrie going to see Bringuier: Dr. Carlos J. Bringuier, *Crime*

Without Punishment: How Castro Assassinated President Kennedy and Got Away With It, (Authorhouse, 2014), page 266.

Ferrie's quote about Garrison running for higher office: Aaron Kohn Memo dated June 12, 1967, based upon a phone call with Bringuier, Papers of the Metropolitan Crime Commission, NARA.

Ferrie quote about a bad publicity campaign: Ibid.

Bringuier quote about Arcacha to John Volz: Ibid.

Garrison quote to Merriman Smith: https://www.maryferrell. org/showDoc.html?docId=60404&search=% 22merriman_smith%22#relPageId=134&tab=page

Garrison telling Hoke May that the troops went to Dallas: Hoke May note dated May 1, 1967, found in the Harold Weisberg Archive; http://jfk.hood.edu/Collection/Weisberg% 20Subject%20Index%20Files/M%20Disk/May%20Hoke% 20Notes/Item%2033.pdf

Propinquity and Clay Shaw's mother: David Chandler interview by Robert Wilson, March 24, 1967, Papers of Irvin Dymond.

Garrison and the training camps: There are a series of memos from Al Oser regarding his search for the training camp.

Garrison examining aerial photographs: Brener, op. cit., page 72.

Quote about Tulane Primate Center: Ibid.

Bringuier quote about "somebody is lying or is a son of a bitch": Aaron Kohn Memo dated June 12, 1967, regarding a phone call with Carlos Bringuier.

Bringuier quote that Oswald was brought to town by conservative Americans: Ibid.

Bringuier quote about Oswald going to Cuba to kill Castro: Ibid.

Bringuier telling Garrison "this was the most ridiculous thing I have heard": Ibid.

Bringuier telling Garrison "somebody's furnishing you wrong information": Ibid.

Bringuier quote that Garrison's investigation would end in zero: Ibid.

Garrison asked Bringuier to take a lie detector test: Ibid.

Bringuier quote asking examiner about ridiculous thing: Ibid.

Garrison saying "so far': Ibid.

Ferrie going to see Bringuier on February 20th: Ibid.

Bringuier quote that Ferrie looked destroyed and sick: Ibid.

Bringuier's wife's miscarriage: Bringuier, op. cit., page 304.

Carlos Quiroga and Lee Harvey Oswald: https://www.maryferrell.org/showDoc.html?docId=800&relPageId=171&search=quiroga

Quiroga asked to come down to DA office: Aaron Kohn investigative report dated April 18, 1968, based upon an interview with Carlos Quiroga on July 25, 1967; Papers of the Metropolitan Crime Commission.

Quiroga quote on investigation going the wrong way: Ibid.

Quiroga offers to "clarify the whole mess": Ibid.

Garrison subpoena to Quiroga: Ibid.

Quiroga quote on touching rifle: Ibid.

Garrison threat to bring him to the Grand Jury: Ibid.

Quotes about "clean his ass": Carlos Quiroga document sent to Aaron Kohn dated March 23, 1969, retrieved from the Gerald Posner archive.

Garrison taped interview: Interview dated January 31, 1967, Papers of Irvin Dymond.

The threatening phone call from Jack Martin and quotes related to it: Kohn memo of April 18, 1968.

Garrison quote about the conspiracy: Quiroga letter to Kohn dated March 23, 1969.

Quiroga telling Garrison to investigate the people who have been lying: Kohn memo dated April 18, 1968.

Quiroga confronting Jack Martin: Ibid.

Quiroga's lie detector test: Kohn memo of April 18, 1969, and Quiroga letter to Kohn March 23, 1969.

Car going around Quiroga's neighborhood: Ibid.

Quiroga subpoena to appear before the Grand Jury: Ibid.

Quiroga Grand Jury testimony: https://www.maryferrell.org/showDoc.html?docId=1204

Quiroga's father: Kohn memo dated April 18, 1968.

Garrison quote "I'm not through with you": Quiroga letter to Kohn dated March 23, 1969.

Quiroga quote that Garrison is insane: Aaron Kohn Investigative Report dated July 27, 1967, regarding an interview with Carlos Quiroga on July 25, 1967.

Endnotes

Carl Pelleck quote on David Lewis: New York Post, February 24, 1967, "Behind The New Orleans Probe," by Carl Pelleck; http://jfk.hood.edu/Collection/White%20Materials/Sylvia%20Meagher%20Clips/SM-027.pdf

Garrison not filing proper paperwork on Gordon Novel: "Novel Will Be Returned—Ohio," *The Times-Picayune*, May 10, 1967.

Novel telling Robert San Anson he will be head of the CIA: Robert Sam Anson, *They've Killed the President: The Search for the Murderers of John F. Kennedy*, (Bantam Books, 1975), page 109.

Novel conviction in 1970: "Eavesdropping Conviction Made," *Las Vega Review-Journal*, November 6, 1970.

Novel arrested by ATF: "Garrison JFK Probe Figure charged in Mardi Gras Plot," *Dallas Morning News*, February 28, 1976.

Novel's conviction overturned: Dick Reavis, "Conspiracy dreams are an FBI nightmare," *San Antonio Express-News*, January 23, 2000, https://culteducation.com/group/1220-waco-davidians/24065-conspiracy-dreams-are-an-fbi-nightmare.html

Gus Russo interview with Gordon Novel: Papers of Gus Russo.

Novel plugging anti-gravity device: https://www.americanantigravity.com/gordon-novel-on-antigravity

Bug installed in Perry Russo's home: The bug was in his stereo, http://www.jfk-online.com/russokirk.html

WAS KERRY THORNLEY THE SECOND OSWALD?

Richard Popkin, *The Second Oswald: A startling alternative to the single assassin theory of the Warren Commission Report*, (Avon, 1966).

Harold Weisberg, *Whitewash: The Report on the Warren Report* (Dell, 1966).

Kerry Thornley and Oswald: https://www.maryferrell.org/showDoc.html?docId=946&search=thornley#relPageId=412&tab=page

Oswald quote that communism was the best: Warren Commission Hearings, Volume XI, page 87, https://www.maryferrell.org/showDoc.html?docId=45#relPageId=97

Thornley quote about someone else speaking Russian: Ibid, page 108, https://www.maryferrell.org/showDoc.html?docId=45#relPageId=118

Thornley quote about disillusionment: Ibid, page 97, https://www.maryferrell.org/showDoc.html?docId=45#relPageId=107

Thornley working as a waiter when JFK killed: Adam Gorightly, *Caught in the Crossfire: Kerry Thornley, Lee Oswald and the Garrison Investigation*, (Feral House, 2014), page 25.

Kerry Thornley, *Oswald* (New Classics, 1965).

Lifton angry with Thornley's depiction of Oswald: David Lifton, "Is Jim Garrison Out of His Mind?" *Open City*, May 31, and June 6, 1968 issues, https://mcadams.posc.mu.edu/lifton1.htm

Lifton called Garrison's office: Ibid.

Heindel statement to Garrison: Statement of John R. Heindel, September 19, 1967; http://jfk.hood.edu/Collection/Weisberg%20Subject%20Index%20Files/H%20Disk/Heindel%20John%20Rene/Item%2001.pdf

Garrison on Heindel lying through his teeth: Lifton, op. cit.

Thornley's eleven-page affidavit: Statement of Kerry Wendell Thornley dated September 23, 1967, Regarding His Warren Commission Deposition; http://jfk.hood.edu/Collection/Weisberg%20Subject%20Index%20Files/T%20Disk/Thornley%20Kerry%20Wendell%20--%20Lifton%20David/Item%2010.pdf

Quote about "persuade Heindel to provide detrimental testimony": Gorightly, op. cit., page 38.

Garrison telling Lifton that we can throw a couple of bricks: Lifton, op. cit.

Lifton meeting Erwin Donald Lewis: Ibid.

Garrison sending Thornley a telegram: Ibid.

Garrison asking Thornley to use a pseudonym: David Lifton, "Thoughts and Comments on Garrison and Thornley," May 2, 1969; https://mcadams.posc.mu.edu/lifton2.htm; Thornley letter to Robert Anton Wilson, dated September 1, 1975, papers of the Metropolitan Crime Commission.

Thornley letter to Garrison: Papers of Edward Wegmann, NARA.

Garrison's new theory on Thornley: Lifton, "Is Garrison Out of His Mind?" op. cit.

Garrison's belief that Thornley's actions were those of a member of a conspiracy: Lifton, "Thoughts and Comments" op. cit.

Garrison subpoena to Kerry Thornley: Harry Connick Papers, NARA.

Thornley dialog with Sciambra: Kerry Thornley, "In the Garrison State (1970)" Gorightly, op. cit., page 186-187.

Andrew Sciambra quote in memo: Memo from Andrew

Sciambra to Jim Garrison dated February 7, 1968, Harry Connick Papers, NARA.

Thornley remembering a conversation with a girlfriend: Gorightly, op.cit., page 188.

Kerry Thornley testimony before Grand Jury: https://www.maryferrell.org/showDoc.html?docId=1207

Lou Ivon yelling at Thornley: Gorightly, op. cit., page 199.

Thornley offer to brainstorm: Ibid, page 201.

Garrison press release on perjury charge: Dated February 21, 1968;   http://jfk.hood.edu/Collection/Weisberg%20Subject%20Index%20Files/T%20Disk/Thornley%20Kerry/Item%2028.pdf

Marine Statements who served with Oswald: Volume VIII of the Warren Commission Hearings and Exhibits, starts on page 315,   https://www.maryferrell.org/showDoc.html?docId=36#relPageId=323

Greg Hill quote on post office boxes: Gorightly, op. cit., page 60.

Propinquity and Kerry Thornley: Diary of Tom Bethell, entry for   February   9,   1968,   https://mcadams.posc.mu.edu/bethell5.htm

Bethell memo to Jim Garrison: http://jfk.hood.edu/Collection/Weisberg%20Subject%20Index%20Files/T%20Disk/Thornley%20Kerry/Item%2049.pdf

Barbara Reid in the Times-Picayune: David Cuthbert, "Bell, Book, Candle Shed Little Friday 13th Light," *The Times-Picayune*, June 13, 1969, http://historiadiscordia.com/barbara-reid-voodoo-practitioner-discordian-society-member-and-dealey-plaza-irregular-part-00001/

Thornley's plea to have Barbara Reid investigated: Gorightly, op. cit., page 195.

FBI report on Thornley: Warren Commission Document 244, page 40, https://www.maryferrell.org/showDoc.html?docId=10647#relPageId=41&tab=page

Barbara Reid letter to Harold Weisberg: Letter dated April 2, 1968; http://jfk.hood.edu/Collection/Weisberg%20Subject%20Index%20Files/R%20Disk/Reid%20Barbara/Item%2012.pdf

Weisberg on Reid being "an accomplished liar": Harold Weisberg letter dated 2/8.73; http://jfk.hood.edu/Collection/Weisberg%20Subject%20Index%20Files/T%20Disk/Turner%20Dione%20Letters%20from%20Houston/Item%2054.pdf

Clint Bolton quotes about Barbara Reid: Gorightly, op. cit., page 192.

Boxley memo on Barbara Reed [sic]: Papers of Edward Wegmann, NARA.

Quote on witnessing the crime of the century: Lifton, "Is Garrison Out of his Mind," op. cit.

Quote about encyclopedia salesman: Gorightly, op. cit., page 202.

Lifton quote about witness recruitment program: Lifton, "Is Garrison Out of his Mind," op. cit.

The witness who saw Thornley at Oswald residence: John Schwegmann letter to Garrison dated February 22, 1968, Papers of Harry Connick, NARA.

Sciambra memo on Jim Serio: Memo dated May 10, 1968, Papers of Jim Garrison, NARA.

Harold Weisberg Letter to Fred Newcomb: http://jfk.hood.edu/Collection/Weisberg%20Subject%20Index%20Files/N%20Disk/Newcomb%20Fred/Item%2017.pdf

Garrison discussion on Thornley in Oswald photograph: New Orleans conference September 21, 1968, between Garrison and his Assistant DA's and investigators, page 66, https://archive.org/stream/GarrisonPapers/New%20Orleans%20Conference%209%3A21%3A1968%2012%20of%2017#page/n77/mode/1up

Reverend Broshears not knowing Ferrie's apartment: http://www.jfk-online.com/dbraybropost.html

Boxley quote on queer waiter: New Orleans conference, September 2, 1968, page 93.

Lou Ivon memo on the Heights of the Oswalds: Memo dated November 14, 1968, Papers of Jim Garrison, NARA.

Tom Bethell on dinner with Jones Harris: Bethell, op. cit., page 65.

Thornley calling for Garrison to bring him to trial: "Tampa writer asks trial in JFK assassination case," *The Tampa Times*, March 3, 1968.

Thornley's guerilla tactics: Gorightly, op. cit., page 87.

Kerry Thornley, *The Idle Warriors*, (IllumiNet Press, 1991).

Jonathan Vankin quote: John Strausbaugh, "Making Book"; http://historiadiscordia.com/kerry-prankster-cia-lsd-jfk/; Jonathan Vankin, *Conspiracies, Coverups & Crimes: From Dallas to Waco*, (Illuminet Press, 1996), page 18-19.

Paul Hoch on Thornley: *Echoes of Conspiracy* newsletter, Volume 13, Number 1; http://www.jfk-online.com/eoc1301exc.html

THE BALLAD OF SLIDIN' CLYDE JOHNSON

Clyde Johnson's idea about calling Garrison: Memo on Clyde Johnson dated January 16, 1969 taken from Edward Wegmann notes; letter from Edward Wegmann to William McNamara, October 6, 1967; Papers of Irvin Dymond.

Johnson calling Garrison's office and his story: Statement of Clyde Johnson dated April 5, 1967; Papers of Richard Billings.

DA showed Johnson about 35 photographs: Ibid.

Why Johnson had not come forward: Ibid.

Ed McMillan's story: Statement of Edward McMillan, dated April 11, 1967, NARA.

Clyde Johnson's new statement: Dated June 5, 1967, NARA.

Garrison paragraph on Johnson allegation: "Ruby is Named as Plot Figure," *The Times-Picayune*, June 6, 1967, https://www.maryferrell.org/showDoc.html?docId=55186&relPageId=240

Times-Picayune quote about Johnson: "Johnson Says Meetings Held," *The Times-Picayune*, June 16, 1967, http://jfk.hood.edu/Collection/Weisberg%20Subject%20Index%20Files/J%20Disk/Johnson%20Clyde/Item%2004.pdf

Johnson quote on not cooperating with Garrison: "Johnson Says He Was Informer for Garrison," *Shreveport Journal*, June 16, 1967.

Johnson quotes on being a hostile witness and "half the truth": Ibid.

Property damage against Southern Bell Telephone and Telegraph: *The Times-Picayune*, June 16, 1967, op. cit.

Johnson talking to NBC: Transcript of NBC interview of Clyde Johnson for June special. Papers of the Metropolitan Crime Commission, NARA.

Court order to particularize further: "Defense Wins on Two Points," *The Times-Picayune*, August 17, 1967, https://www.maryferrell.org/showDoc.html?docId=55187&relPageId=322

Garrison gives a date of September 3, 1963: "Garrison Names Date of Meeting," *Richmond Times-Dispatch*, August 19, 1967.

Letter to Eva Grant: Papers of Edward Wegmann, NARA.

Investigation showed that Ruby was not in Baton Rouge: Letter from Hugh Aynesworth to Irvin Dymond, dated August 30, 1967, Papers of Irvin Dymond; Eva Grant letter to Edward Wegmann, February 1968, Papers of Irvin Dymond.

Eva Grant seeing Ruby in Dallas every day in September: Eva Grant letter to Nicholas Chriss of the L.A. Times, dated September 16, 1967, Papers of Edward Wegmann, NARA.

Lardner quote about Johnson being flaky: George Lardner Jr article on Garrison investigation dated June 17, 1967, Papers of George Lardner, Jr., Library of Congress.

Johnson getting small change from Garrison's office: Gurvich conference, August 29, 1967, Papers of Edward Wegmann, NARA.

Johnson's standard line: Ibid.

Johnson's code: Ibid.

Johnson's rap sheet: Papers of Irvin Dymond.

Johnson an inmate at mental hospital: Edward Wegmann memo on Clyde Johnson dated July 6, 1967, Papers of Edward Wegmann, NARA.

Johnson's car accident: "Johnson Fails to Qualify as Governor," *Baton Rouge States-Times Advocate*, September 16, 1963.

Quote on papers disappearing: Ibid.

Johnson's run for Congress: "Clyde Johnson Killed, Report," *The Times-Picayune*, July 24, 1969.

March 1965 story about Johnson searching people for weapons: "Clyde Johnson Held in Café Search Incident," *Baton Rouge State-Times*, March 10, 1965.

Johnson threatening a black man: "Clyde Johnson Charged with Hitting Negro," *Baton Rouge States-Times Advocate*, March 6, 1967.

Alcock's six overt acts: Kirkwood, op. cit., page 64-65; "Two Jurors Selected For Clay Shaw Trial," *The Times-Picayune*, January 22, 1969.

Johnson quote on being ace-in-the-hole: "Charges Pend in Slaying of La. 'Candidate," *New Orleans States-Item*, August 24, 1969, http://jfk.hood.edu/Collection/White%20Materials/Garrison%20News%20Clippings/1969/69-07/69-07-23.pdf

Johnson arrested for not paying hotel bill: "Clyde Johnson is Hospitalized," *The Times-Picayune*, January 21, 1969.

Defense calling Ed McMillan to testify: Shaw defense memo on witnesses, January 8, 1969, Papers of Irvin Dymond.

Quote about deep-lying roots: "Ralph McMillan is Booked with Manslaughter," *Baton Rouge State-Times Advocate*, July 16, 1969.

Endnote

Irvin Dymond quote about Clyde Johnson: James Kirkwood interview with Irvin Dymond, Papers of James Kirkwood.

EDGAR EUGENE BRADLEY WAS A TRAMP

Thomas Thornhill's letter to Garrison: Letter dated April 10, 1967, Papers of Edward Wegmann, NARA.

Garrison registered under the name Clyde Ballou: Associated Press report, December 21, 1967, NARA.

Package delivered to Garrison: Harold Weisberg letter, dated February 23, 1991; http://jfk.hood.edu/Collection/Weisberg%20Subject%20Index%20Files/S%20Disk/Stone%20Gregg%20Suicide/Item%2003.pdf

Visit to Tom Thornhill's home: Memo from Bill Turner to Jim Garrison, dated February 16, 1968, Papers of Edward Wegmann, NARA.

Quotes about Bradley "harping;" calling his wife from Dallas; had blueprints of the storm drain system; had tried to induce Dennis Mower to take a shot; is a sadist; beats his daughter; and has a habit of pinching women: Ibid.

Quotes about Aydelotte telling Bradley she owned .357; his attempt to recruit her husband; and poisons and booby traps: Memo from Bill Boxley to Jim Garrison dated March 19, 1968, Papers of Edward Wegmann, NARA.

Aydelotte identifying Bradley as one of the tramps: Memo from Bill Turner to Jim Garrison, dated February 16, 1968, Papers of Edward Wegmann, NARA.

Interview with Thornhill: Memo March 19, 1968 op. cit.

Meeting with Dennis Mower: Ibid.

Staff pushing back on Garrison: Diary of Tom Bethell, entry for January 15th, https://mcadams.posc.mu.edu/bethell4.htm; entries for February 13th and 14th, 1968, https://mcadams.posc.mu.edu/bethell6.htm

Charge sheet for Edgar Eugene Bradley: Papers of Edward Wegmann, NARA.

Garrison press release: Dated December 20, 1967, Harry Connick Papers, NARA.

Bradley quote on it being a practical joke: Bradley interview with Joe Pyne on March 7, 1968, Papers of Edward Wegmann, NARA.

"Off Rocker" headline: New Orleans States-Item, December 27, 1967, https://www.maryferrell.org/showDoc.html?docId= 55188&relPageId=207

Bradley quote about Garrison being off his rocker: Dallas Morning News, December 27, 1967.

Bradley quotes after arraignment, "I know I am not guilty": "Bradley Free Without Bond," The Times-Picayune, December 28, 1967.

Bradley quote about being framed: Ibid.

Bradley whereabouts on November 22, 1963: Ibid.

Massive feud between Bradley and Aydelotte: Peter Noyes, Legacy of Doubt: Did the Mafia Kill JFK? (Pinnacle Books, 1973), pages 206-209.

Bradley calling Aydelotte a kook: Ibid, page 207.

Bradley writing Robert Welch: Ibid.

Bradley deposition in Aydelotte lawsuit: Dated December 19, 1967; portions of this document were in the Harry Connick Papers, NARA.

Aydelotte's claim of 400 hours of tape: Aydelotte letter to Jim Garrison, dated December 29, 1967; Papers of Edward Wegmann, NARA.

Dennis Mower only 14 in 1960: Noyes, op. cit., page 202; https://zodiackiller.forumotion.com/t445-pastor-dennis-p-mower

No FBI record of Mower speaking to them: FBI memo dated October 13, 1969, RIF # 124-10369-10021; https://www. maryferrell.org/showDoc.html?docId=62458&search=% 22dennis_mower%22+bradley#relPageId=99&tab=page

Garrison paperwork in support of extraditing Bradley: Affidavit of Jim Garrison, dated January 23, 1968; Affidavit of Max Gonzales, dated January 16, 1968; Affidavit of Roger Craig, dated January 19th, 1968; NARA.

Impossibility of being a tramp and Craig's secret service agent: See diary entry of Tom Bethell for February 13, 1968, https://mcadams.posc.mu.edu/bethell6.htm

Richard Sprague and multiple Bradleys: Richard Sprague letter to Fred Newcomb, dated January 24, 1969; Harold Weisberg Archive.

Richard Sprague about Bradley perhaps having an operation: Richard Sprague letter to Fred Newcomb dated January 9, 1969; Papers of Richard Sprague, Georgetown University.

Quote about Sprague being a threat: Letter to Richard Bernabei from Gary Schoener, the Papers of Richard Bernabei courtesy of researcher Dennis Moricet.

Newspaper report of Craig being shot at: "Bullet Misses Probe Witness," *The Times-Picayune*, November 3, 1967.

Bradley extradition hearing: Jerry Cohen, "Garrison Has Perhaps Irreparably Damaged His JFK Death Probe," *Los Angeles Times*, June 29, 1968.

Peter Noyes trying to find Bradley: Noyes, op. cit., page 103.

Bradley letters to Jim Garrison: Letter dated September 17, 1969, Harry Connick Papers, NARA; Letter dated May 22, 1968, Ibid.

Charges dropped against Bradley: Bob Ussery, "Conspiracy Suit Dropped By Volz," *The Times-Picayune*, June 26, 1970, http://jfk.hood.edu/Collection/White%20Materials/Garrison%20News%20Clippings/1970/70-06/70-06-42.pdf

Roger Craig suicide: "Ex-deputy at Kennedy's death site kills himself," *Austin American-Statesman*, May 17, 1975,

Roger Craig on valium: Magen Knuth, "Roger Craig: Mysterious Death?" https://mcadams.posc.mu.edu/craig_death.htm

Note by Roger Craig's daughter: Courtesy of Todd Vaughan, Email from Roger Craig's daughter via John Simkin, June 13, 2008, https://groups.google.com/forum/m/#!topic/alt.assassination.jfk/3-PfhXeqrjo; Mary Ferrell also posted on the internet a letter saying that Craig was "a very sick young man."

Bradley phone call to Garrison: Letter from Mary Ferrell to Harold Weisberg, dated September 10, 1991; Harold Weisberg Archive, http://jfk.hood.edu/Collection/Weisberg%20Subject% 20Index%20Files/F%20Disk/Ferrell%20Mary%20McHughes/ Item%20032.pdf

Turner admission that Bradley charge was for publicity: Diary of Tom Bethell, entry of February 14, 1968, https://mcadams. posc.mu.edu/bethell6.htm

Garrison lunch with Bradley and book story: Ferrell letter, op. cit.

Endnotes

Reports of another Bradley: Memo on Leslie Norman Bradley by William Gurvich, Papers of Irvin Dymond; Diary of Tom Bethell, entry for February 13, 1968, https://mcadams.posc.mu. edu/bethell6.htm

Roger Craig calling up Irvin Dymond: Wegmann letter to Elmer Gertz, February 2, 1971, Papers of Elmer Gertz.

Pershing Gervais on Max Gonzales: Transcript of Gervais interview with Patricia Lambert for her documentary, May 19, 2000, Papers of Patricia Lambert.

FINALLY, A CHAPTER WITH FLYING SAUCERS!

Anonymous letter to Garrison: Letter dated May 22, 1967; Papers of Gus Russo.

BBB report on Thomas Beckham: The Better Business Bureau of the Greater New Orleans Area newsletter dated October 29, 1962. Harry Connick Papers, NARA.

David Lewis reporting Beckham to the FBI: https://www. maryferrell.org/showDoc.html?docId=62435&relPageId=160& search=%22reported_that%20thomas%20edward% 20beckham%22

Charles Spiesel identifying Beckham: Garrison November 17,

1967 leads memo, found in the Harold Weisberg Archive (lead #50).

Witness from Clinton identifying Beckham: Memo dated January 31, 1968 from Frank Ruiz and Kent Simms regarding Interview with William Dunn, found in the Papers donated by Harry Connick.

Quote from Garrison memo on Beckham handing out Cuban handbills: Garrison November 17, 1967 leads memo, found in the Harold Weisberg Archive (lead #50).

Garrison locating Beckham in Omaha: Memo dated November 13, 1967 from Kent Simms to Louis Ivon regarding Locate Thomas Edward Beckham, HSCA collection, NARA, RIF # 180-10076-10142.

Beckham's Ricky Nelson show: See Greater New Orleans BBB report, op. cit.

Beckham's theft from fabric store: "Beckham Theft Charge Pending," *The Times-Picayune*, February 3, 1968.

Beckham's attempt to hang himself: Memo dated November 19, 1962 from Anthony Vesich, Sr., of the Juvenile Court; Garrison Papers at the New Orleans Public Library.

Beckham's 14-year-old-wife: Letter from Thomas Beckham to Louisiana Attorney General Jack Gremillion dated November 1, 1962; Papers of Gus Russo.

Austin BBB: Newsletter dated February 1966; Harry Connick Papers, NARA.

National Institute of Criminology: Ibid.

Lincoln Nebraska BBB alert: Letter from Lincoln Nebraska BBB to other BBB's dated January 20, 1967 regarding "Dr." Thomas E. Beckham, Harry Connick Papers, NARA; also, alert dated February 15, 1967.

Garrison's quote on "scar on his left cheek": Garrison leads memo, op. cit., lead #65.

Anatomy Charts: Garrison Papers at New Orleans Public Library.

Garrison subpoena to Thomas Beckham: Relevance paragraph for Thomas Beckham, Papers of Edward Wegmann, NARA.

Second anonymous letter: Letter dated January 9, 1968, HSCA document RIF #180-10070-10385.

Robert Lavender memo and quotes: Memo from William Boxley to Jim Garrison dated February 19, 1968 regarding Interview with Bob Lavender, Papers of Gus Russo.

Beckham testimony before Grand Jury: https://www.maryferrell.org/showDoc.html?docId=1175

Alcock quote about Beckham: Diary of Tom Bethell, entry for February 15, 1968, https://mcadams.posc.mu.edu/bethell6.htm

Reports about Crisman and Beckham: See letter from Edd Jeffords of the Citizens Committee of Inquiry dated August 7, 1967; Results of Oregon Check by Fred Newcomb, dated July 18, 1968; Undated Memo on Fred Crisman, Wilbert White and Julio Grassi by Edd Jeffords; NARA; for a series of articles by Edd Jeffords for the Tacoma News Tribune, http://jfk.hood.edu/Collection/Weisberg%20Subject%20Index%20Files/C%20Disk/Crisman%20Fred%20Lee/Item%203.pdf

Gypsy children program: Ibid.

What struck Garrison as important: Garrison has several notations on the undated document from Edd Jeffords on Fred Crisman, op. cit.

Fred Crisman and flying saucers: One of the best overviews of the Maury Island incident is by Charlette LeFevre and Philip Lipson, *The Maury Island UFO Incident: The Story behind the Air Force's first military plane crash*," (self-published, 2014). Dr. Larry Haapanen, who investigated Crisman for Garrison, wrote the forward; see information sheet on Fred Crisman by Paris Flammonde, Papers of Richard Billings; "The Maury Island UFO Incident" by the Editors of Publications International, https://science.howstuffworks.com/space/aliens-ufos/maury-island-incident.htm; "Maury Island No Longer a Mystery: A

UFO Hoax Exposed" by Anthony Bragalia," https://www.
ufodigest.com/article/maury-island-no-longer-a-mystery-a-ufo-
hoax-exposed/

Crisman and Beckham hold Midwest UFO conference: Adam
Gorightly, "The Raymond Broshears Files Part 00003: Flying
Saucer   Attack!"   http://historiadiscordia.com/the-raymond-
broshears-files-part-00003-flying-saucer-attack/

Beckham's American Academy for Professional Arts: "Multi-
Degreed Beckham Gets 'Phony' Tag, 30 Days," *Omaha World-
Herald*, September 26, 1968.

Garrison quotes about Crisman to his investigators: New
Orleans Conference, September 21, 1968, pages 33, 34, https://
archive.org/stream/GarrisonPapers/New%20Orleans%
20Conference%209%3A21%3A1968%2012%20of%
2017#page/n11/mode/1up

Garrison quote on the common denominator: Ibid, page 34.

Hinckle quote: Warren Hinckle, *If You Have a Lemon, Make
Lemonade*, (W. W. Norton & Company, 1974), page 198.

Garrison quote about Oswald and Reily Coffee: New Orleans
Conference, op. cit., page 35.

Departures from Reily Coffee: Papers of Jim Garrison,
NARA.

Garrison memo: "An Analysis of Potential Witnesses Indicating Role of the Military Industrial Complex in the Assassination of President Kennedy," dated September 1968, Papers of
Patricia Lambert.

Norman Gallo: Garrison memo, Ibid.

Crisman teaching in high school on November 22, 1963:
Letter to the HSCA from Stanley Peerboom, Principal of Rainier
High School, dated December 15, 1978, NARA; see also HSCA
Final Report, page 92 & page 607, https://www.maryferrell.org/
showDoc.html?docId=800#relPageId=122

Sprague letter about Crisman: Papers of Richard Sprague,
Georgetown University.

Garrison subpoena to Fred Crisman: Garrison press release dated October 31, 1968, from the Harold Weisberg Archive.

Crisman quotes to the press about Beckham: "There Was a Conspiracy, Crisman Believes," *Tacoma News Tribune*, November 2, 1968.

Crisman testimony to Grand Jury: https://www.maryferrell. org/showDoc.html?docId=1178

Endnote

Gurvich quote about Mel Coffey: Memo dated June 4, 1968, regarding the Reign of Terror, conversation between Gurvich and Wegmann, Papers of Gerald Posner.

ARSENIC AND OLD PERRIN

William Wood talking with a Louisiana State Trooper: William Wood, "Ex-CIA Agent Tells His Role In Garrison's Conspiracy Probe," *National Tattler*, September 1975; NARA.

Garrison discussion with Wood: Ibid.

Quote about Wood understanding the mentality of the agency: George Lardner, Jr., "On the Set of Dallas in Wonderland," *Washington Post*, May 19. 1991, https://www.maryferrell.org/ showDoc.html?docId=6761#relPageId=258

Wood responsible for getting Garrison to believe what he wanted to believe: Diary of Tom Bethell, entry for October 19, 1967, https://mcadams.posc.mu.edu/bethell3.htm

Quotes on "develop the proof": Harold Weisberg, unpublished manuscript; http://jfk.hood.edu/Collection/Weisberg% 20Subject%20Index%20Files/S%20Disk/Stone%20Oliver% 20JFK%20Movie/American%20Historical%20Review/ Item%2001.pdf

Dialog with James Alcock and Jim Garrison: Diary of Tom Bethell, entry for February 22, 1968, https://mcadams.posc.mu. edu/bethell7.htm

History of William Wood: CIA memo RIF # 104-10115-10090; https://www.maryferrell.org/showDoc.html?docId=63675#relPageId=1&tab=page; RIF # 104-10189-10013; https://www.maryferrell.org/showDoc.html?docId=17992

Nancy Perrin Rich testimony before the Warren Commission: Volume XIV, page 330-364, https://www.maryferrell.org/showDoc.html?docId=50#relPageId=338

Nancy Perrin Rich statements to FBI: Warren Commission Exhibits 3058-3059; Volume XXVI, page 615–625, https://www.maryferrell.org/showDoc.html?docId=1142#relPageId=651

Nancy Perrin Rich lie detector test: Warren Commission Exhibit 3062, Volume XXVI, page 632, https://www.maryferrell.org/showDoc.html?docId=1142#relPageId=668

Nancy Perrin Rich as a "habitual liar": Warren Commission Exhibit 3059, op. cit.

Nancy Perrin Rich stories ridiculous: Ibid.

Nancy Perrin Rich described as a psychopathic liar: Ibid.

Robert Perrin calling Louisiana State Police: Report of the Detective Bureau, Criminal Investigative Division, Louisiana State Police, August 28, 1962.

Garrison noting that Boxley lived on the same block as David Ferrie: Garrison notation on Louisiana State Police Report, Harold Weisberg Archive; http://jfk.hood.edu/Collection/Weisberg%20Subject%20Index%20Files/S%20Disk/Stone%20Oliver%20JFK%20Movie/Boxley%20Bill%20Records%20Copies%20Of/Item%2003.pdf

Boxley memo questioning Perrin's suicide: Memo from William C. Boxley to Jim Garrison dated November 22, 1968 regarding Arsenic Death of Robert Lee Perrin; Harry Connick Papers, NARA.

Visit to Rev. A. Kruschevski: Memo from William C. Boxley to Jim Garrison dated November 13, 1968, regarding Nancy Perrin Resume; Harry Connick Papers, NARA; Memo from

William Boxley and Joel Palmer, undated, regarding Rev. A. Kruschevski, Papers of Jim Garrison, NARA.

Garrison's belief that this was most important break: Series of articles about William Wood in the Lubbock Avalanche-Journal, November 1975. Boxley lived in Lubbock.

Boxley's various beliefs about Perrin: Ibid.

Garrison's decision to charge Perrin, Bradley and the three tramps: Weisberg memo on Vincent Salandria dated January 10, 1995; Weisberg letter to Paul Hoch dated September 6, 1991; Weisberg unpublished manuscript, Chapter 21, *The Living Orwell*; Weisberg letter to Oliver Stone, dated February 8, 1991; all from the Harold Weisberg Archive, http://jfk.hood.edu/ Collection/Weisberg%20Subject%20Index%20Files/HW% 20Manuscripts/Inside%20the%20Assassination%20Industry/ Itai-21.pdf

Weisberg quotes regarding Salandria: See above memos.

Weisberg investigation on Perrin-Boxley: Harold Weisberg memo dated December 7, 1968, regarding Boxley reports; Harold Weisberg Archive; http://jfk.hood.edu/Collection/ Weisberg%20Subject%20Index%20Files/S%20Disk/Stone% 20Oliver%20JFK%20Movie/Boxley%20Bill%20Records% 20Copies%20Of/Item%2012.pdf

Salandria quote on explaining to Garrison: E-mail from Vince Salandria dated April 5, 2000 to Joan Mellen and others.

Sciambra quote on Italian dinner: Weisberg memo on Vince Salandria, op. cit.

Turner letter to Larry Haapanen: Harold Weisberg Archive; http://jfk.hood.edu/Collection/Weisberg%20Subject% 20Index%20Files/T%20Disk/Turner%20William%20aka% 20Bill/Item%2031.pdf

Boxley calling Garrison's house: Interview of William C. Wood by George Rennar from August/September 1971, http:// jfk.hood.edu/Collection/Weisberg-Commission%20Documents/

Lardner%20George%20Record%20Copies%20On%20Return%20To/Lardner%2022.pdf

Boxley going to Texas and story of stolen gun: *Lubbock Avalanche Journal*, November 21, 1975; George Rennar interview.

Wood quote on Angola: *Lubbock Avalanche Journal*, November 21, 1975.

Garrison quote that Boxley was an agent on a very high level: "Shaw Trial Set for Jan. 21," *The Times-Picayune*, December 12, 1968, https://www.maryferrell.org/showDoc.html?docId=55189#relPageId=58

Garrison press release on Boxley: Harold Weisberg Archive; http://jfk.hood.edu/Collection/Weisberg%20Subject%20Index%20Files/S%20Disk/Stone%20Oliver%20JFK%20Movie/Boxley%20Bill%20Records%20Copies%20Of/Item%2009.pdf

Weisberg quote that Garrison could not fire himself: Weisberg letter to Premiere Magazine, dated December 17, 1991, http://jfk.hood.edu/Collection/Weisberg%20Subject%20Index%20Files/S%20Disk/Stone%20Oliver%20JFK%20Movie/Premiere/Item%2002.pdf

Endnote:

Joel Palmer message: Facebook message to Fred Litwin April 2020.

GARRISON TAKES THE HSCA FOR A RIDE

Good Night America show with the Zapruder film: https://www.youtube.com/watch?v=nxCH1yhGG3Q

Why Kennedy's head moved backward: https://www.maryferrell.org/showDoc.html?docId=82&search=fpp#relPageId=83&tab=page; see pages 173-174.

Newspaper stories on Good Night America: John J. O'Connor, "TV: Two Programs Exploit Subjects," *New York Times*, March 27, 1975; Earl Golz, "Shooting Gory Sight." *Dallas Morning News*, March 7, 1975.

Interview of Garrison for a week: Memo from S. Jonathan Blackmer to G. Robert Blakey, dated September 1, 1977, regarding Interview with Jim Garrison in New Orleans, NARA.

Garrison's memos to the HSCA, all from NARA:

- July 18, 1977 regarding Thomas E. Beckham.
- July 15, 1977 letter about Morgan City.
- August 16, 1977 letter about deaths of Guy Banister and Clay Shaw.
- August 25, 1977 letter with questions for Beckham.
- August 16, 1977 Memo regarding statements of Perry Russo
- Undated memo listing a variety of leads.
- October 20, 1977 memo regarding Material allegedly seen at Wray Gill's office following assassination.
- Letter dated September 14, 1977 regarding Clay Shaw.
- Letter dated November 8, 1977 regarding Individuals subpoenaed to the Orleans Parish Grand Jury.
- Undated memo regarding Clay Shaw trip to S.F.; subsequent Shaw trip to Portland, Oregon; and F. Lee Crisman factors with regard to Oregon.
- Undated memo regarding Data Correlations of K.T. and L.O. Locations.
- Undated memo regarding Kerry Thornley.

Garrison quotes about Thornley: Garrison memo on K.T. and L.O. Locations.

Second Oswald in Morgan City: Statement of Mrs. Corrine

Verges Villard dated February 28, 1967, Papers of Edward Wegmann, NARA.

Garrison believed this was the 'alternative Oswald': Garrison letter about Morgan City.

Perry Russo hypnosis transcripts: See Garrison August 16. 1977, memo on Perry Russo;

Garrison quotes about Shaw not a 'mere' conspirator: Ibid.

Garrison's fast one on the committee: See his Russo memo; See also essay by David Reitzes, https://mcadams.posc. mu.edu/jimlie4.htm

Portion of Garrison memo: August 16, 1977, memo regarding Perry Russo.

Transcript of first Perry Russo hypnosis session: http:// mcadams.posc.mu.edu/session1.htm

Girnus and Whalen: Memo dated September 18, 1967, from James Alcock to Jim Garrison regarding Edward James Whalen; Memo dated December 7, 1967, from James Alcock to Jim Garrison regarding Edward Julius Whalen, Papers of Jim Garrison, NARA.

So-called FAA flight plan: Papers of Gus Russo.

Girnus rap sheet: https://archive.org/stream/ GarrisonPapers/Girnus%2C%20Edward% 20Julius#page/n7/mode/2up

Whalen quote: Memo on Whalen, op. cit.

Garrison quotes on sources, outright bum, record of arrests, characters with incompetence, and stamped: Garrison letter of September 14, 1977, op. cit.

Garrison quotes on domestic intelligence, flying saucers, chastity, steam-roller, Albert Schweitzer, Mr. Spic & Span: Ibid.

Garrison quote on Crisman being one of the tramps: Memo dated July 18, 1977, regarding Thomas E. Beckham.

Garrison quote on propinquity: Undated memo regarding Clay Shaw trip to S.F.; subsequent Shaw trip to Portland, Oregon; and F. Lee Crisman factors with regard to Oregon.

Garrison quote on Portland being "Crisman home territory": Ibid.

Garrison quote on Crisman being a "high priority investigative target": Ibid.

Garrison quote on "cut-out for anti-Castro operations': Ibid

Garrison quote on pre-assassination scene: Ibid.

Garrison quote on "professionally clandestine operation": Ibid.

Garrison quote on traditional evidence: July 18, 1977, regarding Thomas E. Beckham.

Garrison quote on "application of models": Ibid.

Garrison quote on maintaining national security: Ibid.

Garrison's special interest in Beckham: Ibid.

Garrison quote about film of Beckham at TSBD: Ibid.

Garrison quote about not being optimistic about finding film: Ibid.

Garrison's belief about Beckham being an alternative patsy: Ibid.

Garrison quote about Crisman being more important than Beckham: Ibid.

Beckham being arrested for fraud: "Beck-Stolz Fund Fraud Suspect Held," *Mobile Alabama Press-Register,* February 23, 1977.

Acquittal of Thomas Beckham: "Beckham acquitted," *Mobile Alabama Press-Register,* July 28, 1977.

Beckham claiming to be CIA agent: Ibid.

Beckham marrying couples: "Team Quiet about Beckham Interview on Assassination," *Clarksville Leaf-Chronicle,* August 10, 1977.

Beckham's discussion with HSCA investigators on October 9, 1977: Transcript of Interview conducted at the Holiday Inn-Medical in Jackson, Mississippi, NARA.

Garrison calling Ted Gandolfo: Ted Gandolfo newsletter dated December 29, 1986; See also "The Garrison-Gandolfo

'Smoke & Mirror' Show" by G.J. Rowell in *The Investigator*; Paul Hoch, *Echoes of Conspiracy*, Volume 9, No. 1; See also Paul Hoch, *Echoes of Conspiracy*, Volume 9, Number 1, https:// archive.org/stream/nsia-HochPaulCorrespondence/nsia-HochPaulCorrespondence/Hoch%20Paul% 200941#page/n3/mode/1up

Beckham polygraph test: Email to author from G. Robert Blakey; Joan Mellen, *A Farewell to Justice: Jim Garrison, JFK's Assassination, and the Case That Should Have Changed History,* (Potomac Books, 2005) page 351.

Thomas Beckham deposition before the HSCA: Testimony taken May 24, 1978; RIF # 180-10104-10278, NARA.

HSCA Final Report on Thornley: Volume X, page 125; https://www.maryferrell.org/showDoc.html?docId= 1212#relPageId=129&tab=page

HSCA on Fred Crisman: Letter to the HSCA from Stanley Peerboom, Principal of Rainier High School, dated December 15, 1978, NARA; see also HSCA Final Report, page 92 & page 607.

HSCA on Clinton: HSCA Final Report, page 145; https:// www.maryferrell.org/showDoc.html?docId=800&relPageId= 175&search=%22inclined_to%20believe%22

Paul Hoch quote on Clinton: Echoes of Conspiracy, Volume 13, Number 1; http://www.jfk-online.com/eoc1301exc.html

HSCA quote on "if not Clay Shaw': HSCA Final Report, page 145; https://www.maryferrell.org/showDoc.html?docId= 800&relPageId=175&search=clay_shaw

HSCA conclusion on Garrison: HSCA Final Report, page 142; https://www.maryferrell.org/showDoc.html?docId=800& relPageId=172&search=%22had_been%20fairly% 20criticized%22

Blakey quote that Garrison was a fraud: G. Robert Blakey and Richard N. Billings, *Fatal Hour: The Assassination of President Kennedy by Organized Crime,* (Berkley Books, 1992), page 49.

Blakey quote that the case against Shaw was "flimsy": Ibid, page 193.

Blakey quote that Russo's testimony was "blatantly concocted": Ibid.

National Academy of Sciences report on the ballistics evidence: http://www.jfk-online.com/nas00.html

Gus Russo anecdote about Thomas Beckham: https://mcadams.posc.mu.edu/mellen.htm

Beckham is now a Rabbi: *Remnants of Truth: Revealing Evidence on the Jim Garrison Investigation*, by T.E. Beckh'am, (Echo Communications), Page 20.

Beckham singing under the name Wade Hampton: Letter from T.E. Beckham to Gus Russo dated February 16, 1993, Papers of Gus Russo.

Wade Hampton as the "singing Jew from the Cajun country of Louisiana": Promotional article found in the Papers of Gus Russo.

ON THE TRAIL OF DELUSION

1995 documentary on homosexuals in the movies: *The Celluloid Closet*, 1995 written by Vito Russo.

Norman Mailer on the characterization of homosexuals: Norman Mailer, "The Homosexual Villain," contained in *Norman Mailer: Mind of an Outlaw* (Random House, 2014), page 14.

Tom Clancy in Newsweek: Cover story, "Tom Clancy, Bestseller," August 8, 1988.

Overall gross of JFK film: http://www.boxofficemojo.com/movies/?id=jfk.htm

Quote in the New York Times: Bernard Weinraub, "Hollywood Wonders If Warner Brothers Let 'J.F.K.' Go Too Far," *New York Times*, December 24, 1991.

Jim Garrison, *A Heritage of Stone* (G.P. Putnam & Sons, 1970).

Ralph Schoenman letter to Jim Garrison: See Holland, "The Lie That Linked CIA to the Kennedy Assassination," op. cit.

Garrison sent the first five chapters to McGraw-Hill: Letter to Ms. Gladys Carr, Editor in Chief of McGraw-Hill Trade Division from Jim Garrison, dated September 16, 1982, Papers of Jim Garrison, NARA.

Garrison form letters and quotes: Letter to Mr. Bob Severin dated December 30, 1985, Jim Garrison Papers, New Orleans Public Library. The identical letter is contained in *The Garrison Investigation* by Louis Sproesser, 1995.

Paul Hoch on Henry Hurt's book: Echoes of Conspiracy, Volume 8, #1, dated February 28, 1986; http://smokyhole. org/wb/wb0091.htm

Garrison letter to Ted Gandolfo, Paul Hoch letter to Jim Garrison, Jim Garrison letter to Ted Gandolfo: courtesy of Paul Hoch.

Paul Hoch quote "all his faults or virtues": Paul Hoch, *Echoes of Conspiracy*, Volume 8, Number 2; https://archive.org/stream/ nsia-HochPaulCorrespondence/nsia- HochPaulCorrespondence/Hoch%20Paul% 200936#page/n4/mode/1up

Garrison wanting more information on Fred Crisman: Letter from Garrison to Fred Newcombe, August 6, 1986; Larry Haapanen letter to Garrison September 12, 1986 and October 17, 1986. Description of Garrison telephone conversation with Haapanen; email from Larry Haapanen dated May 5, 2020. Documents courtesy of Larry Haapanen.

Garrison and Prentice Hall: Letter from Jim Garrison to Philip Pochoda, Publisher and Editor-in-Chief of Prentice Hall Press dated November 13, 1986. There are several other letters between Garrison and Pochoda; Papers of Jim Garrison, NARA.

Sylvia Meagher quote about Oswald's aim: Chapter-by-

Chapter commentary by Sylvia Meagher courtesy of researcher John Kelin.

Meagher quotes on New Orleans characters: Letter from Sylvia Meagher to Philip Pochoda dated December 18, 1986, courtesy of researcher John Kelin.

Meagher on the motorcade route: Letter from Sylvia Meagher to Philip Pochoda dated December 27, 1986, courtesy of researcher John Kelin.

Meagher recommending the book be published: Letter of December 18, 1986, op. cit.

Pochoda rejection letter to Garrison: Letter dated January 9, 1987, Papers of Jim Garrison, NARA.

Pochoda wrote to me: Email from Philip Pochoda dated March 17, 2020.

Pochoda's bigger problem: Rejection letter op. cit.

Garrison's reply to Pochoda: Letter dated January 15, 1987, Papers of Jim Garrison, NARA.

Garrison's complaint but his last waltz with an Agency asset: Basic cover letter re: Simon's Letter, dated July 14, 1987, Papers of Jim Garrison, NARA.

CovertAction Information Bulletin and Philip Agee: Agee was on the Board of Advisors. https://covertactionmagazine.com/index.php/archives/, https://www.washingtonpost.com/archive/politics/1978/08/03/worldwide-effort-being-launched-to-destabilize-cia/2455deb0-99b9-4439-8ff4-2263c228b0be/

Mitrokhin Archive on CovertAction: Christopher Andrew & Vasili Mitrokhin, *The KGB in Europe and the West: The Mitrokhin Archive*, (Penguin Books, 2000), pages 303-305.

Garrison quote on Charles Spiesel: Garrison, op. cit., page 237.

Garrison on Permindex: Garrison, op. cit., pages 87-90.

Garrison on the three tramps: Garrison, op. cit., pages 207-213.

Garrison on Thornley as second Oswald: Garrison, op. cit., pages 65-74.

Garrison on witnesses still dying: Garrison, op. cit., page 273; See Garrison's interview with *NBC* on September 22, 1967, where he says that up to 35 people have died mysteriously, Papers of the Metropolitan Crime Commission.

Garrison on killers being protected by Dallas police: Garrison, op. cit., page 277, 202-203.

Garrison on post office being a CIA meeting place: Garrison, op. cit., pages 72, 26.

Garrison rejecting lie detector test for Perry Russo: Garrison, op. cit., page 152.

Garrison on motorcade route: Garrison, op. cit., page 101-103.

Paul Hoch quote on Garrison's book: Echoes of Conspiracy, Volume 11, Number 1; https://archive.org/stream/nsia-HochPaulCorrespondence/nsia-HochPaulCorrespondence/Hoch%20Paul%200958#page/n5/mode/1up

Rosemary James calling Garrison's book fiction: Transcript of Patricia Lambert interview of Rosemary James for her documentary, August 25, 2000, Papers of Patricia Lambert.

Oliver Stone buys rights to "On the Trail of the Assassins": Vincent Bugliosi, *Reclaiming History: The Assassination of President John F. Kennedy*, (W. W. Norton & Company, 2007), page 1352.

Oliver Stone likens Garrison's book to a Dashiell Hammett whodunit: Richard Bernstein, "Film; Oliver Stone, Under Fire Over the Killing of J.F.K." *New York Times*, July 28, 1991, https://www.nytimes.com/1991/07/28/movies/film-oliver-stone-under-fire-over-the-killing-of-jfk.html

Stone purchases rights to Crossfire by Jim Marrs: Paul Hoch on Oliver Stone and Jim Garrison, Excerpt from Paul Hoch, *Echoes of Conspiracy*, Volume 13, Number 1, Note 38; http://www.jfk-online.com/eoc1301exc.html

Stone's belief that Garrison tried to "force a break in the case": Robert Sam Anson, "The Shooting of JFK," *Esquire*, November, 1991;   https://classic.esquire.com/article/1991/11/1/the-shooting-of-jfk

Stone's quote on the film being "worth the sacrifice of one man": Ibid.

Scenes from the film JFK: Oliver Stone & Zachary Sklar, *JFK: The Documented Screenplay*, (Applause Books, 1992). The screenplay in this book varies from the actual film.

Broshears   never   met   Ferrie: http://www.jfk-online.com/dbraybropost.html

William Morris claim about Jack Ruby: Transcript of interview between William Boxley, William Martin, and William Morris, dated July 14, 1967, of a conversation two days earlier, Papers of Jim Garrison, NARA, https://archive.org/stream/GarrisonPapers/Interview%20of%20William%20A.%20Morris%2C%207%3A12%3A67%201%7%20of%2017

Quote "At times, however, we had to put words in Ferrie's mouth to write the scene": Oliver Stone & Zachary Sklar, *JFK: The Documented Screenplay*, (Applause Books, 1992), page 88.

The Advocate on JFK: David Ehrenstein, "JFK—A New Low for Hollywood," *The Advocate*, January 14, 1992.

Quote on gratuitous orgy scene: John Weir, "FILM: Gay-Bashing, Villainy and the Oscars," *The New York Times*, March 29, 1992, https://www.nytimes.com/1992/03/29/movies/film-gay-bashing-villainy-and-the-oscars.html

Oliver Stone reply to the David Ehrenstein of The Advocate: Stone & Sklar, op. cit., page 511; see also the exchange of letters between David Ehrenstein and Zachary Sklar in *Cineaste*, December 1992.

Quote from the Gay & Lesbian Alliance for Defamation: *GLAAD Bulletin*, January/February 1992, https://digital.library.unt.edu/ark:/67531/metadc916872/m1/1/

Scene with "X" in JFK: Stone & Sklar, op. cit., pages 105-114.

Kennedy and Vietnam: National Security Memorandum #273, http://mcadams.posc.mu.edu/viet16.htm; See also Stanley Karnow, "JFK: Oliver Stone and the Vietnam War," http://mcadams.posc.mu.edu/karnow.htm

Kennedy quote to Walter Cronkite: Ibid.

Kennedy quote to Chet Huntley: Ibid.

Robert Kennedy oral history interview on Vietnam: http://mcadams.posc.mu.edu/vietnam.htm

George Lardner quote about William Gibbons: Letter to Harold Weisberg, dated July 28, 1991, Harold Weisberg Archive.

Prouty and the Military Intelligence Group: Memo from Tim Wray to Jeremy Gunn of the Assassinations Record Review Board regarding Army Intelligence in Dallas; https://www.maryferrell.org/showDoc.html?docId=205283&relPageId=1&search=tim_112dalla.wpd

Kennedy's planned speech in Dallas: "Context: Kennedy and Foreign Policy," http://mcadams.posc.mu.edu/context1.htm

Michael Beschloss quote: Michael R. Beschloss, "Assassination and Obsession," *Washington Post*, January 5, 1992.

L. Fletcher Prouty as a consultant to the Lyndon LaRouche organization: Edward J. Epstein, "The Assassination Chronicles," op. cit., page 578.

L. Fletcher Prouty consulting for lawyers working for the Church of Scientology: Ibid.

L. Fletcher Prouty speaking at the 1990 Convention of the Liberty Lobby: Ibid.

L. Fletcher Prouty appearances on Liberty Lobby radio: Anti-Defamation League report on Willis Carto from 2013.

L. Fletcher Prouty on Advisory Board: Sara Diamond, "Populists' Tap Resentment of the Elite," *The Guardian*, July 3, 1991.

L. Fletcher Prouty book: *The Secret Team: The CIA and its Allies in Control of the United States and the World* was published by the Institute for Historical Review (IHR) in 1991.

The IHR was founded by David McCalden and William Carto, the head of the Liberty Lobby.

L. Fletcher Prouty presenting at the Liberty Lobby's annual Board of Policy convention: Epstein, op. cit., page 579.

Prouty letter about Israeli threats and unrest: Letter from L. Fletcher Prouty to Dennis Effle, dated December 26, 1989; Papers of Gus Russo.

Prouty's remark about the Holocaust: Robert Sam Anson, "The Shooting of JFK," *Esquire*, November, 1991.

Jane Rusconi memo: Memo to Oliver Stone, Alex Ho, Clayton Townsend from Jane Rusconi, dated July 23, 1991, regarding Fletcher Prouty/Liberty Lobby, Papers of Gus Russo.

Oliver Stone excusing Prouty: Hollywood & History: Bill Rockwood, "The Debate Over 'JFK," November 19, 2013, https://www.pbs.org/wgbh/frontline/article/hollywood-history-the-debate-over-jfk/

Letter from L. Fletcher Prouty to Charles: Papers of Richard Sprague, NARA.

Jim Garrison's introduction of L. Fletcher Prouty to Oliver Stone: "Oliver Stone Discusses His Film JFK

and Introduces the Real "Man X," L. Fletcher Prouty, *JFK: The CIA, Vietnam, and the Plot to Assassinate John F. Kennedy* (Carol Publishing Group, 1992), page xvii, http://www.prouty.org/stone/stone_x.htm

Prouty quote about Stone phone call: Preface to Prouty's book, *JFK: The CIA, Vietnam, and the Plot to Assassinate John F. Kennedy.*

Leonard C. Lewin, *Report from Iron Mountain* (Dial Press, 1967).

Report from Iron Mountain as a hoax: Victor Navasky, "Conspiracy Theory Is a Hoax Gone Wrong," *New York Magazine*, November 17, 2013; https://web.archive.org/web/20120419001730/http://www.silverbearcafe.com/private/Navasky.html

Lewin admits to hoax in the New York Times Book Review: Leonard Lewin, "Report from Iron Mountain: The Guest Word," *New York Times Book Review*, March 19, 1972.

Prouty's quote on the Iron Mountain Group Report: L. Fletcher Prouty, JFK: *The CIA, Vietnam, and the Plot to Assassinate John F. Kennedy* (Carol Publishing Group, 1992), page 5.

Stone's introduction to Prouty's book: Ibid.

Oliver Stone quote on Mr. Hitler: L. Fletcher Prouty, JFK: *The CIA, Vietnam, and the Plot to Assassinate John F. Kennedy* (Carol Publishing Group, 1992).

Stone on General Y: JFK: *The Documented Screenplay*, see pages 181-183; Max Boot, *The Road Not Taken: Edward Lansdale and the American Tragedy in Vietnam,* (Liveright, 2018), page 421.

Prouty quote on Lansdale planning Dallas and masterminding the coverup: Fletcher Prouty letter to Harold Weisberg, dated April 4, 1989, Harold Weisberg Archive, http://jfk.hood. edu/Collection/Weisberg%20Subject%20Index%20Files/P% 20Disk/Prouty%20L%20Fletcher/Item%2035.pdf

Max Boot quote about Landale: *The Road Not Taken*, op. cit., page 423.

Lansdale quote about Prouty: Cecil B. Curry, Edward Lansdale: *The Unquiet American*, (Houghton Mifflin, 1988), page 384.

Prouty quote on the middle tramp: Prouty letter to Harold Weisberg, dated April 4, 1989.

Prouty letter to Richard Sprague wondering who the tramp was: Prouty letter to Richard Sprague, dated January 5, 1974, Papers of Richard Sprague, NARA.

Prouty belief that FDR was murdered: https://prouty.org/comment1.html

Prouty belief that he had seen a UFO: http://www.prouty.org/coment16.html

Prouty on the death of Diana: http://mcadams.posc. mu.edu/27.htm

Prouty on flechette: https://mcadams.posc. mu.edu/prouty_tum.htm

Lambert quote on Prouty: Patricia Lambert letter to James Phelan, dated August 2, 1993, Papers of Patricia Lambert.

Clay Shaw's relationship with the CIA: Max Holland, "The Lie That Linked CIA to the Kennedy Assassination: The Power of Disinformation," op. cit.

New Orleans investigation of Clay Shaw's death: http:// mcadams.posc.mu.edu/death9.htm

George Will on Oliver Stone: George Will, "Is Oliver Stone an intellectual sociopath, indifferent to truth," *Milwaukee Sentinel*, December 20, 1991, https://www.washingtonpost. com/archive/opinions/1991/12/26/jfk-paranoid-history/ 1353d5cd-9d26-4088-acf7-d3ba5a0f8a0d/

George Lardner, Jr. on JFK: George Lardner, Jr., "On the Set: Dallas in Wonderland," *The Washington Post*, May 19, 1991; George Lardner, Jr., "The Way It Wasn't: In 'JFK,' Stone Assassinates the Truth," *Washington Post*, December 20, 1991, http:// jfk.hood.edu/Collection/Weisberg%20Subject%20Index% 20Files/S%20Disk/Stone%20Oliver%20JFK%20Movie/ Reviews%20Comments%20Stories%2012-20%20--%2022-92/ Item%2002.pdf

Oliver Stone discussion with Christopher Hitchens: Tad Friend, "Oliver Stone's Chaos Theory," *The New Yorker*, October 22, 2001, https://www.newyorker.com/magazine/ 2001/10/22/oliver-stones-chaos-theory

Oliver Stone on Jewish control of media: "Oliver Stone: Jewish control of the media is preventing free Holocaust debate," *Haaretz*, July 26, 2010, https://www.haaretz.com/jewish/1. 5152427

*Oliver Stone quote "Israel has f***** up American foreign poli-*

cy": Ben Child, "Oliver Stone apologizes for 'antisemitic' remarks," *The Guardian*, July 27, 201, https://www.theguardian.com/film/2010/jul/27/oliver-stone-apologises-antisemitic-remarks

Oliver Stone quote that "I had to apologize": Andrew Goldmanov, "Oliver Stone Rewrites History—Again," *The New York Times Magazine*, November 22, 2012, https://www.nytimes.com/2012/11/25/magazine/oliver-stone-rewrites-history-again.html

Stone's documentary "Commandante" and interview with Anne Louis Bardach: Anne Louis Bardach, "Oliver Stone's Twist: Is the director's latest film soft on Castro?" http://www.slate.com/articles/news_and_politics/interrogation/2004/04/oliver_stones_twist.html, April 14, 2004.

Foreign Policy magazine on "South of the Border": Elizabeth Dickinson, "The Oliver Stone Show," *Foreign Policy*, June 24, 2010, https://foreignpolicy.com/2010/06/24/the-oliver-stone-show/

Ron Radosh on "South of the Border": Ron Radosh, "More on Oliver Stone's latest Travesty, South of the Border," *Pajamas Media*, June 26, 2010, https://www.wsj.com/articles/SB10001424052748704911704575326901733289566

Foreign Policy magazine on Mi Amigo Hugo: Jeffrey Tayler, "Oliver Stone's Disgraceful Tribute to Hugo Chavez," *Foreign Policy*, May 13, 2014, https://foreignpolicy.com/2014/05/13/oliver-stones-disgraceful-tribute-to-hugo-chavez/

Oliver Stone asks Putin to be his Daughter's Godfather: Allison Quinn, *The Daily Beast*, July 19, 2000, https://www.thedailybeast.com/oliver-stone-asks-vladimir-putin-to-be-his-daughters-godfather

Stone on Russia law outlawing homosexual propaganda: Corey Atad, "Oliver Stone Defends Himself After Calling Russian Anti-LGBTQ Law 'Sensible," July 26, 2019; https://etcanada.com/news/479731/oliver-stone-defends-himself-after-calling-russian-anti-lgbtq-law-sensible/

Stone quote on Putin as a stabilizing force in Syria: Holly-wood movie director Oliver Stone praises Putin for Syria intervention on trip to Saudi Arabia, October 30, 2019; https://english.alaraby.co.uk/english/news/2019/10/30/oliver-stone-praises-putins-syria-intervention-on-saudi-trip

Oliver Stone on United States as evil empire: Alexi Druzhnin, "Oliver Stone: United States is 'the Evil Empire,'" *Sputnik News*, January   31,   2020;   https://sputniknews.com/us/2020013110781899951-oliver-stone-interview/

Anna Nelson quote about Jim Garrison: Transcript of Patricia Lambert interview of Anna Nelson for her documentary, dated August 29, 2000; Papers of Patricia Lambert.

Douglas Horne's five-volume work: *Inside the Assassination Records Review Board: The U.S. Government's Final Attempt to Reconcile the Conflicting Medical Evidence in the Assassination of JFK—Volume I-V*, 2009.

Oliver Stone on alteration of Zapruder Film: Paul Joseph Watson, "Oliver Stone: Zapruder Film Was Altered," InfoWars, November 6, 2013; https://www.infowars.com/oliver-stone-zapruder-film-was-altered/

Zavada report on the authenticity of the Zapruder Film: http://rochester.nydatabases.com/story/zavada-report-jfk-assassination-evidence

Dying man confession to Oliver Stone: Mark Zoller Seitz, *The Oliver Stone Experience*, (Harry N. Abrams, 2016), page 457.

Oliver Stone quotes on confession: Ibid.

Endnotes

Willie O'Keefe being a composite character: http://www.jfk-online.com/jfk1ookeefe.html

ARRB interview of Prouty: Dated September 24, 1996, the interview was conducted by Christopher Barger, http://documents.theblackvault.com/documents/jfk/NARA-Oct2017/ARRB/CBARGER/WP-DOCS/PROUTY11.WPD.pdf

GARRISON'S FORGOTTEN VICTIM - MAJOR LOUIS BLOOMFIELD

Scene in JFK on Paese Sera and CMC: JFK: *The Documented Screenplay*, op. cit., page 82-83.

Max Holland quote on "beyond KGB's wildest imagination": Transcript of Max Holland's interview with Patricia Lambert for her documentary, August 23, 2000.

Le Devoir articles on Clay Shaw: "La Pravda: le CIA avait sous ses ordres Clay Shaw, accuse d'avoir complote contre J.F.K." *Le Devoir*, March 8, 1967; "L'enquete du procureur Garrison sur l'assassinat de Kennedy conduira-t-elle a Montreal?" *Le Devoir*, March 16, 1967.

English translations of Paese Sera articles from Jim Garrison: https://catalog.archives.gov/OpaAPI/media/7564842/content/arcmedia/dc-metro/jfkco/641323/jfk-garrison-071/jfk-garrison-071.pdf

Clark Blaise letter to Robert Scheer: Letter dated June 22, 1967, The Papers of Jim Garrison, NARA, https://archive.org/stream/GarrisonPapers/Shaw%20III-World%20Trade%20Center%20%28Italy%29#page/n27/mode/2up

Ramparts references Le Devoir: William Turner, "The Garrison Commission," *Ramparts*, January, 1968; http://jfk.hood.edu/Collection/White%20Materials/Garrison%20News%20Clippings/1968/68-01/68-01-002.pdf

Letter to Jim Garrison from Professor Klaus Hermann: Donated Papers of Bill Boxley/William Wood, NARA.

Garrison conference talking about James Earl Ray: Garrison conference, op. cit., September 21, 1968, page 164, https://archive.org/stream/GarrisonPapers/New%20Orleans%20Conference%209%3A21%3A1968%2012%20of%2017#page/n173/mode/1up

Stone and Sklar writing about Garrison's resources: Oliver

Stone & Zachary Sklar letter to *The Wilson Quarterly*, dated May 25, 2001, Papers of Patricia Lambert.

Flammonde quote that Bloomfield was "active in the espionage arm of the U.S. government": Paris Flammonde, *The Kennedy Conspiracy: An Uncommissioned Report on the Jim Garrison investigation*, Meredith Pres, 1969, page 218-219.

Jim Garrison quote on Bloomfield: Jim Garrison, op. cit., page 88-89.

Garrison quoting from Le Devoir as if it is different from Paese Sera: Ibid.

Jim Garrison on Jules Kimble: Jim Garrison, op. cit., page 118.

CIA document RIF # 104-10437-10083: https://www.maryferrell.org/showDoc.html?docId=8170#relPageId=1&tab=page

Joan Mellen claims the articles had been in the works for months: Joan Mellen, op. cit., page 139.

Fanti told Professor Paul Mitchinson: Paul Mitchinson blogpost, January 23, 2006 (from a 2001 article)

Max Holland quote on Paese Sera series of articles: reply by Max Holland to readers from his article "The JFK Lawyer's Conspiracy," *The Nation*, March 2006, https://www.thenation.com/article/archive/november-22-1963-you-are-there/

Mellen's discussion of 2003 CIA document: Mellen, op.cit., page 389.

CIA document RIF # 180-10143-10220: https://www.maryferrell.org/showDoc.html?docId=31932#relPageId=1&tab=page

CIA document claiming Shaw was a "highly paid CIA contract source": RIF # 104-10428-10104; https://www.maryferrell.org/showDoc.html?docId=7302#relPageId=1&tab=page

Jefferson Morley making a big deal out of this document:

https://jfkfacts.org/who-was-the-only-man-to-ever-face-legal-charges-in-jfks-assassination/#more-18380

CIA document saying that Shaw was not remunerated: https://www.maryferrell.org/showDoc.html?docId=55187& search–Reel_24+1994.04.12.12#relPageId=9&tab=page

CIA document on the Pravda article: https://www.maryferrell.org/showDoc.html?docId=53420#relPageId=5&tab=page

CIA document offering to put CIA agent on staff of Permindex: RIF #104-10181-10114; https://www.maryferrell.org/showDoc.html?docId=185094#relPageId=3&tab=page

Mantello letter to Clay Shaw: Papers of Clay Shaw, NARA.

CIA quotes on Permindex: CIA document RIF #104-10181-10114, see link above.

Quote on George Mantello being unscrupulous: Ibid.

Larger quote on Mantello's loyalty to his Jewish co-religionists: ibid.

Mantello as first secretary of El Salvador: Journal News, Hamilton Ontario, February 28, 2010.

Complete history of George Mantello: David Kranzler, *The Man Who Stopped The Trains to Auschwitz: George Mantello, El Salvador and Switzerland's Finest Hour*, (Syracuse University Press, 2000); https://youtu.be/a9BhvuKu9RI

The United States Holocaust Memorial Museum has three volumes of Mantello documents: https://www.ushmm.org/collections/the-museums-collections/collections-highlights/mantello-rescue-mission, https://collections.ushmm.org/search/catalog/irn98208

Mantello honorary doctorate from Yeshiva University: https://www.nytimes.com/1992/05/06/world/george-mandel-montello-is-dead-special-envoy-90-rescued-jews.html

For more on George Mantello: "El Salvador's Holocaust Heroes" by John Lamperti, https://math.dartmouth.edu/~lamperti/Holocaust_Heroes.pdf

Castellanos named Righteous Among the Nations at Yad Vashem: https://www.jewishpress.com/sections/features/ rescued-by-el-salvador-a-little-known-holocaust-tale/ 2019/01/16/

Mantello's arrest in May 1944: Kranzler, op. cit., page 73.

Quote from John Winant: Ibid, page 33.

Jewish Community write Mantello: Ibid, page 234.

Formal inquiry into Mantello: Ibid, page 242-249.

Formal inquiry conclusion: Ibid, page 247.

Mantello's denial of a visa: Ibid, page 239.

Rothmund on "the Jew": Thomas Stephens, "The Boat is Full: 75 years Later," https://www.swissinfo.ch/eng/jewish-refugee-policy_-the-boat-is-full---75-years-later/43531288

American consulate on Mantello: Foreign Service Despatch dated February 1, 1957 from the American Consulate in Basel to the Department of State, Papers of Gus Russo.

Conspiracy authors using the term "Jewish refugee racket": James DiEugenio, *Destiny Betrayed: JFK, Cuba, and The Garrison Case,* (Skyhorse Publishing, 212), page 386; Joan Mellen, op. cit., page 138; William Davy, *Let Justice Be Done: New Light on the Jim Garrison Investigation,* (Jordan Publishing, 1999), page 97.

Consulate dispatch on lack of negative results on Mantello: Foreign Service Despatch, dated April 9, D1958 from Amconsul Basel to The Department of State, Papers of Gus Russo.

Patricia Lambert quote on Garrison being a tool of communist propaganda: Patricia Lambert, "The Permindex Story," unpublished paper, Papers of Patricia Lambert.

Clay Shaw and Permindex: See the Papers of Clay Shaw at NARA; Don Carpenter, *Man of a Million Fragments: The true story of Clay Shaw,* (Donald H. Carpenter, 2014), pages, 191, 310.

Clay Shaw as a domestic contact of the CIA: CIA RIF# 104-10013-10308; see also Reel 17, Folder G—Clay Shaw from the

CIA available at the Mary Ferrell Archive (RIF#: 1994.05.09.10:43:33:160005), https://www.maryferrell.org/showDoc.html?docId=55053#relPageId=1

Papers of Louis Mortimer Bloomfield: National Archives of Canada, Louis M. Bloomfield, MG31, E 25.

Maurice Phillips and the Bloomfield Archive: http://somesecretsforyou.blogspot.com/

John Kowalski and the Bloomfield Archive: https://kennedysandking.com/news-items/john-kowalski-sues-over-release-of-louis-mortimer-bloomfield-papers

Article in Il Messaggero: Retrieved from the *Il Messaggero* archives for March 5, 1967.

Canadian Dimension letter to Louis Bloomfield: http://somesecretsforyou.blogspot.com/2010/04/

Lyndon LaRouche publication on Bloomfield: Retrieved from the Canadian Jewish Archives, Montreal; published in *Executive Intelligence Review*, Volume 21, No. 48, December 2, 1994.

Bloomfield letter to Isadore G. Alk: Retrieved from the Bloomfield Archive, Library & Archives Canada.

Macleans article on Dope, Inc: Andre McNicholl, "Paranoia and power: the marshalling of a U.S. cult, *Macleans Magazine*, October 29, 1979.

Louis Bloomfield letter to the RCMP: Louis Bloomfield Archive, Library & Archives Canada.

Louis Bloomfield biographical details: Various documents from Bloomfield's Papers.

Bloomfield in the Canadian Military: Lou Seligson, "Lawyer knows boundaries at home and around the world," *Canadian Jewish News*, October 6, 1978.

Bloomfield named first Jewish Knight of Grace: Biographical details from the Bloomfield Archive.

Quote on St. John's Ambulance: *Canadian Jewish News*, op. cit.

John Diefenbaker letter to Louis Bloomfield: Bloomfield Archive, Library & Archives Canada.

Death of Louis Bloomfield: https://www.jta.org/1984/07/23/archive/louis-bloomfield-dead-at-78

Endnotes
_____

Discharge of Jules Kimble from the U.S. Military: FBI report of January 15, 1968. They note that his "records indicate that in October 1960, he was given a diagnosis of "schizoid personality, chronic, moderate; characterized by bizarre, vague somatic complaints and difficulty in relationship to others," https://www.maryferrell.org/showDoc.html?docId=9925&search=%22schizoid_personality%22+kimble#relPageId=352&tab=page

Changing story of Jules Kimble: Memo dated September 6, 1967, from Louis Ivon to Jim Garrison, regarding Conversation with Jules Rocco Kimble, Papers of Jim Garrison, NARA.

Project   QK/Enchant: https://www.cia.gov/library/readingroom/docs/DOC_0000904662.pdf

Ferenc Nagy and his anti-fascist coalition: Geoff Swain, Eastern Europe Since 1945, (Red Globe Press, 2017) page 45; https://www.britannica.com/biography/Ferenc-Nagy

Carlo   d'Amelio: https://it.m.wikipedia.org/wiki/Carlo_d'Amelio

CONCLUSION: THE ATTEMPT TO REHABILITATE JIM GARRISON

They all suffer from "invincible ignorance": James Phelan used this term in a telephone conversation with Patricia Lambert on August 11, 1991, Papers of Patricia Lambert. For a good review of William Davy's book, check out David Reitzes' review, http://www.jfk-online.com/davy1.html

Patricia Lambert on Joan Mellen: https://mcadams.posc.mu.edu/mellen.htm

DiEugenio on Clyde Johnson: DiEugenio, op. cit., page 294.

Mellen on Clyde Johnson: Mellen, op. cit., page 300-301.

Davy on Clyde Johnson: Davy, op. cit., page 310.

Joan Mellen letter to Harold Weisberg: Letter dated May 7, 2001, Harold Weisberg Archive, http://jfk.hood.edu/Collection/Weisberg%20Subject%20Index%20Files/M%20Disk/Mellen%20Joan/Item%2010.pdf

Weisberg reply to Joan Mellen: Letter dated June 20, 2001, Harold Weisberg Archive, link above.

James DiEugenio on Leander D'avy: DiEugenio, op. cit., page 387; Researcher Tracy Parnell has also written about D'avy, http://wtracyparnell.blogspot.com/2017/03/leander-davy.html

Leander D'avy deposition to the HSCA: Interview of Leander D'avy by Belford Lawson and Jack Moriarty, dated June 23, 1977, RIF # 180-10108-10188, NARA.

Leander D'avy on Jack Ruby: Memo from Belford Lawson to Robert Tanenbaum dated July 8, 1977, regarding Alleged Anti-JFK Co-conspirators in the New Orleans area; Eyewitness Account of a Meeting with LHO, David Ferrie, and Three Tramps, RIF # 180-10087-10474, NARA.

Leander D'avy on Fred Crisman: Interview of Leander D'avy by Bob Buras and L. J. Delsa on December 16, 1977. RIF # 180-10114-10154, NARA.

Questions about D'avy's credibility: July 8, 1977, memo from Belford Lawson, op.cit.

William Morris signed an affidavit: DiEugenio, op. cit., page 210.

William Morris interview: Dated July 12, 1967, interview of William Morris by William Boxley and William Martin at the Wynne State Farm, Texas Department of Corrections, Papers of Jim Garrison, NARA, op. cit.

DiEugenio on Virginia Johnson: DiEugenio, op. cit., page 387.

Virginia Johnson statement: Memo dated March 22, 1967,

from C. J. Navarre, Investigator to Louis Ivon regarding Interview Mrs. Virginia Johnson, Papers of Edward Wegmann, NARA.

Second Virginia Johnson interview: Memo from Gary Sanders, Investigator to Louis Ivon regarding Virginia Johnson, Clay Shaw's Maid, dated January 16, 1968, NARA.

Mrs. Jessie Parker testimony: Her testimony was not transcribed, but is described by James Kirkwood in his book, *American Grotesque*, pages 348-350.

Military escort at VIP Room: Memo from Andrew Sciambra to Jim Garrison dated April 2, 1968, regarding Interview with Captain John Warren, Papers of Irvin Dymond.

One employee did recognize Shaw's picture: Memo from Andrew Sciambra to Jim Garrison dated April 2, 1968, regarding Interview with Mr. Theodore Herrera, State Department, Papers of Irvin Dymond; Memo from Andrew Sciambra to Jim Garrison dated April 2, 1968, regarding Interview with Mr. and Mrs. Ross Pope. He picked out Gordon Novel as the man he saw at the airport, Papers of Irvin Dymond; Memo from James Alcock to Jim Garrison dated November 17, 1967, regarding Mr. Alfred Moran, Papers of Edward Wegmann, NARA.

Turner memo on Thomas Breitner: Papers of Edward Wegmann, NARA; See also interview report, March 29, 1967 regarding Clay Shaw—Possible contacts in Bay area by Bill Turner, Ibid.

Breitner called the Berkeley Police Department: Memo regarding Thomas Breitner from Holloway Associates to Edward Wegmann dated February 15, 1969, Papers of Edward Wegmann, NARA; there is also another undated memo on Breitner as well.

Breitner's claim his life was threatened by people with poison darts: Ibid.

Breitner letter about CIA harassment: Secret Service file, RIF # 180-10065-10379, NARA; https://www.maryferrell.org/

showDoc.html?docId=147379&search=
breitner#relPageId=194&tab=page

James DiEugenio on Perry Russo: DiEugenio, op. cit., pages 217-219.

James Phelan wrote to DiEugenio's publisher: Letter to Ms. Ellen Ray dated October 9, 1992, Papers of Irvin Dymond.

DiEugenio on Clay Shaw's notebook: DiEugenio, op. cit., page 237.

Clay Shaw's notebook in Garrison's book: Garrison, op. cit., pages 147-148.

Page from Clay Shaw's notebook: You can find copies of Shaw's notebook in various sources like the Papers of Gus Russo, https://archive.org/stream/GarrisonPapers/Clay%20Shaw%20Notebooks#page/n51/mode/1up

Blackmer's memo on interview with Garrison and subsequent quotes: Memo from S. Jonathan Blackmer to G. Robert Blakey, dated September 1, 1977, RIF # 180-10105-10199, NARA.

DiEugenio quote about Blackmer's memo: DiEugenio, op. cit., page 332.

DiEugenio quote on three stage program: DiEugenio, op. cit., page 229.

DiEugenio quote about Gurvich being CIA: DiEugenio, op. cit., page 231.

DiEugenio quote about Novel being an experienced Agency operative: DiEugenio, op. cit., page 232.

DiEugenio quote about Novel being a target for Allen Dulles: Ibid.

DiEugenio on Novel's lawyers being paid by the CIA: DiEugenio, op. cit., page 263.

DiEugenio's second stage: DiEugenio, op. cit., page 229.

DiEugenio quote about a "covert team": DiEugenio, op. cit., page 239.

Sheridan as a "trusted Kennedy family operative": Quote by David Reitzes, https://mcadams.posc.mu.edu/cia_garrison.htm

Edward Kennedy quote about Walter Sheridan: Ibid.

DiEugenio quote about Jim Phelan: DiEugenio, op. cit., page 249.

Hugh Aynesworth trip to Cuba: NARA Record Number: 1994.05.06.08:44:58:780005; https://www.maryferrell.org/showDoc.html?docId=55194&relPageId=30&search=Science-Aviation_reporter%20for%20the%20Dallas%20Mornin

Weisberg letter to Joan Mellen in April 2000: Letter dated April 27, 2000; Harold Weisberg Archive.

Weisberg letter to Mellen with quote "did more than enough to himself": Letter dated October 18, 2001, Harold Weisberg Archive.

David Reitzes quote: http://mcadams.posc.mu.edu/cia_garrison.htm

DiEugenio's last stage: DiEugenio, op. cit., page 229.

DiEugenio quotes on "quashed subpoenas," "flipped witnesses," and "physically assaulted witnesses": James DiEugenio presentation at CAPA November, 22, 2019; https://kennedysandking.com/images/pdf/FBI-JFK-Garrison-2019.pdf

DiEugenio quote on documents "originated in the office of Richard Helms": DiEugenio, op. cit., page 294.

Tanenbaum seeing documents which then vanished: Ibid.

Ramsey Clark interest in Garrison investigation: Max Holland, *The Kennedy Assassination Tapes: The White House conversations of Lyndon B. Johnson regarding the assassination, the Warren Commission, and the aftermath*, (Alfred A. Knopf, 2004), pages 389-410.

Lyndon Johnson calling Ramsey Clark: Holland, op. cit., page 389. Quote about "interfering or obstruction" is on page 397.

Clark calling Johnson and quote about "erratic people": Holland, op. cit., page 402.

CIA memo from June 1967: Memo dated June 6, 1967, regarding Garrison TV interview of 21 May 1967 and 28 May

1967,   https://www.maryferrell.org/showDoc.html?docId=
101296&search=%22attacked_CIA+more+vehemently%
22#relPageId=4&tab=page

Shaw's legal team felt he was up against a "stacked deck":
Patricia Lambert, "Edward Wegmann and the Bonderman
Memorandum," sample chapter from a book proposal dated June
13, 2005, page 3, Papers of Patricia Lambert.

Wegmann and Dymond meet with Jack Miller: Ibid, page 15.

Quote about "steer them to the true facts": Ibid, page 16.

Miller speaks with Lawrence Houston: Ibid.

*Quote about Department of Justice and "safety of our execu-
tive privilege"*: CIA memo dated September 26, 1967 regarding
Garrison Group Meeting No 2; RIF # 104-10428-10022;
https://www.maryferrell.org/showDoc.html?docId=6514

Wegmann and Dymond meet with Nathaniel Kossack: Ibid,
also see RIF # 104-10189-10373 titled "Cable re: Clay Shaw
attorneys," which lists the names they would like information on.

Quote about "strong plea for investigative assistance":
Lambert, op. cit., page 18.

CIA memo from Donovan Pratt: Memo dated September 25,
1967, regarding Garrison Investigation; https://www.maryferrell.
org/showDoc.html?docId=101491&search=draft_memo+re+
federal+assistance+to+clay+shaw#relPageId=1&tab=page

Pratt's suggestion to study Warren Report: Ibid.

Quote about executive privilege: Memo dated September 29,
1967, from Lawrence Houston to The Director regarding Clay
L. Shaw's Trial and the Central Intelligence Agency; https://
www.maryferrell.org/showDoc.html?docId=101471&search=
9%2F29%2F1967_Houston%2C+
Lawrence#relPageId=1&tab=page

Quotes on "no action": Ibid.

Problem for Clay Shaw's lawyers: Ibid.

Routing slip from Lawrence Houston dated 2 October 1967:
https://www.maryferrell.org/showDoc.html?docId=101471&

search=9%2F29%2F1967_Houston%2C+
Lawrence#relPageId=1&tab=page

Wegmann phone call to Robert Wick: Memo from R. E.
Wick to Mr. DeLoach dated March 9, 1967; https://www.
maryferrell.org/showDoc.html?docId=
62403#relPageId=67&tab=page

FBI learns Wegmann wants to come to meet the Director:
Memo from A. Rosen to Mr. DeLoach dated April 17, 1967;
https://www.maryferrell.org/showDoc.html?docId=
62412#relPageId=86&tab=page

*Quotes about FBI happy to accept information but could not
offer any assistance*: Ibid.

Garrison and the falsification of his National Guard record:
https://www.muckrock.com/news/archives/2017/aug/02/jim-
garrison-fbi-jfk/

Documents related to his National Guard record: https://
www.muckrock.com/foi/united-states-of-america-10/jim-
garrison-24631/#file-97848

Wegmann meeting with Robert Kennedy: Bonderman memo,
op. cit., page 18, Papers of Patricia Lambert, her source is an
interview with William Wegmann on October 11, 2004.

Civil rights complaint to John Doar: Letter to John Doar from
Edward Wegmann, William Wegmann and Irvin Dymond dated
December 1, 1967, Papers of Irvin Dymond.

Wegmann and Dymond meeting with Pollak and Kirby:
Bonderman memo, op. cit., page 22.

Quote from letter from Wegmann: Bonderman memo, op. cit.,
page 24.

Response from Pollak: Ibid.

Shaw complaint to U.S. District Court in New Orleans:
Bonderman Memo, op. cit., pages 24-25; Shaw v. Garrison, et al.,
Civil Action #68-1063, Complaint May 27, 1968.

David Bonderman quotes: Bonderman Memo., op. cit., pages
28-29.

Patricia Lambert quote about throwing Shaw to the wolves: Ibid, page 31.

Kennedy decides to step up covert operations in June 1963: Russo, op. cit., page 162; Davison, *Oswald's Game*, (W. W. Norton & Company, 1983), page 180-181.

Anti-Castro Cubans shell a Cuban factory: Davison, op. cit., page 181.

Two planes dropped bombs on Cuba: Ibid, page 182.

Fidel Castro speech on September 7, 1963: "Castro Blasts Raids on Cuba," *The Times-Picayune*, September 9, 1963, https://www.history-matters.com/archive/jfk/wc/wcvols/wh22/pdf/WH22_CE_1348.pdf

Davison quote on Becket: Davison, op. cit., page 183.

Rolando Cubela and his embedded message: Davison, op. cit., page 243; Gus Russo and Stephen Moulton, *Brothers In Arms: The Kennedys, The Castros, and the Politics of Murder*, (Bloomsbury, 2008), page 12.

Kennedy's outstretched arm to Cuba: Russo, op. cit., page 234-236.

Richard Helms quote about a "feint"; Russo, op. cit., page 237.

Gus Russo quote on Garrison getting it backward: Gus Russo, "Who is Jim DiEugenio, 1999; http://jfkfiles.blogspot.com/2008/09/who-is-jim-dieugenio.html

Paul Hoch quote: Patricia Lambert note on conversation with Paul Hoch, dated November 12, 1993, Papers of Patricia Lambert.

Michele Metta, CMC, *The Italian Undercover CIA and Mossad Station and The Assassination of JFK*, 2018.

CIA document excerpt: RIF # 104-10181-10114, https://www.maryferrell.org/showDoc.html?docId=157805#relPageId=1&tab=page

Metta quotes on Gershom Peres: Metta, op. cit., page 118.

Metta quote on Shimon Peres: Metta, op. cit., page 122-123.

Metta quote on Israeli leaders seeing Kennedy as the enemy: Metta, op. cit., page 123.

Metta quote "plague the destiny of Israel' and his admonitions: Metta, op. cit., page 168.

Oliver Stone quote on fascism: https:// youtu.be/7rOF_1ZKOuc

Oliver Stone on Syria as a stabilizing force: Jon Gambrell, "US *filmmaker Oliver Stone Praises Putin for role in Syria, October 30, 2019*, https:// apnews.com/bb5501b2fff7472092aa39ba86f814c3

Destiny Betrayed mini-series: https://variety.com/2019/tv/ global/agc-television-picks-up-worldwide-oliver-stones-jfk-destiny-betrayed-1203368818/

Tilting at windmills: https://www.phrases.org.uk/meanings/ tilting-at-windmills.html

Endnotes

Harold Weisberg and VIP Room witnesses: Harold Weisberg Archive, http://jfk.hood.edu/Collection/Weisberg%20Subject% 20Index%20Files/S%20Disk/Shaw%20Clay%20Airport% 20Party/Item%2002.pdf, http://jfk.hood.edu/Collection/ Weisberg%20Subject%20Index%20Files/S%20Disk/Shaw% 20Clay%20Airport%20Party/Item%2001.pdf

CIA report on Gordon Novel: NARA identification number 1993.08.11.10:28:32:840007; https://www.maryferrell.org/ showDoc.html?docId=101448&search=%22gordon_dwane+ novel%22#relPageId=1&tab=page

Tanenbaum claim to have seen a video of Oswald and others at training camp: DiEugenio, op. cit., page 116.

J. Edgar Hoover notation on memo: https://www.maryferrell. org/showDoc.html?docId=62403#relPageId=67&tab=page

Made in the USA
Monee, IL
10 October 2020